Harmonizing Experience and Value Creation in the AI-Driven World

Nasser Hamed Al Harrasi
https://orcid.org/0000-0003-4456-0926
University of Technology and Applied Sciences, Oman

Zahra Sultan Al Habsi
University of Technology and Applied Sciences, Oman

IGI Global
Scientific Publishing
Publishing Tomorrow's Research Today

Published in the United States of America by
IGI Global Scientific Publishing
701 East Chocolate Avenue
Hershey, PA, 17033, USA
Tel: 717-533-8845 | Fax: 717-533-7115
Website: https://www.igi-global.com E-mail: cust@igi-global.com

Library of Congress Cataloging-in-Publication Data

Names: Al Harrasi, Nasser Hamed, 1988- editor | Al Habsi, Zahra Sultan, 1983- editor
Title: Harmonizing experience and value creation in the AI-driven world / edited by: Nasser Hamed Al Harrasi, Zahra Sultan Al Habsi.
Description: Hershey PA : IGI Global Scientific Publishing, [2027] | Includes bibliographical references. | Summary: "This book explores how organizations can align people, customers, and purpose within AI-enabled environments. It examines how AI reshapes employee experience, customer journeys, and organizational value creation, offering human-centered frameworks, theoretical insights, and practical models for responsible and effective AI transformation"-- Provided by publisher.
Identifiers: LCCN 2026003457 (print) | LCCN 2026003458 (ebook) | ISBN 9798337382821 hardcover | ISBN 9798337382838 paperback | ISBN 9798337382845 ebook
Subjects: LCSH: Artificial intelligence--Industrial applications
Classification: LCC TA347.A78 H3577 2026 (print) | LCC TA347.A78 (ebook)
LC record available at https://lccn.loc.gov/2026003457
LC ebook record available at https://lccn.loc.gov/2026003458

British Cataloguing in Publication Data
A Cataloguing in Publication record for this book is available from the British Library.

Table of Contents

Detailed Table of Contents

This chapter analyses the strategic fit between the artificial intelligence (AI) and digital transformation to fill the value gap that has existed in the organizations over time. Based on the Resource-Based View (RBV) and Dynamic Capabilities Theory, this paper relies on a multi-case qualitative research on the financial, healthcare, and manufacturing sectors to identify how AI is reshaping the processes and capabilities within the organizations. The findings indicate that automation does not suffice to develop sustainable value, but that one can develop digital fluency and ethical governance that will strike a balance between algorithmic accuracy and human experience. The final result of this study is a strategic model according to the idea of the Intelligence-Led Differentiation that is the roadmap of the way in which leaders could align technological change with the qualitative value creation.

Artificial intelligence (AI) is reshaping organizations beyond technological change, influencing how work is designed, services are delivered, and values are enacted. This chapter argues that employee experience (EX), customer experience (CX), and organizational purpose are interconnected through shared AI-enabled design choices rather than separate domains. Building on a sociotechnical perspective, it develops the EX–CX–Purpose Alignment Framework, positioning employee experience as a key link between internal workforce dynamics and external service outcomes. Three propositions are advanced: algorithmic authority reduces perceived fairness without voice mechanisms; declines in employee experience precede customer experience deterioration; and institutionalized purpose strengthens alignment. Drawing on insights from India's service sectors, the chapter highlights how misalignment undermines trust and performance, and outlines implications for HR leadership, governance, and capability development.

AI-based companies are beginning to realize that to create value in a meaningful way, they must pair technology with the people who will use it. This chapter examines a people-based approach to creating value. This chapter examines a people-based approach to creating value by integrating employees' feelings about their work (employee experience), customers' feelings about the experience with the company (customer experience), and the company's main goal or purpose. While AI can help companies with efficiency, smart decisions, and personalization, the gap between how well people are treated, customers' feelings about the experience with the company, and the purpose of the company can hinder success. The chapter shows that companies must create AI-based systems that allow people to do their best work with the help of AI, create trust with the people who work for the company, create a sense of meaningful work for the people who work for the company, and create tremendous value for the customer.

This chapter examines how Artificial Intelligence (AI) is transforming human work experiences, job roles, and workplace organization. The purpose of this chapter is to explore how AI-driven technologies reshape work through automation, human–machine collaboration, and changing skill demands. The chapter discusses how employees are increasingly expected to contribute through creativity, adaptability, and ethical judgment as routine and analytical tasks are augmented by AI. It also addresses challenges related to trust, accountability, employee well-being, and organizational culture, including concerns about monitoring, job insecurity, and stress. In addition, the chapter explores how AI is influencing Human Resource Management, shifting attention toward ethics, people management, and organizational change. By integrating theoretical perspectives and empirical research, this chapter provides a foundation for understanding AI's impact on work and offers insights for sustainable and employee-centered technology adoption.

The increasing use of Artificial Intelligence in the organizational system is changing how work is being designed, experienced, and valued. This chapter examines the AI-enabled organizations on human-based views, which are in the sense, meaning, agency, and employee experience. It extends past efficiency-based discourses, and understands AI as a socio-technical collaborator that has an influence on autonomy, trust and engagement in its design and governance. The chapter is based on the wisdom of various fields and existing case studies regarding the significance of developing a transparent, participatory, and ethically regulated AI infrastructure that can strengthen meaningful work, rather than diminish meaningful work. The review illuminates the concept that sustainability of the production of value in the AI-based world is grounded on the equilibrium between the technological smartness and human dignity, empowerment, and corporate intent.

The rapid integration of Artificial Intelligence (AI) in financial technology (FinTech) has transformed the way financial services are delivered, experienced and evaluated by consumers. AI-driven applications such as chatbots, robo-advisors, fraud detection systems and personalized financial recommendations are reshaping customer interactions while simultaneously redefining value creation. However, the increasing reliance on AI has also raised concerns regarding trust, transparency and the absence of human touch, leading to varying degrees of consumer skepticism. This study adopts an exploratory and descriptive research design using an interview-based approach to examine how users perceive AI-enabled FinTech services in terms of trust, experience and value co-creation. The findings reveal a dual perception among users while AI enhances convenience, efficiency and personalization, concerns regarding data privacy, algorithmic opacity and reduced human interaction influence trust levels.

Preface

INTRODUCTION

Artificial Intelligence (AI) has emerged as one of the most transformative forces shaping contemporary organizations, industries, and societies. Beyond its technological capabilities, AI is fundamentally redefining how individuals interact with organizations, how value is created, and how experiences are designed and delivered. As organizations increasingly integrate AI into their strategic operations, customer engagement models, workplace environments, and decision-making processes, the relationship between technological advancement and human experience has become a critical area of inquiry. Harmonizing Experience and Value Creation in the AI-Driven World was developed to explore this evolving relationship and provide interdisciplinary perspectives on how organizations can achieve meaningful, responsible, and sustainable value creation in an AI-enabled era.

The rapid adoption of AI technologies has introduced both unprecedented opportunities and complex challenges. While AI offers capabilities such as automation, personalization, predictive analytics, and enhanced decision support, its successful implementation depends on addressing essential human considerations, including trust, transparency, employee well-being, ethical governance, and organizational purpose. This edited volume examines how AI can be leveraged not only as a technological resource but also as a catalyst for improving human experiences, strengthening organizational capabilities, and fostering innovative approaches to value creation. The contributing authors present theoretical insights, conceptual frameworks, empirical investigations, and practical applications across diverse sectors, highlighting the importance of maintaining balance between technological intelligence and human-centered approaches.

This book is intended for researchers, academics, practitioners, policymakers, and organizational leaders seeking to understand the multidimensional impacts of

AI on experience and value creation. By bringing together perspectives from management, marketing, human resources, finance, retail, tourism, healthcare, sports, and emerging markets, this volume offers a comprehensive examination of AI-driven transformation. We hope that the discussions presented in this book will encourage continued dialogue on responsible AI adoption and inspire organizations to design AI ecosystems that enhance human potential, organizational resilience, and sustainable value creation.

CHAPTER OVERVIEW

The chapters in this book collectively examine the intersection of AI, human experience, and value creation across organizational and industry contexts. Beginning with the strategic implications of AI-driven transformation, the volume explores how organizations can integrate emerging technologies while preserving human-centered principles. The chapters progress from organizational capabilities and employee experiences to customer engagement, industry-specific applications, and broader societal considerations, demonstrating the interconnected nature of AI adoption and human value creation.

Chapter 1, "AI Advancements and Digital Transformation: Reshaping Organizational Processes, Capabilities, and Strategic Directions," examines the strategic relationship between AI and digital transformation. Drawing on the Resource-Based View and Dynamic Capabilities Theory, the chapter explores how organizations across financial services, healthcare, and manufacturing can move beyond automation toward intelligence-led differentiation. It emphasizes the importance of digital fluency, ethical governance, and strategic alignment in achieving sustainable organizational value.

Chapter 2, "Re-centering Human Experience in AI-Driven Organizations: An EX–CX–Purpose Alignment Framework," introduces a framework connecting employee experience, customer experience, and organizational purpose. The chapter highlights how AI-enabled organizational decisions influence trust, fairness, and performance, emphasizing the need for alignment between internal workforce experiences and external customer outcomes.

Chapter 3, "Human-Centred Value Creation—Aligning Employee Experience, Customer Experience, and Purpose in AI-Driven Organisations," further explores people-based approaches to AI-enabled value creation. The chapter discusses how organizations can integrate AI capabilities with employee empowerment, meaningful work, and customer value while maintaining trust and human connection.

Chapter 4, "Human Experience in AI-Enabled Workplaces: Examining How AI Impacts Employee Roles, Collaboration, Skills, Well-being," investigates the transformation of workplace structures, employee roles, and skill requirements. The chapter considers the implications of AI adoption for collaboration, organizational culture, employee well-being, and responsible human resource management.

Chapter 5, "Working with Intelligent Systems—Reimagining Meaning, Agency, and Experience in AI-Enabled Organizations," examines AI as a sociotechnical collaborator and considers its influence on autonomy, trust, engagement, and meaningful work. The chapter emphasizes transparent, participatory, and ethically governed AI systems that support human dignity and empowerment.

Chapter 6, "Human-Centered AI and Value Co-Creation in FinTech—Exploring Consumer Trust, Experience and Perceived Value," explores AI adoption in financial technology and its impact on consumer relationships. The chapter examines how AI-driven services such as chatbots, robo-advisors, and fraud detection systems influence trust, personalization, and perceptions of value.

Chapter 7, "Scaling Personalization in Ecommerce through Machine Learning for Hyper Relevant Customer Engagement," investigates the role of machine learning in creating personalized digital commerce experiences. The chapter presents an integrated framework addressing ethical AI, explainability, customer privacy, organizational readiness, and trust in scalable personalization strategies.

Chapter 8, "AI-Driven Immersive Technologies for Sustainable Consumer Experience and Value Creation in Retail and Tourism," examines how AI-enabled immersive technologies contribute to consumer engagement and sustainable value creation. The chapter highlights the role of personalization, experiential design, and human-centered governance in shaping future retail and tourism experiences.

Chapter 9, "Human-Centered AI Transformation in Emerging Markets: Integrating Institutional Conditions, Organizational Purpose, and Employee Experience," explores the contextual challenges associated with AI implementation in emerging economies. The chapter emphasizes the importance of institutional environments, stakeholder relationships, organizational purpose, and employee experiences in enabling successful AI transformation.

Chapter 10, "Human Experience in AI-Enabled Workplace: An AI-Enabled Communication and Diagnostic Support Case Study Within Veterinary Clinics in Ukraine," provides an applied perspective through a qualitative case study of AI adoption in veterinary clinics. The chapter demonstrates how AI can enhance communication, documentation, and diagnostic preparation while also addressing implementation challenges related to governance, training, privacy, and human oversight.

CONCLUSION

As AI continues to transform industries and organizational practices, the central challenge is not simply technological adoption but the creation of meaningful alignment between intelligent systems and human needs. The chapters presented in this volume demonstrate that successful AI transformation requires organizations to consider the experiences of employees, customers, communities, and other stakeholders. AI must be approached as an enabler of human capability rather than a replacement for human judgment, creativity, and purpose.

The contributions within this book highlight that responsible AI implementation depends on principles of transparency, ethical governance, inclusivity, and continuous learning. Across workplaces, markets, and industries, organizations must develop strategies that integrate technological innovation with human-centered design. Whether through enhanced employee experiences, personalized customer interactions, immersive consumer environments, or improved organizational decision-making, AI-driven value creation is most effective when technology and humanity are considered together.

Looking ahead, the future of AI will be defined by organizations' ability to harmonize technological advancement with human experience. The perspectives presented in Harmonizing Experience and Value Creation in the AI-Driven World provide a foundation for understanding this evolving relationship and encourage scholars and practitioners to pursue AI strategies that are innovative, responsible, and sustainable. By placing human experience at the center of AI transformation, organizations can create systems that not only improve efficiency but also strengthen trust, purpose, and long-term value creation.

Chapter 1

AI Advancements and Digital Transformation: Reshaping Organizational Processes, Capabilities, and Strategic Directions

Shikha Khullar
http://orcid.org/0009-0000-5598-3145
Poornima University, India

Astri Dwi Andriani
http://orcid.org/0000-0003-3951-4829
Strategic Research Institute, Asia Pacific University of Technology and Innovation, Malaysia

Arun Arora
http://orcid.org/0000-0002-8976-0633
Lloyd Business School, India

ABSTRACT

This chapter analyses the strategic fit between the artificial intelligence (AI) and digital transformation to fill the value gap that has existed in the organizations over time. Based on the Resource-Based View (RBV) and Dynamic Capabilities Theory, this paper relies on a multi-case qualitative research on the financial, healthcare, and manufacturing sectors to identify how AI is reshaping the processes and capabilities within the organizations. The findings indicate that automation does not suffice to develop sustainable value, but that one can develop digital fluency and ethical governance that will strike a balance between algorithmic accuracy and

DOI: 10.4018/979-8-3373-8282-1.ch001

human experience. The final result of this study is a strategic model according to the idea of the Intelligence-Led Differentiation that is the roadmap of the way in which leaders could align technological change with the qualitative value creation.

1. INTRODUCTION

The world is currently facing a major disruption era, shifting the landscape of digital transformation from a passive digitalization movement to an active artificial intelligence-centric paradigm, or what we now know as AI. Several experts, such as Chui et al., predict that Generative AI and Large Language Models (LLMs) will contribute USD 4.4 trillion annually to the economy (Chui et al., 2023). This, of course, requires organizations to adapt their data processing methods, transforming raw data into predictive insights and creative innovations. (Andriani, 2025) Davenport and Mittal (2022) state that AI is now reengineering value chains into more dynamic entities with continuous algorithmic feedback. Furthermore, AI also assists humans in decision-making. In other words, AI will analyze and predict for companies operating in the financial and logistics sectors. Relying on AI will predict market dynamics with more than 90% accuracy (Davenport & Mittal, 2022).

The phenomenon has shifted the dynamic and culture of the organization, where generative AI predictive modeling has made strategic planning superior, shifting from deterministic forecasting to probabilistic forecasting then ultimately helping companies process non-linear variables that affect the company in real time – for example geopolitical changes in a country. Nevertheless, every single change produces side effects, where one of them is creating stochastic conflict on the structural between natural culture of the organization and the strong AI capability which often hampers the artificial intelligence implementation in an organization, as the strong AI capability's pace has outpaced most of the organization's conventional managers in a company. This value gap will remain a crucial challenge when organizational culture adapts to technology according to Fischer and friends (2020). A mere handful of organizations are able to translate this investment into measurable and tangible results. This was aggravated by the fears of many elements in an organization who had belief that humans would be replaced by machines. This phenomenon is called “technological alienation” (Brynjolfsson et al., 2021).

Brynjolfsson and others (2021) emphasize that technological alienation occurs when AI is used by companies to replace or replace humans, not as a tool or additive to complement human work. The systemic inability to align human experience and AI will inevitably result in a decline in organizational performance, leading to a stagnation in strategic performance. Critical and skeptical views of artificial intelligence were also fueled by the phenomenon of AI black boxes. In the world of artificial intelligence, especially deep learning, decisions are made based on input without transparency. It becomes so complex that humans cannot understand it. On the other hand, more and more aspects of the organization doubt artificial intelligence because it lacks human empathy.

Meanwhile, a major challenge for organizations in using AI is customer brand loyalty, even though organizations possess a wealth of consumer and brand information, even as technology becomes increasingly sophisticated. To address this dilemma, companies and organizations must shift their mindset and shift the current organizational culture, focusing not only on utilizing artificial intelligence for automation but also on experience architecture and augmentation. By applying Dynamic Capability Theory and Human-Computer Interaction (HCI), leaders in companies and organizations can use artificial intelligence as an agent to align shared value creation and operational system efficiency. Ultimately, AI is expected to become an agent in bridging the value gap and achieving digital maturity. Human-AI collaboration improves organizational trust and employee productivity (Khullar et al., 2026).

2. LITERATURE REVIEW

2.1 Resource-Based View

The adaptability of business models in today's digital era depends on strategic resource configurations that can adeptly respond to market changes (Fischer et al., 2020). Ultimately, creating the foundation of a robust business model requires a Resource-Based View (RBV) when conducting strategic analysis within the VRIO model. Mikalef & Gupta (2021) consider artificial intelligence a strategic asset that can calibrate competitive advantage through advanced data processing. If utilized optimally, it can increase productivity by 5-6 percent (Mikalef & Gupta, 2021).

Of course, the existence of artificial intelligence will never be separated from the role of humans themselves. True competitive advantage is the synergy between humans and artificial intelligence. More precisely, it is the combination of insights generated by artificial intelligence with the complex social knowledge of humans. This synergy will ensure that the value gap between technology and humans is properly filled, ultimately creating a robust system that competitors cannot replicate. This is known as knowledge by view (KBV), a knowledge-based perspective capable of openly integrating multiple models/systems. Explainable AI improves transparency and stakeholder trust (Khullar et al., 2026).

Although artificial intelligence (AI) has become increasingly popular in the business world due to its relative advantages for companies, Marr (2023) cautions that institutional use of AI must address data ethics and the reputation of algorithms.

This issue is also increasingly highlighted by countries in the European Union, which are currently focusing on global regulations regarding the legal use of AI. Now, we will observe the exciting change. This change puts us in a bit of a frenzy of awareness about the greater dynamism required to be digitized. In this regard, machine AI, analogous to machine predictive analytics and machine generative AI, enables organizations to reimagine branding processes. They can also be readily available for creating value-added prototypes in a volatile market, as proposed by Sjodin and her team in 2020.

The ultimate power that is most valuable is the human experience. Human experience is the most valuable of all because it is impossible to replace it with sophisticated technologies such as artificial intelligence. Orthogenic construction will never, ever be able to develop the empathy or judgments that resembling those of mankind. A company's strategic advantage lies in its ability to utilize artificial intelligence by analyzing large amounts of data. A company's strategic advantage lies in its ability to perform tasks with others. Companies that succeed in balancing this will build what is referred to as Experience Assets, which are extremely difficult to replicate by other companies. Toward achieving future success, the next generation of leadership must become Company Orchestrators, more competent in managing resources and exploiting human experiences, and themselves meet the VRIO criteria by orchestrating rather than accumulating them.

Finally, AI-related benefits are linked to the Organizational Learning Cycle, which is associated with path independence. The development model of AI has historically been given birth to barriers to entry for newcomers, which lacks the appropriate institutional intelligence. Through RBV, AI transfiguration offers organizations the chance to repay speculative investments to a model where technology plays a key role in sustaining value creation. The art of comprehensively combining value and experience as two sides of the same strategy ensures that AI-centric development is not fragile, sluggish, or discontinuous.

2.2 Dynamic Capability Theory

In a volatile digital landscape, maintaining competitive advantage is achieved through a continuous process of strategic renewal, driven by the ability to sense digital trends, capitalize on opportunities, and transform organizational structures (Warner & Wager, 2020). Sensing: This is the application of machine learning to identify weak signals in consumer behavior to shift the company's mindset to a fast-learning architecture where algorithms act as the peripheral nervous system to predict turbulence. Mastery: The shift between insight and action, namely the application of generative planning strategies with the help of LLM to test thousands of scenarios in a single effort.

Digital transformation research is significantly more effective when companies with rigid organizational structures integrate AI technologies, digital transformation, digitization, and digital transformation (Verhoef et al., 2021). This requires versatile organizational flexibility to once again allocate capital and talent in the form of human resources to AI projects without any obstacles. The final and most important key is transformation, which will replace continuous structural renewal until the workforce is able to experience the same growth as AI. This will require a transition to algorithmic governance and cross-functional partnerships between data scientists and subject matter experts.

By comprehensively integrating AI into the DNA of a social enterprise, an organization will be able to build a path-dependent advantage that cannot be achieved without AI acquisition and that supports the continuation of AI as an integral part of inner-circle work. Synergy contributes to the realization of what is known as ambidextrous capabilities: the ability to leverage existing AI to maximize efficiency while simultaneously looking to the future for innovation. Organizations that successfully balance the exploration of new digital technologies with the simultaneous utilization of existing assets—unidimensional digital ambidexterity—deliver significantly higher performance than those focused solely on one dimension (Vaska et al., 2021). Furthermore, sensing should encompass ethical standards and detecting algorithmic bias to gain social license. Proactive adherence to international requirements such as ISO/IEC 42001 helps transform compliance from a cost center to a strategic source of institutional trust.

Finally, experience and values align with "Learning Speed" and "Ecosystemic Value Creation." When AI-driven collective intelligence is viewed as a dynamic capability, companies are always ready for disruption. While the RBV recognizes AI as a valuable resource, DCT provides a way to manage that resource sustainably, aligned with human experience. This is the key to sustainable value in an AI-driven world (Andriani & Siripipatthanakul, 2025).

2.3 The Idea of Creating Shared Value in the AI Era

Within the last stepping stone of this framework, Value Co-Creation is reorganized, i.e. organizations are moving away off a linear delivery system to an AI-driven ecosystem. Devoiced under the developed Service-Dominant Logic framework, the value is generated through the active relational combination of resources, and service interactions in an intricate, technology-enabled, actor-actor (A2A) ecosystem (Vargo and Lusch, 2020). It is a three-way collaborative process of companies, customers, and independent AI agents during the AI era. The shift enables the provision of the most personalized value based on the data with the help of data-driven insights, which enhances long-term customers engagement and lifetime value in online markets significantly (Mustak et al., 2021).

The foundations of this paradigm lie in the so-called Value Feedback Loop, in which the raw material would be user interactions, and it would be refined to produce the service improvements that would be continual. Contrary to traditional tools, AI-powered services are enhanced throughout the usage; every clue and correction will tailor the algorithm to the particular circumstances of the user. This makes users smart prosumers. Relational transparency, assuring the user of the confidence in the way their information will be utilized in order to generate value, closes the psychological gap of the Value Gap to work. The value-in-exchange is changed into strategic value-in-experience. AI also serves as a coordinator, which carries less cognitive burden, allowing human beings to concentrate on high-value problems that are empathetic.

According to Chui et al. (2023), such kind of cooperation will boost the labor productivity by 0.5-3.4 in a year. But this takes the human element to ensure control and the AI remains an assistant, rather than a replacement to human aspect of the service. To do so, organizations will have to model an Open AI Architecture that allows interacting with a variety of streams of data ecosystems.

The leadership problem is to keep up " Agentic Harmony, the narrow border between human beings and machines. In case AI is over invasive, it may become the risk of Value Destruction and resistance to the users. One needs truly strategic skills in order to devise systems that allow human involvement because technology cannot just be a blank partner in the innovative process. Finally, both Resource-Based View (assets) and Dynamic Capabilities (agility) are connected with Shared Value Creation that offers the Purpose of transformation. In the case of AI, value is generated via the unlimited potentials of matching machine accuracy with human innovativeness. Through this philosophy, firms will make sure that online transformation is a radical change in the way they produce and maintain human value and satisfaction in the world that is becoming more complex.

3. METHOD

The third part of this chapter changes the focus on the theory abstraction to the empirical rigor by relating the qualitative multiple case study design with the research conducted on how AI is regulated within an organizational setting. The qualitative approach is in a unique position to answer this research question because it allows conducting a more profound study of complex phenomena in suitable conditions through which a deeper analysis of the lived experiences of participants can be conducted (Dawadi et al., 2021).

Since the transformation driven by AI is a relatively modern and dynamic phenomenon, a case study approach offers the details that would be required in order to indicate how various organizational cultures and structural backgrounds influence the success rates of AI integration. This study is based on a multiple case study design, according to which an analytical unit of each case is used to either confirm or refute the theoretical framework that is developing, which enhances the strength and transferability of the results (Saldaña, 2021).

The purposive sampling strategy was used to select the cases, including organizations in three different industries (Financial Services, Healthcare and Advanced Manufacturing) with a minimum of 36 months of recorded investment in AI-driven digital transformation. The cross-sectoral approach will enable to find out the overall trends in the success of AI and industry peculiarities, especially the regulation and the complexity of data. Quantitative data indicate that with varying adoption levels, these three industries are driving AI investment in the market today; the financial sector alone will amass to a $100 billion AI investment by 2026 (Chui et al., 2023).

Through a study on the leaders in this highly competitive environment, this paper pinpoints the most appropriate dynamic capabilities required to fill the Value Gap, so as to reach a mindful balance between practitioner experience and end-user experience. This study will be designed based on diverse data gathering processes, where triangulation will be used to guarantee the soundness and authenticity of the fact. The selection of the basic data sources will be semi-structured interviews with C-level executives, Chief Information Officers (CIOs), and senior project managers in charge of AI implementation. Such insights are supplemented with secondary data, including internal white papers, annual reports, and digital transformation roadmaps. This is a multi-layered data collection wherein it can be compared between the official organizational discourse and the real experience in the real-life implementation.

In order to achieve internal validity, the chain of evidence was rigorously built, which enabled mapping all theoretical propositions across a range of empirical observations related to the different cases under analysis (Gustafsson, 2020). The analysis phase was made through Thematic Synthesis with the help of Qualitative Data Analysis Software (QDAS), including NVivo. It starts with the open coding whereby the raw data is categorized into specific events and concepts which is followed by the axial coding which assists in establishing the connection between the Resource-Based View (RBV) and the Dynamic Capabilities themes. The most significant component of this methodology is the cross-case synthesis factor that aims at establishing convergence and non-convergence patterns in various industries. The analysis (e.g.) determines whether the structure behind Sensing capabilities in healthcare (predictive diagnostics) resembles the Sensing capabilities in finance (fraud detection) or whether the special ethical requirements of healthcare prescribe a special Transformation course.

It is the comparative optics that needs to be created in order to create a framework that is robust enough to act in the globalized digital economy. Member checking and peer review will be used to make the study as reliable as possible, the qualitative counterpart of consistency. Initial findings will be analyzed by the industry practitioners to make sure that the interpretations are congruent to the organizations. Moreover, the methodology considers the so-called contextual sensitivity: AI transformation is affected by regional laws (such as GDPR, the AI Law of the European Union). This rigor in methodology will guarantee that the final product, the AI-Experience-Value framework is not merely a pile of anecdotes but a science-based tool that will give actionable strategic advice. The goal is to provide a testable roadmap for organizations that need to navigate the complexities of the mid-2020s business world in the context of a balanced approach between technical efficiency and human-centered value.

4. RESULT

4.1. Reshaping Organizational Processes Through AI

The results of various case study analyses indicate that AI-assisted organizational process restructuring is not a gradual process, but rather a radical reengineering of the value chain (Sharipudin et al., 2024). Autonomous compliance has already been designed to be manufactured in the financial services industry, as it shifts to AI-based intelligence, which outcompetes past automation. Analyzing transactions with predictability has already helped companies reduce false positive rates in detecting fraudsters by up to 45 percent and allowed analysts to focus on priority first-level investigations (Davenport and Mittal, 2022). This change is an indicator that AI-enabled process reformatting will transform employees into more effective strategy enforcers, not machines that read input data at all. This leads to a flexible, less narrow, and well-defined organizational process shifting to a dynamic process that responds to data input in real time.

The most important thing in the healthcare industry is also the least important thing in the healthcare industry. Lemungul, the hospital has already been able to achieve a level of synchronized speed and accuracy of results that was previously impractical due to the impossibility of implementing a deep learning model in diagnostic imaging. Evidence shows that integrating AI into clinical workflows optimizes these radiology assessments, potentially accelerating data processing by up to 30% and maintaining diagnostic precision above 95% through advanced algorithm analysis (Bohr & Memarzadeh, 2020). This is an evolution of the process, not replacing physicians, although it is more appropriate to reform the clinical experience with longitudinal data and second opinion proposals. This combination of technical expertise and human expertise is the source of the primary production of value, where patient outcomes are prioritized alongside operational efficiency. AI inference combined with IoT supports real-time data analytics and smart decision-making (Khullar & Tank, 2026).

The Advanced Manufacturing case study highlights another aspect of process change, based on the shift from Preventive Maintenance to Prescriptive Maintenance. In systems like that, AI tends not to simply predict when the machine will fail; it will also predict when not to change operational specifications that are required to optimize the increase in life time. Thanks to the combination of IoT sensors and generative AI interfaces, shop floor managers can query production line conditions, fundamentally democratizing access to data (Albasrie et al., 2024). Quantitative analysis of the described cases indicates that the transformation can help reduce unplanned downtime by approximately 20 percent, which has a direct impact on company profits. This re-engineering of the industry's processes marks a shift toward the Intelligence-as-a-Service model of internal organizational structure (Andriani et al., 2021).

The core strategic process emerging from these findings is known as Human-Centered Automation. The most successful implementations across any sector are those that explicitly create AI interfaces in a way that enhances the "User Experience" (UX). Organizations can save up to 25 percent of average employee hours by using Large Language Models (LLMs) to address complex documentation and administrative overhead (Chui et al., 2023). This time is then reallocated to high-value activities such as customer relationship management and innovation brainstorming. Thus, process redefinition becomes more of an experience than a technical activity, with the primary value gained being the freeing up of human mental capacity for more meaningful tasks.

Furthermore, statistics show that the "Value Gap" is filled as organizations evolve from the "Point Solution" stage to the Systemic AI Integration stage. Most large, low-performing companies implement AI as a one-off solution to a specific problem, and the most successful organizations consider AI the foundation of their operational structure. A systemic approach also enables what is known as Cross-Functional Synergy, where data provided by the marketing department is automatically used to implement supply chain changes through AI-based broadcast models. Empirical evidence shows that organizations that achieve deep systemic integration of AI capabilities realize significantly higher returns on digital investments compared to companies operating with isolated or fragmented AI applications (Mikalef & Gupta, 2021). This is a strategic direction that emphasizes the Horizontal Capabilities element, which plays a crucial role in contemporary enterprises.

The new organizational process identified by this analysis is significantly called Algorithmic Governance. It encompasses decision-making power, artificial intelligence models, auditing, validation, and monitoring of these models. This is achieved in the financial industry through the enforcement of back-testing regulations along with rigorous bias detection to meet ethical requirements. Case studies show that organizations with stronger AI-based governance structures tend to experience slower and less stringent regulatory progress and higher levels of stakeholder trust. Governance in this process is not a bottleneck, but rather a Value Guardian, enforcing the sustainability of AI transformation and balancing the need for speed with the need for security.

Mascul Ali, organizational reengineering, is driving a shift in Strategic Agility. In digital transformation, conventional strategies are periodic, top-down, and often tedious; in the AIDi era, strategies are bottom-up, integrating real-time market information. Predictive analytics, in the global economy, enables companies to develop Continuous Strategic Sensing, allowing them to reimagine product offerings or supply chain pathways at the micro level. This type of agility is a direct consequence of how AI can evolve through the use of non-linearity, a form of elitism that competitors can develop, which imposes itself on the speed of sudden decision-making, rather than simply the size of the resource.

A key aspect of this finding is the importance of orchestrating experiences in customer-facing processes. After using AI to create highly personalized journeys, organizations no longer enjoy immunity from mass marketing, except in Segment One. In one case study, companies that implemented AI to personalize experiences through AI increased their satisfaction levels by 15 percent due to their ability to design more relevant and timely interactions. Definition: The shared value between AI and customers is a hallmark of the Experience Economy, where the primary product is the valuable experience itself. The ability to coordinate this technical power with a deep understanding of human psychology is recognized as a key strategic strength. However, reengineering such processes, such analysis, warns, enables, captivates, structures, diverts, from, warns, mercurun segal, segal, menintining, miserikkan, pada, kehudang serta, kehudang, dan, pada, meninkuktur, suktur, pada, ningkuktur, suktur. Organizations that rely too heavily on AI and eliminate human oversight risk facing major problems, where workers no longer understand the logic behind it; it is simply what they are told to do. Today, successful companies are launching Knowledge Retention Cycles, where young professionals can periodically revise AI logic. This ensures that organizations are ambidextrous enough to harness AI's efficiencies, yet still able to use critical thinking to solve high-stakes problems and make ethical decisions.

The process of transforming organizational processes driven by AI is defined, in short, as AI, which means a more significant shift towards an Augmented Intelligence Environment. This environment is characterized by fluid data flows, a high degree of strategic agility, and a deep commitment to the human experience. Results in the financial, healthcare, and manufacturing sectors demonstrate that AI Alchemy is a highly effective tool when applied to align algorithms with the empathy and creativity of the human workforce. This holistic process will generate sustainable value created by a true AI-driven digital transformation from 2026 onward.

The combination of Robotic Process Automation (RPA) with Artificial Intelligence (AI) represents a step toward Operational Intelligence and eliminates the limitations of conventional automation, which, at best, merely mimics human keystrokes. Historically, conventional HG automation has operated in silos, with RPA bots capable of only line-based tasks, with pre-defined rules, and failing miserably when unstructured information or process variability is encountered. For a clearer picture of this transformation, readers are encouraged to refer to the Intelligence Evolution Roadmap in diagram form, as shown in the diagram below. This visual representation envisions a significant shift from isolated and stagnant systems to a more holistic cognitive architecture where machine learning and natural language processing models are placed directly into the automation cycle, transforming isolated tasks into autonomous, flexible, and self-optimizing ecosystems.

Figure 1. The Evolution of Intellegence

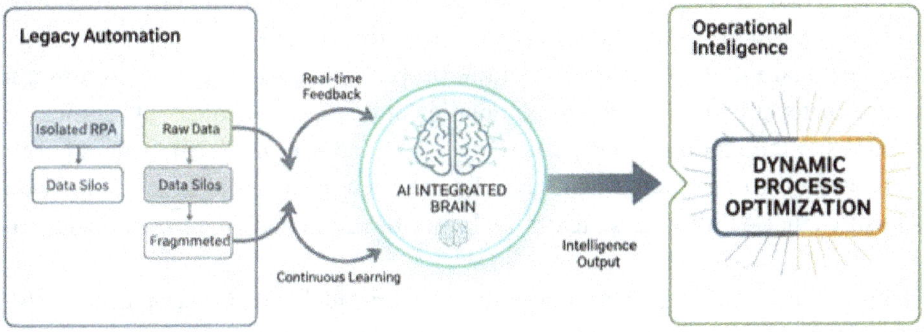

The above diagram 1 depicts the dynamic transfer of data energy of an organisation between the legacy automation techniques and the so-called cognitive brain, which synthesizes the unstructured inputs to form Dynamic Process Optimization. As per the visual flow, it not only changes the reactive character of the traditional RPA but also introduces proactive intelligence that can anticipate bottlenecks and reorganize the workflows without human intervention. This change, which the glowing arrow to AI represents, implies that automation cannot be passed as an efficiency tool anymore, but as a strategic asset, as it will enable the company to enhance its dynamic capabilities by providing feedback, which, in its turn, hindered organizational agility in the past. More so, the evolutionary process, shown in the figure above, illustrates how the operational values and human experience will be aligned with the help of dynamic optimization output used as a bottom-up layer. As the complexity of the underlying cognitive processing is removed by the use of AI-integrated system processes, this roadmap demonstrates that organizations liberate human resources to dedicate themselves to more strategic orchestration. The diagram highlights the fact that all these technical flows are coordinated so that they do not conflict but rather complement each other to create a robust architecture in which the technological capabilities and the human based values go hand in hand. This fit will assist in reinforcing operational excellence in overall strategic direction of the company in the AI-driven world.

4.2. Build Capacity of Organisation New

According to the shift toward an AI-inclusive architecture (rather than a traditional digital architecture), the new organizational form of capability development requires the development of new capabilities that are overly excessive with technical expertise. A crucial aspect of this evolution is digital literacy, which encompasses not only the ability to use tools but also a holistic understanding of how AI can be used to deliver strategic outcomes. In the case study analyzed, organizations that have succeeded in closing the gap, now referred to as the Value Gap, treat digital literacy as a form of tribute, not as competition from local IT. Quantitative analysis of the financial industry indicates that the proportion of high-level digital literacy among non-technical personnel in companies increases the scale of AI projects 12 percent faster than their counterparts (Davenport and Mittal, 2022). This capability facilitates the use of a common language between information seekers and providers and ensures that AI programs are driven by the desire to push the limits through the goal of creating value in organizations.

Digital literacy, along with a new strategy, is Ethical Data Governance. With AI models increasingly relying on large-scale and sensitive databases, data integrity management has emerged as the ultimate source of institutional trust. While ethical governance is no longer a burden, it is becoming increasingly prevalent in the healthcare sector. Patient participation in digital health programs increases because users feel secure about how their information is handled. Companies that have implemented transparent and auditable algorithms for data usage policies have already reported significant improvements in patient participation. This ethical capacity, inclusively, takes place within the Resource-Based View and thus classifies it as a resource that is uncommon and not matched anywhere, introducing a competitive buffer of reputational risk that is habitually bred by the efforts of AI-based businesses.

Furthermore, this information serves as a prelude to the importance of Adaptive Learning Architectures as a source of critical organizational power. The ability to unlearn and relearn on a large scale is a crucial mechanism for maintaining a landscape where the lifespan of technical skills is declining at a rate accelerated by Large Language Models (LMLs). Examples in the manufacturing sector indicate that the most tangible company is one that replaces regular training sessions with what is known as the Continuous Learning Cycle, which is integrative to the extent of being a digital employee. This competency will prepare manpower to work in AI, accompanying emerging technologies to become a system based on agents with progressive advancement at any time. Indonesia suggests that companies currently focusing on this learning cycle also contribute 20 percent to employee retention due to high levels of digital disruption (World Economic Forum, 2024).

The fourth capability identified is Algorithm Orchestration, which refers to an organizational framework for coordinating human talent and autonomous AI agents. This represents an advanced understanding of task decomposition, identifying which aspects of a process are most effectively handled by machine accuracy, which require empathy, and which require human decision-making. The study revealed that successful companies have developed Orchestration Playbooks, defining where the transition between human and machine occurs, drastically reducing operational wait times. This is crucial in ensuring operational resilience because it prevents unnecessary reliance on the system, which can lead to costly disruptions when a black swan event occurs at a time when historical data ceases to be relevant.

Data sovereignty and curatorial excellence are key capabilities, as companies don't simply acquire ready-made data, nor strategically manage their proprietary data sets. With the commoditization of basic AI models, data is company-specific, creating unique brand value. According to case studies, organizations that are more successful in building strength around the introduction of AI are those that have already developed the capacity to clean, label, and protect assets unique to them. This transformation of raw information into strategic data assets plays a curatorial role, promoting the company's unique advantage in specific markets.

Human-Centered Design Thinking has also become a requirement that is obligatory to organizations of the contemporary times. This includes the capability to be able to create an AI system with a focus on the experience of the user, whether to be of service to a worker or to a customer. Implementing an ethnography principle and concept can reduce the level of introduction of technology, and this may go to an extent of increasing its adoption, as the use of AI increases its application level. New publications indicate that AI implementation with a focus on design that is user-centric and civic empathy at a high level reduces risk incidence of the so-called

Shadow IT; when AI is implemented in a legitimate manner, workers tend not to seek an alternative design-independent system and are not perceived as obstructionist (Fischer et al., 2020).

Apart from design, Strategic Planning and Scenario Modeling have also been once again defined as capabilities that can be performed by AI. Predictive Simulation has already become a tool that will be used by organizations to train to face the future, to make them glad that they can create various strategies to respond under different circumstances, responsive to a variety of situations in a concerted effort. This will allow companies to switch to the tightly structured Dynamic Strategy model that will be upgraded in time with the introduction of new data to the deepest parts of AI.

Further, interdisciplinary collaboration has already shifted away from the skills that are difficult to achieve to capabilities that are highly desirable to the success of AI. The value gap is typically greatest when data science groups are left to work separately from business units. This study, however, reveals that organizations integrating AI are those that create so-called bilingual teams, teams where members feel equally comfortable discussing neural network design and financial reports. This teamwork capability facilitates AI transformation led by business, not driven by technology, a key difference that defines the difference between projects that can increase organizational profitability and projects that will simply become experimental projects.

The ninth capability identified in this paper is the ability to manage the aspect of algorithmic accountability. Organizations need to have established processes to address the accountability issues of human involvement in AI systems increasingly performing autonomous tasks in procurement, lending, and diagnostics. This also includes the formation of an in-house AI Ethics Board and explainable AI (XAI) technical protocols. According to case studies, the possibility of achieving a 40 percent higher score on getting the approval of a product based on AI nova increases the chances of a company releasing a particular decision by 40 percent. This competency overcomes barriers between technical and social extremes, and ensures the strategy of strategic alignment of the enterprise that is social-oriented.

The transition to the AI-oriented enterprise is linked to a massive reorganization of the process of formulating strategic decisions, eradication of the subjective bias, and transition to the models of analytical precision. The type of decision-making in the classical organizational framework is based on limited information and executive instincts, this may be rather untrustworthy with the current markets becoming more complicated. To picture such a dramatic change, the readers are advised to look at the From Intuition to Predictive Insight Matrix that can be seen in the figure below. This matrix is a roadmap of what a legacy decision-making has restricted, and what a Decision-Making Co-Pilot architecture can offer, within the framework of combating experience-based and probabilistic situations: incredible exploratory freedom, as AI and human intelligence harmonize

Figure 2. Between Intuition and Predictive Foresight

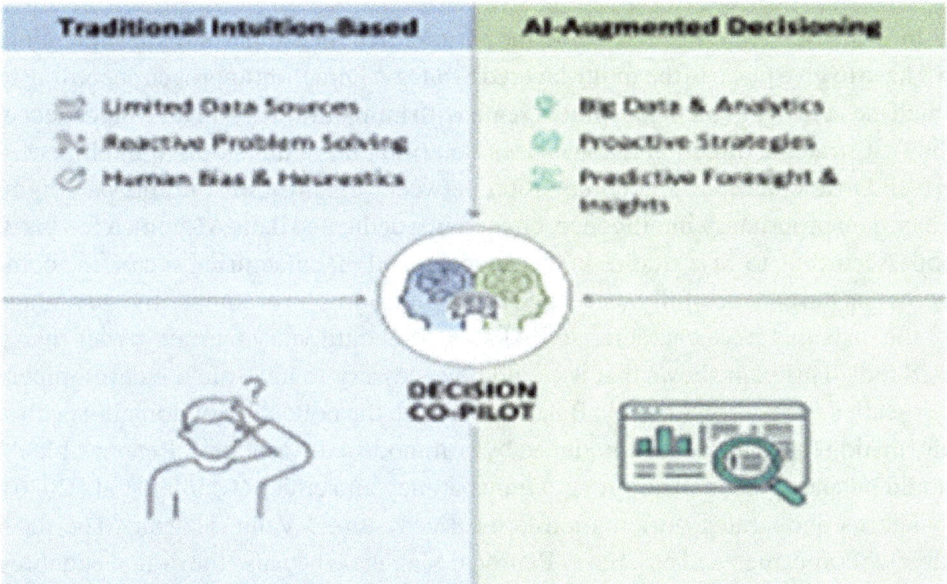

The above diagram represents the multidimensional advantages of moving away to a focused and data-driven approach of approach to strategy and not guesswork. The adoption of AI-enhanced decision-making, the application of big data analytics and predictive modeling to transform organizations into a Fast-Relevant to Fast-Proactive mode, is also exhibited at the right hemisphere of the matrix. The explanation of Decision Co-Pilot is that the concept is not to eliminate people in automated cycles but to make a complex supporting tool that could identify patterns that are not seen by the naked eye. Nonlinear variable analysis assists the matrix in knowing how organizations will attain optimum results within a considerably reduced cognitive bias and information overload among human beings. Moreover, the above diagram emphasizes the fact that AI-decision-making alignment creates a more appropriate strategic path of contemporary businesses. Critical decisions in the traditional version were often made under the circumstances of extreme urgency; yet, in an AI-powered system, a firm base of Evidence-Based Leadership is provided. This change is not only concerned with making a single decision better, but the whole strength of the organization is to be transformed so as to become more strategically agile. This matrix supports the need to show how, in the future, organizational direction is not only is the data driving the organization but also combined with a vision of sustainable value and a more positive stakeholder experience.

4.3. Strategic Direction in an AI-Driven World

In an artificial intelligence world, the paradigm of traditional and linear planning will have to give place to the multi-layered Strategic Direction approach according to which the idea of balancing technical scale with human values will take precedence. The first strategic direction that has been determined is a transition to Intelligence-Driven Differentiation. The competition between organizations, in this paradigm, is based on proprietary intelligence, created in a dedicated data-AI-human feedback loop. According to case studies in the financial and manufacturing sector, the companies that have successfully succeeded in attaining long-term competitive advantage are the ones that have characterized AI as a co-evolutionary partner, rather than a fixed tool. This plan shows that it would be necessary to invest in the development of so-called long-term Strategic Bastions through the collection of domain-specific information that cannot be reproduced by commodified AI models. Responsible AI should balance personalization with transparency and ethics (Khullar et al., 2026).

The second strategy orientation is the Ecosystemic Value Sharing. The most effective companies will emerge as Platform Managers because the digital economy is more interconnected and depends on AI to allow the value exchange between a network of partners, suppliers, and customers that is large. Such a tendency will bend the efficiency of organizations to the external synergies, in which AI-based APIs and data-sharing standards will yield a type of Network Effect that will benefit all parties involved. It is advised in the study that over fifty percent of the world value creation will be in these AI-enhanced ecosystems in 2026 and that interoperability and collaborative innovation plans, instead of close and proprietary systems, are essential.

The third course is Hyper-Personalization-At-Scale Shift with user experience becoming a strategic indicator. Organisations can move to the stage of individualised value propositions in real time and across aggregated market segments using generative AI and predictive models. The Strategy One segment will involve a radical re-engineering of the marketing and service functions in order to move intrusive advertising to proactive and positive interventions. According to the latest data of digital health implementation, hyper-personalized AI assistants can contribute significantly to patient engagement, and clinical results indicate that there is a significant improvement in adherence to the treatment protocol when personalized interfaces are applied (Bohr and Memarzadeh, 2020).

The fourth strategic direction is to Institutionalize Strong and Ethical AI Leadership. The idea of Ethics-Based Design approach as a regulatory one and due to the increased awareness of the risks of algorithmic bias and data leaks, it has become a crucial concept in the industry. Those organizations that are keen on making sure that their AI initiatives are in line with the global moral principles like the ISO/IEC 42001 are establishing some form of a Social Capital institution to cushion them during market restructuring. The instructions stress the idea that the Value Gap is frequently a Trust Gap and must be removed through a unique concept of leadership that is responsive to the needs of the algorithmic efficacy and accountable to human values and societal prosperity.

In addition, the study reveals that Organizational Ambidexterity is a sustainable positioning strategy. This guidance suggests that firms can optimize their business nature through the automation of their business based on AI (exploitation) and engage in entirely new kinds of business due to the new AI technologies (exploration). The above cases indicate that firms that are said to be ambidextrous are 30 times more probably to endure a shake-up in the industry because they can be restructured to change paths in their activities without losing their fundamental sources of income. The dual strategy is narrowed down with the help of scenario modeling based on AI, which will give the hint on how to find the balance between the short-term stability and long-term innovation.

Radical Human Enhancement should be the workforce strategic direction. This will entail a shift in the workforce paradigm to be shifted to a paradigm in which AI is in place as a cognitive framework that will broaden human possibilities and capabilities to new degrees of creativity and strategic decision-making. Plans in this field are connected with what is known as Experience Architecture that will enable the employees, reduce burnout, and establish a Human-AI Synergy culture. The companies that specialize in this trend discover that AI is more useful in terms of value of human capital when it is engaged in repetitive tasks, and that Human Excellence is found in the occupations with high degrees of empathy and high levels of moral uncertainty.

One of the components of this strategic direction involves the implementation of Dynamic Governance Model. Unlike in the traditional governance systems in the past, AI governance has to be through a Direct Governance system where the control system should be dynamic as the algorithms it controls. It implies real-time auditing of AI results and the continuous re-optimization of the risk parameters, which is facilitated by incoming data. The scenarios of high-stakes systems such as financial and health care show that dynamic governance could reduce Model Risk by at least 60, avoiding AI exploration of unsafe operation space in fluctuating market conditions. This agility of governance is one of the keys to resilience in the operations in the mid-2020s.

The eighth strategic direction is Sustainable AI Transformation, which deals with the environmental and social cost of AI computing. The energy consumption of Large Language Models (LLMs) makes them change to the so-called Green AI and Small Language Models (SLM) that are less carbon-intensive but remain high-performance. The given direction makes the corporate AI strategies work in line with global ESG (Environmental, Social, and Governance) objectives, so that the delivery of digital value does not adversely affect the health of planet. Those firms that are on the forefront of sustainable AI are more popular among institutional investors, which provide them with lower costs of capital and better brand image.

The second, or direction, is Algorithmic Transparency and Explainability (XAI) development. In order to stay in a competitive advantage, the companies must make sure that their AI systems are not black boxes, but can be explained to the employees and authorities. This plan includes coming up with Interpretable Architectures which are correctable by human beings. This orientation plays a key role in sustaining the presence of Knowledge in the institutions where organizations see the reasoning behind the reasons of their decision making and how the institutions adjust to the changing environment. This paper highlights the fact that transparency is an intermediate variable between technical efficiency and human trust.

To sum up, this chapter has examined the paradigm change in digital transformation to an AI-driven transformation and defined the essential, so-called Value Gap, as well as the concept of Dynamic Capabilities that will help to fill the value gap. The numerous studies indicate that when applied to fit algorithms to the richness of the human experience, AI Alchemy is the most potent. Ecosystem co-creation, AI-inspired separate differentiation, and human-focused improvements can help organizations surmount the value gap to the sustainable and purposeful value-generation future. The final purpose of an AI-based world will not be to substitute human experience but to synchronize it with the technological progress and build compassionate and effective corporations.

Customer Experience (CX) development in the digital era is a strategic shift in terms of moving a generic interaction to a mutual comprehension of personal consumer needs. The traditional paradigm restricted an organization to the techniques of Mass Marketing in which only one value proposition is aired to a large audience with the likelihood of minimal engagement and massive resources wastage. In order to imagine the extent of such an overhaul, the readers are asked to consider the "Segment of One" Personalization Funnel shown in the illustration below. The funnel illustrates how the customer journey is continuously being refinanced by targeting broader segments and further narrowing down to the pinnacle of Shared Experience Value Creation by means of AI-driven precision.

Figure 3. Personalization Funnel segments

The diagram3 above shows how AI is a transformational filter that reduces a plethora of behavioral information to actionable and highly personalized interactions. The shift in the focus on the segmented marketing to the segment one is facilitated by real-time predictive modeling as in the scenario of the funnel narrowing as the organizations are able to predict the individual preferences even before they are pronounced out. The diagram underscores the fact that at this last stage there is no longer a transactional relationship between a company and its customers but rather symbiotic. Such a high degree of personalization means that every single point of makes a different impact on the user experience, which allows closing the gap between technical efficiency and human emotional satisfaction.

Moreover, the development of the strategy presented in the diagram above highlights the fact that an individualization of the "Experience" is the most viable means of fueling the long-term "Value." Mass marketing has usually considered the customers as the passive receivers of the information, though the AI-enabled channels show that it has changed to active value co-creation. Together with a strategy of having customized services according to the individual context of the user, organizations will be able to experience a 15-20 percent boost in customer loyalty and retention rates. This alignment, as shown in the flowchart, shows that when under AI is adopted to identify individual uniqueness, the strategic direction generated by it is not only optimal to shareholder value but also to enhance human experience in the digital economy.

5. DISCUSSION: INTEGRATING EXPERIENCE AND VALUE

The results show that the achievement of organizations has shifted past a trade-off in technical efficiency and human satisfaction to a strategic harmony model. Value is created in an AI-driven environment by having systems that enhance human capability but not automate labor. The reduction of the Value Gap through the use of AI at the expense of experience results in a strategic renewal. The use of predictive analytics and generative AI is most suitable under the conditions of human judgmental support rather than the replacement of moral judgment and situation awareness. Centrally located is Experience -Value Synchronicity: There is a direct correlation between employee and customer experiences and shareholder value. Experience of sectors demonstrates that AI sustainable returns are not only based on the reduction of costs, but in fact, the restoration of the Human Premium the ability to think and feel in complex ways (Andriani and Siripipatthanakul, 2026). AI boosts the contribution of human beings by lessening cognitive load, enhancing culture, and contributing to long-term organizational stability. AI turns data into assets of strategic insights, reducing uncertainty by sensing and responding in real-time. However, predictive ability should not be based on scientific moralism; technology that is not connected to human meaning is likely to be alienated and lose its reputation. AI architectures focused on purpose, in turn, establish a sense of trust and bring quality talent on board.

With dynamic capabilities, AI entails an element of feedback which becomes part of the strategic processes and makes them relevant and agile. Algorithms are efficient to increase margins, although continued benefit requires gains to be reinvested in experience improvement. Transparency and explainability in ethics is thus a strategic resource, which strengthens stakeholder trust and institutional legitimacy. The discussion also highlights the Cognitive Ambidexterity whereby precision based on data is offset by human interpretation. Evidence-based decisions are supported by hybrid intelligence, which does not eliminate the professional intuition. The AI-supported knowledge architectures enable faster information exchange, create horizontal hierarchies, and become more responsive to changes in the market.

This is further aligned by sustainability. The AI-optimized operations would provide support to the environmental objectives and enhance the ESG performance. Generative strategic planning puts leaders on their toes, allowing them to see systemic risks and protect long-term value. Finally, AI-based competitive advantage is, after all, not technological but cultural. Digital maturity indicates the considered combination of machine intelligence and human intent. This reinforcing cycle is represented in figure 4 the AI Alchemy Synergy Framework: the institutional trust, workforce empowerment, customer loyalty, and shareholder value develop simultaneously. The idea of sustainable transformation is thus a result of the ongoing process of harmonizing the Values and Experiences, as AI enhances the human potential but does not substitute it.

Figure 4. Synergy Framework

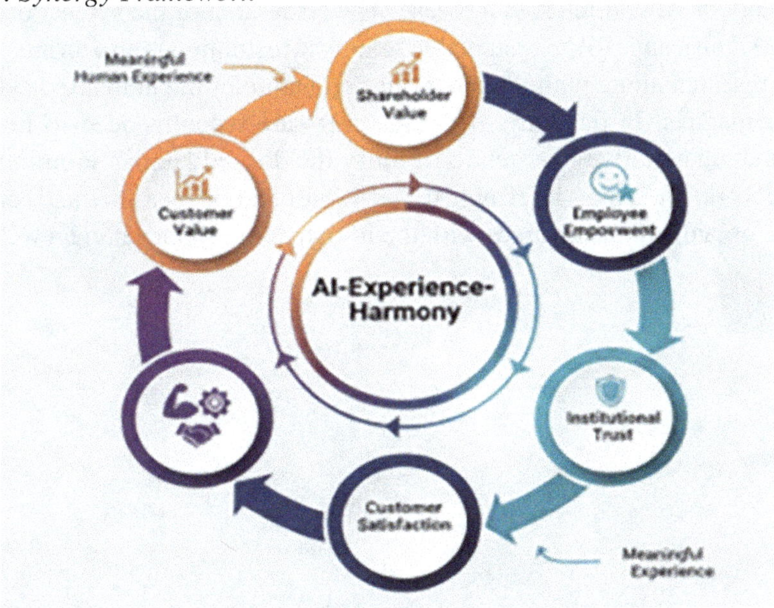

6. CONCLUSION & FUTURE RESEARCH

On the whole, the chapter is a valuable theoretical and empirical contribution to the discourse on AI-driven digital transformation, as it has incorporated the Resource-Based View, Dynamic Capability Theory, and Service-Dominant Logic into one framework, which was called AI-Experience-Value. Theoretically, this study puts AI in the role of an active facilitator of value co-creation, as it involves active use of machine intelligence and human experience to help bridge the so-called Value Gap, by aligning the two. Practically, the findings form a strategic roadmap of organizational leaders, as sustainable competitive advantage in the mid-2020s will be founded on Digital Capability and Ethical Governance, and not necessarily on computing scale. The examples of companies in the financial, healthcare, and manufacturing industries that have successfully achieved a balance between shareholder value and meaningful user experiences make this piece a guiding light in determining the way to achieve the actual digital maturity in the tumultuous global economy. Notwithstanding such findings, this study recognizes the following limitations: First, the study is a qualitative research that may be restricted to the small businesses or nonprofits because of the study only covering three different industry sectors. It is more than that, the long-term stability of the given strategic direction is the sphere that has to be investigated more. Additional investigation is required as the development of AI continues to increase. The discussion of the subject of Agentic AI and its significance to the sustainable scientific institution is also an area of focus in future research along with the cross-cultural nature of the human-AI synergy in emerging markets. In this case, the researchers are recommended to implement longitudinal quantitative research to quantify the desired Human Premium of AI-enhanced workflows, thus, informing the co-value creation measures and complying the future organizational changes with the initiative to enhance human well-being.

REFERENCES

Albasrie, A. D. A., Himawan, I. S., & Sharipudin, C. (2024). Sustainable wellness tourism in Indonesia (Case study on health tourism development at Hanara Wellbeing Center Bandung). *Media Konservasi, 2S*(3), 435–435. DOI: 10.29244/medkon.29.3.435

Andriani, A. D. (2025). The future of digital content: AI-generated texts, images, videos, and real-time production. In *Impacts of AI-Generated Content on Brand Reputation* (pp. 149–176). IGI Global Scientific Publishing. DOI: 10.4018/979-8-3373-4327-3.ch006

Andriani, A. D., Mulyana, D., Dida, S. C., & Wahyudin, U. (2021). The role of healing environment in reducing the stress of patients with non-communicable disease. *Journal of Natural Science, Biology, and Medicine, 12*(3), 300–306. DOI: 10.4103/jnsbm.JNSBM_12_3_7

Andriani, A. D., C Siripipatthanakul, S. (2025). Strategic Governance Communication and Green Indicators for Digital Business Sustainability.

Andriani, A. D. C., & Siripipatthanakul, S. (2026). Technology-Driven Organization Policies: E-Waste Governance Framework. In Technology Policy and Its Impact on Green Governance and Sustainability (pp. 31-62). IGI Global Scientific Publishing.

Bohr, A. C., & Memarzadeh, K. (2020). *Artificial Intelligence in Healthcare*. Academic Press.

Brynjolfsson, E., Rock, D. C., & Syverson, C. (2021). The productivity J-curve: How intangible capital signals errors in future efficiency statistics. *Science, 371*(6525), 161–164.

Chui, M., Hazan, E., Roberts, R., Singla, A., Smaje, K., Sukharevsky, A., Kwakye, J. C., & Wright, G. (2023). *The economic potential of generative AI: The next productivity frontier*. McKinsey Global Institute.

Davenport, T. H. C., & Mittal, N. (2022). *All-in on AI: How smart companies win big with artificial intelligence*. Harvard Business Review Press.

Dawadi, S., Shrestha, S. C., & Giri, R. A. (2021). Mixed-methods research: A discussion on its types, challenges, and ethics. *Journal of Practical Studies in Education, 2*(2), 25–36. DOI: 10.46809/jpse.v2i2.20

Fischer, M., Imgrund, F., Janina, C. C., & Winkelmann, A. (2020). Strategy followed by structure: Antecedents of business model adaptability in the digital age. *International Journal of Information Management*, *52*, 102095.

Gustafsson, J. (2020). Single case studies vs. multiple case studies: A comparative study. Academy of Business. *Engineering and Science*, •••, 1–15.

Khullar, S., Baghel, R. S., & Swami, P. (2026). Human-AI collaboration: Balancing trust, emotion, and productivity. In *AI hallucination management in the enterprise metaverse*. IGI Global Scientific Publishing., DOI: 10.4018/979-8-3373-7534-2.ch003

Khullar, S., Kate, C., Rao, A. S., Sharrif, U. H., Gupta, A., & Kaliappan, S. (2026). Explainable intelligence for ethical human-centric AI: Trust modeling using gradient boosting. In *Proceedings of the 2026 5th International Conference on Innovative Practices in Technology and Management (ICIPTM)* (pp. 1–9). IEEE. DOI: 10.1109/ICIPTM69057.2026.11465350

Khullar, S., Sobhan, A., Tank, N., & Swami, P. (2026). From personalization to responsibility: AI-driven adaptive learning environments. In *Ethical leadership and pedagogical transformation in AI-driven education*. IGI Global Scientific Publishing., DOI: 10.4018/979-8-2600-1840-8.ch010

Khullar, S., & Tank, N. (2026). Integrating AI inference with IoT and big data for smart city solutions. In *Harnessing AI inference for intelligent decision-making in real-time dataflows*. IGI Global Scientific Publishing., DOI: 10.4018/979-8-3373-7046-0.ch009

Marr, B. (2023). *Future skill: The 20 skills and competencies everyone needs to succeed in a digital world*. Wiley.

Mikalef, P. C., & Gupta, M. (2021). Artificial intelligence capability: Conceptualization, measurement calibration, and link to competitive advantage. *MIS uarterly*, *45*(1), 335–359.

Mustak, M., et al. (2021). Deep learning in marketing: A review and research agenda.

Saldaña, J. (2021). *The coding manual for qualitative researchers*. SAGE Publications.

Sharipudin, M. N. S., Rejab, M. M., Tugiman, N., Indiyati, D., C Andriani, A. D. (2024). The influence of digital communication technology on university branding: An understanding of open and distance learning (ODL) from students' perspectives. Jurnal Komunikasi: Malaysian Journal of Communication.

Vargo, S. L. C., & Lusch, R. F. (2020). Service-dominant logic 2025. *International Journal of Research in Marketing*, *37*(1), 1–10.

Vaska, S.. (2021). Digital transformation: Lessons from organizations that have successfully balanced exploration and exploitation. *Frontiers in Psychology*, *12*, 629864.

Verhoef, P. C., Broekhuizen, T., Bart, Y., Bhattacharya, A., Dong, J. ., Fabian, N., & Haenlein, C. (2021). Digital transformation: A multidisciplinary reflection and research agenda. *Journal of Business Research*, *122*, 889–901. DOI: 10.1016/j.jbusres.2019.09.022

Warner, K. S. C., & Wäger, M. (2020). Building dynamic capabilities for digital transformation: An ongoing process of strategic renewal. *Long Range Planning*, *53*(3), 101910.

World Economic Forum. (2024). The future of jobs report 2024. Geneva: WEF.

Chapter 2
Re-centering Human Experience in AI-Driven Organizations:
An EX-CX-Purpose Alignment Framework

Sakshi Mann
http://orcid.org/0009-0002-8238-5268
School of Business, Indira University, Pune, India

Shikha Mann
http://orcid.org/0000-0003-0395-9164
School of Business, Indira University, Pune, India

ABSTRACT

Artificial intelligence (AI) is reshaping organizations beyond technological change, influencing how work is designed, services are delivered, and values are enacted. This chapter argues that employee experience (EX), customer experience (CX), and organizational purpose are interconnected through shared AI-enabled design choices rather than separate domains. Building on a sociotechnical perspective, it develops the EX–CX–Purpose Alignment Framework, positioning employee experience as a key link between internal workforce dynamics and external service outcomes. Three propositions are advanced: algorithmic authority reduces perceived fairness without voice mechanisms; declines in employee experience precede customer experience deterioration; and institutionalized purpose strengthens alignment. Drawing on insights from India's service sectors, the chapter highlights how misalignment undermines trust and performance, and outlines implications for HR leadership, governance, and capability development.

DOI: 10.4018/979-8-3373-8282-1.ch002

1. INTRODUCTION: THE HUMAN STAKES OF AI-DRIVEN TRANSFORMATION

Artificial intelligence has moved out of pilot projects and into everyday operations. Recruitment systems filter applications before any human reads them, performance dashboards update continuously, and customer interactions run through automated routing. What was called innovation a few years ago is now routine infrastructure.

Much of the discussion around AI still centres on efficiency, scale, and predictive accuracy. These matter, but they leave a more immediate question unanswered: what does this transformation mean for the people who work inside these systems and the people served by them? The question is hard to answer partly because nobody experiences AI as a standalone technology.

In practice, AI arrives through organizational arrangements. Employees meet it as task allocation tools, shifting targets, skill-matching platforms, and evaluation mechanisms that run on algorithmic inputs. Customers meet it as mediated interactions that prioritize speed and consistency, sometimes at the cost of flexibility. People are not simply interacting with technology. They deal with organizational choices that have been written into technological systems.

When AI is introduced as a technical upgrade, its human implications get considered later, if at all. Yet the effects run deep. Roles change, discretion narrows, and accountability blurs. Employees ask where decision boundaries sit and whether decisions can be questioned. Customers ask the same when automated processes fail or produce outcomes no one can explain. As Kellogg et al. (2020) note, algorithmic systems do not remove control. They redistribute it in ways that are less visible and therefore harder to challenge.

Organizational responses are uneven. HR concentrates on reskilling and workforce readiness. Customer-facing functions push automation and personalization. Leadership talks about ethics and purpose. Each effort has value, yet they rarely connect. Systems built for efficiency raise pressure on employees. Value statements sit uneasily beside the way algorithmic decisions are actually made. HR policies lag the pace of technological change (Malik et al., 2023).

These tensions are easy to see in large service-driven contexts such as India's business process and customer support sectors. Practitioner observations from high-volume support environments suggest that performance dashboards can update faster than managerial feedback cycles. Targets shift before expectations are understood, and employees are left unsure how they are being evaluated and by whom.

This chapter addresses three gaps. First, employee experience (EX), customer experience (CX), and AI governance are usually studied separately, even though the same design choices shape all three. Second, little conceptual work positions HR as the connecting mechanism between internal employee realities and external customer outcomes in AI-enabled environments (Malik et al., 2023; Kim et al., 2025). Third, emerging economy settings, particularly India's large-scale service and business process sectors, remain underrepresented in the algorithmic governance literature despite the insight they offer at scale (Economic Survey of India, 2024–2025).

From this standpoint, EX is more than a supporting factor. In digitally mediated environments, performance depends not only on technological capability but on whether people systems are designed to work with that technology. When AI is deployed purely for optimization, without attention to discretion, employment relationships, and ethical responsibility, trust weakens. Not immediately. Over time.

Different outcomes are possible. Practitioner observations from Indian service-sector settings suggest that organizations which involve HR in technology design decisions face fewer disconnects between system outputs and employee expectations. Where HR systems support judgment, encourage learning, and clarify accountability, AI can serve both organizational performance and human dignity. These outcomes depend on deliberate choices in design and governance (Floridi et al., 2018; Fenwick et al., 2024).

1.1 Conceptual Development Approach

This chapter is conceptual. The framework was developed through an integrative synthesis of published literature, in the sense described by Torraco (2005) and Jaakkola (2020), rather than through primary data collection. Four literature domains were reviewed: employee experience and work design under algorithmic management; service management research on the employee-customer interface, including the service-profit chain and emotional labor; organizational purpose, ethics, and responsible-AI governance; and strategic human resource management, with particular attention to the Ability-Motivation-Opportunity tradition and procedural justice theory.

The three central constructs, EX, CX, and organizational purpose, were selected because each recurs across these literatures as a point at which AI adoption produces consequences that efficiency metrics miss, and because the relationships among the three remain undertheorized when studied separately. The propositions state relationships that appear consistently across these domains but have not been formally tested in AI-enabled service settings. They are testable statements, not findings.

The chapter also draws on the authors' professional experience in corporate HR roles and continuing industry engagement with Indian service-sector organizations. These observations were not collected through formal research. No interviews were conducted and no organizational records were accessed. Where such observations appear, they are contextual illustrations, signalled with wording such as "practitioner observations from Indian service-sector settings suggest," and are supported with published evidence wherever it exists.

Two terms are used deliberately. "AI-driven transformation" refers to the broader process of organizational change associated with AI adoption. "AI-enabled" describes the systems, functions, and organizations in which AI operates alongside human judgment.

1.2 Structure of the Chapter

The argument runs in three strands. The first examines how AI reshapes EX through work design, authority, fairness, and career sustainability. The second treats CX as an output of service systems in which human and technological elements interact. The third examines organizational purpose as an ethical foundation and a guide for decision-making in AI adoption. The strands come together in the EX-CX-Purpose Alignment Framework, supported by three propositions. The chapter closes with implications for HR leaders, organizations, and policymakers, and directions for future research.

2. REIMAGINING EMPLOYEE EXPERIENCE IN AI-ENABLED ORGANIZATIONS: AN HR ARCHITECTURE PERSPECTIVE

2.1 Employee Experience as a Systemic Outcome

Discussions of AI adoption usually frame EX narrowly, as a matter of perception: do employees trust the tools, do they feel comfortable with automation. Perceptions matter, but they are not where experience comes from. Employee experience is also produced by how employment systems are structured and governed.

In this chapter, EX means the cumulative quality of an employee's interactions with the organization's systems, processes, and relationships across the employment life cycle (Plaskoff, 2017). Several neighboring constructs get used interchangeably with it, and they should not be. Engagement is the psychological presence and energy a person brings to a role (Kahn, 1990). Job satisfaction is an evaluative attitude toward the job. Well-being concerns physical and psychological health. Meaningful work is the sense that one's work carries significance (Rosso et al., 2010). These are outcomes that a given employee experience may produce or erode. EX itself is the designed and lived condition from which they emerge. The distinction matters because AI systems act directly on that condition, on how work is allocated, evaluated, and rewarded, and only through it on the attitudes that follow.

HR research has long shown that employee attitudes and behaviors are produced by combinations of formal and informal arrangements: recruitment practices, performance management, reward structures, career pathways (Appelbaum, Bailey, Berg, & Kalleberg, 2000). As AI enters recruitment screening, task allocation, performance evaluation, and learning platforms, it joins this architecture. It does not merely support work. It reshapes the employment relationship itself.

This view has deep roots in socio-technical systems theory. Early studies of British coal mining found that redesigning the technical organization of work while ignoring its social organization damaged both output and morale (Trist & Bamforth, 1951). The design principle that emerged, joint optimization, holds that technical and social subsystems must be designed together, because improving one while neglecting the other degrades the whole (Cherns, 1976). AI presents the same problem in sharper form, since here the technical subsystem itself makes decisions. An algorithm can be accurate and still produce poor outcomes if the surrounding arrangements for discretion, explanation, and accountability are left undesigned. The chapter treats joint optimization as a baseline assumption, consistent with the sociotechnical turn in recent HRM scholarship, where technology is an active shaper of work rather than a neutral tool (Kim et al., 2025).

The question, then, is not whether employees hold favorable attitudes toward AI. It is what kind of employment relationship these systems produce over time. Do they expand learning and participation, or narrow discretion and reinforce control? EX is a lived outcome of system design, not a by-product of individual perception.

2.2 Work Design and the Redistribution of Authority

One visible shift concerns how authority is exercised. Managers once interpreted performance, adjusted expectations, and allocated work with context in mind. Algorithmic systems automate parts of this interpretive role. Tasks are assigned in real time, metrics update continuously, and workflow optimization runs inside daily operations.

In large Indian IT services and business process organizations, including BFSI firms, AI-driven task allocation has improved coordination and scale. Practitioner observations from these settings suggest a shift in how authority is felt. Performance targets appear system-generated rather than negotiated. Thresholds change without visible discussion, and deviations require justification even when the underlying logic is unclear. Control is present, but its source is harder to locate.

Research on algorithmic management finds the same pattern: control is redistributed, not removed, and becomes harder to question (Kellogg et al., 2020). Duggan et al. (2023) observe comparable dynamics in the gig economy, where app-based control can mirror and sometimes intensify traditional managerial structures.

When employees cannot tell where automated decision-making ends and human judgment begins, they start treating system outputs as fixed, and perceived autonomy erodes. Clarity about decision rights and accountability is therefore not administrative housekeeping. Without it, efficiency gains come at the cost of commitment.

2.3 Fairness, Voice, and Procedural Justice

As authority becomes technologically mediated, fairness concerns sharpen. Employees judge processes as well as outcomes. Procedural justice theory holds that decisions are more likely to be accepted when processes are transparent, consistent, and allow meaningful voice (Lind & Tyler, 1988).

AI-enabled HR systems now influence high-stakes decisions: candidate screening, performance ranking, reward allocation. They are presented as objective. But objectivity without explainability feels arbitrary. When decision criteria shift dynamically or stay opaque, even accurate outcomes read as unfair.

Practitioner observations from large service and banking organizations in India illustrate the tension. Employees must explain performance shortfalls flagged by AI dashboards, while changes in system parameters arrive without any comparable explanation. Bankins et al. (2022) find that employees judge AI-made HR decisions through the lens of interactional justice, and that perceptions of respectful treatment differ sharply depending on whether a human or an AI makes the decision.

Voice mechanisms are therefore essential, not optional. Formal appeals, human review, and accessible explanations reinforce legitimacy. Where these are absent, employees keep complying, but engagement becomes brittle.

Voice also needs to begin earlier than the appeal stage. Most discussions of voice under algorithmic management concentrate on what happens after a decision. Participation before and during deployment matters at least as much. Employees who test allocation rules, flag unworkable thresholds during pilots, and review dashboards before rollout catch design errors that no appeal process will later reach. Socio-technical design has long treated such participation as a condition of workable systems, not a courtesy (Cherns, 1976). In this chapter, voice covers both stages: participation in design, testing, and monitoring, and contestation of decisions once made.

The relationship between algorithmic authority and perceived fairness will not be uniform. It plausibly depends on decision accuracy, task type, transparency of criteria, employee participation in design, and the trust employees already place in management. Proposition 1 is framed as conditional, not deterministic.

Proposition 1: Algorithmic authority is likely to reduce employees' perceived procedural justice where decision criteria are opaque and voice mechanisms are weak. This effect is expected to weaken, and may reverse, where explanation processes, appeal pathways, defined human override authority, and employee participation in system design are institutionalized. Its strength is also expected to vary with decision accuracy, task type, and pre-existing trust in management.

2.4 Skill Governance and Career Sustainability

AI-enabled organizations are described as learning-oriented. Predictive systems identify skill gaps, recommend training, and classify employees by expected adaptability. This allows personalized development. It also introduces new control.

Predictive labels can harden. Practitioner accounts from Indian IT services and BFSI organizations undergoing digital transformation suggest that mid-career employees are uneasy about algorithmic skill tagging. Positioned as developmental, such classifications can quietly steer career mobility once treated as fixed assessments.

The Ability-Motivation-Opportunity (AMO) framework helps here (Appelbaum et al., 2000). AI touches all three components: it shapes capability through training recommendations, signals expectations through metrics, and regulates opportunity through access to roles and projects. In many cases AI strengthens Ability through targeted learning while constraining Opportunity by narrowing role pathways. Dima et al. (2024) show that AI can enhance capability development and simultaneously standardize career trajectories.

Sustaining careers under these conditions requires preserving agency. Learning systems should support dialogue rather than replace it, and career pathways must stay adaptable. In a labour market the size of India's service sector, early restrictions on mobility compound for years.

2.5 Well-Being and the Hidden Costs of Optimization

The well-being implications of AI receive far less attention than the productivity claims. Continuous monitoring, real-time feedback, and predictive systems can intensify work without formally increasing workload.

In digitally enabled financial services environments in India, frontline work is tightly structured. Interactions are timed, responses follow AI prompts, escalation rules are predefined. Each element improves efficiency. Together they compress recovery space: the short intervals between interactions in which employees reset attention, finish follow-up work, and regain composure before the next demand. When systems schedule work back to back, those intervals disappear while measured workload stays constant.

Automation can reduce routine demands and still introduce new strain: alert fatigue, the effort of interpreting system outputs, the wear of constant visibility (Parker & Grote, 2022; Bienefeld et al., 2025). Well-being here is not an individual matter. It is a property of work design. When systems reward speed and consistency without accounting for cognitive and emotional load, stress gets built into the workflow, and no downstream wellness programme removes it.

2.6 Designing AI-Enabled HR Systems With Human Intent

Reimagining EX requires deliberate design. Employees need to know which decisions are automated, who owns system parameters, and how exceptions are handled. Human judgment stays central wherever contextual understanding is required.

Organizations also need to evaluate AI beyond immediate efficiency. A capability-focused approach asks how these systems contribute to long-term employability and adaptability (Fenwick et al., 2024).

HR sits at the centre of this work. Design choices embedded in AI systems shape authority, fairness, learning, and well-being at the same time. Employee experience is not a reaction to technology. It reflects how these systems are governed.

Table 1. Dimensions of Employee Experience in AI-Enabled Organizations

EX Dimension	AI-Driven Challenge	HR Design Imperative	Key Reference
Work Design & Authority	Algorithmic task allocation reduces visible human authority; justification asymmetry between employee deviations and system recalibrations	Define clear decision rights; specify human override mechanisms; ensure system logic is communicated	Kellogg et al. (2020); Duggan et al. (2023)
Fairness & Procedural Justice	Opaque algorithmic criteria undermine legitimacy; high-stakes decisions lack explainability	Build appeal and review pathways; involve employees in system design and testing; pair algorithm updates with explanation processes	Lind & Tyler (1988); Bankins et al. (2022)
Skill Governance	Predictive skill tags may harden into fixed career labels; AI shifts AMO balance toward Ability while constraining Opportunity	Treat learning analytics as conversation tools; preserve skill negotiability and career flexibility	Appelbaum et al. (2000); Dima et al. (2024)
Well-Being	Continuous monitoring and system-paced work compress discretion; emotional and cognitive load intensifies	Integrate well-being metrics upstream; design recovery space into workflow architecture	Parker & Grote (2022); Bienefeld et al. (2025)
Capability Development	Short-term efficiency optimization may narrow future employability and limit workforce adaptability	Invest in capability as long-term strategic asset; avoid over-reliance on algorithmic skill foreclosures	Fenwick et al. (2024); Dima et al. (2024)

Note: EX = Employee Experience; AMO = Ability–Motivation–Opportunity framework. Table 1 synthesizes the principal dimensions of employee experience affected by AI-enabled HR systems, with theoretical anchors and HR design responses.

3. CUSTOMER EXPERIENCE AS WORKFORCE DESIGN IN AI-DRIVEN ORGANIZATIONS

3.1 Reframing Customer Experience Through an HR Lens

In AI-driven organizations, CX is discussed in technological terms: personalization algorithms, chatbot capability, predictive analytics, digital platforms. These matter, but the framing hides a basic fact. Even services mediated by intelligent systems are delivered by people working inside organizational structures.

CX is produced through workforce design. It depends on how much discretion employees hold, how their performance is measured, and how far they can respond to what a customer actually needs. When AI systems define prompts, escalation routes, and decision thresholds, they set the conditions under which employees can exercise judgment. CX cannot be separated from HR architecture (Malik et al., 2023). Service quality reflects system accuracy and the room employees have to act within system boundaries.

The connection between EX and CX runs through identifiable mechanisms, not vague spillover. Service research has long tied internal work conditions to external service outcomes, through the service-profit chain (Heskett et al., 1997) and through evidence that employees' perceptions of service climate predict customers' perceptions of quality (Schneider et al., 1998). In AI-enabled settings, six mechanisms stand out. Frontline discretion decides whether an employee can leave the script when the situation demands it. Emotional availability decides whether composure and empathy survive system-paced work. Interpretive capability lets an employee judge when an AI recommendation does not fit the case in front of them. Service-recovery authority decides whether a failure is fixed on the spot or joins an escalation queue. Employee continuity matters because attrition resets relational knowledge, leaving customers with people who lack context. And willingness to exercise voice decides whether frontline staff report system faults before customers hit them repeatedly. Each is a workforce design choice before it becomes a service outcome.

The relationship shows itself when operational metrics hold steady while customer satisfaction falls. What looks like a service problem is usually a design problem.

This leads to the following proposition, framed as a contribution claim rather than a strict temporal sequence, since establishing that EX decline comes before CX decline would require longitudinal evidence.

Proposition 2: Deterioration in employee experience under AI-enabled systems is likely to contribute to subsequent deterioration in customer experience. When workforce architecture limits discretion, compresses recovery space, or weakens relational capability, service quality is expected to decline even where operational performance indicators remain stable.

3.2 Frontline Roles Under Algorithmic Structuring

Across banking, telecommunications, healthcare, and public services, AI has reshaped frontline work. Decision-support tools assist credit approvals, fraud systems flag irregularities, triaging algorithms rank customer cases. Consistency and speed improve. The enactment of the role changes with them.

Practitioner accounts from Indian BFSI organizations undergoing digital transformation, including large private banks on AI-supported platforms, suggest that frontline work increasingly feels like operating the system rather than solving the customer's problem. AI defines "next best actions," and escalation paths sit inside predefined workflows. Discretion exists, but conditionally.

Employees remain responsible for outcomes while their room to interpret and adapt shrinks. Work design research links such redesign to both engagement and strain, particularly in roles with limited task variety (Parker & Knight, 2024). The consequences reach customers. When frontline roles are defined around compliance, interactions turn procedural. Efficiency rises while relational depth and trust thin out. Professional judgment needs space to operate if service quality is to hold.

3.3 Capability Beyond Technical Literacy

AI in service delivery expands capability requirements in ways training programmes rarely reflect. Most initiatives teach technical use: following workflows, reading dashboards, entering data accurately. Necessary, not sufficient.

Effective service in AI-mediated environments also rests on interpretive and relational capability. Interpretive capability means assessing AI recommendations critically, recognizing when system logic does not fit the situation, and explaining constraints in plain terms. Relational capability means sustaining trust, empathy, and responsiveness inside interactions partly shaped by automation. Together they underpin workable human-AI service encounters (Mortati & Viana Mundstock Freitas, 2026). Organizations that train only for compliance struggle when exceptions arise. Those that build interpretive and relational capability hold service quality under algorithmic conditions.

3.4 Emotional Labor Under Algorithmic Conditions

Service work has always involved emotional labor: regulating one's emotions to meet organizational expectations (Hochschild, 1983). AI does not remove the requirement. It changes how it is experienced.

Algorithmic performance systems track speed, volume, and accuracy in detail. They barely register emotional strain. Employees are expected to stay composed and empathetic while working at system-defined speeds, so emotional regulation becomes continuous rather than occasional. A structural tension follows: performance systems reward measurable output while relational effort stays invisible. Interactions grow efficient and less meaningful at the same time. Sustaining emotionally viable work is a design responsibility (Parker & Knight, 2024), which means emotional load belongs inside performance metrics, workflow structures, and support mechanisms, not in the aftermath.

3.5 Trust, Accountability, and the Human Interface

Discussions of AI and trust dwell on data privacy and technical transparency. In service contexts, customers care about something more basic: accountability. When AI systems deny credit, flag transactions, or delay claims, customers rarely want a technical explanation. They want to know whether a human can review the decision and take responsibility. The point is sharpest in India's financial services and public sectors, where algorithmic decisions affect access to essential services. Formal compliance with system rules does not translate into perceived fairness.

Customer contestability therefore deserves the same attention as employee voice. Customers affected by high-stakes automated decisions, a rejected loan application, a frozen account, a delayed insurance claim, need four things: an explanation they can understand, a route to human review, a way to correct wrong records, and an escalation path when review fails. An organization that builds appeal rights for its employees but leaves its customers facing a chatbot wall has solved half of the contestability problem. In the framework developed in Section 5, customer contestability sits alongside employee voice within the same governance layer.

A related tension appears on the employee side of the interface. Employees are held responsible for outcomes they are not empowered to change. HR systems shape this interface by defining discretion, escalation pathways, and protection for employees who question system decisions. Where employees can intervene, they act as intermediaries between AI systems and human needs. Where they cannot, they become conduits of automation.

3.6 Integrating Workforce Design and Customer Outcomes

In AI-enabled organizations, CX is inseparable from workforce design. Treating CX as a technology or branding initiative overlooks the employment systems that carry it. Decisions about automation, personalization, and predictive analytics need to be weighed against their effects on autonomy, capability development, and well-being. When HR leaders enter AI design decisions early, trade-offs between efficiency and relational quality get addressed while they are still cheap to fix. When workforce architecture and service logic align, AI supports trust instead of eroding it.

Table 2. Frontline Workforce Capabilities for AI-Mediated Service Delivery

Capability Domain	Description	Risk When Absent	HR Design Response
Technical Literacy	Ability to use AI tools, interpret dashboards, and follow structured workflows	Process errors, inefficient use, over-reliance on system outputs	System training, user-centred design, workflow-aligned onboarding
Interpretive Capability	Ability to assess AI outputs contextually and explain decisions	Rigid service encounters, poor handling of exceptions, customer frustration	Scenario-based training, case learning, reflective supervision
Relational Capability	Ability to sustain empathy and trust in structured interactions	Transactional service, weakened loyalty, loss of relationship quality	Emotional intelligence development, discretion-preserving role design
Escalation Authority	Ability to override or adapt system outputs when required	Employees act as system conduits, accountability gaps	Clear override rules, governed frontline discretion

Note: The capability domains are mutually reinforcing. Interpretive and relational capabilities are particularly interdependent in non-routine service encounters.

3.7 Bridging Reflection: From Experience to Purpose

The analysis so far shows AI reshaping employee experience and, through workforce design, customer experience. One pattern repeats. The decisive factor is not the technology, but the organizational logic embedded in it: how authority, discretion, capability, and accountability are configured.

A larger question follows. If AI systems shape both work design and service delivery, what principles guide the systems themselves? Efficiency alone cannot. When algorithms set thresholds, allocate authority, and rank outcomes, they encode organizational values, and those values need an explicit governing framework. Organizational purpose stops being a narrative statement and becomes a structural requirement. The next section takes this up directly.

4. PURPOSE AS THE ETHICAL AND STRATEGIC ANCHOR OF AI ADOPTION

4.1 Moving Beyond Purpose as Rhetoric

Organizational purpose has re-emerged as a central theme in AI adoption, presented as an ethical guide and a reference point for responsible innovation. In practice it frequently stays symbolic: visible in mission statements and leadership communication, absent from everyday decision-making.

Purpose also needs separating from four neighboring terms it gets merged with. A mission statement describes what the organization does. Values name the behaviors it says it prizes. Ethics statements and responsible-AI policies declare standards it intends to meet. Purpose, as used here, is the reason the organization exists in a form capable of governing decisions. It becomes meaningful only when translated into decision rights, resource allocation, accountability for outcomes, and the ability of affected people to contest decisions. A firm can hold a polished mission, published values, and a responsible-AI policy and still lack purpose in this operational sense, because none of those documents settles who may override an algorithm or what happens when someone objects.

The gap widens in AI-enabled environments. Algorithmic systems scale decisions, automate thresholds, and redistribute authority. Once decisions are embedded in systems, values become operational rules. What an organization stands for shows up in how its algorithms allocate opportunity, distribute risk, and define acceptable outcomes, not only in what it says. Where purpose lacks structural anchoring, efficiency dominates and fairness recedes. Floridi et al. (2018) argue that ethical legitimacy comes from consistent, visible practice rather than declaration, and the stakes are highest in employment, where algorithmic decisions touch career progression, dignity, and economic security.

4.2 Embedding Purpose in Governance and Decision Rights

AI raises a governance challenge beyond regulatory compliance. As algorithmic systems influence hiring, performance differentiation, and workforce planning, authority operates through technological mediation. The question is not whether AI is used but how responsibility is structured around it. Who can override automated recommendations? How are disputes handled? Where does accountability sit when outcomes go wrong?

Human oversight illustrates the difference between formal and operational purpose. Many governance frameworks require a human in the loop. The presence of a person is not oversight. An employee reviewing algorithmic outputs can only do the job under specific conditions. They need authority to change the outcome, not merely record an objection. They need enough expertise to understand what the system is doing, and enough time to apply it; a reviewer clearing hundreds of flagged cases an hour is ratifying, not reviewing. They need information in a form they can interpret, protection from retaliation when they challenge outputs, and documented accountability so responsibility is traceable. Absent these conditions, oversight is rubber-stamp review, and the purpose written into governance documents stops at the page.

Mökander and Floridi (2023) show that effective AI governance connects existing organizational processes so ethical reflection runs through the whole AI lifecycle rather than surfacing at deployment. In many rapidly digitalizing Indian organizations, AI arrives to improve scale while governance structures evolve more slowly. When purpose is not embedded in HR decision frameworks, and appeal or oversight processes stay vague, responsibility diffuses. Purpose-driven governance does not slow automation. It puts structure around it. Mökander et al. (2022) find that organizations achieve stronger governance by adapting and connecting existing mechanisms rather than inventing new ones.

4.3 Ethical AI as an Employment Relationship Issue

Ethical AI debates focus on data privacy, transparency, and compliance. Necessary, but incomplete, because algorithmic systems shape employment relationships directly: task allocation, performance evaluation, promotion, career continuity. Stahl et al. (2016) argue that ethical responsibility extends past technical accuracy to the power dynamics and human consequences built into system use.

From an HR perspective, ethical AI runs through procedural justice and legitimacy. Employees accept algorithmic decision-making when processes are fair and consistent with organizational values (Floridi et al., 2018). The ILO (2025) identifies five recurring principles across global AI ethics frameworks: beneficence, non-maleficence, justice, autonomy, and explicability. All five carry extra weight in employment, where power imbalances and long-term consequences are pronounced. Purpose, in this setting, is not abstract. It is enacted through HR systems that determine fairness, transparency, and accountability in daily practice.

4.4 Leadership, Moral Distance, and Algorithmic Delegation

AI can create moral distance. When decisions are informed by algorithms, responsibility appears less direct; outcomes get attributed to system logic rather than organizational choice. Delegating decision support to AI does not delegate ethical responsibility. Restructuring, performance evaluation, and opportunity allocation remain organizational actions, whatever predictive system supports them.

HR has a specific job here. Leadership accountability frameworks, governance processes, and performance systems must keep responsibility human. When AI influences high-stakes outcomes, accountability needs to be visible and traceable. Practitioner observations from Indian service-sector settings suggest that organizations which keep clear ownership of AI-mediated decisions hold their ethical commitments more steadily over time. Purpose survives delegation when delegation strengthens judgment instead of replacing responsibility.

4.5 Purpose, Capability Development, and Long-Term Employability

A persistent tension separates short-term efficiency from long-term employability. Intelligent systems optimize immediate performance and can quietly constrain future opportunities when capability development is deprioritized. A purpose-driven approach treats workforce adaptability as central to sustainability: learning systems, reskilling, and career pathways should expand future possibilities, not just patch current gaps.

The point is acute in India, where a large service workforce is undergoing rapid digital transformation. The Economic Survey of India (2024–2025) notes that AI adoption may disproportionately affect lower- and middle-income workers unless matched by institutional investment in skill development. Organizations that treat employability as a strategic commitment rather than a by-product of efficiency are better placed to build durable workforce systems.

4.6 Purpose as Strategic Integrator

Purpose plays an integrative role. It gives organizations a basis for weighing trade-offs between efficiency and fairness, automation and discretion, short-term gains and long-term durability. Embedded through HR governance and leadership accountability, purpose becomes a strategic resource rather than a slogan, connecting workforce design, service delivery, and technological capability into one coherent system. In AI-enabled environments, purpose is not a layer added to strategy. It is the framework through which systems are evaluated, adjusted, and legitimized.

5. THE EX-CX-PURPOSE ALIGNMENT FRAMEWORK FOR AI-DRIVEN ORGANIZATIONS

5.1 Why Alignment Is the Central HR Challenge

AI-driven transformation rarely touches one part of an organization. Intelligent systems reshape how employees work, how customers experience service, and how values are enacted in decisions, all at once. Responses, though, stay compartmentalized: HR runs workforce readiness, service units redesign customer journeys, leadership communicates ethical intent. Each effort may be well developed. They do not connect.

The problem is not only fragmentation of effort but fragmentation of logic. AI systems run on shared decision architectures. The algorithm that shapes internal performance evaluation may also shape customer prioritization; a predictive model built for personalization can simultaneously affect workforce scheduling. EX, CX, and purpose are wired together through common technological infrastructure (Malik et al., 2023).

Misalignment surfaces fast. Employees working under tightly paced, system-driven conditions struggle to deliver relationally meaningful service. Customers meet outcomes that contradict stated values. Purpose statements lose credibility when operational decisions say something else. These are not isolated glitches. They are design incoherence. From an HR perspective, alignment is a structural requirement, not a soft value.

5.2 Conceptual Foundations of the Framework

The EX-CX-Purpose Alignment Framework rests on three premises.

First, employee experience enables customer experience. Service quality is produced under conditions set by HR systems: roles, incentives, discretion boundaries, metrics, learning opportunities. When AI alters those conditions, it indirectly shapes customer outcomes. Adaptability and ethical sensitivity cannot be expected from employees whose work design restricts judgment or removes recovery space. This extends the service-profit chain (Heskett et al., 1997) into algorithmically mediated environments.

Second, customer experience is organizational values in action. Customers do not read mission statements. They judge outcomes: what gets approved, denied, escalated, automated. Those outcomes are increasingly set by algorithmic rules, so purpose is enacted through operational design rather than communication.

Third, purpose must be institutionalized to function as a governance anchor. It has to shape decision rights, accountability structures, and capability investment, or it stays symbolic. Together the premises position HR as the integrative mechanism where experience and value creation meet.

The framework's relationship to established models can be stated precisely. It extends the service-profit chain (Heskett et al., 1997) by specifying the mechanisms through which internal conditions reach customers under algorithmic mediation, and by adding purpose as a governance layer the chain does not contain. It applies the joint-optimization principle of socio-technical systems theory (Trist & Bamforth, 1951; Cherns, 1976) to settings where the technical subsystem itself makes decisions, a condition the original theory never faced. It builds on strategic HR architecture (Lepak & Snell, 1999) by treating HR systems as design instruments for AI-mediated work rather than complements to technology. It takes its fairness logic from procedural justice theory (Lind & Tyler, 1988) but moves the analysis from managerial decisions to algorithmic ones, where explanation and appeal must be designed rather than assumed. And it differs from responsible-AI governance frameworks (Floridi et al., 2018; Mökander & Floridi, 2023) by locating governance inside the employment relationship, in decision rights, voice, and accountability, rather than in principles external to it. The distinctive claim is the integration: none of these models connects EX, CX, and purpose within a single alignment structure.

Figure 1 presents the framework. Two kinds of relationship appear in it. Primary alignment links, drawn as solid double-headed arrows, are relationships HR systems design and govern directly: the hub's connections to workforce architecture, service enactment, and ethical governance. Secondary or indirect links, drawn as dashed lines, are relationships transmitted through the domains rather than designed directly, such as the influence of EX on CX through the frontline mechanisms in Section 3.1, or the enactment of purpose in work design and service outcomes. The hub sits inside a dashed boundary representing cross-functional governance, because HR coordinates alignment but does not own every decision within it. Markers P1 to P3 locate the three misalignment patterns discussed in Section 5.4.

Figure 1. The EX-CX-Purpose Alignment Framework for AI-Driven Organizations

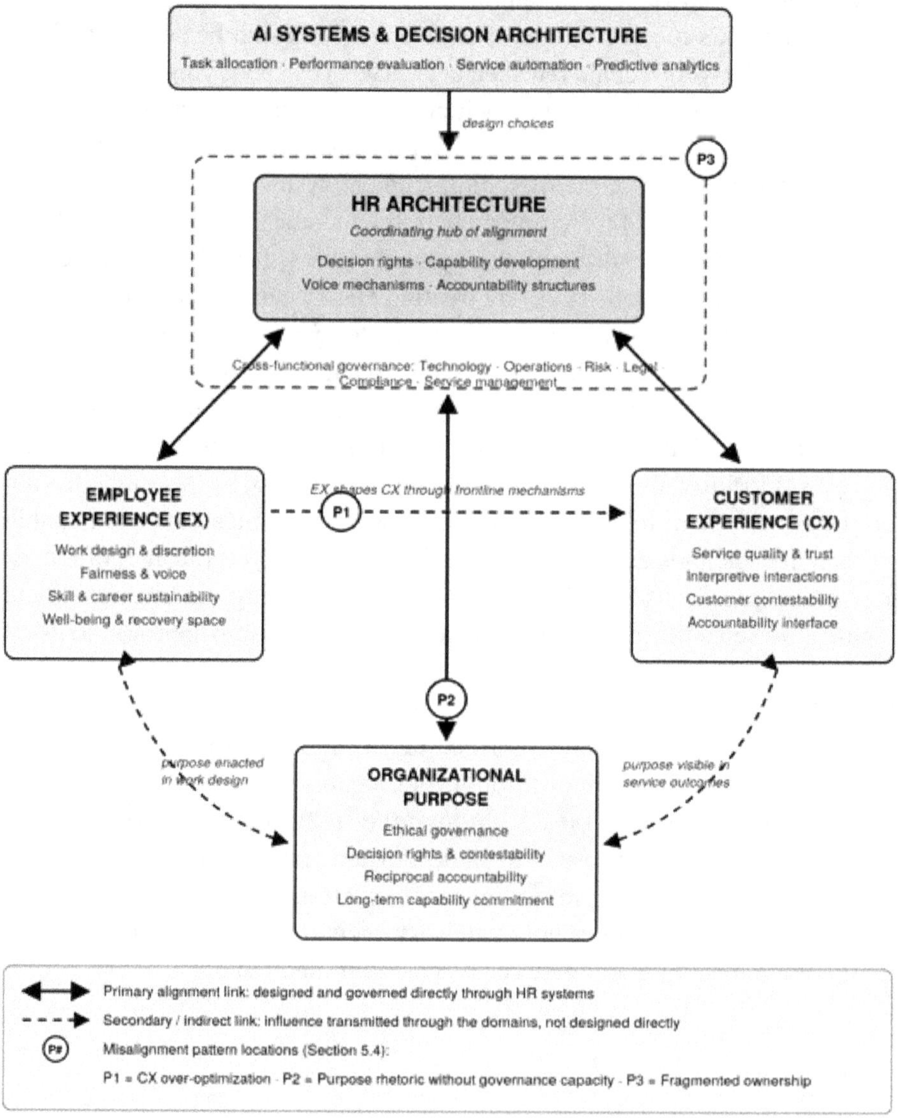

Note. Solid double-headed arrows show primary alignment links: relationships designed and governed directly through HR systems. Dashed arrows show secondary or indirect links: influence transmitted through the domains rather than designed directly. The dashed boundary indicates that HR architecture coordinates alignment within cross-functional governance involving technology, operations, risk, legal, compliance, and service-management functions. Markers P1 to P3 locate the three misalignment patterns described in Section 5.4. Misalignment in any domain propagates across the system. Figure prepared by the authors.

5.3 Core Components of the Alignment Framework

The framework treats EX, CX, and purpose as dynamically interconnected. Alignment exists when workforce architecture, service delivery, and ethical governance reinforce each other.

Workforce Architecture and Employee Experience

Workforce architecture is how roles, authority, skills, and incentives are structured in AI-mediated environments. Intelligent systems alter it by increasing performance visibility, redefining tasks, and reshaping discretion; in some contexts, capability expands, in others it narrows. Organizations that achieve alignment do not design HR systems around efficiency indicators alone. They preserve discretion in roles requiring contextual judgment, treat capability development as long-term investment, and count emotional and relational labor as performance (Parker & Knight, 2024). When workforce architecture buys speed at the expense of autonomy and recovery, employee experience deteriorates, and the deterioration does not stay contained. It travels into service quality and ethical outcomes. Efficiency can be engineered. Commitment cannot.

Service Enactment and Customer Experience

In AI-enabled organizations, customer experience emerges from interactions between people and systems. Frontline employees act as interpreters of algorithmic outputs: they explain automated decisions, manage system constraints, and absorb customer frustration when outcomes look inflexible. Alignment means designing service roles that support this mediating function. Technical competence is not enough; employees need interpretive capability to contextualize AI recommendations and relational capability to hold trust under structured conditions. They also need authority. Without the ability to override or adapt system outputs, employees become procedural executors. Scripted compliance buys consistency and stays fragile whenever situations deviate from patterns.

Ethical Governance and Organizational Purpose

Purpose anchors the framework by defining acceptable trade-offs between efficiency, experience, and responsibility. Ethical governance clarifies decision rights, assigns accountability, and establishes review and contestability mechanisms for employees and customers alike. Effective governance connects existing structures across the AI lifecycle rather than bolting ethics on (Mökander & Floridi, 2023).

One mechanism deserves formal status within the framework: reciprocal accountability. Section 2 identified a justification asymmetry in algorithmically managed work. Employees must explain deviations from system expectations while systems are recalibrated without comparable explanation. Reciprocal accountability corrects the asymmetry by holding the system to standards symmetrical with those applied to people. Parameter changes are logged and explained. System performance is reviewed against defined criteria, just as employee performance is. When an employee's override of an algorithmic recommendation proves correct, the record feeds back into the evaluation of the system, not only of the person. Reciprocal accountability sits inside ethical governance and doubles as a diagnostic: an organization that audits its people more rigorously than its algorithms is misaligned by design.

HR institutionalizes these mechanisms through leadership evaluation, policy design, and workforce planning that reflect ethical commitments alongside performance goals. Purpose loses credibility when responsibility is shifted onto systems. In aligned organizations, purpose shapes system design rather than staying at the level of communication.

Proposition 3: Organizations that institutionalize purpose through governance mechanisms, including explicit decision rights, accountability structures, reciprocal accountability for AI systems, and contestability processes for AI-mediated outcomes, are likely to demonstrate stronger EX-CX alignment than organizations in which purpose remains communicative rather than operational. HR is positioned as the coordinating function for these mechanisms, operating jointly with technology, operations, risk, legal, and compliance functions rather than in isolation.

5.4 Three Misalignment Patterns

The framework highlights three recurring patterns, marked P1 to P3 in Figure 1.

Pattern 1: CX over-optimization. Heavy investment in automation and personalization while employee experience is neglected. Discretion narrows, recovery space shrinks, capability development slows. Service quality may improve at first; strain accumulates and performance eventually declines.

Pattern 2: Purpose rhetoric without governance capacity. Public commitments to fairness or inclusion alongside opaque systems with no audit or appeal mechanism. The gap between stated values and operational reality becomes visible. Floridi et al. (2018) call this ethics "bluewashing."

Pattern 3: Fragmented ownership. Technology teams deploy systems, HR manages workforce effects, service units handle customer outcomes, and no integrative oversight exists. Local efficiencies rise while overall coherence declines.

Alignment is not automatic. It requires deliberate design and continuous governance.

Table 3. The EX–CX–Purpose Alignment Framework: Domains, Components, and Diagnostic Indicators

Framework Domain	Core Component	Aligned State	Misaligned State	HR Design Priority
Employee Experience (EX)	Workforce Architecture	Clear decision rights; preserved discretion; long-term capability focus; well-being integrated	Opaque control; compliance-driven roles; reskilling treated as individual burden	Clarify accountability; invest in capability; embed well-being in performance systems
Customer Experience (CX)	Service Enactment	Interpretive and relational roles supported; override authority present	Scripted compliance; constrained discretion; unresolved system mismatch	Build interpretive capability; enable frontline judgment
Organizational Purpose	Ethical Governance	Decision rights reflect values; accountability visible; review mechanisms operational	Purpose remains symbolic; governance lags deployment; responsibility diffused	Embed purpose in governance; reinforce leadership accountability

Note. HR Architecture acts as the integrative mechanism across domains. Misalignment in one domain propagates across the system.

5.5 Boundary Conditions

The framework's relationships will not hold with equal force everywhere. Seven conditions plausibly moderate them. Service intensity: the EX-to-CX link should be strongest where value is created in direct human interaction, weaker in asset-heavy or purely transactional services. Task complexity: discretion and interpretive capability carry more weight in non-routine work than in standardized processing. Employee skill level shapes how much interpretive capacity exists to begin with. Customer vulnerability raises the stakes of contestability; a delayed food order and a denied insurance claim are not equivalent. National labour protections determine how much voice is institutionally guaranteed rather than organizationally granted. AI-governance maturity determines whether the mechanisms the framework calls for already have an organizational home. And the extent of algorithmic autonomy, whether systems recommend or decide, changes how much oversight is demanded.

These conditions also mark where the framework travels with caution. It was developed with high-volume, labour-intensive service settings in view; its weights may differ in capital-intensive or fully automated contexts, and each condition can be treated as a testable moderator.

5.6 HR Leadership and the Work of Alignment

Alignment is not a one-time initiative. As AI systems evolve, their effects on experience, fairness, and accountability shift with them. HR leaders therefore need to move past implementation roles and steward coherence across domains: entering AI design decisions early, questioning trade-offs, and making sure gains in predictive efficiency do not erode employability, dignity, or trust. The work also involves convening the other holders of the problem. Technology owns the systems, operations owns the workflows, and risk, legal, and compliance own the exposure. HR's distinctive contribution is to hold the employment relationship steady across all of them.

Alignment is iterative. It depends on feedback loops, cross-functional dialogue, and the willingness to adjust systems when misalignment shows. HR becomes a strategic integrator not because it owns technology, but because it shapes the employment relationship.

5.7 Contribution of the Framework

The framework makes three contributions. It advances an HR-centered view of AI adoption that integrates employee and customer experience, closing the first gap identified in the introduction. It reframes organizational purpose as a governance mechanism embedded in employment systems rather than a communication tool. And it offers a diagnostic approach: the misalignment patterns, boundary conditions, and the reciprocal accountability test give organizations concrete points of examination before ethical, service, or performance breakdowns occur. The contribution is most relevant in India's service-intensive, rapidly digitizing economy, where the scale and speed of AI adoption amplify both risks and opportunities.

6. IMPLICATIONS FOR PRACTICE, POLICY, AND FUTURE RESEARCH

6.1 Implications for HR Leadership

The analysis points to a shift in how HR leadership engages with AI-driven transformation. AI is not a standalone technological initiative with indirect people implications. It is a systemic force reshaping work design, authority, and accountability. As algorithmic systems influence hiring, performance evaluation, learning pathways, and workforce planning, HR leaders cannot stay confined to implementation. Even where technology ownership sits elsewhere, the outcomes carry ethical, experiential, and strategic consequences squarely within HR's domain (Fenwick et al., 2024).

Four priorities follow. First, HR leaders need a seat in AI design discussions before deployment; the consequential decisions, thresholds, classification logic, and escalation rules, are made at design. Second, HR must work with technology, operations, risk, legal, and compliance to establish clear accountability for AI-mediated decisions, specifying responsibility, oversight mechanisms, and conditions for human intervention; as Section 4.2 argued, oversight is meaningful only when reviewers hold real authority, expertise, time, and protection. Third, HR leaders need to safeguard human judgment in decisions affecting careers, dignity, and employability. This is not a rejection of automation but the condition of its legitimacy. Fourth, HR professionals need governance literacy as a core capability: competence in ethics, system design, and algorithmic accountability alongside analytics.

6.2 Organizational Implications: Designing for Coherent Value Creation

At the organizational level, the design goal is coherence, not isolated optimization. AI transformation progresses unevenly. Automation and analytics advance fast; performance management, rewards, and development practices move slowly. The gap produces misalignment between employee experience, service quality, and values.

Two design principles follow. First, organizations should test whether AI-driven performance metrics support the behaviors they claim to want. Metrics narrowed to speed, volume, or predictive accuracy quietly weaken relational behavior, contextual judgment, and learning. The reciprocal accountability test in Section 5.3 offers a starting point: systems should face the same standard of explanation and review they impose on people. Second, reskilling and capability development are shared organizational responsibilities, not individual burdens. AI adoption redistributes pressure across roles, hitting frontline and mid-level employees hardest, and sustainable transformation depends on collective accountability for adaptation rather than expecting individuals to absorb disruption alone.

6.3 Institutional and Policy-Level Implications

The implications extend past individual organizations. Policy frameworks pay limited attention to the employment consequences of AI-driven decision-making in hiring, performance evaluation, and restructuring. Institutional mechanisms supporting algorithmic accountability, rights to explanation, appeal, and meaningful human review, can strengthen trust without constraining innovation, and they matter on both sides of the service encounter: for employees subject to algorithmic evaluation and for customers subject to high-stakes automated decisions.

The issues are salient in India, where AI adoption intersects with large-scale service employment and platform work. The Economic Survey of India (2024–2025) points to the need for coordinated action among government, industry, and academia to manage AI-driven labor transitions with attention to equity and social protection. India is not a uniform context, though. Conditions differ across sectors, occupations, firm sizes, and contractual arrangements; a permanent employee in a large IT services firm, a contract worker in business-process operations, and a platform-based gig worker occupy very different positions. Policy responses, and the framework's application, must account for this variation rather than treating the Indian service sector as one setting.

Educational and professional institutions have a role too. Preparing HR professionals for AI-enabled environments means expanding competency models past analytics into governance, ethics, and socio-technical system design.

6.4 Future Research Directions

The chapter develops a conceptual framework supported by propositions. Empirical validation is the obvious next step, in four directions.

First, the propositions need systematic testing: the conditional relationship between algorithmic authority and procedural justice (P1), the proposed contribution of EX deterioration to subsequent CX decline (P2), and the role of purpose institutionalization in EX-CX alignment (P3). Proposition 2 in particular requires longitudinal designs, since only time-ordered data can establish whether EX decline comes before CX decline; multi-level designs would strengthen the testing of all three.

Second, the boundary conditions in Section 5.5 can be examined as moderators: governance maturity, service intensity, task complexity, employee skill level, customer vulnerability, national labour protections, and the degree of algorithmic autonomy. Knowing which of these most alters the framework's relationships would sharpen both its theory and its use.

Third, comparative research across institutional contexts is needed, examining how the EX-CX-Purpose relationship operates in emerging economies such as India against high-income contexts with stronger labor protections.

Fourth, methodological diversity matters. Qualitative and ethnographic approaches suit the question of how employees experience algorithmic authority day to day, and sector-specific case studies tracing AI design decisions through employee experience to customer outcomes can illuminate the processes described here.

7. CONCLUSION: RE-CENTERING HUMAN EXPERIENCE IN THE AGE OF INTELLIGENT SYSTEMS

Artificial intelligence is called transformative for its speed, scale, and predictive capability, and these do reshape competitive strategies and operating models. But the most lasting effects of AI adoption are neither purely technical nor immediately visible. They are relational and organizational.

AI does not simply automate tasks. It reorganizes authority, reshapes discretion, and reframes how performance is judged and services delivered. Above all, it changes how organizational values are enacted in everyday decisions, gradually and without announcement.

Treating AI transformation as a technical project with downstream people implications gets the direction of influence backwards. The effectiveness and legitimacy of AI depend on the coherence of the people systems it operates through. Where algorithmic systems enter employment relationships without attention to accountability, fairness, or capability development, efficiency gains coexist with declining trust. Where workforce design, service delivery, and governance are deliberately aligned, AI supports organizational resilience rather than strain.

The EX-CX-Purpose Alignment Framework offers an integrative way to see these dynamics. Its core argument is simple to state and hard to implement: employee experience, customer experience, and organizational purpose are not independent outcomes but interlinked consequences of shared design choices. Algorithms do not distinguish internal from external stakeholders. They encode priorities that hit both at once. Misalignment builds slowly, showing up in exhausted employees, fragile service interactions, and values statements disconnected from operational reality. Rarely is this deliberate neglect. Mostly it is fragmented decision-making.

Alignment takes deliberate integration. It asks HR leaders to move upstream into AI design conversations and to convene technology, operations, risk, legal, and compliance around a shared view of the employment relationship. It asks leadership accountability to stay human even when decisions are technologically mediated. And it asks organizations to treat capability development and employability as strategic commitments, not corrective responses.

Sustainable value creation in AI-driven organizations depends on whether technological sophistication is matched by institutional maturity. Intelligent systems can optimize processes. They cannot sustain dignity at work, trust in service relationships, or ethical consistency. Those remain the result of human design choices, and HR, as steward of the employment relationship, is uniquely positioned to shape them.

KEY TAKEAWAYS FOR HR LEADERS AND PRACTITIONERS

The following principles summarize the chapter's practical implications:

- **Position HR upstream:** Engage in AI design decisions before implementation. Design choices determine employee and customer outcomes.
- **Clarify decision rights:** Specify which decisions are automated, who can override systems, when human review is required, and where accountability lies.
- **Safeguard procedural fairness:** Pair high-stakes algorithmic decisions with explanation, appeal, and review mechanisms, and involve employees in system design, testing, and monitoring, not only in post-decision appeals.
- **Apply reciprocal accountability:** Hold systems to the standards they impose on people. Log and explain parameter changes, review system performance against defined criteria, and feed successful human overrides back into system evaluation.
- **Extend contestability to customers:** Give customers affected by high-stakes automated decisions an understandable explanation, a route to human review, a way to correct errors, and an escalation path.
- **Build interpretive and relational capability:** Train employees in judgment, algorithmic literacy, and communication, not only in system use.
- **Treat employability as a strategic asset:** Design learning systems that expand future opportunities, not only correct immediate skill gaps.
- **Measure what matters:** Include relational, emotional, and learning-oriented behaviors in performance systems, not only speed and accuracy.
- **Institutionalize purpose:** Translate values into governance structures, decision rights, and accountability mechanisms. Purpose has to operate within systems to guide AI responsibly.

ACKNOWLEDGMENT

The authors used an AI assistant to support language editing, verification of bibliographic records, and the graphical preparation of Figure 1 based on the authors' original design. All arguments, the conceptual framework, the propositions, and the final text were developed, reviewed, and approved by the authors, who take full responsibility for the content.

REFERENCES

Appelbaum, E., Bailey, T., Berg, P., & Kalleberg, A. L. (2000). *Manufacturing advantage: Why high-performance work systems pay off.* Cornell University Press.

Bankins, S., Formosa, P., Griep, Y., & Richards, D. (2022). AI decision making with dignity? Contrasting workers' justice perceptions of human and AI decision making in a human resource management context. *Information Systems Frontiers, 24*(3), 857–875. DOI: 10.1007/s10796-021-10223-8

Bienefeld, N., Keller, E., & Grote, G. (2025). AI interventions to alleviate healthcare shortages and enhance work conditions in critical care: Qualitative analysis. *Journal of Medical Internet Research, 27*, e50852. DOI: 10.2196/50852 PMID: 39805110

Cherns, A. (1976). The principles of sociotechnical design. *Human Relations, 29*(8), 783–792. DOI: 10.1177/001872677602900806

Dima, J., Gilbert, M.-H., Dextras-Gauthier, J., & Giraud, L. (2024). The effects of artificial intelligence on human resource activities and the roles of the human resource triad: Opportunities and challenges. *Frontiers in Psychology, 15*, 1360401. Advance online publication. DOI: 10.3389/fpsyg.2024.1360401 PMID: 38903456

Duggan, J., Carbery, R., McDonnell, A., & Sherman, U. (2023). Algorithmic HRM control in the gig economy: The app-worker perspective. *Human Resource Management, 62*(6), 883–899. DOI: 10.1002/hrm.22168

Economic Survey of India. (2024–2025). *Harnessing AI for India's workforce development.* Government of India, Ministry of Finance. https://www.pib.gov.in/PressReleasePage.aspx?PRID=2097907

Fenwick, A., Molnar, G., & Frangos, P. (2024). Revisiting the role of HR in the age of AI: Bringing humans and machines closer together in the workplace. *Frontiers in Artificial Intelligence, 6*, 1272823. Advance online publication. DOI: 10.3389/frai.2023.1272823 PMID: 38288334

Floridi, L., Cowls, J., Beltrametti, M., Chatila, R., Chazerand, P., Dignum, V., Luetge, C., Madelin, R., Pagallo, U., Rossi, F., Schafer, B., Valcke, P., & Vayena, E. (2018). AI4People—An ethical framework for a good AI society: Opportunities, risks, principles, and recommendations. *Minds and Machines, 28*(4), 689–707. DOI: 10.1007/s11023-018-9482-5 PMID: 30930541

Heskett, J. L., Sasser, W. E.Jr, & Schlesinger, L. A. (1997). *The service profit chain: How leading companies link profit and growth to loyalty, satisfaction, and value*. Free Press.

Hochschild, A. R. (1983). *The managed heart: Commercialization of human feeling*. University of California Press.

International Labour Organization. (2025). *Governing AI in the world of work: A review of global ethics guidelines*. International Labour Organization. https://www.ilo.org/resource/article/governing-ai-world-work-review-global-ethics-guidelines

Jaakkola, E. (2020). Designing conceptual articles: Four approaches. *AMS Review, 10*(1–2), 18–26. DOI: 10.1007/s13162-020-00161-0

Kahn, W. A. (1990). Psychological conditions of personal engagement and disengagement at work. *Academy of Management Journal, 33*(4), 692–724. DOI: 10.2307/256287

Kellogg, K. C., Valentine, M. A., & Christin, A. (2020). Algorithms at work: The new contested terrain of control. *The Academy of Management Annals, 14*(1), 366–410. DOI: 10.5465/annals.2018.0174

Kim, S., Khoreva, V., & Vaiman, V. (2025). Strategic human resource management in the era of algorithmic technologies: Key insights and future research agenda. *Human Resource Management, 64*(2), 447–464. DOI: 10.1002/hrm.22268

Lepak, D. P., & Snell, S. A. (1999). The human resource architecture: Toward a theory of human capital allocation and development. *Academy of Management Review, 24*(1), 31–48. DOI: 10.2307/259035

Lind, E. A., & Tyler, T. R. (1988). *The social psychology of procedural justice*. Plenum Press. DOI: 10.1007/978-1-4899-2115-4

Malik, A., Budhwar, P., & Kazmi, B. A. (2023). Artificial intelligence (AI)-assisted HRM: Towards an extended strategic framework. *Human Resource Management Review, 33*(1), 100940. Advance online publication. DOI: 10.1016/j.hrmr.2022.100940

Mökander, J., & Floridi, L. (2023). Operationalising AI governance through ethics-based auditing: An industry case study. *AI and Ethics*, *3*(2), 451–468. DOI: 10.1007/s43681-022-00171-7 PMID: 35669570

Mökander, J., Sheth, M., Gersbro-Sundler, M., Blomgren, P., & Floridi, L. (2022). Challenges and best practices in corporate AI governance: Lessons from the biopharmaceutical industry. *Frontiers of Computer Science*, *4*, 1068361. Advance online publication. DOI: 10.3389/fcomp.2022.1068361

Mortati, M., & Viana Mundstock Freitas, G. (2026). AI in service design: A new framework for hybrid human–AI service encounters. *Journal of Service Research*, *29*(1), 81–96. Advance online publication. DOI: 10.1177/10946705251344387

Parker, S. K., & Grote, G. (2022). Automation, algorithms, and beyond: Why work design matters more than ever in a digital world. *Applied Psychology*, *71*(4), 1171–1204. DOI: 10.1111/apps.12241

Parker, S. K., & Knight, C. (2024). The SMART model of work design: A higher order structure to help see the wood from the trees. *Human Resource Management*, *63*(2), 265–291. DOI: 10.1002/hrm.22200

Plaskoff, J. (2017). Employee experience: The new human resource management approach. *Strategic HR Review*, *16*(3), 136–141. DOI: 10.1108/SHR-12-2016-0108

Rosso, B. D., Dekas, K. H., & Wrzesniewski, A. (2010). On the meaning of meaningful work: A theoretical integration and review. *Research in Organizational Behavior*, *30*, 91–127. DOI: 10.1016/j.riob.2010.09.001

Schneider, B., White, S. S., & Paul, M. C. (1998). Linking service climate and customer perceptions of service quality: Test of a causal model. *The Journal of Applied Psychology*, *83*(2), 150–163. DOI: 10.1037/0021-9010.83.2.150 PMID: 9577232

Stahl, B. C., Timmermans, J., & Mittelstadt, B. D. (2016). The ethics of computing: A survey of the computing-oriented literature. *ACM Computing Surveys*, *48*(4), 55. Advance online publication. DOI: 10.1145/2871196

Torraco, R. J. (2005). Writing integrative literature reviews: Guidelines and examples. *Human Resource Development Review*, *4*(3), 356–367. DOI: 10.1177/1534484305278283

Trist, E. L., & Bamforth, K. W. (1951). Some social and psychological consequences of the Longwall method of coal-getting. *Human Relations*, *4*(1), 3–38. DOI: 10.1177/001872675100400101

Chapter 3
Human-Centred Value Creation:
Aligning Employee Experience, Customer Experience, and Purpose in AI-Driven Organisations

Muhammad Usman Tariq
http://orcid.org/0000-0002-7605-3040
University College Cork, Ireland

ABSTRACT

AI-based companies are beginning to realize that to create value in a meaningful way, they must pair technology with the people who will use it. This chapter examines a people-based approach to creating value. This chapter examines a people-based approach to creating value by integrating employees' feelings about their work (employee experience), customers' feelings about the experience with the company (customer experience), and the company's main goal or purpose. While AI can help companies with efficiency, smart decisions, and personalization, the gap between how well people are treated, customers' feelings about the experience with the company, and the purpose of the company can hinder success. The chapter shows that companies must create AI-based systems that allow people to do their best work with the help of AI, create trust with the people who work for the company, create a sense of meaningful work for the people who work for the company, and create tremendous value for the customer.

DOI: 10.4018/979-8-3373-8282-1.ch003

INTRODUCTION

In recent years, numerous companies in various industries have undergone numerous changes because of the rapid adoption and growth of artificial intelligence (AI). The idea of AI was originally viewed to aid in the automation of business or to be used for data-oriented tasks. However, today, it is an essential element of how businesses operate (Szostak, 2025). AI is now an element of how decisions are made, customer service is provided, employees are managed, and the future is planned. This has created what is referred to as an "AI-driven company system," which is a complex system that utilizes computer programming, digital tools, knowledge, and business processes to create business value (Hasani et al., 2025). AI is no longer viewed as a technology system unto itself but is now an element of how both employees and customers perform their tasks. Moreover, AI is now an element of how services are performed. As the system continues to grow, the question of how technology can be used to strengthen the human element of business also grows. The primary reason companies have implemented technology in the past is to be more efficient.

From the first machines that aided factories in data technology today, companies have generally sought ways to save money, do things faster, and be more productive. This was also true for AI technology when it was first implemented. It was used to make companies more efficient by automating tasks, improving supply chains, and allowing companies to process large amounts of data faster than humans could process (Papadopoulou & Kotsi, 2025). This is not only good for business but also makes people wonder about the role of workers, the quality of their jobs, and how customers are understood by them. When technology is implemented primarily for efficiency, it can sometimes create a disconnect between the company and the people who are helping it be successful. Workers can begin to feel like they are just numbers on a screen, and customers can be helped quickly but not feel that they are being understood. Given these issues, many experts and business leaders are now considering the larger purpose of technology.

There is a focus on ensuring that technology is used to increase human value. This means that companies can only be successful if technology is used in ways that enable people to do their work better, make their work more meaningful, and help them build better relationships with customers and their communities. Instead of taking over human capabilities, such as judgment, creativity, or kindness, technology can be used to enable these capabilities (Hasani et al., 2025). In this regard, technology can take over boring tasks that allow people to focus on more important work, such as solving problems, working together, or coming up with new ideas. On the other hand, technology can be used to enable better customer service by understanding people's needs, predicting what they need, or delivering faster service.

This change from being efficient to being more human-focused is indicative of how companies think about value.

The traditional way that companies are run was based on being successful based on profit and efficiency. However, nowadays, companies are run in a way that their environment is just as important. For instance, customers today want companies that are honest, transparent, and responsible. Employees today want a workplace that allows them to feel that they matter (Viljakainen et al., 2025). This means that value is no longer just about being efficient; it is also about providing a good human experience, both inside and outside the company. For instance, a company might implement a smart tool that helps the company work better together or a bad monitoring tool that makes the employee feel like they are being watched or like they are not being trusted. The other part of the value equation is customer experience.

Customers may seek kindness, understanding, and a sense of connection, which are usually provided through human interaction. Organizations must, therefore, strike a balance between smart system usage and sensitivity to ensure a positive customer experience. The relationship between employees and customer experience is strong. Employees who are well supported, appreciated, and in control are more likely to provide good and caring customer experiences. Employees who are overwhelmed by technology or feel excluded from decision-making may have difficulty providing positive experiences.

In a company with an AI system, this relationship is further complicated, as both employees and customers use the same technology. If a company can design an effective AI system, it can simultaneously enhance both experiences. For example, an AI system could provide employees with information about what customers like or need, helping them provide more relevant and personalized assistance. In addition to employee and customer experience, a company's purpose is now a significant element in creating value in a human-friendly way. Purpose refers to what a company is fundamentally about, aside from making money. It reflects what a company values, its contributions, and its long-term aspirations, which in turn shape how a company behaves. In terms of AI, a company's purpose will influence how it uses technology. Companies with strong purposes are more likely to consider the ethical aspects of AI, such as fairness, honesty, and responsibility. Companies with strong purposes are more likely to build technology for good rather than for profit. The increased significance of an organization 's purpose demonstrates how society expects businesses to be more responsible, especially in a world that is increasingly digital in nature. When considering how AI influences jobs, personal information, and decision-making, businesses are being called on to lead responsibly (Papadopoulou & Kotsi, 2025). Those invested in businesses, such as workers, customers, government bodies, and communities, are observing how businesses are using technology more closely than ever before. Businesses that incorporate purpose into their use of technology can build more trust and credibility, both within their own business and beyond its walls. Businesses that are more concerned with making technology go faster without considering how it will impact people may lose trust and experience challenges with those they are working with. In this sense, the central idea of this chapter is that companies that use AI must look beyond the quality of their technology (Tariq, 2026).

Value creation should center on people, and a full picture is needed to understand how value is created. This picture recognizes that AI can work well when the experiences of the people who work there, the experiences of the people who use their services, and the purpose of the organization align. The purpose is the rule for using technology properly. The experiences of the people who work there help them use AI to deliver good services. The experiences of the people who use the services will create loyalty to the organization that will last a long time. In this chapter, we explore how businesses can develop and manage their artificial intelligence systems to ensure that people's value is prioritized, including new technology (Hasani et al., 2025). The chapter explores the changing relationship between people at work and technology and how fair rules, kind leaders, and inclusive businesses are essential. By focusing on people's experiences as the key to their artificial intelligence strategy, businesses can turn the challenges of technological changes into opportunities for better connection, growth, and success. By doing so, they can ensure that the future of work and services is both smart and deeply human.

CONCEPTUAL FOUNDATIONS OF HUMAN-CENTERED VALUE

This chapter makes a contribution by bringing the value-creation thinking into AI supported organizational contexts. The service-profit chain has a strong correlation between the employee experience and customer satisfaction and organizational performance, whereas in this chapter, the author suggests that AI alters the mechanisms by which this relationship works. Value creation is created by the employee's engagement, service quality, algorithmic transparency, human oversight, data governance, customer trust, employee autonomy and organizational purpose in the context of the organization that is designed with AI. The chapter thus presents a value creation ecosystem for humans and AI, which harmonizes employee experience, customer experience and purpose with responsible AI-enabled systems. The growing integration of artificial intelligence into organizational life has led many scholars and practitioners to rethink value creation and maintenance in contemporary workplaces. As technology continues to advance in terms of capabilities, successful organizations are realizing that value creation is no longer a product of technology alone. Rather, value creation is a product of the interplay between individuals, technology, and organizational value (Schmager et al., 2025). In this regard, human-centered value creation has become a prominent concept for thinking about value creation in contemporary workplaces that significantly leverage technology. Three key dimensions; employee experience, customer experience, and organizational purpose–constitute the core of this value creation model. Employee experience is an important concept in thinking about the future of work, particularly in organizations where artificial intelligence plays a significant role in shaping people 's daily activities. Figure 1 presents the chapter's core conceptual model. It positions organizational purpose as the guiding layer that shapes how AI-enabled systems are designed and used.

Figure 1. Human-Centered AI Service Ecosystem Model

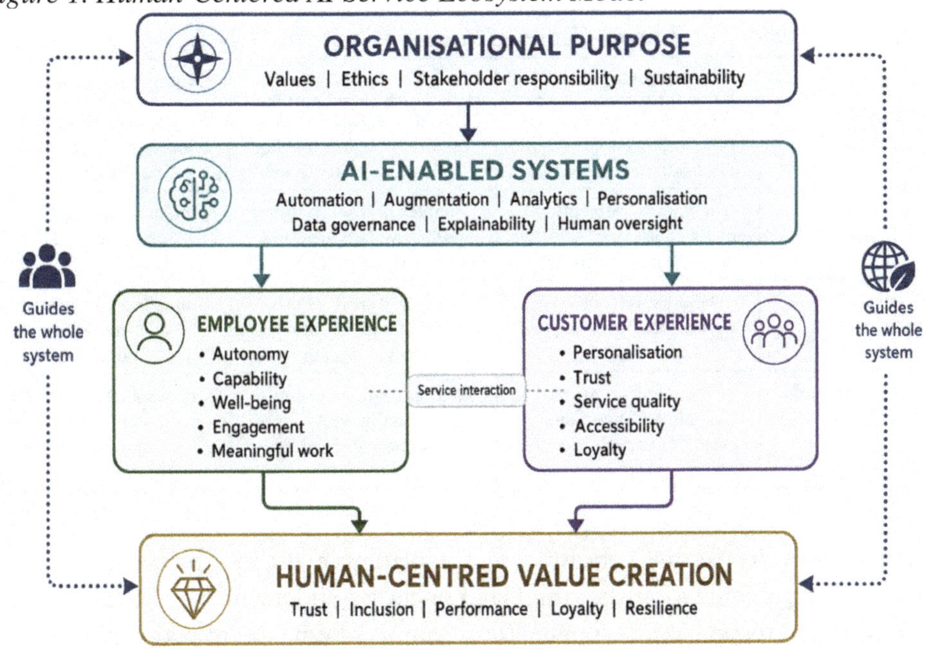

In most organizational studies, job satisfaction or employee engagement has been used as a measure of positive employee experiences in the workplace (Hasani et al., 2025). Employee experience provides a more encompassing and holistic view of how people experience their work environment in an organization. In a system where decision-making processes are influenced by algorithms, employees' experience is influenced not only by the organizational culture but also by the technology used.

When an AI system is transparent, supportive, and considers employees' needs, employees' productivity can increase, making work more fulfilling. For instance, the system can free employees from repetitive work, giving them more time to engage in more interesting aspects of their work, whether it is related to creativity, analysis, or interaction with others (Ramkissoon et al., 2025). Employees can use the system to obtain instant information that can guide them to make better decisions, which can increase their confidence and competence. However, if employees perceive the AI system as a control mechanism, they may perceive the organization as restricting their freedom. Employees may perceive the system as constantly evaluating them, which can cause stress or demotivation. The design of algorithmically mediated environments also has ethical and transparency implications that affect customer experience in important ways. Table 1 provides overview of dimensions of human-centered value creation in AI-driven organizations.

Table 1. Dimensions of Human-Centered Value Creation in AI-Driven Organizations

Dimension	Description	Role of AI	Organisational Impact
Employee Experience (EX)	Employees' perceptions of work, technology, and organisational environment	Automates routine tasks, supports decision-making, enhances productivity	Improves engagement, job satisfaction, and performance
Customer Experience (CX)	Customers' perceptions across interactions with the organisation	Enables personalisation, predictive services, and faster responses	Enhances satisfaction, trust, and loyalty
Organisational Purpose	The organisation's core values and reason beyond profit	Guides ethical AI use, responsible innovation, and strategic direction	Builds trust, legitimacy, and long-term sustainability
Interrelationship (EX–CX–Purpose)	Interaction between employee experience, customer experience, and purpose	AI aligns employee tools, customer insights, and organisational values	Creates a cycle of value creation and continuous improvement

For instance, if customers are aware that algorithms play a role in decision-making processes in an organization, they might be concerned about whether such algorithms are ethical and responsible. Organizations that use human-centered design for AI development and implementation acknowledge the need for transparency and ethical governance in their decision-making processes (Hasani et al., 2025). Organizations can use AI to respect customer rights and interests, build strong relationships, and satisfy customers. In addition to employee and customer experiences, organizational purpose is another strategic element that helps drive value creation. Organizational purpose is defined as the underlying reason for an organization to exist beyond financial performance. Purpose is a set of underlying principles that drive strategic decisions, cultural dynamics, and interactions with key stakeholders. The purpose is particularly important for an organization considering the adoption of AI, because it can be a key driver for considering the broader impact of the technology. Without a sense of purpose, an organization may be driven solely by technological prowess or performance improvements. Having a well-articulated purpose helps the organization navigate the complexities that arise from the changes brought about by new technologies.

This helps the organization determine whether new AI technologies align with its values and long-term goals. For example, an organization that has defined its purpose as improving the human experience may choose to adopt technologies that make the organization more accessible to people with disabilities. Purpose may also be a powerful tool for uniting people within an organization. When people feel that the work they do is contributing to a larger purpose, they may become more engaged. Purpose helps create a better human experience within the organization (Papadopoulou & Kotsi, 2025). The relationship between how employees feel about their jobs, how customers feel about the services they receive, and the reason for the company's existence is extremely strong. These three elements are related and affect each other in several ways. If employees are well supported by their company's environment, leaders, and tools, they are more likely to be kind and caring when assisting customers. This helps them to develop better relationships with the people they serve. In contrast, if employees are not well supported by their company's environment, leaders, and tools, it can affect the way they serve customers.

When customers are happy with the service they receive and feel that the company truly cares about them, it makes employees proud to be part of that company. This creates a cycle in which employees work even better because they know that customers are happy with the service they are receiving. The company's mission or reason for existing helps to bring all this together. This gives a sense of purpose for the company to exist and how it can best serve people. In businesses that use AI, it is necessary to maintain this balance (Szostak, 2025). Leaders must ensure that the technology is for employees as well as customers, not against them. If the technology is for the people and is aligned with the company's values, it can aid in creating meaningful experiences. Therefore, the key idea is that better technology does not have to mean better people's well-being separately. By focusing on linking employees' experience, customers' experience, and the purpose of the business in an honest way, a great workplace can be created.

CONCEPTUAL APPROACH

This chapter is written as a conceptually and practically based summary. It builds on recent and foundational knowledge about human centred AI, responsible AI, employee experience, customer experience, purpose and stakeholder value creation and socio-technical work design. This chapter does not include primary empirical data. Rather, it brings together these literatures and proposes a three pillar value creation approach for human-centred AI. The framework was developed by taking a literature review approach to identify common themes: the need to build human capabilities, the need to design intelligent systems responsibly, and the need for the integration of AI adoption with organizational purpose and value for stakeholders.

AI AS AN ENABLER AND DISRUPTOR OF VALUE CREATION

Artificial intelligence has altered how organizations create, deliver, and experience value. While it creates new opportunities for efficiency and innovation, it also brings complex challenges that affect how organizations and people relate to one another. Artificial intelligence creates new forms of value and alters how people and organizations perform tasks and make decisions. The key is to examine how organizations perform and how people feel about their tasks by considering how automation and decision algorithms affect organizations (Wang et al., 2026). The key is to examine how organizations perform and how people feel about their tasks by considering how automation and decision algorithms affect organizations. The impact of smart systems on the daily lives of people at work goes beyond how much is being created and moves towards the social and ethical aspects. Automation has always gone hand in hand with technology advancement. This is because technology has enabled the automation of tasks that could not be automated before.

In the past, automation was used for simple tasks. From an organizational perspective, the benefits of automation include a smoother working environment and the opportunity for workers to focus on creative or interesting tasks. Simultaneously, AI not only replaces people but also helps them. This process is known as augmentation. There are many jobs in which people are aided by AI tools to obtain more information, suggestions, or even predictions (Pappas & Vassilakopoulou, 2025). Other tools can also help doctors, engineers, and bankers make better decisions. In all such cases, AI tools help people involved in making better decisions by providing more information. This is beneficial, as it improves people's skills. This is a good thing. The next major impact of AI is on how it can help make better decisions. Currently, many companies use algorithms to analyze their data. Table 2 provides details of AI role and its key features.

Table 2. AI as an Enabler and Disruptor of Organizational Value

AI Role	Key Features	Benefits (Enabler)	Risks (Disruptor)	Implications for Organisations
Automation	Replaces repetitive tasks with machine processes	Increases efficiency and reduces workload	Job displacement concerns and reduced human engagement	Need for reskilling and job redesign
Augmentation	Supports human decision-making with insights and recommendations	Enhances human capabilities and decision quality	Over-reliance on AI outputs	Promote human–AI collaboration and critical thinking
Algorithmic Decision-Making	Uses data-driven models for organisational decisions	Improves speed and consistency of decisions	Bias, lack of transparency ("black box")	Require ethical governance and explainability
Personalisation & Prediction	Analyses customer data to anticipate needs	Improves customer experience and service relevance	Privacy concerns and perceived intrusion	Balance personalisation with data ethics
Surveillance & Monitoring	Tracks employee performance and behaviour	Enables performance optimisation	Reduces trust and increases stress	Ensure transparency and fair use policies

Although algorithms are seen as unbiased, their output is also heavily determined by the data on which they are based. This means that if the data is biased in some way, algorithm-based decisions could be biased too, perhaps even increasing them. People in the workplace and customers may not be aware of algorithm-based decisions, especially if they are based on complex algorithms that are seen as 'black boxes' of decision-making (Hasani et al., 2025). This can cause confusion and affect levels of trust in algorithms. Therefore, rules need to be developed to ensure that these decisions are clear, fair, and based on ethical principles. AI has also changed the way organizations relate to customers through personalization and prediction. In the online world, organizations obtain a large amount of information on how customers behave, what they like, and what they do. AI can use this information to predict what a customer might need next. Personalization tools can use this information to provide customers with information on products they might need. For example, an online store might suggest products to a customer based on what they have purchased or looked at previously. This can make the customer happy and encourage them to return to the organization to do more business.

Predictive analytics can also accomplish the same. It can enable an organization to predict what a customer might need next. Tools that use AI can predict what the customer might need next. This can be done by looking at trends. Tools that use AI can predict what a customer might need next by analyzing trends. This can make the customer happy (Viljakainen et al., 2025). This can enable the organization to provide the customer with the best service. However, there are some concerns.

Customers might feel uncomfortable if the organization knows too much about them. There are some issues related to the information used by the organization. In addition to the ways in which AI influences the interaction between people and organizations, AI also influences the nature of work.

The use of smart technology has several effects on the nature of work. With the use of AI, many jobs are changing, with the main effect being that many people are left with jobs that are more complex and require more analysis, creativity, or teamwork. In some situations, people are required to learn how to use AI tools, with the main goal being to understand what the algorithms suggest, as well as their own judgment. This presents a learning opportunity, with the main effect being that the organization must invest more in training its employees. The emergence of workplaces with AI technologies has underscored the significance of digital literacy, data interpretation skills, and flexible problem-solving skills. Employees are not only required to be familiar with the use of such technologies but also need to be capable of critically evaluating the results produced by AI technologies. Otherwise, they are likely to view the imposition of performance criteria by AI technologies or the restriction of their individual choices as a loss of professional freedom. Despite the many advantages of AI in the generation of value, its widespread adoption presents several risks that organizations must carefully navigate. One such risk in the context of AI is the potential for dehumanization. Customers who interact only through technology feel that the company does not really care for them. Employees who interact only through technology can feel that the company does not really care for them. Another important risk that has been identified in the context of AI is the potential for bias in algorithmic systems. One such potential for bias in AI is that because AI learns from data that are available to it, there can be a potential for social inequalities that exist in organizations to be reflected in the AI. For instance, a recruitment system that learns from data available in the past can end up being biased against certain groups. Another challenge that may arise in AI-enabled workplaces is surveillance. Erosion of trust may be the biggest challenge in the long term if AI systems are not implemented with adequate consideration of human values (Schmager et al., 2025). Trust plays a significant role in building relationships among organizations, workers, and customers. When people perceive a system, especially a technological one, as fair, transparent, and responsible, they are more likely to trust and accept it (Tariq, 2025).

MECHANISMS LINKING EX, CX, AND PURPOSE

The growing trend towards the integration of artificial intelligence in organizations has created a greater need to explore how changing dynamics within an organization affect both employees and customers. While technology continues to provide new avenues and opportunities for organizations, the underlying process in which value is created remains closely linked to human interactions and relationships. Modern discussions surrounding employee and customer experience can be linked to earlier theories that established the impact that underlying dynamics in an organization have on the external world. One such theory is the service-profit chain theory, which is based on the underlying principle that employee satisfaction results in an enhanced quality of service, which in turn results in increased customer loyalty and profits (Tokic & Csivre, 2026). While this remains the underlying principle in an AI-driven world as well, the dynamics in which this is created have changed. The use of technology has altered the way in which employees perform their duties and how customers interact with an organization. Traditionally, in service environments, the service-profit chain model emphasized the significance of positive work environments, employee engagement, and leadership in satisfying customers.

There are several mechanisms that can explain the link between employee experience and customer experience. First, frontline discretion gives employees the flexibility to rely on their judgment if the AI recommendations don't adequately address the emotional and contextual requirements of customers. Second, emotional involvement will impact service quality because personnel who feel trusted, supported and capable are more likely to communicate with care and confidence. Thirdly, service recovery relies on employees' abilities to have the authority and information to solve customer issues if an automated system fails. Fourth, the extent to which the insights generated are understood and applied in a responsible way and converted into valuable customer support depends on the capability of the employees. These mechanisms illustrate that AI is not the end of the EX–CX relationship, it's an alteration of circumstances, of how the EX–CX relationship generates value.

In AI-enabled service environments, these employee-level dynamics are likely to be more complex, given that employees are likely to be engaged in interactions with technology that could affect service delivery. To reinterpret the service-profit chain model in AI-enabled service environments, it is important to note that technology is likely to be part of the service environment to which both customers and employees are exposed. In environments where AI technology is likely to positively contribute to employee service delivery, for example, by providing positive contributions that are easily understandable, employees are likely to be in a better position to deliver quality services to customers (Hasani et al., 2025). This is because when employees are confident that technology is not limiting them, but is instead a positive contributor to service delivery, they are likely to be engaged positively in delivering services to customers. This empowerment does not come from technology per se, but from being able to utilize that technology effectively. When employees are enabled to use technology in ways that combine their own understanding and empathy, customers tend to have a more unique and genuine experience, thus showing the link between employee experience and customer experience. Trust is another key mechanism that connects employee experience, customer experience, and organizational purpose.

In an environment where algorithms play a role in decision making and interaction, trust is vital in ensuring that people not only accept the technological systems they are using but also trust the algorithms themselves. For instance, employees must trust the algorithms they use to ensure that they are not replaced unfairly by the AI they use. Customers need to trust the algorithms they use to ensure that the organizations they work with use the information in the most appropriate manner. Transparency plays an important role in this process (Mehter et al., 2025). With the complexity of AI tools, organizations are facing a new challenge that involves providing explanations for the way algorithmic decisions are made and how data are used to produce insights (Mourtzis et al., 2022).

Organizations that incorporate ethical considerations in the development of AI strategies have demonstrated a sense of responsible innovation. Such a sense of responsible innovation tends to resonate with the organizational workforce as well as consumers. Organizational purposes, therefore, act as a framework that enables the incorporation of trust, transparency, and ethical considerations into AI-based strategies. Therefore, purpose plays a critical role in guiding organizational leaders in the development of AI strategies. Organizational purposes that focus on the betterment of humans, responsible innovation, and contribution to society tend to have a significant impact on the development of AI strategies. Organizational leaders with a sense of purpose that focuses on responsible innovation may develop strategies that incorporate AI to empower organizational employees, customers, and the broader community. Therefore, this purpose ensures that organizational innovation in technology is not based on efficiency and competitiveness. The link between how employees feel about their work, how customers feel about their experience, and the purpose of the organization is enhanced through feedback. Feedback loops enable organizations to learn and improve. Customer satisfaction in service organizations can be an indicator of how well employees and technology work together. When customers provide positive feedback, employees appreciate it, thereby increasing their motivation. When employees appreciate their contributions, they are likely to be involved in and committed to the purpose of the organization. Customer interactions are an information source that can be used to detect trends in satisfaction, services, or even product consumption (Alamelu & Motha, 2026). In contrast, employee feedback, performance monitoring, and technology enable employees to understand what they are going through. When organizations use these different sources of information, they are in a better position to understand the relationship between employee engagement and customer outcomes, as well as the relationship between customer feedback and what is happening inside the organization. For instance, high employee engagement could be related to high customer loyalty, and low customer satisfaction could be related to what is happening inside the organization (Aitken et al., 2025).

It is worth noting that these feedback loops are not only about technology but also about how people in the organization understand and interpret feedback. The people in charge and employees need to understand what the feedback is showing and how the practices, technologies, and values in the organization influence it. When organizations encourage dialogue and teamwork to solve problems, they are in a better position to convert feedback into opportunities for continuous improvement. When employees understand that their feedback is used to improve the organization, they are more likely to be engaged and committed (Maindola et al., 2026). Technology provides new opportunities to use information to improve decision-making. However, the effectiveness of these opportunities depends on their integration into human work and service systems. When organizations focus on empowering people, building trust, being transparent, and being responsible, AI can help bring people and customers closer together rather than driving them apart. Through these connections, organizations can create a cycle of engaged employees who create meaningful experiences for customers, loyal customers, and the ability of the organization to continue to grow and thrive in line with its purpose.

DESIGNING HUMAN-CENTERED AI ORGANIZATIONS

Many organizational leaders today face the problem of how to harness the power of advanced technology without losing sight of the human foundations of work and service. In many organizations, digital transformation efforts are traditionally geared towards improving efficiencies, reducing costs, and gaining a competitive advantage. However, these are not the only benefits that can be achieved by an organization. These benefits are not a true reflection of the real potential that can be achieved with the use of AI. Purpose gives a sense of direction to an organization on how to use AI, what benefits to aim for, and what effect it should have on employees and customers. An organization with a purpose to improve the community may be different from one with a purpose to be a leader in the market (Balaji, 2025). In the former case, the digital transformation process may be geared towards ensuring accessibility, transparency, and inclusiveness. Purpose-driven transformation is also important, as it enables management to deal with the ambiguity that often accompanies the use of technology.

It is important to note that the use of AI technologies may affect the workforce and decision-making processes. In this case, the workforce may feel that the use of technology is disruptive. Therefore, purpose plays a significant role, as it enables the workforce to understand the connection between the use of technology and the purpose of the organization. Another important aspect of creating human-centered AI organizations is the establishment of ethical governance. It is important to note that AI technologies can process vast amounts of data and impact decision-making. In this case, the decision may impact on the workforce, customers, and the organization. Therefore, it is important to establish the use of ethical AI governance, as it ensures that the use of technology is transparent and that the decision-making process is fair. In this case, the workforce and the organization will understand the use of technology. In the traditional view of technological innovation, technology design is often left to experts or managers (Schmager et al., 2025). However, the design of AI technologies affects many aspects of an organization. For example, the design of technology may impact how employees or customers interact with it. Involving customers or employees in the design process provides organizations with valuable insights into how technology may be used to solve real problems, as opposed to assumptions.

The involvement of employees in co-creation is significant because they may have valuable knowledge about customers. Employees engaged in the design of AI systems could also create a sense of ownership, which could encourage them to embrace technology (Hasani et al., 2025). This enables organizations to design digital technology that is both efficient and empathetic. For instance, customers may find automated customer support technology helpful; however, they may still want to speak to a real person when the issue is complicated or emotionally taxing. Co-creation helps an organization understand this and design the system accordingly. The development of AI knowledge enables employees to be confident when dealing with technology. When people are aware of the ways in which AI tools produce information, they can use such information along with their own expertise to make informed decisions.

These are important for building effective relationships with customers and other employees. By providing learning opportunities for employees, companies can assist them in becoming effective employees in a workplace that incorporates both humans and technology. Finally, to develop AI systems that focus on people, there needs to be a complete plan, including purpose, rules, involvement, and learning. Technology, by itself, does not create value; however, it must be part of a business culture that values people and teams. When changes to digital technologies are driven by purpose, supported by ethical rules, inspired by the ideas of many, and informed by strong technological knowledge, AI becomes a technology for helping people grow, rather than for limiting them (Szostak, 2025). Organizations that use these principles to guide their use of AI and digital technologies are more likely to earn the trust of their people and customers. They demonstrate to people that the future of AI in businesses is not about replacing technology but about using technology and human experiences in a thoughtful way.

GOVERNANCE SAFEGUARDS FOR HUMAN-CENTERED AI

The AI organizations that are built with humans need governance safeguards that can protect the employees and customers. Firstly, effective human oversight should be kept for decisions relating to customers' access to, or treatment in, services, employment and eligibility, as well as decisions on the complaints and appeals process and their resolution, and decisions concerning price. Where human dignity, fairness or rights are involved, AI can be used to assist in making these decisions but should not be the final decision-maker.

Secondly, employees and customers should know how to appeal when automated decisions affect them. This encompasses the right to know the reason behind a decision, to ask for a human review of the decision and to challenge decisions that seem incorrect or unfair. Third, regularly review AI performance with bias audits to ensure that AI systems deliver non-biased results for groups. Fourth, privacy and data governance should determine what data is collected, the purpose of the collection, the length of time data is kept, and who has access to it. Lastly, there is a need for organizations to keep an eye on AI surveillance. Productivity dashboards, behavioral tracking & customer analytics can help with decision making but can also erode trust if used as too much control. Transparency, proportionality, accountability and stakeholder participation are the four key characteristics of human-centered AI governance.

STRATEGIC FRAMEWORK FOR ALIGNMENT

As more businesses use artificial intelligence, the importance of aligning technology with human values becomes clearer. Many businesses invest heavily in technology, but the real value of technology lies in how it fits with people and the business's primary objectives. If these three parts do not match, artificial intelligence may increase speed; however, it may not necessarily make things worthwhile. Therefore, it is important for businesses to have a clear plan that helps them maintain a good balance between technology, people's skills, and the business's primary objectives (Balaji, 2025). A good way to think about this balance is to use a three-pillar model that focuses on people's skills, smart systems, and alignment with the business's primary objectives. All three parts are important for change in the business, and the way they work together makes the entire plan strong. The first part of the model is about human skills.

This refers to the involvement of people as active participants when AI is implemented in the company. Although AI can perform many tasks and assist in decision-making, it cannot replace human skills such as creativity, understanding others, making ethical decisions, and making complex decisions. Therefore, companies need to assist the people involved in developing the skills required to work well with technology (Anitha et al., 2026). These skills include not only knowing how to work with technology well but also staying happy and healthy, having independence in the workplace, being able to adapt to new things, and learning. If the people involved understand how new technology helps the company achieve its goals, they are likely to embrace new ideas rather than resist them. Training and learning are important in this regard.

Workers in AI-enabled companies must read the data, check AI suggestions, and then decide using a combination of technology and real-life knowledge. This requires more than the ability to use technology; it requires strong thinking and problem-solving abilities (Espinosa Gámez, 2026). Organizations that emphasize providing opportunities for training and learning ensure that workers feel confident in using technology. However, it is also important to consider workers' well-being. Changes in technology may lead to more stress, more work, and feelings of being left behind by workers. Supporting workers by understanding leadership, work culture, and flexible work arrangements ensures that they remain engaged and motivated during significant changes. Another important aspect of human skill is the freedom to make decisions. Figure 2 translates the conceptual argument into a practical strategic framework.

Figure 2. Three-Pillar Strategic Framework

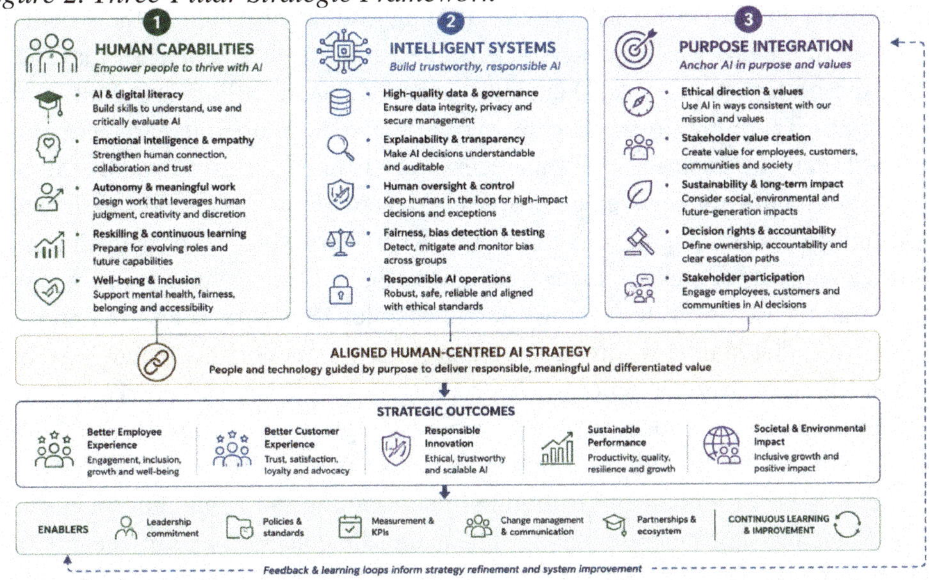

Workers are more creative and enthusiastic about their tasks when they are given the freedom to make their own decisions and use AI in real-life tasks. Although AI can provide suggestions or guesses, these must be interpreted in terms of business and society. By allowing workers to take the lead in tasks with AI assistance, a company can obtain the best from AI and humans (Muridzi & Dhliwayo, 2026). This aspect of human skills ensures that workers are important in creating value for a company, not only in being passive in changes. The second part of this model concerns smart systems. Smart systems are technologies that help AI systems make decisions and provide services to people. Smart systems are software programs, data platforms, tools for analyzing data, and rules that help digital systems run well. Many companies have invested significantly in smart systems because data is now one of the most valuable assets in the digital world.

AI tools require a large amount of data to make predictions and provide insights, and the quality of these insights depends on the accuracy and completeness of the data (Passalacqua et al., 2025). Guidelines for data management are called data governance, and they are essential in ensuring that data are used honestly and ethically. These guidelines include how data can be used, who is responsible for ensuring that data are accurate, and how data privacy and security can be ensured. Without guidelines, companies can misuse data and make poor decisions based on false data.

In addition to data systems, companies must ensure that they design and use AI tools in their work processes. Therefore, technology that is too advanced and not well integrated with the way the company works may lead to a slower process. An example is if employees are asked to use the suggestions provided by the AI but are not aware of the process by which these suggestions are obtained. They may either ignore these suggestions or use them without analyzing them (Pepple & Muthuthantrige, 2026). Therefore, for a company to be effective in its use of smart technology, it should focus on ensuring that this technology is not only user-friendly but also encourages teamwork between employees and technology. Rules and standards are important for smart systems. As the use of AI is increasing, with its use to guide many decisions affecting employees and customers, it is important for a company to ensure that its use of this technology is responsible. Therefore, rules are important for ensuring that standards are set to ensure that the use of this technology by a company is responsible and not just focused on ensuring that the process is faster. The third part of this model is about purpose integration, in which technological changes are integrated with the company's main values and its role in society.

The purpose of a company is to guide its decisions and goals. For instance, in using AI technology, purpose integration ensures that technology projects not only help a company grow economically but also positively in terms of its role in society and the environment. A company's cultural purpose helps it decide whether a technology fits its long-term mission (Viljakainen et al., 2025). Moreover, the integration of purpose helps the organization retain the trust of various stakeholders. Sustainability is likely to feature prominently in this pillar. AI technologies require enormous computational power, and digital infrastructure is likely to have a negative environmental impact. Another aspect of purpose integration is stakeholder impact.

Technology has an impact not only on employees and customers but also on stakeholders, the community, and the government. Therefore, the impact of technology strategy on stakeholders should be analyzed. Involving stakeholders in the conversation regarding the AI initiative may help identify the concerns and opportunities that may arise. When stakeholders feel that their voices are heard, they may become more inclined to trust the organization's motives. Although the three pillars; human capability, intelligent systems, and purpose integration; represent unique aspects of the organization, the real value of the pillars is found in their alignment (Balaji, 2025). Organizations should ensure that they invest as much as they invest in technology in their people and values. To do this, a roadmap may be developed that outlines the transformation process. In the first part of the process, the organization may evaluate the current state of the organization. The following stage involves the development of basic capabilities.

Organizations may develop training programs to improve digital literacy, enhance data infrastructure, and develop a framework for the use of ethical AI. Pilot programs provide opportunities for organizations to test the outcomes of new technologies on employees, customers, and the results achieved. Governance metrics, such as ethical

AI standards, transparency, and sustainability, reflect the organizational commitment to human and ethical values in the innovation process. Assessing these factors helps an organization make the necessary adjustments to ensure that alignment remains strong across all three pillars. In an environment in which technology is constantly and rapidly changing, alignment is not something that an organization achieves once and then forgets (Hasani et al., 2025). It is an ongoing process that requires an organization to learn and adapt to achieve an appropriate balance between human potential, intelligent systems, and organizational purpose, and to turn the disruptive power of AI on its head to drive value creation that is both sustainable and human centric.

When purpose has an impact on specific organizational decisions, it enters into the realm of being operational. The purpose needs to influence the funding of AI projects, the performance metrics prioritized, the decision rights, accountability, and who is involved in the activities. For instance, an organization with a commitment to inclusion should not review AI based on speed or cost savings; it should also consider how AI will enhance accessibility, minimize bias and safeguard vulnerable users. Likewise, voice, mechanisms to appeal to customers, privacy protection and impact on the environment should all be included in decisions regarding AI investments for a purpose-driven organization.

IMPLICATIONS FOR LEADERSHIP AND SUSTAINABLE PERFORMANCE

The traditional role of leadership in an organization is to ensure that resources are used effectively, work is completed effectively, and everything runs smoothly. While these aspects remain important, the emergence of technology, particularly artificial intelligence, has complicated the role of leadership. It is no longer simply about being proficient in technical skills or making sound decisions. Instead, it is about understanding people's emotions, wants, and connections with each other and customers in response to technological changes. It involves learning how to lead in a manner that effectively links technology, people, and values. However, to become a good leader in the digital world, one must understand that technology does not function autonomously. This is based on people's decisions regarding the use of technology (Schmager et al., 2025). Leaders play a significant role in influencing people's decisions regarding technology use to prevent harm to an organization's culture. Leaders should not only consider AI to enhance efficiency but also view the broader picture, including the people they serve. When leaders consider things from a human perspective, they should analyze how technology use affects people's perceptions of their jobs, learning opportunities, and overall well-being. An important aspect of human-centered leadership is the ability to articulate the role of technology in the context of an organization's objectives.

Changes associated with technology often result in ambiguity, especially for employees who may be concerned about their survival or their ability to keep up with new skill sets. Leaders who can tell a story about the importance of technology and how it helps the business achieve its objectives over the long term can help employees realize the positive impact of AI rather than its negative impact as a replacement for their jobs (Szostak, 2025). By relating the benefits of technology to values such as good service, helping the world, or protecting the environment, a sense of purpose can be instilled in people to support change rather than resist it. Trust is another significant aspect of leadership in technology-using organizations.

As algorithms become part of the process of evaluating people, interacting with customers, and running businesses, people may wonder whether they are fair and transparent. Therefore, leaders must ensure that the use of technology such as AI is ethical and that the process is understandable. In this way, people in the organization and customers will trust leaders, as they are open to the use of technology. In addition to building trust, leaders must ensure a balance between efficiency and empathy (Balaji, 2025). Technology such as artificial intelligence is often adopted in organizations to improve efficiency in terms of decision-making, speed, and cost reduction. While these are crucial for helping organizations remain competitive, leaders must ensure that they achieve efficiency without compromising empathy. Leaders may compromise the dignity of the people in the organization and customers to improve efficiency.

Employees experiencing digital change may be anxious, unsure about what is happening, or even frustrated. A leader with empathy towards employees can reduce their level of resistance. The leader may provide training, encourage employees to discuss how digital change is affecting them, or ensure that employees feel heard when they express their concerns. A leader with empathy may also understand the emotions of customers. Although customers interact with the company through the Internet, they still need to feel understood, heard, and treated with empathy (Hasani et al., 2025). The leader with empathy helps in the creation of AI that allows customers to feel this way rather than relying on the automated responses of the AI. It also means that there is a need to consider the way things are done. Leaders need to consider where technology can help the most, as well as where humans can still make a difference. For instance, leaders may consider whether machines can help in performing some of the simpler jobs so that people can have more time for jobs that require judgment, creativity, and communication (Hwang et al., 2026). In customer service, for example, machines may help in answering simpler questions; however, humans may still have to help in answering more complicated questions. Another significant aspect of leadership is the creation of a culture in which learning and adapting are normal. It is important to recognize that AI and technology are dynamic, meaning that organizations must continuously change their plans and capabilities to remain successful. A culture in which people are naturally inclined to learn helps people in the organization view technology as an enabler for growth rather than a disruptor. Creating such a culture helps organizations remain more resilient.

In contrast, organizations with cultures in which people are inclined to learn, experiment, and collaborate are better positioned to succeed as technology and other dynamics change. This will help build organizational resilience by maintaining good relationships both within the organization and with external stakeholders, such as customers. When employees feel valued, they are more likely to share their ideas, notice problems, and work together to solve them. Similarly, customers will be loyal to an organization if they know that the organization's values and goals are sound, even if things are changing or uncertain. These relationships are the foundation upon which organizations can work to overcome problems without losing the trust of stakeholders. In terms of strategy, human-centered leadership can help build an organization's lasting competitive advantage (Schmager et al., 2025). While many organizations are using similar technologies, it is how well those technologies are embedded in the organization's culture and relationships that will make the real difference. Technology does not necessarily equate with success because another organization could easily do the same. However, another organization cannot easily create an environment in which employees feel free to use technology in an intelligent and thoughtful way. Leaders who are human-centered are those who can create such an environment, in which innovation is not just short-term but ongoing. The key to remain competitive as the use of AI increases will be to combine skills with fairness and an awareness of society. Customers and policymakers are observing how organizations handle their use of data, unfairness in algorithms, and the privacy of personal information. Leaders who demonstrate that they care not only avoid trouble but also gain a reputation for being good to work with. This can be a major advantage for organizations competing for customers, where trust and openness are extremely important.

Ultimately, the use of AI will shape organizations' views on what success means to them. Human-centered leadership will inspire organizations to measure their success not only by money but also by how well they connect with employees, customers, and the community. When this kind of leadership exists, changes brought about by digital technology are seen as an opportunity to improve not only how well an organization works but also how people feel. In the long term, businesses that combine new technology with human-centered leadership are more likely to continue to thrive (Papadopoulou & Kotsi, 2025). They are building a workplace in which people feel they can really make a difference, a customer experience in which people feel they are being heard and respected, and a strategy in which technology works well with their main values. This is why human-centered leadership makes digital transformation not only a technical challenge but also a route to being a strong, fair, and competitive organization.

LIMITATIONS AND FUTURE RESEARCH

This chapter is of a conceptual nature, and does not empirically test the proposed framework. It aims to connect the dots on the literature and offer a framework for comprehending the process of value creation from the human perspective in AI-powered organizations. Future studies should explore the impact of the three human capabilities pillars and their relationship with intelligent systems and purpose in different industries, from an empirical perspective, on employee experience, customer experience and organizational performance.

Additionally, there is a need for further studies on the mechanisms between employee experience and customer experience in AI service environments. Research might focus on the impact of frontline discretion, emotional involvement, employee skill, service recovery and trust on customer outcomes with the use of AI. Stakeholder tensions that need to be explored in future work include tensions between efficiency and well-being, personalization and privacy, automation and security in jobs, innovation and environmental sustainability.

CONCLUSION

The ways in which companies are using artificial intelligence has led people to think differently about the value of technology. Traditionally, artificial intelligence has been viewed to increase efficiency, automate tasks, and improve the effectiveness of operations. Although these factors remain important, they represent a limited way of thinking about artificial intelligence and its value to people and companies. When artificial intelligence is used effectively, it becomes a means of creating more value rather than reducing costs. It becomes a way to enable people to achieve more, to create more personalized and engaging experiences for customers, and to achieve the objectives of the company in a way that benefits the inside and the outside of the company. This new way of thinking requires people and companies to think differently about technology. They must view technology to work alongside human experiences, responsibility, and company objectives. Artificial intelligence should be viewed as something that helps people, not replaces them (Szostak, 2025). Organizations that use AI in this manner provide an environment in which the technology can aid people's creativity, problem-solving skills, and relationships.

Employees who can use AI to make better decisions can provide more thoughtful personalized results. Customers who use AI can experience efficiency along with the feeling that they are understood, which can then allow for more engagement than just the provision of a service. The company's purpose is an important part of this new understanding of AI.

Purpose helps to inform how AI is used in a company, beyond its financial or operational benefits. AI with purpose considers not only how AI can improve efficiency but also how it can improve its impact on people and society. For example, a company's purpose might be to be fair to its customers. AI might then be used to improve access to services, diversity in hiring practices, or sustainability. In these companies, the technology strategy is balanced with the human resource strategy. Another aspect of AI as a value creator is the way it integrates different parts of the company. AI systems gather data to enable better decision-making, process improvement, and customer engagement. However, humans must use the gathered data to improve the business. Employees must trust and understand AI to respond better to the gathered data, enhancing the customer experience and the business. This demonstrates the value of AI as a value creator (Schmager et al., 2025). Therefore, AI might simply be a "numbers game" rather than a game of results. Considering ethics is important for maintaining the value of a company over a long period of time. Various challenges are associated with the use of AI, such as bias, transparency, privacy, and accountability. Some companies ignore these challenges, and as a result, they might lose the trust of their employees, customers, and other stakeholders.

To help people work with AI, companies must invest in learning, development, and empowerment. This will enable people to use AI smartly and responsibly. This combination of human ability and AI technology will enhance a company's ability to innovate, problem-solve, and provide a unique experience that will set it apart from others. In the future, research opportunities in this field will be vast and cover many fields. One research opportunity is the balance between the use of AI and humans to perform work, depending on the type of business. Researchers investigate how the level of AI decision-making affects employees' empowerment, motivation, and engagement, as well as customer satisfaction and business success (Hasani et al., 2025). Another research opportunity is the ethical governance of AI, including how businesses can avoid bias, ensure transparency, and establish accountability for the use of AI. Researchers should investigate how a business's purpose affects its use of AI and its impact on trust, social impact, and stability. They should explore establishing general rules for building businesses that prioritize people in the use of AI.

REFERENCES

Aitken, J., Böhme, T., & McAsh, E. (2025). Co-Creation of Societal Benefits Through Human-Centered Design and Management of Dynamic Capabilities in Oyster Farm Communities. *Strategic Change*, *34*(1), 93–101. DOI: 10.1002/jsc.2611

Alamelu, R., & Motha, C. S. (2026). A causal evaluation framework for aligning employee experience with organisational resilience: Insights from fuzzy DEMATEL and MICMAC. In *Employee experience management for organizational resilience* (pp. 423–446). IGI Global Scientific Publishing.

Anitha, K., Amala, J., & El Gareh, F. (2026). AI-enhanced organisational culture and its effect on employee engagement: Building proficiencies for sustainable decision making. In *Building AI-driven decision making competencies for sustainability* (pp. 1–28). IGI Global Scientific Publishing.

Balaji, K. (2025). Human-centric innovation: Building sustainable organizations for Industry 5.0. In *Human-centric, sustainable, and resilient organizations in the digital age* (pp. 101–124). IGI Global Scientific Publishing. DOI: 10.4018/979-8-3693-8181-6.ch005

Espinosa Gámez, M. (2026). Emotional intelligence: A human-centred AI perspective. In *Handbook of human-centered artificial intelligence* (pp. 1–65). Springer Nature Singapore.

Hasani, N., Hosseini, A., Ashjazadeh, Y., Diederichs, V., Ghotb, S., Riggio, M., Hansen, E., & Nasir, V. (2025). Outlook on human-centred design in Industry 5.0: Towards mass customisation, personalisation, co-creation, and co-production. *International Journal of Sustainable Engineering*, *18*(1), 2486343. DOI: 10.1080/19397038.2025.2486343

Hwang, B. N., Puntha, P., & Jitanugoon, S. (2026). Human-centric AI: Transforming service ecosystems for inclusivity and excellence in resource-constrained contexts. *Journal of Service Theory and Practice*, *36*(3), 1–55. DOI: 10.1108/JSTP-01-2025-0017

Maindola, S., Bangwal, D., Singh Oberoi, S. S., & Kumar, R. (2026). Transforming hospitality 5.0: A systematic review of AI's impact on employee experience and well-being. *International Journal of Quality and Service Sciences*, *18*(2), 1–26. DOI: 10.1108/IJQSS-09-2025-0245

Mehter, A. K., Kumar, V. R., & Mehta, M. (2025, October). A hybrid intelligence approach for customer-centric product development and marketing. In *2025 2nd International Conference on Artificial Intelligence and Knowledge Discovery in Concurrent Engineering (ICECONF)* (pp. 1–8). IEEE. DOI: 10.1109/ICECONF65644.2025.11379515

Mourtzis, D., Panopoulos, N., Angelopoulos, J., Wang, B., & Wang, L. (2022). Human centric platforms for personalized value creation in metaverse. *Journal of Manufacturing Systems, 65*, 653–659. DOI: 10.1016/j.jmsy.2022.11.004

Muridzi, G., & Dhliwayo, S. (2026, February). Satisfaction: Systematic literature review. In *Embracing technological agility in accounting and business (*Vol. 2*): Proceedings of the 6th International Conference of Accounting and Business iCAB, Cape Town 2025* (p. 249). Springer Nature.

Papadopoulou, I., & Kotsi, M. (2025). Customer experience in the era of AI: Harnessing AI and technology for a human future that works. *Journal of Airport Management*, *20*(1), 6–26. DOI: 10.69554/GPJS4492

Pappas, I. O., & Vassilakopoulou, P. (2025). Human value alignment in AI. In *Handbook of human-centered artificial intelligence* (pp. 1–33). Springer Nature Singapore. DOI: 10.1007/978-981-97-8440-0_7-1

Passalacqua, M., Pellerin, R., Magnani, F., Doyon-Poulin, P., Del-Aguila, L., Boasen, J., & Léger, P. M. (2025). Human-centred AI in Industry 5.0: A systematic review. *International Journal of Production Research*, *63*(7), 2638–2669. DOI: 10.1080/00207543.2024.2406021

Pepple, D., & Muthuthantrige, N. (2026). Artificial intelligence, innovation and the new architecture of exploitation: Towards reconfiguring humanness in the age of algorithmic labour. *Journal of Innovation & Knowledge*, *11*, 100878. DOI: 10.1016/j.jik.2025.100878

Ramkissoon, T., Jairam, A., & Hosein, P. (2025, October). AI-driven personalization as a disruptive strategy for the creation of new business models. In *2025 IEEE International Conference on Technology Management, Operations and Decisions (ICTMOD)* (pp. 1–6). IEEE. DOI: 10.1109/ICTMOD66732.2025.11371941

Schmager, S., Pappas, I. O., & Vassilakopoulou, P. (2025). Understanding human-centred AI: A review of its defining elements and a research agenda. *Behaviour & Information Technology*, *44*(15), 3771–3810. DOI: 10.1080/0144929X.2024.2448719

Szostak, M. (2025). Aesthetic insight into humanistic management and AI: Research perspectives. In *AI and humanistic management* (pp. 13–58).

Tariq, M. U. (2025). Harnessing Technology to Combat Bias: Innovative Tools and Techniques in HR. In Kanwal, S. (Ed.), *Navigating Bias in Human Resource Management* (pp. 155–184). IGI Global Scientific Publishing., DOI: 10.4018/979-8-3693-7132-9.ch006

Tariq, M. U. (2026). Bridging the Digital and Human Divide: Fostering Inclusion and Well-Being in Tech-Driven Workplaces. In Achour, Z. (Ed.), *Leading Inclusive Workplaces Through Digital Transformation and Organizational Change* (pp. 139–168). IGI Global Scientific Publishing., DOI: 10.4018/979-8-3373-5127-8.ch005

Tokic, V., & Csivre, A. (2026). Shaping tomorrow's digital banking: From technology to human-centric transformation. *Journal of Digital Banking*, *10*(3), 202–213. DOI: 10.69554/IBDY8945

Viljakainen, A., Silmukari, J., Roto, V., Čaić, M., & Aromaa, S. (2025). AI and the future of industrial work: A framework for enhancing employee experience from satisfaction to flourishing. *Behaviour & Information Technology*, •••, 1–13. DOI: 10.1080/0144929X.2025.2596889

Wang, Y., Zhong, M., Sharma, P., & Niu, D. F. (2026). The impact of human-centred artificial intelligence on firms' workforce demand in Industry 5.0 transition. *Enterprise Information Systems*, *20*(2), 2595706. DOI: 10.1080/17517575.2025.2595706

KEY TERMS AND DEFINITIONS

Customer Experience: Customers' holistic perceptions across all organizational interactions.

Employee Experience: Employee perceptions of the work environment, culture, and technology.

Human-Centered Value Creation: Designing organizational systems that prioritize human well-being and value.

Chapter 4
Human Experience in AI-Enabled Workplaces: Examining How AI Impacts Employee Roles, Collaboration, Skills, Well-Being

Aida Mehrad
http://orcid.org/0000-0003-4364-5709
C3S Business School, Barcelona, Spain

ABSTRACT

This chapter examines how Artificial Intelligence (AI) is transforming human work experiences, job roles, and workplace organization. The purpose of this chapter is to explore how AI-driven technologies reshape work through automation, human–machine collaboration, and changing skill demands. The chapter discusses how employees are increasingly expected to contribute through creativity, adaptability, and ethical judgment as routine and analytical tasks are augmented by AI. It also addresses challenges related to trust, accountability, employee well-being, and organizational culture, including concerns about monitoring, job insecurity, and stress. In addition, the chapter explores how AI is influencing Human Resource Management, shifting attention toward ethics, people management, and organizational change. By integrating theoretical perspectives and empirical research, this chapter provides a foundation for understanding AI's impact on work and offers insights for sustainable and employee-centered technology adoption.

DOI: 10.4018/979-8-3373-8282-1.ch004

CHAPTER OVERVIEW

This chapter analyzes changes in human work experiences driven by Artificial Intelligence (AI). It investigates how rapidly advancing intelligent technologies are redefining the meaning of work, its organization, and the nature of job roles. As AI systems assume more cognitive, analytical, and routine tasks, traditional job roles and boundaries are evolving (Brynjolfsson & McAfee, 2014; Davenport & Ronanki, 2018). These developments form part of a broader digital transformation, with AI distinguished from earlier automation by its support for adaptive decision-making, predictive analytics, and large-scale collaboration between humans and machines (Makridakis, 2017). AI is thus conceptualized not merely as a tool but as a transformative force affecting work processes, power dynamics, and employee experiences.

The chapter also looks at how using AI changes employee roles, teamwork, and the skills people need at work. As algorithms take over tasks such as data analysis, scheduling, recruitment screening, and performance monitoring, employees are expected to focus more on creative thinking, sound judgment, emotional intelligence, and ethical decision-making (Autor, 2015; Raisch & Krakowski, 2021). This shift means workers need to keep learning new skills, making adaptability and digital know-how key for future jobs, according to the World Economic Forum (WEF) (2023). The chapter also discusses new ways in which people and AI work together in teams, which raises important questions about trust, transparency, accountability, and control (Jarrahi, 2018).

The chapter also investigates the impact of AI-driven workplace changes on employee well-being and organizational culture. Although AI can reduce workloads, enhance decision-making, and increase work flexibility, it may also elevate pressure, intensify monitoring, and contribute to job insecurity, stress, or feelings of dehumanization if implemented improperly (Moore, 2019; Tarafdar et al., 2019). These challenges underscore the necessity of responsible, people-centered AI adoption. Furthermore, the chapter explores transformations in Human Resource Management (HRM) prompted by AI, with HR shifting from routine functions toward emphasis on people, ethics, and change management (Kaufman, 2020; Tursunbayeva et al., 2022). By integrating theoretical frameworks and recent empirical studies, the chapter establishes a comprehensive foundation for understanding AI's influence on work and guiding organizations toward sustainable, inclusive, and employee-focused technology use.

1. INTRODUCTION

Artificial Intelligence (AI) is rapidly expanding within organizations, transforming the structure, experience, and management of work (Fenwick et al., 2024). AI-enabled workplaces, where intelligent systems support decision-making, automate routine tasks, and enhance human capabilities, are increasingly prevalent across sectors and regions (Alsaif & Sabih Aksoy, 2023; Babashahi et al., 2024). Advances in machine learning, natural language processing, and predictive analytics drive this digital transformation, reshaping employee roles, teamwork, and the skills necessary for success in these environments (Babashahi et al., 2024; Jarrahi, 2025).

A significant consequence of AI adoption in the workplace is the transformation of employee roles and the skills required. As AI assumes responsibility for repetitive, data-intensive tasks, employees focus more on creative thinking, problem-solving, and interpersonal skills (Alsaif & Sabih Aksoy, 2023). Therefore, employees need a combination of technical expertise, critical thinking, emotional intelligence, and strategic problem-solving abilities. This shift affects training methods and career development pathways. Furthermore, emerging job categories at the intersection of technology and people management increase the importance of AI governance, data analysis, and ethical oversight within human resources (Financial Times, 2025).

Beyond altering individual roles, AI reshapes collaboration and team dynamics. Intelligent systems facilitate real-time coordination, enhance information sharing, and, in some cases, replace traditional team structures, fostering novel forms of human-AI collaboration. These interactions create complex relationships between humans and AI, rendering trust, transparency, and adaptability critical concerns for researchers and managers. Additionally, AI adoption introduces challenges such as job insecurity, technostress, mental health issues, and diminished autonomy (Sadeghi, 2024; Financial Times, 2025). Recent empirical studies indicate that AI's impact on well-being varies across demographic groups, job roles, and organizational contexts, highlighting the need for nuanced analysis (Nakavachara, 2025). Ethical AI implementation, characterized by transparency, fairness, and employee participation, is essential to promote positive psychological outcomes and organizational commitment.

These complex transformations are closely linked to the evolution of Human Resource Management (HRM) practices. With AI systems integrated into recruitment, performance appraisal, learning and development, and talent analytics, HRM is shifting from administrative and operational functions to strategic stewardship of workforce capabilities and organizational culture (Fenwick et al., 2024). HR professionals increasingly manage ethical dilemmas, facilitate human–technology integration, and cultivate environments where AI enhances employee experience and organizational effectiveness rather than undermining them.

The interaction among AI, human experience, and management practices demonstrates that work is undergoing significant changes in the twenty-first century. Researchers, business leaders, and policymakers must understand these changes to leverage AI's benefits, protect workers' well-being, promote teamwork, and ensure digital transformations result in fair, people-centered workplaces.

Human Experience in the Era of AI-Enabled Workplaces

The rapid adoption of Artificial Intelligence (AI) in organizations has initiated a new era characterized by interdependence between humans and technology. In AI-enabled workplaces, intelligent systems have become integral to key work processes, decision-making, and human resource functions, transforming both job execution and employee experience. Unlike earlier automation that primarily replaced manual or routine tasks, contemporary AI influences cognitive processes, interpersonal relationships, and management practices. This transformation is altering employee roles, collaboration dynamics, required skills, and overall well-being (Brynjolfsson & McAfee, 2017; Raisch & Krakowski, 2021). These developments necessitate a detailed examination of employee experiences in digital work environments and the corresponding adaptations in Human Resource Management (HRM). According to Reddy and Kumar (2025) AI is becoming an increasingly important part of everyday life, changing how people communicate, make decisions, and experience emotions. Tools like chatbots, virtual assistants, and recommendation systems make things more convenient and efficient. Still, these technologies can also lead to social isolation, reduced empathy, and excessive dependence on machines. AI has changed how people interact across social media, digital marketing, and customer service. In mental health, AI shows promise but raises ethical concerns about privacy, algorithmic bias, and the loss of human warmth. While AI offers many benefits, it also creates challenges that require attention to maintain strong human relationships and emotional well-being. In addition, Boyd and Markowitz (2026) argued that artificial intelligence can foster emotional investment, simulate understanding, or potentially replace human interaction. Instead of providing a single solution,

AI integration has profound implications for workplace design and organizational culture. Employees are increasingly required to work alongside AI systems, making human–AI collaboration a central feature of daily tasks. This shift challenges traditional role boundaries, requiring individuals to develop advanced digital literacy, critical thinking, and decision-making skills. Simultaneously, managers must rethink supervisory approaches and performance evaluation, balancing algorithmic outputs with human judgment. The interplay between AI recommendations and human decision-making creates both opportunities for enhanced productivity and risks related to overreliance, algorithmic bias, and diminished employee autonomy (Jarrahi, 2018; Tursunbayeva et al., 2022).

Moreover, AI adoption affects employee well-being and engagement in nuanced ways. While AI can alleviate repetitive workloads and support personalized learning, it also introduces stressors such as job insecurity, continuous monitoring, and constant adaptation to new technologies. The psychological and social impacts of AI-mediated work necessitate proactive HRM strategies, including transparent communication, training initiatives, and mechanisms to maintain trust and motivation. By addressing these human-centered considerations, organizations can harness AI's potential without compromising employee satisfaction, mental health, or long-term performance (Moore, 2019; Vrontis et al., 2022). These challenges underscore the importance of integrating technological advancements with a holistic understanding of human factors in contemporary work environments.

Purpose and Scope of the Chapter

This chapter analyzes how AI-enabled workplaces transform employees' work experiences. It addresses employee roles, teamwork, skills, well-being, and the development of human resource management (HRM) practices. The approach adopts a human-centered and socio-technical perspective rather than a solely technology-focused one. It acknowledges that AI's impact depends not only on technological factors but also on organizational structures, management practices, and employees' perceptions of these changes (Jarrahi, 2018; Vrontis et al., 2022).

The chapter uses research from human resource management, organizational behavior, information systems, and future-of-work studies. It examines both the benefits of AI, such as job support, improved teamwork, and data-based HR decisions, and the challenges, including technostress, job insecurity, ethical concerns, and risks of employee monitoring (Moore, 2019; Tarafdar et al., 2019). The goal is to provide a balanced view of how AI-driven changes can help create workplaces that are sustainable, inclusive, and employee-focused.

Artificial Intelligence (AI) denotes computational systems capable of executing tasks that typically require human intelligence, including learning, reasoning, pattern recognition, and decision-making (Russell & Norvig, 2021). In organizational contexts, AI encompasses applications such as machine learning, natural language processing, predictive analytics, and intelligent automation.

AI-enabled workplaces are organizational environments in which AI technologies are systematically integrated into work processes, decision-making tools, and management practices. This integration influences how tasks are assigned, monitored, and evaluated (Davenport & Ronanki, 2018). Such workplaces exemplify digital transformation, defined as the use of digital technologies to alter organizational structures, operations, and value creation (Vial, 2019). Employee experiences in these settings—including job roles, autonomy, collaboration, skill utilization, well-being, and perceptions of fairness and meaning—are increasingly shaped by interactions with algorithmic systems and data-driven management practices (Guest, 2017).

Finally, Human Resource Management (HRM) covers the policies, practices, and systems for managing people in organizations. With AI, HRM is becoming more strategic and ethical, leveraging workforce analytics, AI oversight, skill development, and the management of how people and technology work together (Kaufman, 2020; Tursunbayeva et al., 2022). After this introduction, the chapter puts AI-enabled work in the wider context of digital transformation and the future of work. It reviews the main theories about human–AI interaction and work redesign. Later sections examine how employee roles are changing, new ways people and AI work together, and shifts in the skills needed. The chapter also discusses how AI affects employee well-being and job quality, and how HRM is evolving in digital workplaces. It ends by summarizing key points, considering management and ethical issues, and suggesting areas for future research.

2. AI-ENABLED WORKPLACES AND DIGITAL TRANSFORMATION

Digital transformation constitutes a defining characteristic of contemporary organizations, fundamentally altering value creation, work organization, and interactions between employees and technology. Artificial Intelligence (AI) is central to this transformation, surpassing traditional digital tools by enabling systems to learn, adapt, and make data-driven decisions. Workplaces enabled by AI represent a significant departure from earlier computerization and automation, as intelligent technologies increasingly affect operational efficiency, human roles, social relations, and managerial practices (Vial, 2019; Raisch & Krakowski, 2021). These developments not only reshape how work is performed but also challenge organizations to rethink the design of tasks, responsibilities, and performance metrics in a way that aligns with technological capabilities.

The integration of AI into organizational processes demands a reconfiguration of employee competencies and collaborative structures. Employees must acquire new skills, including data literacy, digital problem-solving, and adaptive decision-making, while managers must navigate the balance between algorithmic recommendations and human judgment. This dynamic transforms traditional hierarchies and decision-making models, fostering environments in which human–AI collaboration becomes a core element of workflow. Furthermore, AI-driven insights offer the potential to optimize resource allocation, enhance productivity, and personalize employee experiences, but they also introduce risks related to overreliance, ethical concerns, and unintended bias (Jarrahi, 2018; Tursunbayeva, Di Lauro, & Pagliari, 2022).

Beyond operational and skill-related implications, AI adoption has significant social and psychological consequences for employees. The presence of intelligent systems in daily work can alter communication patterns, team cohesion, and employee autonomy, influencing motivation, engagement, and overall well-being. Organizations must therefore adopt human-centered approaches to technology integration, emphasizing transparency, trust-building, and continuous learning opportunities. By doing so, firms can leverage AI not only as a driver of efficiency but also as a catalyst for sustainable workforce development and employee satisfaction, ensuring that digital transformation supports both organizational goals and human capital (Moore, 2019; Vrontis et al., 2022).

2.1 From Automation to AI-Enabled Work

Previous technological advancements primarily emphasized mechanization and automation, targeting routine and manual tasks. Although these technologies increased productivity, their influence on cognitive and relational aspects of work remained limited (Autor, 2015). In contrast, AI systems perform complex analytical, predictive, and communicative functions, enabling direct participation in knowledge-intensive and decision-oriented tasks (Davenport & Ronanki, 2018). By engaging with cognitive and interpersonal dimensions of work, AI transforms not only what tasks are performed but also how they are approached, fostering environments that require continuous learning, problem-solving, and human–machine collaboration (Brynjolfsson & McAfee, 2017).

This transition has accelerated the rise of AI-enabled workplaces, where algorithmic systems support or influence activities such as scheduling, performance evaluation, customer interaction, recruitment, and learning and development. Unlike previous automation, AI systems operate in real time and at scale, seamlessly embedding themselves into daily workflows and decision-making processes (Jarrahi, 2018). This integration creates opportunities for efficiency, personalization, and predictive insights, but also introduces complexities regarding trust, accountability, and the alignment of AI outputs with organizational objectives.

As a result, employees must continually adapt to working alongside intelligent technologies, reshaping professional identities, skill requirements, and work expectations. The evolving interface between humans and AI demands not only technical competencies but also socio-emotional skills, such as collaboration, communication, and ethical reasoning. Organizations are therefore tasked with designing work environments and HR practices that support this dynamic, including training programs, participatory decision-making, and strategies to maintain well-being and engagement in AI-mediated work contexts (Moore, 2019; Vrontis et al., 2022). The rise of AI-enabled workplaces thus represents both a challenge and an opportunity, requiring a careful balance between technological capability and human-centered management.

2.2 AI as a Socio-Technical System

A comprehensive understanding of AI-enabled workplaces necessitates moving beyond a purely technological perspective toward a socio-technical view of digital transformation. Socio-technical systems theory emphasizes that organizational outcomes emerge from the interaction between technological infrastructures and social systems, including people, structures, and cultures (Trist & Bamforth, 1951; Parker & Grote, 2022). This perspective highlights that technology alone does not determine work outcomes; rather, its impact is shaped by how it is designed, implemented, and governed within the organizational context. By integrating human, technical, and organizational factors, socio-technical thinking provides a holistic framework for analyzing the complexities of AI adoption in contemporary work environments.

AI systems inherently embed assumptions, values, and power relations that influence how work is monitored, evaluated, and controlled (Kellogg et al., 2020). For instance, algorithmic management tools can standardize processes and enhance efficiency, yet they also carry the risk of reducing employee autonomy, increasing workload intensity, or reinforcing existing biases if deployed without transparency or meaningful employee input. These tensions demonstrate that technology is never neutral; its design and use reflect organizational priorities and cultural norms, which in turn shape employee experiences, engagement, and performance outcomes.

Consequently, AI-enabled workplaces should be conceptualized as dynamic ecosystems where human agency, organizational practices, and technological capabilities continuously interact. Employees are not merely passive recipients of AI-driven processes but active participants who interpret, adapt, and sometimes resist technological interventions. Organizations that recognize this interplay can better align AI implementation with human-centered objectives, promoting collaboration, ethical governance, and sustainable performance. Understanding these socio-technical dynamics is essential for designing workplaces where AI augments rather than diminishes human potential, supporting both organizational effectiveness and employee well-being.

2.3 Digital Transformation and the Future of Work

AI-enabled workplaces are a core component of broader digital transformation strategies that aim to enhance organizational agility, innovation, and competitiveness. Digital transformation involves not only adopting new technologies but also fundamental changes in organizational structures, leadership models, and cultural norms (Vial, 2019). In this context, AI acts as both a driver and an enabler of new work arrangements, including remote and hybrid work, data-driven decision-making, and flexible career paths.

These developments are central to ongoing debates about the future of work. While AI has the potential to augment human capabilities, improve job quality, and support more personalized and meaningful work experiences, it also raises concerns about job displacement, skill polarization, and inequality (OECD, 2023; World Economic Forum [WEF], 2023). The outcomes of AI-driven digital transformation, therefore, depend on organizational choices regarding investment in skills development, ethical governance, and inclusive HRM practices.

The future of work in AI-enabled environments remains undetermined. Organizations play a pivotal role in determining whether AI adoption results in human-centered workplaces that enhance employee well-being and collaboration or in technology-driven systems that prioritize efficiency over human experience (Raisch & Krakowski, 2021). This highlights the need to examine AI-enabled workplaces through an integrative lens that considers technological, human, and managerial dimensions simultaneously.

3. THEORETICAL PERSPECTIVES ON HUMAN–AI INTERACTION AT WORK

A strong theoretical foundation is crucial for understanding how technology interacts with social systems, shapes work design, and impacts employee outcomes in AI-enabled workplaces. Without such a foundation, analyses risk focusing narrowly on technological capabilities while neglecting the human, social, and organizational dimensions that ultimately determine the success and consequences of AI adoption. By grounding research and practice in theory, scholars and practitioners can better anticipate the implications of AI for work processes, employee experience, and organizational performance.

This section explores three interrelated theoretical perspectives that are particularly relevant to analyzing human–AI interactions at work: sociotechnical systems theory, human–AI collaboration and augmentation theory, and job design and work transformation theories. Sociotechnical systems theory emphasizes the interplay between technological systems and social structures, highlighting that organizational outcomes result from the alignment—or misalignment—between these components. Human–AI collaboration and augmentation theories focus on the ways intelligent systems extend human capabilities, redistribute tasks, and influence decision-making processes. Finally, job design and work transformation theories examine how technological changes alter task characteristics, skill requirements, and employee motivation.

Together, these perspectives provide a comprehensive framework for examining how AI reshapes employee roles, collaboration patterns, skill demands, and overall well-being within digitally transformed organizations. By integrating insights from multiple theoretical lenses, researchers and practitioners can capture the complex and multifaceted effects of AI in the workplace. This approach not only illuminates the potential benefits of AI adoption, such as enhanced productivity and knowledge work augmentation, but also identifies risks, including increased work intensity, ethical dilemmas, and challenges to employee autonomy. Ultimately, such a framework supports the design of human-centered AI workplaces that balance technological innovation with employee development, engagement, and well-being.

3.1 Sociotechnical Systems Theory

Sociotechnical systems (STS) theory offers a foundational lens for understanding AI-enabled workplaces by highlighting the need to jointly optimize social and technical systems. Introduced by Trist and Bamforth (1951), STS theory argues that both organizational performance and employee well-being rely on the alignment between technological infrastructures and social components, such as work roles, organizational structures, and employee needs. Rather than treating technology as an external force that dictates work outcomes, STS theory emphasizes the reciprocal and dynamic interaction between humans and technology.

In AI-enabled workplaces, STS theory is particularly relevant because AI systems are embedded in decision-making, coordination, and control processes. Algorithmic systems shape task allocation, performance monitoring, and decision-making, thereby influencing power dynamics and employee autonomy (Kellogg et al., 2020). From a sociotechnical perspective, the effects of AI on human experience are determined by organizational choices regarding workflow design, employee involvement in implementation, and the balance between efficiency and human-centered values (Parker & Grote, 2022).

STS theory suggests that misalignment between AI technologies and social systems can result in negative outcomes, such as technostress, resistance, lower job satisfaction, and reduced trust in management. Conversely, AI adoption guided by participatory design, transparency, and supportive human resource practices can enhance job quality, learning opportunities, and overall employee well-being (Pasmore et al., 2019). Thus, STS theory provides a vital framework for understanding AI not merely as a technical innovation but as a socio-organizational transformation.

3.2 Human–AI Collaboration and Augmentation Theory

Human–AI collaboration and augmentation theory emphasizes complementarity rather than substitution between humans and intelligent systems. While early automation narratives often portrayed technology as replacing human labor, recent research shows that AI frequently enhances human capabilities by supporting decision-making, improving accuracy, and expanding cognitive capacity (Davenport & Kirby, 2016; Raisch & Krakowski, 2021).

Jarrahi (2018) frames human AI interaction as a form of symbiotic collaboration, where humans and AI systems contribute distinct yet complementary strengths. AI is particularly effective at processing large datasets, identifying patterns, and generating predictions, whereas humans provide contextual understanding, ethical judgment, creativity, and emotional intelligence. Optimal collaboration in AI-enabled workplaces occurs when tasks are deliberately allocated to leverage these complementary capabilities, rather than pursuing full automation.

However, human AI collaboration also brings challenges, including issues of trust, explainability, and accountability. Employees need to understand and rely on AI recommendations without falling into overdependence—a phenomenon known as automation bias (Raisch & Krakowski, 2021). Augmentation theory highlights the importance of transparency, human oversight, and continuous skill development to ensure that AI enhances, rather than diminishes, human contributions. From a human resource management perspective, this theory underscores the need to design roles, training programs, and performance systems that promote collaborative intelligence. It also draws attention to psychological factors involved in working alongside AI, such as shifts in identity, perceived competence, and sense of control, all of which are critical to the human experience in AI-enabled environments.

3.3 Job Design and Work Transformation Theories

Job design and work transformation theories provide valuable insight into how AI reshapes the employee experience by influencing task characteristics, skill requirements, and motivational conditions. Classical job design frameworks, such as the Job Characteristics Model (Hackman & Oldham, 1976), propose that meaningful work arises from factors like autonomy, task significance, skill variety, and feedback. The implementation of AI can either strengthen or weaken these characteristics, depending on how it is integrated into work processes.

AI has the potential to reduce repetitive or cognitively demanding tasks, enabling employees to focus on more meaningful and creative work (Autor, 2015). Conversely, algorithmic management systems may limit autonomy, increase monitoring, and standardize work, which can diminish job enrichment and elevate stress levels (Moore, 2019). Work transformation theories highlight that AI-driven changes should be accompanied by deliberate job redesign to preserve motivation and employee well-being.

Recent research emphasizes proactive and adaptive job design in dynamic digital environments. Parker and Grote (2022) argue that work design in AI-enabled workplaces should prioritize learning, adaptability, and employee participation to effectively manage ongoing technological change. This approach aligns with the Job Demands–Resources (JD–R) model, which suggests that AI can function either as a job resource—providing decision support and reducing workload—or as a job demand, contributing to cognitive overload and technostress, with significant implications for employee well-being (Bakker & Demerouti, 2017).

Together, job design and work transformation theories indicate that AI does not automatically enhance or diminish work quality. Instead, its impact on the human experience depends on how tasks are restructured, the level of employee autonomy, and the organization's commitment to supportive human resource practices, including reskilling, participatory design, and ethical governance.

4. TRANSFORMATION OF EMPLOYEE ROLES IN AI-ENABLED WORK ENVIRONMENTS

The integration of Artificial Intelligence (AI) into organizational processes is fundamentally reshaping employee roles by transforming task structures, decision-making authority, and occupational boundaries. Rather than simply eliminating jobs, AI modifies the nature and significance of work through complex processes of automation, augmentation, and job redesign. These changes challenge traditional role definitions and compel organizations to rethink the allocation of responsibilities, autonomy, and skills within human–machine systems (Autor, 2015; Raisch & Krakowski, 2021). This section examines how employee roles evolve in AI-enabled workplaces, with a focus on task reconfiguration, shifts in responsibility and decision-making, and the creation of new or hybrid occupations.

4.1 Task Automation, Augmentation, and Job Redesign

AI-enabled technologies drive substantial changes in job design by enabling varying degrees of task automation and augmentation. Automation occurs when AI systems fully take over human involvement in specific tasks—typically those that are routine, repetitive, or data-intensive—such as transaction processing, scheduling, or basic customer service interactions (Brynjolfsson & McAfee, 2017). While automation can improve efficiency and reduce human error, it may also narrow job scope if not paired with intentional job redesign.

Augmentation, on the other hand, involves AI systems that enhance rather than replace human performance. In augmented roles, AI acts as a decision-support tool, offering insights, predictions, and recommendations that guide human judgment (Davenport & Kirby, 2016). For example, in professional and managerial settings, AI-driven analytics help employees interpret complex datasets, enabling more informed and timely decisions. Augmentation often increases task complexity and cognitive demands, underscoring the need for targeted training and clearly defined roles (Jarrahi, 2018).

Job redesign is a critical organizational response to these shifts. Effective redesign involves restructuring tasks to ensure meaningful work, skill variety, and autonomy, in accordance with established job design principles (Hackman & Oldham, 1976). In AI-enabled workplaces, redesign must account for ongoing technological change and the evolving division of labor between humans and machines. When organizations proactively shape roles to leverage uniquely human strengths—such as creativity, empathy, and ethical reasoning—AI adoption is more likely to enhance job quality and enrich work experiences rather than diminish them (Parker & Grote, 2022).

4.2 Shifts in Responsibility, Autonomy, and Decision-Making

AI-enabled workplaces bring significant changes to responsibility and decision-making authority. As AI systems increasingly influence or automate decisions related to task allocation, performance evaluation, and resource distribution, questions arise about accountability and the level of autonomy employees retain (Kellogg et al., 2020). In some cases, AI can enhance autonomy by reducing administrative burdens, enabling employees to focus on higher-value work. In other situations, algorithmic management systems may limit discretion by standardizing workflows and closely monitoring performance.

Decision-making processes are similarly transformed. AI-driven recommendations can improve decision quality by reducing bias and increasing consistency; however, they may obscure the reasoning behind decisions if the systems lack transparency or explainability (Raisch & Krakowski, 2021). This opacity can lead to overreliance on algorithms, weakening critical thinking and professional judgment—a phenomenon known as automation bias. Consequently, employees must navigate new forms of accountability, overseeing AI outputs while remaining responsible for final decisions.

These changes have important implications for role clarity, trust, and psychological safety. To maintain employee autonomy and confidence in AI-enabled workplaces, organizations need clear governance structures, transparent AI systems, and explicit delineation of human versus algorithmic responsibilities (Parker & Grote, 2022; Tursunbayeva et al., 2022).

4.3 Emergence of New Roles and Hybrid Occupations

AI-enabled workplaces bring significant changes to responsibility and decision-making authority. As AI systems increasingly influence or automate decisions related to task allocation, performance evaluation, and resource distribution, questions arise about accountability and the level of autonomy employees retain (Kellogg et al., 2020). In some cases, AI can enhance autonomy by reducing administrative burdens, enabling employees to focus on higher-value work. In other situations, algorithmic management systems may limit discretion by standardizing workflows and closely monitoring performance.

Decision-making processes are similarly transformed. AI-driven recommendations can improve decision quality by reducing bias and increasing consistency; however, they may obscure the reasoning behind decisions if the systems lack transparency or explainability (Raisch & Krakowski, 2021). This opacity can lead to overreliance on algorithms, weakening critical thinking and professional judgment—a phenomenon known as automation bias. Consequently, employees must navigate new forms of accountability, overseeing AI outputs while remaining responsible for final decisions.

These changes have important implications for role clarity, trust, and psychological safety. To maintain employee autonomy and confidence in AI-enabled workplaces, organizations need clear governance structures, transparent AI systems, and explicit delineation of human versus algorithmic responsibilities (Parker & Grote, 2022; Tursunbayeva et al., 2022).

5. HUMAN–AI COLLABORATION AND CHANGING PATTERNS OF WORK

As AI becomes an integral component of organizational processes, human work increasingly involves collaboration with intelligent systems. Unlike traditional automation, which primarily replaces repetitive or routine tasks, AI enables hybrid forms of work where humans and machines interact to achieve shared goals. These collaborations often combine human creativity, judgment, and socio-emotional skills with AI's computational speed, predictive power, and pattern recognition capabilities. By blending these complementary strengths, AI-augmented work extends the potential of knowledge-intensive tasks, problem-solving, and decision-making within organizations (Jarrahi, 2018; Davenport & Ronanki, 2018).

These human–AI interactions reshape work patterns, team dynamics, and organizational structures. AI systems can influence task allocation, workflow sequencing, and communication channels, requiring employees to coordinate not only with colleagues but also with intelligent technologies. This shift impacts both operational aspects—such as efficiency, accuracy, and resource optimization—and relational dimensions, including collaboration quality, role clarity, and employee autonomy. Employees and managers must therefore adapt to evolving responsibilities, interpret AI-generated insights critically, and integrate algorithmic recommendations with human judgment.

The transformation of work through human–AI collaboration has significant implications for trust, accountability, and team performance. Trust in AI systems is essential for employees to rely on automated recommendations and support decision-making without excessive skepticism or overreliance. At the same time, accountability structures must clarify responsibility for outcomes when tasks are shared between humans and machines, addressing ethical, legal, and performance-related concerns. Understanding these dynamics allows organizations to design work environments that maximize the benefits of AI augmentation while maintaining transparency, fairness, and effective teamwork. Such an approach ensures that human–AI collaboration enhances both productivity and employee experience rather than creating unintended risks or workplace tensions.

5.1 AI as a Collaborative Partner

In AI-enabled workplaces, intelligent systems act as collaborative partners rather than mere tools. AI technologies offer real-time recommendations, predictive analytics, and decision support that enhance human cognitive capabilities. For instance, in fields like marketing or finance, AI can process large datasets to identify trends or risks, while humans contribute contextual understanding, ethical judgment, and creative problem-solving (Raisch & Krakowski, 2021). This partnership is often described as augmented intelligence, highlighting the synergy between machine efficiency and human insight (Davenport & Kirby, 2016).

Effective human–AI collaboration requires employees to develop new skills, including algorithmic literacy, data interpretation, and the ability to critically assess AI outputs. Roles are becoming increasingly dynamic, with humans taking on supervisory or interpretive responsibilities over AI-generated results. These changes emphasize the need for targeted training, organizational support, and clear role definitions to maximize the benefits of human–AI collaboration (Vrontis et al., 2022).

5.2 Trust, Transparency, and Explainability

A key determinant of effective human–AI collaboration is trust. Employees' willingness to rely on AI recommendations hinges on their confidence in the system's accuracy, fairness, and reliability (Lee & See, 2004). When AI decision-making is opaque or lacks transparency, trust can be eroded, resulting in resistance, misuse, or overreliance—a set of issues collectively referred to as automation bias (Raisch & Krakowski, 2021).

To mitigate these challenges, organizations should prioritize explainability and interpretability in AI systems. Explainable AI (XAI) approaches help employees understand how AI arrives at its conclusions, enabling them to intervene when necessary and fostering stronger human–machine collaboration (Gunning, 2017). From a management perspective, building trust also requires clear governance, ethical oversight, and participatory design that actively involves employees in shaping how AI is used within their roles.

5.3 Team Dynamics and Hybrid Work Structures

Human–AI collaboration transforms team dynamics and work patterns. AI systems can serve as mediators, coordinators, or knowledge repositories, shaping information flow and interactions among team members (Jarrahi, 2018). Teams increasingly operate in distributed, data-driven ways, with humans focusing on tasks that require creativity, empathy, or strategic judgment, while AI manages analytical and operational processes.

These hybrid work arrangements have significant implications for organizational culture and management. Leaders must cultivate environments that promote collaboration across human–AI boundaries, support continuous learning and adaptation, and address potential social tensions arising from perceived imbalances in human–machine contributions (Parker & Grote, 2022). Successful collaboration also requires aligning AI outputs with human objectives, ensuring that employees maintain agency and decision-making authority. For instance, the companies in developed countries have changed their method and mostly focused on team dynamics. For example, software companies employ developers who work remotely from various countries, whereas product managers and designers are required to attend the office two days per week (Ford et al., 2021). Also, they emphasize that remote software teams benefited from increased autonomy and flexible scheduling. In contrast, Olson and Olson (2000) argue that geographic distance can reduce communication quality and coordination efficiency. This contrast suggests that the success of hybrid work may depend on organizational communication systems and team maturity rather than hybrid structures alone.

5.4 Implications for HRM Practices

The integration of AI into collaborative work processes has profound implications for Human Resource Management (HRM). Traditional HRM practices focused on recruitment, training, and performance management must now adapt to the realities of hybrid human–AI work environments. This includes designing programs for re-skilling and upskilling employees to work effectively alongside intelligent systems, redefining roles to incorporate AI-augmented tasks, and updating performance evaluation frameworks to account for both human contributions and the oversight or interpretation of AI outputs (Tursunbayeva, Di Lauro, & Pagliari, 2022). By doing so, HRM ensures that employees remain competent, confident, and engaged in increasingly technologically mediated workplaces.

For instance, performance metrics in AI-enabled settings may need to extend beyond traditional productivity indicators to capture skills such as adaptability, problem-solving, ethical decision-making, and effective collaboration with AI systems. HRM practices must therefore balance operational efficiency with the development of human skills that complement AI capabilities. Additionally, organizations must address the psychosocial aspects of work, monitoring cognitive load, stress, and engagement as employees navigate environments where AI mediates tasks, provides recommendations, or enforces performance standards (Moore, 2019). This requires proactive approaches to well-being, including supportive policies, feedback mechanisms, and interventions that prevent overload and foster sustainable work practices.

In summary, human–AI collaboration represents a fundamental shift in the nature of work and the role of HRM. While AI can enhance efficiency, decision-making, and the quality of data-driven insights, it also necessitates rethinking team structures, trust mechanisms, and employee management practices. Organizations that successfully integrate AI into work processes are those that design HRM systems to optimize both performance outcomes and the overall employee experience, creating environments where humans and intelligent technologies can collaborate effectively and sustainably.

6. SKILLS, COMPETENCIES, AND WORKFORCE CAPABILITY DEVELOPMENT IN AI-ENABLED WORKPLACES

The growing integration of Artificial Intelligence (AI) into organizational processes is reshaping the skills, competencies, and overall capabilities required of the workforce. As AI systems take on tasks that are repetitive, data-intensive, or analytical, the nature of human work shifts toward roles that emphasize judgment, problem-solving, and socio-emotional competencies. Employees are increasingly expected to collaborate with intelligent systems, interpret algorithmic outputs, and apply insights to complex, context-dependent decisions. This evolving landscape challenges traditional notions of job design and requires a strategic approach to workforce development (Brynjolfsson & McAfee, 2017; Jarrahi, 2018).

As tasks become increasingly automated or augmented, employees must adjust to evolving job demands by developing both digital proficiency and distinctly human abilities. Critical thinking, creativity, communication, and emotional intelligence emerge as essential skills that enable employees to complement AI capabilities rather than compete with them. Additionally, adaptability and continuous learning are critical for employees to navigate changing technologies, organizational processes, and expectations. Organizations that fail to support skill development risk widening capability gaps and reducing workforce engagement, while those that proactively cultivate these competencies enhance both individual and organizational performance.

Human Resource Management (HRM) plays a central role in building a workforce equipped for AI-driven workplaces. HRM strategies must focus on identifying skill gaps, designing targeted learning programs, fostering a culture of continuous development, and embedding digital literacy across the organization. Initiatives such as AI-focused training, cross-functional collaboration, mentorship programs, and competency mapping can help employees acquire the skills needed to thrive in hybrid work environments. By aligning HRM practices with the demands of AI-augmented work, organizations can ensure that their workforce remains agile, capable, and prepared to leverage technology for innovation, productivity, and sustainable performance.

6.1 Evolving Skills and Competencies

The adoption of AI is transforming the nature of work by moving the focus away from routine and manual activities toward more complex cognitive, analytical, and social tasks. As a result, technical skills—such as data literacy, coding, and the ability to interpret AI outputs—are becoming increasingly important across a wide range of roles (WEF, 2023). However, technical expertise alone is not enough. The true human advantage lies in capabilities that complement AI, including problem-solving, creativity, ethical judgment, and effective interpersonal communication (Raisch & Krakowski, 2021).

The concept of T-shaped skills—characterized by broad knowledge across multiple disciplines coupled with deep expertise in a specific area—has gained particular significance in AI-driven workplaces. Employees are increasingly expected to integrate their domain expertise with analytical and digital capabilities to engage effectively with AI systems (Davenport & Kirby, 2016). Alongside this, adaptive expertise and a commitment to continuous learning are essential, as the rapid evolution of AI technologies demands that employees regularly refresh and expand their knowledge and skillsets (OECD, 2023).

6.2 Role of HRM in Workforce Capability Development

Human Resource Management (HRM) is pivotal in preparing employees for the demands of AI-enabled work. Effective HRM strategies should encompass reskilling, upskilling, and ongoing professional development to maintain productivity and engagement (Tursunbayeva et al., 2022). For instance, HRM can utilize AI-driven tools to personalize learning experiences through people analytics, recommending training programs that address individual skill gaps and align with career goals (Vrontis et al., 2022).

Equally important is cultivating a learning-oriented organizational culture that promotes experimentation, collaboration, and reflection. In AI-driven workplaces, employees often encounter uncertainty regarding task allocation, decision-making authority, and job security. Supportive HR practices—such as coaching, mentoring, and cross-functional teamwork—enable employees to build confidence in collaborating with AI systems and strengthen resilience amid continuous change (Moore, 2019; Parker & Grote, 2022).

6.3 Strategic Approaches to Workforce Transformation

Several strategic approaches have emerged to align workforce capabilities with the goals of AI-enabled organizations. One foundational approach is competency mapping and gap analysis, which involves systematically assessing current employee skills against those required for AI-augmented roles. By identifying gaps in technical proficiency, cognitive abilities, and socio-emotional competencies, organizations can design targeted reskilling and upskilling initiatives that address specific workforce needs. This ensures that training investments are efficient and that employees acquire capabilities that directly support the organization's AI-driven objectives (Kaufman, 2020).

Another critical strategy involves building learning ecosystems and microlearning platforms. Digital learning environments, which include on-demand modules, interactive simulations, and bite-sized training, provide employees with flexible, continuous opportunities to develop relevant skills. These platforms are particularly effective in hybrid or AI-integrated workplaces, where work schedules, geographic dispersion, and rapidly changing technologies demand just-in-time learning. By embedding skill development into the flow of work, organizations support continuous learning and reinforce employee adaptability (OECD, 2023).

In addition, organizations are increasingly adopting human–AI co-learning and dynamic career path redesign. Human–AI co-learning involves employees working alongside AI systems to interpret outputs, provide feedback, and refine algorithms, creating a reciprocal learning cycle that enhances both human expertise and AI performance (Jarrahi, 2018). Simultaneously, career path redesign moves away from traditional linear trajectories toward flexible, lattice-like structures. These career frameworks emphasize hybrid roles, cross-functional skills, and ongoing professional growth, empowering employees to navigate AI-driven workplaces successfully while fostering engagement and adaptability (World Economic Forum, 2023). Collectively, these strategies enable HRM to proactively align workforce development with organizational goals, ensuring that human-centered practices remain integral in AI-enabled work environments.

6.4 Implications for Employee Experience

Investing in workforce capability development has a profound effect on the employee experience in AI-enabled workplaces. Well-designed training, reskilling, and upskilling programs help employees feel more confident in their roles, increase job satisfaction, and enhance perceived employability. These programs are particularly important in AI-driven environments, where technological changes can create uncertainty, disrupt familiar routines, and introduce new cognitive and social demands. By providing structured support, organizations can reduce stress, anxiety, and resistance to change, helping employees navigate technological transformations with greater ease and resilience (Moore, 2019).

Beyond mitigating stress, capability development empowers employees to collaborate effectively with AI systems, which can enhance the meaningfulness of their work. As employees gain proficiency in interpreting AI outputs, integrating algorithmic insights, and contributing to AI-mediated processes, they experience a stronger sense of mastery and accomplishment. This not only improves performance but also fosters engagement, motivation, and commitment to organizational goals. In this way, learning initiatives and skill development become mechanisms for strengthening the human–AI partnership, rather than simply supporting technical adoption (Raisch & Krakowski, 2021).

Ultimately, workforce capability development is both a strategic and human-centered priority. By aligning employee skills with the demands of AI-enabled work, organizations not only drive operational efficiency and innovation but also cultivate well-being, resilience, and a positive organizational culture. This dual focus ensures that technology enhances rather than undermines the employee experience, creating sustainable and mutually beneficial outcomes for both workers and organizations.

For the role of AI and workers well-being in Scientific Reports that has been issued in 2025, is a longitudinal empirical analysis, meaning it tracks the same population trends over a long period (2000–2020) rather than capturing a single snapshot in time. It uses large-scale German labor survey data, which allows researchers to observe how workplace changes linked to AI exposure evolve over two decades. Workers in AI-intensive roles experience different effects than those in low-AI environments.

7. EMPLOYEE WELL-BEING AND PSYCHOLOGICAL IMPACTS OF AI-ENABLED WORK

The integration of Artificial Intelligence (AI) into workplaces carries wide-ranging implications for employee well-being, producing both positive and negative psychological effects. On the positive side, AI can improve efficiency, reduce repetitive tasks, and support decision-making. However, it can also create challenges related to job security, workload, autonomy, and social interaction. For organizations striving for human-centered and sustainable AI adoption, understanding these dynamics is essential (Moore, 2019; Tursunbayeva et al., 2022). This section examines the impact of AI on employee well-being, the psychological processes driving these effects, and strategies to mitigate potential negative outcomes.

7.1 Positive Impacts on Employee Well-Being

AI-enabled workplaces can positively impact employee well-being by enhancing human capabilities and alleviating cognitive and physical demands. By automating repetitive or low-value tasks, employees are able to concentrate on more meaningful, creative, or strategic work, which boosts job satisfaction and perceived autonomy (Brynjolfsson & McAfee, 2017; Jarrahi, 2018). AI also supports more accurate and efficient decision-making, helping to reduce stress linked to uncertainty or complex information processing (Raisch & Krakowski, 2021).

Moreover, workplace AI can facilitate personalized learning, career development, and engagement through people analytics and adaptive training programs, enabling employees to acquire new skills and navigate evolving roles effectively (Vrontis et al., 2022). When applied thoughtfully, these AI-driven initiatives foster a sense of mastery, competence, and professional growth—core factors that contribute to psychological well-being (Deci & Ryan, 2000).

7.2 Potential Risks and Psychological Challenges

While AI offers numerous operational and strategic benefits, its adoption also introduces significant risks to employee well-being. As AI reshapes task allocation, employees may face job insecurity, role ambiguity, and uncertainty regarding career trajectories. These shifts can generate anxiety, reduce confidence, and increase the perceived threat of redundancy, particularly in highly automated or algorithmically managed workplaces (OECD, 2023; World Economic Forum, 2023). Employees may also struggle to adapt to evolving performance expectations, new skill requirements, and continuous learning demands, all of which can exacerbate workplace stress.

Algorithmic management systems, while designed to enhance efficiency and consistency, can inadvertently intensify workloads and reduce autonomy. Constant monitoring, automated performance evaluations, and prescriptive task allocations may heighten perceptions of micromanagement, eroding employee control over work processes and contributing to burnout (Kellogg et al., 2020; Moore, 2019). Additionally, overreliance on AI outputs—sometimes referred to as automation bias—can undermine critical thinking and decision-making skills, leading employees to defer judgment to machines even in ethically or socially complex situations. These factors create a dual cognitive burden: managing one's tasks while simultaneously interpreting, validating, or correcting AI-generated recommendations (Raisch & Krakowski, 2021).

AI adoption can also disrupt social and relational aspects of work. By reducing opportunities for human-to-human interaction, collaborative problem-solving, and informal knowledge sharing, AI may inadvertently foster isolation or weaken social support networks, particularly in remote or hybrid work environments (Jarrahi, 2018). Such disruptions can negatively affect team cohesion, trust, and engagement, compounding psychological strain. Taken together, these challenges illustrate the dual-edged nature of AI in the workplace: while it offers efficiency and enhanced decision-making, poorly implemented AI can amplify stressors, undermine autonomy, and threaten employee well-being, highlighting the critical need for thoughtful design, governance, and HRM interventions.

7.3 Mediators and Moderators of Well-Being Outcomes

Research indicates that the psychological effects of AI on employees are shaped by a combination of individual, technological, and organizational factors. Key determinants include role clarity, perceived autonomy, trust in AI systems, and perceptions of fairness in AI-driven decision-making processes. When employees clearly understand how AI will impact their responsibilities and feel confident in their ability to interact effectively with intelligent systems, they are more likely to experience positive outcomes, such as enhanced engagement, satisfaction, and performance (Parker & Grote, 2022; Tursunbayeva et al., 2022). Furthermore, AI systems that are transparent, explainable, and aligned with human objectives foster trust and reduce uncertainty, mitigating potential stress and cognitive overload (Gunning, 2017).

Organizational culture and Human Resource Management (HRM) practices play a crucial moderating role in shaping these psychological effects. Supportive interventions—such as participatory design, collaborative decision-making, mentoring, and ongoing learning opportunities—help employees adapt to AI-driven changes, build competence, and maintain well-being in technologically enhanced work environments (Moore, 2019). These practices also reinforce perceptions of fairness and inclusion, ensuring that AI adoption complements human contributions rather than undermining them.

Conversely, the absence of transparency, punitive algorithmic monitoring, or insufficient training can exacerbate stress, anxiety, and disengagement. When AI systems are perceived as opaque or controlling, employees may feel disempowered, mistrustful, or fearful of error, increasing cognitive and emotional strain. These dynamics highlight the ethical and managerial responsibility of organizations to implement AI in a human-centered manner, ensuring that technological advancements support both organizational performance and employee well-being.

7.4 Strategies to Promote Well-Being in AI-Enabled Workplaces

To promote employee well-being in AI-enabled workplaces, organizations can implement several key strategies:

Human-Centered AI Design – Engaging employees in AI implementation to ensure systems support and enhance human work rather than restrict it (Pasmore et al., 2019). Transparent and Explainable Systems – Leveraging explainable AI to build trust, understanding, and confidence in machine-generated recommendations (Gunning, 2017). Reskilling and Continuous Learning – Offering ongoing opportunities for skill development to strengthen competence, adaptability, and career security (OECD, 2023; Vrontis et al., 2022). Well-Being-Oriented HRM Practices – Aligning AI adoption with initiatives that safeguard workload balance, autonomy, social support, and psychological safety (Parker & Grote, 2022). By integrating these employee-centered practices with technology, organizations can maximize AI's potential to enhance productivity while fostering resilience, engagement, and overall well-being.

8. EVOLUTION OF HRM PRACTICES IN AI-ENABLED WORKPLACES

The incorporation of Artificial Intelligence (AI) into organizational operations requires a significant transformation of Human Resource Management (HRM) practices. AI is changing how organizations attract, manage, develop, and retain talent, while also reshaping performance management, decision-making, and employee engagement strategies (Vrontis et al., 2022; Tursunbayeva et al., 2022). This section examines the evolution of HRM in AI-enabled workplaces, emphasizing strategic workforce management approaches, the use of people analytics, and the alignment of HRM practices with both employee experience and organizational goals.

8.1 Strategic HRM in AI-Enabled Workplaces

The integration of Artificial Intelligence (AI) has fundamentally transformed Human Resource Management (HRM), shifting it from a primarily administrative role to a strategic function within organizations. Modern HR practices increasingly leverage AI to support data-driven decision-making, optimize workforce allocation, and detect emerging talent needs with greater accuracy (Davenport et al., 2020). AI-enabled systems provide real-time insights into employee performance, learning progress, and potential skill gaps, enabling HR professionals to make proactive rather than reactive decisions. This transition allows HR to contribute directly to organizational agility and long-term strategic planning, rather than focusing solely on routine administrative tasks (Bersin, 2019).

In AI-driven environments, strategic HRM extends beyond operational efficiency to actively shape human–AI collaboration. By anticipating future skill requirements, redesigning roles to complement intelligent systems, and fostering adaptive learning, HR ensures that employees are equipped to work effectively alongside AI. This proactive approach not only improves individual and team performance but also promotes employee engagement and well-being by providing clarity, training, and support in navigating evolving work demands.

Moreover, the incorporation of AI into HR processes enhances workforce planning and talent management capabilities. Organizations can identify high-potential employees, predict future workforce needs, and develop tailored development pathways, ensuring a strong alignment between human capital and organizational objectives. By embracing AI as a strategic enabler, HR emerges as a key driver of competitiveness in digital and AI-enabled workplaces, shaping not just human resources but the broader organizational capacity to adapt, innovate, and thrive in a technologically evolving landscape.

8.2 AI-Enhanced Recruitment, Selection, and Talent Management

Recruitment and selection have been profoundly reshaped by the use of AI technologies. Organizations now rely on AI-powered tools to automate resume screening, assess candidates through predictive analytics, and reduce certain forms of bias, leading to more efficient and potentially fairer hiring outcomes. Despite these advantages, important ethical challenges persist. Issues such as transparency, accountability, and algorithmic fairness remain central concerns, as biased training data or opaque decision processes can reinforce existing inequalities in hiring (Raghavan et al., 2020).

At the same time, talent management practices are undergoing significant change. AI-driven people analytics allow organizations to generate deeper insights into employee performance, engagement levels, retention risks, and learning needs. These insights enable HR professionals to create more personalized development plans, tailor career progression pathways, and implement targeted interventions that improve both employee engagement and overall satisfaction (Tursunbayeva et al., 2022).

8.3 Learning, Development, and Capability Building

AI-enabled workplaces place a strong emphasis on continuous learning and reskilling to keep pace with rapid technological advancements. Traditional, one-off training programs are no longer sufficient; instead, HRM practices are evolving toward adaptive learning ecosystems that leverage digital platforms, microlearning modules, and AI-driven personalization (OECD, 2023). By analyzing employee performance data, learning patterns, and skill gaps, HR can recommend targeted upskilling initiatives, ensuring that employees acquire the competencies required to succeed in increasingly AI-augmented roles. This data-informed approach also enables organizations to anticipate emerging skills needs, aligning workforce development with both technological change and strategic business objectives.

Beyond individual skill development, human–AI co-learning is gaining prominence as a critical strategy for workforce capability building. These initiatives encourage employees to interact with AI systems in ways that enhance both human expertise and machine performance, creating a continuous feedback loop of mutual learning (Jarrahi, 2018). By engaging with AI outputs, employees refine their analytical, problem-solving, and decision-making skills, while AI systems improve through iterative feedback, resulting in more effective collaboration and operational outcomes.

Importantly, this co-learning approach emphasizes not only technical skill acquisition but also the development of distinctly human capabilities such as ethical judgment, critical thinking, and experiential learning. By fostering these complementary skills, organizations ensure that AI augments rather than replaces human agency, preserving employee autonomy and promoting meaningful engagement in AI-driven workplaces. In this way, adaptive learning ecosystems and human–AI co-learning collectively support workforce resilience, adaptability, and long-term organizational performance.

8.4 Performance Management and Employee Experience

AI is fundamentally transforming performance management practices in organizations. Traditional evaluation methods, which were often periodic, retrospective, and subjective, are increasingly being complemented or replaced by continuous, data-driven assessments. AI systems can monitor key performance indicators, track project outcomes, analyze collaboration patterns, and identify trends in real time, enabling managers to provide more timely, personalized, and objective feedback (Bersin, 2019). This shift allows for a more proactive approach to performance management, helping employees understand expectations, recognize areas for improvement, and enhance overall productivity.

However, integrating AI into performance management also raises critical ethical and psychological concerns. Continuous monitoring can create perceptions of surveillance, reduce autonomy, and generate anxiety if employees feel their every action is being tracked. Moreover, algorithmic systems may inadvertently encode biases in performance evaluations or fail to account for contextual nuances, potentially undermining fairness (Kellogg et al., 2020). Addressing these challenges requires transparent system design, clear communication about AI's role in evaluations, and mechanisms that allow human judgment to complement algorithmic insights.

When implemented thoughtfully, AI-enabled performance management can strengthen both organizational outcomes and the employee experience. By combining data-driven insights with a human-centered HRM approach, organizations can enhance motivation, support professional growth, and maintain well-being, while still ensuring accountability and high performance. Ultimately, AI has the potential to transform performance management from a punitive or administrative task into a continuous, collaborative, and development-focused process.

8.5 Ethical Considerations and Governance in AI-Driven HRM

The development of HRM in AI-enabled workplaces also brings ethical, legal, and governance considerations to the forefront. Algorithmic decision-making must align with principles such as fairness, accountability, transparency, and inclusivity (Raghavan et al., 2020). As a result, HR professionals are taking on greater responsibility for overseeing AI systems, auditing algorithms, and ensuring compliance with data protection and privacy regulations.

Effective ethical governance not only helps reduce potential risks but also builds employee trust in the use of AI. By promoting transparency and responsible use, organizations can foster a more positive and inclusive workplace culture while supporting the broader adoption of AI technologies (Davenport et al., 2020).

8.6 Integrative Perspective

In summary, HRM in AI-enabled workplaces is increasingly defined by strategic alignment, human-centered approaches, and ongoing skill development. By utilizing AI for predictive analytics, personalized learning, and performance management, organizations can boost productivity, engagement, and employee well-being. Simultaneously, upholding ethical principles, transparency, and employee autonomy ensures that HRM remains both effective and socially responsible in the context of digital transformation.

9. CONCLUSION AND FUTURE DIRECTIONS

The introduction of Artificial Intelligence (AI) in the workplace marks a significant transformation in work processes, employee collaboration, and human capital management. This chapter has explored the diverse effects of AI on job roles, collaborative practices, skills and competencies, employee well-being, and HRM practices within digitally transformed organizations. The analysis underscores that AI is more than a technological advancement—it serves as a catalyst for organizational, human, and societal change, necessitating careful integration to optimize benefits while minimizing potential risks.

9.1 Key Insights

Transformation of Employee Roles: AI reshapes work by automating repetitive tasks, augmenting human decision-making, and creating hybrid roles that combine technical expertise with human-centered skills. This shift calls for job redesign, redefinition of responsibilities, and adjustments to autonomy and decision-making authority, altering traditional occupational boundaries (Autor, 2015; Raisch & Krakowski, 2021).

Human–AI Collaboration: AI acts as a collaborative partner, enhancing human capabilities while demanding new competencies in algorithmic literacy, trust, and ethical oversight. Effective collaboration relies on transparent and explainable AI systems, as well as adaptive organizational cultures that support continuous learning and empower employee agency (Jarrahi, 2018; Gunning, 2017).

Skills and Workforce Capability Development: AI-driven workplaces require both technical and human-centric skills. Employees need data literacy, critical thinking, creativity, and emotional intelligence, while organizations must implement ongoing learning, reskilling, and adaptive capability-building programs (OECD, 2023; Vrontis et al., 2022).

Employee Well-Being: AI can reduce monotonous work and boost productivity, but it may also introduce challenges such as job insecurity, work intensification, and reduced social interaction. HRM strategies emphasizing transparency, ethical governance, participatory design, and skill development can mitigate these risks and support psychological well-being (Moore, 2019; Parker & Grote, 2022).

Evolution of HRM Practices: AI is transforming HRM from a primarily administrative function to a strategic one. Recruitment, performance management, learning and development, and talent management are increasingly data-driven and personalized, yet human-centered oversight remains essential to ensure fairness, ethical integrity, and employee engagement (Davenport et al., 2020; Tursunbayeva et al., 2022).

Collectively, these insights highlight that AI's influence on work extends beyond technology to social and organizational domains. Effective AI integration requires organizations to balance efficiency and innovation with employee experience, ethical standards, and strategic workforce planning.

9.2 Implications for Practice

1. Human-Centered AI Design: AI systems should be developed to enhance, not replace, human capabilities, ensuring employees maintain meaningful roles, decision-making authority, and autonomy.
2. Ethical Governance and Transparency: Implementing transparent, explainable AI and clear accountability structures is essential to build trust and minimize biases.
3. Reskilling and Lifelong Learning: Ongoing learning and capability development programs are crucial to help employees adapt to changing roles and sustain employability.
4. Integration of HRM and AI Strategy: HR functions should strategically leverage AI tools for workforce planning while preserving human judgment and maintaining ethical oversight.
5. Well-Being-Focused Interventions: Organizations need to monitor factors such as workload, social interaction, and role clarity to reduce stress and promote employee engagement in AI-enabled workplaces.

9.3 Future Research Directions

- Despite increasing research on AI in the workplace, several areas require further exploration:
- Longitudinal Impacts of AI: There is a need for studies examining the long-term effects of AI adoption on employee roles, well-being, and career development trajectories.
- Sector-Specific Dynamics: AI's influence differs across industries, and research should investigate how contextual factors shape adoption, collaboration, and skill requirements.
- Human–AI Trust and Ethical Decision-Making: Additional research is necessary to understand how trust, explainability, and ethical considerations affect human–AI interactions and organizational outcomes.
- Integration of AI with HRM Strategy: Future studies could identify best practices for aligning AI adoption with strategic HRM objectives, employee experience, and organizational culture.
- Societal and Policy Implications: Research should also examine regulatory frameworks, labor market transformations, and broader societal consequences resulting from AI-enabled workplace changes.

9.4 Final Thoughts

AI-enabled workplaces present significant opportunities to improve productivity, decision-making, and employee experience. However, capturing these benefits demands a balanced, human-centered approach that accounts for technological capabilities alongside organizational culture, workforce skills, ethical governance, and employee well-being. By thoughtfully integrating AI with HRM practices, organizations can effectively navigate digital transformation while building resilient, adaptive, and engaged workforces prepared to thrive in an AI-driven future.

REFERENCES

Alsaif, A., & Sabih Aksoy, M. (2023). AI-HRM: artificial intelligence in human resource management: a literature review. *Journal of Computing and Communication, 2*(2), 1–7. DOI: 10.21608/jocc.2023.307053

Autor, D. H. (2015). Why are there still so many jobs? The history and future of workplace automation. *The Journal of Economic Perspectives, 29*(3), 3–30. DOI: 10.1257/jep.29.3.3

Babashahi, L., Barbosa, C. E., Lima, Y., Lyra, A., Salazar, H., Argôlo, M., Almeida, M. A., & Souza, J. M. (2024). AI in the workplace: A systematic review of skill transformation in the industry. *Administrative Sciences, 14*(6), 127. DOI: 10.3390/admsci14060127

Bakker, A. B., & Demerouti, E. (2017). Job demands–resources theory: Taking stock and looking forward. *Journal of Occupational Health Psychology, 22*(3), 273–285. DOI: 10.1037/ocp0000056 PMID: 27732008

Bersin, J. (2019). HR technology disruption: AI and the future of work. Deloitte Insights. https://www2.deloitte.com/us/en/insights/focus/human-capital-trends/2019/ai-in-hr.html

Boyd, R. L., & Markowitz, D. M. (2026). Artificial Intelligence and the Psychology of Human Connection. Perspectives on psychological science: a journal of the Association for Psychological Science, 21(2), 192–220. https://doi.org/DOI: 10.1177/17456916251404394

Brynjolfsson, E., & McAfee, A. (2014). *The second machine age: Work, progress, and prosperity in a time of brilliant technologies.* W. W. Norton & Company.

Brynjolfsson, E., & McAfee, A. (2017). *Machine, platform, crowd: Harnessing our digital future.* W. W. Norton & Company.

Davenport, T. H., Guha, A., Grewal, D., & Bressgott, T. (2020). How artificial intelligence will change the future of marketing. *Journal of the Academy of Marketing Science, 48*(1), 24–42. DOI: 10.1007/s11747-019-00696-0

Davenport, T. H., & Kirby, J. (2016). Just how smart are smart machines? *MIT Sloan Management Review, 57*(3), 21–25.

Davenport, T. H., & Ronanki, R. (2018). Artificial intelligence for the real world. *Harvard Business Review, 96*(1), 108–116.

Deci, E. L., & Ryan, R. M. (2000). The "what" and "why" of goal pursuits: Human needs and the self-determination of behavior. *Psychological Inquiry, 11*(4), 227–268. DOI: 10.1207/S15327965PLI1104_01

Fenwick, A., Molnar, G., & Frangos, P. (2024). Revisiting the role of HR in the age of AI: Bringing humans and machines closer together in the workplace. *Frontiers in Artificial Intelligence, 6*, 1272823. DOI: 10.3389/frai.2023.1272823 PMID: 38288334

Ford, D., Storey, M.-A., Zimmermann, T., Bird, C., Jaffe, S., Maddila, C., Butler, J., Houck, B., & Nagappan, N. (2021). A tale of two cities: Software developers working from home during the COVID-19 pandemic. *Empirical Software Engineering, 26*(4), 70. Advance online publication. DOI: 10.1007/s10664-021-09984-3

Guest, D. E. (2017). Human resource management and employee well-being: Towards a new analytic framework. *Human Resource Management Journal, 27*(1), 22–38. DOI: 10.1111/1748-8583.12139

Gunning, D. (2017). Explainable artificial intelligence (XAI). Defense Advanced Research Projects Agency (DARPA). https://www.darpa.mil/program/explainable-artificial-intelligence

Hackman, J. R., & Oldham, G. R. (1976). Motivation through the design of work: Test of a theory. *Organizational Behavior and Human Performance, 16*(2), 250–279. DOI: 10.1016/0030-5073(76)90016-7

Jarrahi, M. H. (2018). Artificial intelligence and the future of work: Human–AI symbiosis in organizational decision making. *Business Horizons, 61*(4), 577–586. DOI: 10.1016/j.bushor.2018.03.007

Jarrahi, M. H. (2025). *Research on human–AI collaboration and the future of work (profile)*. Wikipedia.

Kaufman, B. E. (2020). The future of HRM: A systems perspective. *Human Resource Management Review, 30*(4), 100685. DOI: 10.1016/j.hrmr.2019.100685

Kellogg, K. C., Valentine, M. A., & Christin, A. (2020). Algorithms at work: The new contested terrain of control. *The Academy of Management Annals, 14*(1), 366–410. DOI: 10.5465/annals.2018.0174

Lee, J. D., & See, K. A. (2004). Trust in automation: Designing for appropriate reliance. *Human Factors, 46*(1), 50–80. DOI: 10.1518/hfes.46.1.50.30392 PMID: 15151155

Makridakis, S. (2017). The forthcoming artificial intelligence (AI) revolution: Its impact on society and firms. *Futures, 90*, 46–60. DOI: 10.1016/j.futures.2017.03.006

Moore, P. V. (2019). OSH and the future of work: Benefits and risks of artificial intelligence tools in workplaces. *Policy and Practice in Health and Safety*, *17*(2), 1–15. DOI: 10.1080/14773996.2019.1657171

Nakavachara, V. (2025). AI and worker well-being: Differential impacts across generational cohorts and genders [Preprint]. arXiv.

OECD. (2023). *OECD employment outlook 2023: Artificial intelligence and the labour market*. OECD Publishing.

Parker, S. K., & Grote, G. (2022). Automation, algorithms, and beyond: Why work design matters more than ever in a digital world. *Applied Psychology*, *71*(4), 1171–1204. DOI: 10.1111/apps.12241

Pasmore, W., Winby, S., Mohrman, S. A., & Vanasse, R. (2019). Reflections: Sociotechnical systems design and organization change. *Journal of Change Management*, *19*(2), 67–85. DOI: 10.1080/14697017.2018.1553761

Raghavan, M., Barocas, S., Kleinberg, J., & Levy, K. (2020). Mitigating bias in algorithmic hiring: Evaluating claims and practices. *Proceedings of the 2020 Conference on Fairness, Accountability, and Transparency*, 469–481. DOI: 10.1145/3351095.3372828

Raisch, S., & Krakowski, S. (2021). Artificial intelligence and management: The automation–augmentation paradox. *Academy of Management Review*, *46*(1), 192–210. DOI: 10.5465/amr.2018.0072

Reddy, S. M., & Kumar, B. R. (2025). Artificial intelligence and the human experience: Impacts on social behavior and mental processes. *Chinese Medicine*, *25*(1), 89–111. PMID: 40524220

Russell, S., & Norvig, P. (2021). *Artificial intelligence: A modern approach* (4th ed.). Pearson.

Sadeghi, S. (2024). Employee well-being in the age of AI: Perceptions, concerns, behaviors, and outcomes [Preprint]. arXiv.

Tarafdar, M., Cooper, C. L., & Stich, J. F. (2019). The technostress trifecta—Techno eustress, techno distress and design: Theoretical directions and an agenda for research. *Information Systems Journal*, *29*(1), 6–42. DOI: 10.1111/isj.12169

Trist, E. L., & Bamforth, K. W. (1951). Some social and psychological consequences of the longwall method of coal-getting. *Human Relations*, *4*(1), 3–38. DOI: 10.1177/001872675100400101

Tursunbayeva, A., Di Lauro, S., & Pagliari, C. (2022). People analytics—A scoping review of conceptual boundaries and value propositions. *International Journal of Human Resource Management, 33*(2), 357–388. DOI: 10.1080/09585192.2019.1659492

Vial, G. (2019). Understanding digital transformation: A review and a research agenda. *The Journal of Strategic Information Systems, 28*(2), 118–144. DOI: 10.1016/j.jsis.2019.01.003

Vrontis, D., Christofi, M., Pereira, V., Tarba, S., Makrides, A., & Trichina, E. (2022). Artificial intelligence, robotics, advanced technologies and human resource management: A systematic review. *International Journal of Human Resource Management, 33*(6), 1237–1266. DOI: 10.1080/09585192.2020.1871398

World Economic Forum. (2023). The future of jobs report 2023. World Economic Forum.

Chapter 5

Working With Intelligent Systems: Reimagining Meaning, Agency, and Experience in AI-Enabled Organizations

Dusmuxammedova Nozima
Termez University of Economics and Service, Termez, Uzbekistan

S. Aarthi
http://orcid.org/0009-0006-9064-2091
Marwadi University, Rajkot, India

Shodiyeva Yulduz
Bukhara State Medical Institute, Bukhara, Uzbekistan

Khidirov Nodir Giyosalievich
Tashkent State University of Economics, Tashkent, Uzbekistan

R. N. Ravikumar
http://orcid.org/0009-0009-3705-1681
Jain (Deemed to be) University, Bangalore, India

Mirzayev Bobur
Alfraganus University, Tashkent, Uzbekistan

ABSTRACT

The increasing use of Artificial Intelligence in the organizational system is changing how work is being designed, experienced, and valued. This chapter examines the AI-enabled organizations on human-based views, which are in the sense, meaning, agency, and employee experience. It extends past efficiency-based discourses, and understands AI as a socio-technical collaborator that has an influence on autonomy, trust and engagement in its design and governance. The chapter is based on the wisdom of various fields and existing case studies regarding the significance of developing a transparent, participatory, and ethically regulated AI infrastructure that can strengthen meaningful work, rather than diminish meaningful work. The

DOI: 10.4018/979-8-3373-8282-1.ch005

review illuminates the concept that sustainability of the production of value in the AI-based world is grounded on the equilibrium between the technological smartness and human dignity, empowerment, and corporate intent.

1. INTRODUCTION

The rapid spread of Artificial Intelligence (AI) across organizations is transforming how work is organized, managed, and experienced. AI-based systems increasingly mediate decision-making, performance assessment, task allocation, and knowledge generation, thereby redefining traditional human roles in organizations. Although the prevailing narrative tends to explain such changes in terms of productivity, efficiency, and automation, these approaches can be quite misleading because they do not deal with the human implications of embracing AI (Akinnagbe, 2024). Work is not simply a technical act but an important social practice that is determined by agency, identity and purpose. With smarter systems that take up more of the cognitive and managerial processes, concerns begin to emerge on how the employees perceive and understand their work, how they feel in control, and how they maintain their involvement in the AI-mediated space. This chapter defines AI not as an impartial instrument but as a socio-technological partner, the design and regulation of which have a direct impact on the experience of employees. The chapter answers the ever-increasing worries about the problem of dehumanization, algorithmic control, and ethical erosion in AI-powered companies through foregrounding meaning, agency, and lived experience (Jarrahi et al., 2023). It claims that sustainable value creation in the AI-driven world demands meticulous calibration between technological smartness and human decency, with the necessity of upfront, participative, and ethically sensible ways of engaging with AI in organizations.

1.1 AI and Work Transformation

Artificial Intelligence is essentially changing the organization processes by increasing or eliminating human judgment in recruitment, coordinating tasks, managing performance, and executing strategic plans. The intelligent systems are becoming more of a decision-support or decision-making agent that redefines the workflow and redistributes authority in human-machine configurations. This is not just a transformation of routine activities or the automation of them, but rather it is a transformation of cognitive and relational aspects of work, which has an impact on interpersonal interaction, learning, and value creation among workers (Riedl, 2019). With the implementation of AI systems in the organizational structures, they revise the skill needs and role structures, as well as work time cycles. On the one hand, it can be stated that these changes guarantee more efficient and responsive organization; on the other hand, new reliance on the algorithmic system and reorganization of the forces in organizations are introduced. The employees must also adjust to new technologies as well as logics of assessment and control enshrined in AI-based systems. To comprehend this change, it is necessary to get beyond technological determinism to study how organization decisions about the design, application, and governance of AI change work experiences and organizational performance.

1.2 Meaning, Agency, and Experience

The coming of smart systems into organizational existence poses urgent questions regarding the ways of employees to get a sense of meaning and agency in their work. Algorithms can cause employees to lose control of their tasks, lose a sense of purpose, or have ambiguity about responsibility when they affect task allocation, the way managers evaluate performance, or the decisions they make (Anisha Estherita & Vasantha, 2024). Meaningful work is traditionally based on perception of contribution, mastery, and self-determination, but the basis of such work may be broken through algorithmic mediation by clouding the rationales of decisions and restricting the voice of employees. Agency is also not immune since the workers work their way through systems that bind discretion and at the same time require flexibility and adherence. Such processes do not conform to traditional conceptions of human experience when it comes to workplaces, since it is placed in the context of interactions with opaque data-driven systems (Kiverstein et al., 2022). The problematization of meaning and agency allows one to take a more critical look at AI-powered workplaces and note the conflicts between the rationality of efficiency and human values. To eliminate these concerns, it is important to consider employee experience as the primary design parameter, and not an indirect consequence of technological adoption.

1.3 Scope and Contribution

This chapter discusses AI-enabled organizations with human-centered approach, which is how intelligent systems generate meaning, agency, and experience of the employee. It also adds to the field of interdisciplinary scholarship as it combines the views of management studies, organizational psychology, human-computer interaction and digital ethics. The chapter does not view AI as a separate piece of technology, but as a socio-technical partner, which is part of organizational cultures, governance, and leadership practices. The chapter goes a step further in developing conceptual clarity as the author connects the AI design options to employee views of justice, confidence, and autonomy. The chapter is designed as a conceptual review with secondary-case analysis. It synthesizes peer-reviewed literature, organizational reports, and published case evidence to examine how AI-enabled systems influence meaning, agency, autonomy, fairness, trust, and employee experience in organizations. The chapter presents theoretical background, conceptual framing, secondary-case interpretation, and managerial implications to support a structured book-chapter discussion. In such a way, it provides both analysis and practicality that can be added to the current discussions on how organizations can use AI to create sustainable value without compromising human dignity and participation.

2. BACKGROUND TO THE STUDY

The context of this research lies within the increasing pace of introducing technologies of Artificial Intelligence into the functioning of organizations and management. Organizations have over time shed off the primitive information technologies, and are now implementing sophisticated intelligent systems that have the capability of learning, predicting, and making decisions independently. The development has escalated the controversies of control, accountability and human relevance in digitally mediated workplaces. Although the initial implementation of technology was focused on its efficiency, the modern AI systems are becoming defining of the work strategy and relationships (Dican, 2025). This change requires a more analytical approach that will take into consideration both social, psychological, and ethical aspects of AI application. The literature background has shown an increasing disintegration of the relationship between technological capability and organizational readiness in dealing with the human consequences. Bias, monitoring, loss of trust and spreading of skills have been highlighted as problems, calling for a more responsible and human-friendly use of AI. Understanding of these dynamics is the foundation for investigation into how the intelligent systems can enhance or reduce human agency and experience. Building on this background, the study moves to a discussion of the conditions under which the use of AI is aligned with the organization's values, employee health, and long-term value creation.

2.1 Evolution of Intelligent Systems

Intelligent systems in organisations has been linked to the shift of rule-based automation to data-driven and learning based technologies. First ones were transaction processing and efficiency gains oriented systems that were able to provide support to repetitive and structured tasks. Modern systems can perform many elements of complex thinking such as pattern recognition, prediction, and optimization of decisions, with the help of recent advancements in machine learning and analytics

(Sigfrids et al., 2022). Consequently, smart systems are actively being used in areas where human discretion has long been considered, such as talent management, risk assessment and strategy planning. Such development has transformed the organizational architectures by incorporating intelligence in workflows, platforms, and other managerial tools. Nevertheless, greater system independence has also made the process less transparent and more reliant on algorithmic results. The contexts of organizations determine the way these systems are understood and applied by making them either appear as supportive mechanisms or control mechanisms. This evolution is imperative to understand how intelligent systems change the relations of power, responsibility, and human experience in the contemporary organizations. Table 1 Overviews some significant steps of intelligent system evolution and its evolving functions in organizational work.

Table 1. Evolution of AI Work Systems

Stage	Dominant Technologies	Role of AI in Work	Impact on Employees
Automation Era	Rule-based systems, RPA	Task execution and process automation	Reduced manual effort, limited autonomy
Analytics Era	ML, predictive analytics	Decision support and forecasting	Improved efficiency, increased cognitive load
Algorithmic Management Era	Recommender systems, scoring models	Task allocation, performance evaluation	Reduced discretion, role ambiguity
Augmentation Era	Explainable AI, decision-support AI	Human–AI collaboration	Enhanced judgment, skill transformation
Human-Centered AI Era	Participatory, ethical AI systems	Socio-technical partner	Reinforced meaning, agency, and trust

2.2 Human–AI Collaboration

Socio-technical perspectives focus on the interaction between social structures and technological systems, rather than assuming that organizational outcomes are produced by technology alone. In this perspective, human-AI work is defined by task design, organizational practices and governance structures that define the distribution of intelligence between humans and machines. Smart systems are not only characterized by a set of preset functions but they also affect the decision-making process, communication and the behavior of the employees. Socio-technical approaches emphasize on alignment between the capabilities of the system and the needs of human beings especially in the maintenance of autonomy and interpretability (Sartori & Theodorou, 2022). AI systems should not be built without regard to the social context, or they will cause opposition, abuse, or disengagement. On the other hand, participatory design and adaptive governance may allow effective cooperation where AI will complement human abilities. This point of view supports the necessity to interpret AI-enabled work as a dynamic formation of human judgment and machine intelligence, which develops in learning and organizational practice (Ravikumar & Aarthi, 2025c). Table 2 Maps the aspects of technology and social factors that affect human-AI interaction in organizations.

Table 2. Human–AI Collaboration Dimensions

Dimension	Technological Aspect	Social / Organizational Aspect
Task Design	AI-supported workflows	Human discretion and interpretation
Decision Authority	Algorithmic recommendations	Managerial and employee judgment
Transparency	Explainability mechanisms	Trust and sense-making
Control	Automated monitoring	Perceived autonomy
Learning	Adaptive systems	Skill development and role evolution

2.3 Challenges in AI Adoption

The implementation of AI in the organizations leads to a set of ethical, psychological and managerial issues which are not purely technical performance. Such ethical issues as algorithmic bias, insufficient transparency, and intrusive surveillance practices are likely to cause a lack of trust and dignity in the employees. Employees might also be psychologically anxious, lose control or identity as smart systems reinvent job and performance standards. At the managerial level, the leaders experience difficulty in maintaining efficiency targets and promoting fairness, accountability and welfare of the employees (Khan et al., 2023). The AI adoption when poorly regulated may widen power inequalities and destroy the company culture. To overcome these issues, there must be intentional governmental practices, moral control, and executive dedication to human principles. The successful application of AI is not only based on the level of technology but includes thoughtful organizational practices, the focus on including and explaining as well as ongoing dialogue (Reinhardt, 2023). These difficulties create an imperative contextual framework of how Artificial Intelligence would boost or harm meaningful and interesting work experiences.

3. RESEARCH OBJECTIVES AND QUESTIONS

The research questions of this chapter are designed in a systematic way so that it can lead towards a systematic study about the Human impacts on the introduction of Artificial Intelligence in the organizational environment. Beyond efficiency-based narratives, the objectives are on the impact of AI-powered systems on worker meaning, agency, and experience at work, and identify organizational conditions where ethical and human values are generated. These goals will drive the interdisciplinary analysis of concepts and literature compilation and discussion of case studies in the chapter. The chapter is guided by the following research objectives:

- To examine how AI-enabled systems influence employees' sense of meaning, purpose, and role identity within contemporary organizations.
- To analyze the impact of AI-driven decision-making and algorithmic management on employee agency, autonomy, and everyday work experience.
- To investigate employee perceptions of fairness, transparency, and trust in interactions
  with intelligent systems.
- To identify organizational, cultural, and leadership practices that enable human-centered and ethically grounded AI adoption.
- To propose conditions under which AI can function as an augmenting socio-technical collaborator that supports sustainable value creation rather than human displacement.

3.1 Research Questions

This chapter is guided by the following research questions:

RQ1: How do AI-enabled systems influence employees' meaning, role identity, and engagement?

RQ2: How do algorithmic decision-making and monitoring affect agency, autonomy, fairness, and trust?

RQ3: What organizational design and governance conditions support human-centered AI adoption?

RQ4: How can AI contribute to sustainable organizational value without reducing human dignity?

3.2 Definition of Key Concepts

In this chapter, meaning refers to the employee's sense that work has purpose, value, and personal or organizational significance. Agency refers to the ability of employees to make choices, influence work outcomes, and participate in decisions affected by AI systems. Autonomy means the freedom to decide how tasks are performed and how AI recommendations are interpreted or applied. Fairness is the feeling that decisions made with AI are justifiable, unbiased, consistent and transparent. Trust is the confidence of employees in AI systems, management, and the organization's use of AI that it is reliable, responsible, and ethical. Engagement is a state of emotional, cognitive and behavioral involvement of employees in their work. These are key to understanding the nature of the role of AI-enabled systems in employee experience, role identity and in human-centred value creation in organizations.

4. CONCEPTUAL MODEL

The theoretical framework that was developed in this chapter is an AI-facilitated work system in which the technological possibilities, the organizational forms and the human experience are intricately linked. The model takes a different approach to AI than viewing it as an autonomous or deterministic action; it highlights the relational processes between intelligent systems and employees, wherein meaning, agency, and experience are created in the process (Mabrouk, 2024). The model incorporates three fundamental dimensions and these are human-AI interaction, organizational design and governance, and the results at the levels of employees. The model proposes that AI systems influence work experience through both functional performance and the values embedded in their design, visibility, and governance. The model predicts human experience as one of the key consequences of AI adoption by connecting AI design options and governance policies to fairness perceptions, trust perception, and autonomy. It is a conceptualization that allows analyzing the way AI can either augment or limit meaningful work in a structured way. The model also operates as an interpretive resource in understanding the secondary case evidence and uniting resources in other fields with the justification that the ethical, human-based AI is central to the creation of sustainable organizational value (Ahmad et al., 2025). Figure 1 demonstrates how AI design and governance, organisational context and human-AI interaction combine to influence the experience outcomes of employees, namely, fairness, meaning, autonomy, and make sustainable organisational value creation possible.

Figure 1. Human-Centered AI Work Model

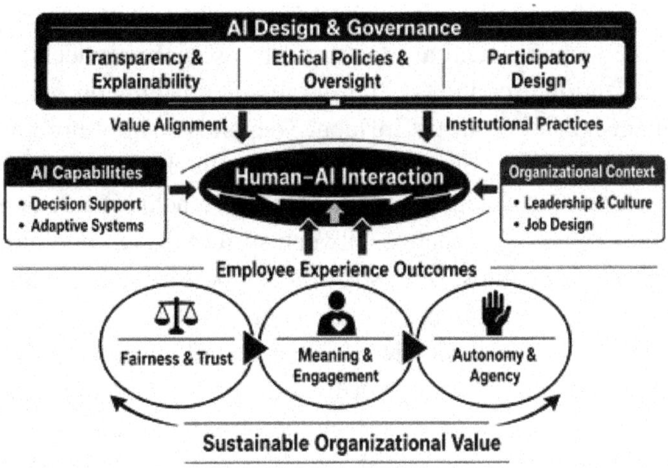

4.1 Theoretical Novelty of the Model

The novelty of the model lies in linking AI design and governance with employee-level psychological outcomes through a socio-technical pathway. Unlike efficiency-based AI adoption models, this framework positions meaning, agency, fairness, trust, and engagement as central outcomes of organizational AI implementation. The model shows that AI does not shape employee experience by itself. Instead, its impact depends on transparency, human discretion, participatory governance, leadership support, and ethical organizational practices. This makes the model useful for understanding how AI can either strengthen or weaken human-centered work.

4.2 Propositions

P1: Transparent and explainable AI systems are more likely to strengthen employee trust.

P2: AI systems that preserve human discretion are more likely to support employee agency and autonomy.

P3: Participatory AI governance improves perceptions of fairness and organizational legitimacy.

P4: AI adoption produces sustainable value when productivity gains are balanced with human dignity and employee engagement.

4.3 Human–AI Interaction as a Socio-Technical System

The interaction between human and AI is also discussed as a socio-technical system where the technological artefacts and the social practices are co-evolved within the organizational contexts. The intelligent systems do not work without human participants, on the contrary, influence depends on how employees perceive, believe, and interact with algorithmic results (Aarthi et al., 2025). This school of thought acknowledges the fact that work results are achieved through the correspondence/or lack of correspondence between system design and human abilities. AI systems organize decision spaces, stipulate the performance goals, and mediate the flow of information, thus predetermining cognition and behavior of employees (Herrmann & Pfeiffer, 2022). Meanwhile, human judgment, knowledge and situational awareness will continue to be critical in the interpretation and subsequent actions of AI-driven insights. A socio technical framing emphasizes on the value of flexibility, representativeness and shared learning in human AI collaboration. Such systems, when modeled in a manner to enable sense-making and discretion, can add to human agency. On the other hand, systems that are not well integrated can create dependence, resistance or disengagement which sabotages meaningful work experiences.

4.4 AI Design and Experience

The aspects of AI design and governance are extremely important in defining the experience of intelligent systems by employees in the workplace. The design considerations concerning transparency, explainability, and user control do affect the perception of AI systems as a helpful tool or as a surveillance and control mechanism (Ravikumar & Aarthi, 2025a). This is further mediated by governance structures that set accountability, oversight and ethical limits in using AI. In combination, design and governance dictate the degree of decentralization of decision-making between humans and machines, which have a direct impact on perceptions of autonomy and fairness (Sigfrids et al., 2023). With well-developed policies and inclusive decision-making and ethics, workers would feel more trusted and involved in the work process with AI systems in place. On the other hand, non-transparent algorithms and control by a small number of people may destroy trust and reduce agency. This framework highlights the necessity of AI adoption within an organization being responsible by stating specifically that AI design and governance is directly correlated with the experience of employees. Technology does not produce employee experience; rather it is a product of managerial and ethical decisions.

4.5 Ethical AI-Enabled Work

The given conceptual framework of meaningful and ethical AI-enabled work combines the human values with the technological intelligence to promote responsible organizational practice. In essence, the framework puts meaning, agency, and dignity at the center of the AI adoption, and not as secondary considerations (Ma et al., 2025). It underlines that an ethical AI can be obtained not merely with the help of technical compliance, but also with participatory design, open decision-making and constant learning. The framework relates the organizational culture, leadership commitment and job design to how the employees feel about the purpose and the power. The AI systems are presented as collaborative aids of skill building and sense-making, as opposed to being replacements of human judgment. The ethical issues like bias reduction, responsibility and privacy are incorporated at every level of the framework. With its focus on technology innovation and human-centered values, the framework provides a systematic framework that organizations wishing to leverage AI without dehumanizing valuable work and its continued generation (Familoni, 2024). The following table 3 shows the main elements and connections of the suggested human-centered AI conceptual model.

Table 3. AI Design and Employee Experience

Layer	Key Elements	Employee Experience Outcome
AI Design	Transparency, explainability, usability	Understanding and confidence
Governance	Policies, accountability, oversight	Fairness and trust
Organizational Context	Leadership, culture, ethics	Psychological safety
Job Design	Augmentation, flexibility	Meaningful engagement
Outcomes	Balanced human–AI interaction	Sustainable value creation

5. LITERATURE REVIEW

The discussion of Artificial Intelligence in organizational settings has also grown at a fast pace as evidence of increased attention to the way smart systems transform the work, management, and worker experience. The initial research mostly focused on the productivity increase, put up automation possibilities and efficiency results, presenting AI as a neutral technological object. Recent research has moved more towards exploring the social, psychological, and ethical consequences of AI-assisted work which is in line with the issues to do with meaning, agency and the dignity of humans (Xavier et al., 2025). This changing literature emphasizes the fact that the implementation of AI is not just a technical change, but a restructuring of work design, power dynamics, and sense making. Socio-technical and human-centered approaches to research are becoming more common because it is now acknowledged that the outcome of organizations relies on the design, governance, and experience of intelligent systems among employees. Three streams of literature that can be related especially in this larger discussion are: algorithmic management and work design, meaningful work and agency in digital environments, and transparency-oriented participatory AI practices (Prabagar et al., 2025).

5.1 Foundational Theoretical Perspectives

Theories which underpin analysis of AI-enabled work are used to enhance this analysis in this chapter. AI is understood as an element of a broader socio-technical system consisting of individuals, technology, organizational processes and structures. The concept of meaningful work theory contributes to understanding how employees feel meaningful, how they feel like they are contributing, and how they will feel as a part of their role when AI impacts their work. The discussion of autonomy, competence and agency is supported by self-determination theory which indicates that the employees' engagement remains when they are given choices and opportunities for skill development. Organizational justice theory contributes to the understanding of fairness, trust, and legitimacy in AI-informed decision-making processes, particularly when they are transparent and accountable. Work design theory provides a platform to assess the impact of AI on tasks, discretion and responsibilities. In this light, it is helpful to consider the monitoring, control, surveillance, and diminished employee voices as discussed in algorithmic management literature. The theories complement each other and are central to the focus of the chapter on meaning, agency, fairness, trust and engagement. Table 4 summarizes the major theoretical perspectives used to explain meaning, agency, fairness, trust, and employee experience in AI-enabled organizations.

Table 4. Theories for Human-Centered AI

Theory Area	Use in This Chapter
Socio-technical systems theory	Explains AI as part of work systems, not only as technology
Meaningful work theory	Defines meaning, purpose, and role identity
Self-determination theory	Explains autonomy, competence, and agency
Organizational justice theory	Explains fairness, trust, and legitimacy

continued on following page

Table 4. Continued

Theory Area	Use in This Chapter
Work design theory	Explains job redesign, discretion, and task changes
Algorithmic management literature	Explains surveillance, control, and performance monitoring

5.2 AI, Management, and Work Design

Intelligent system and algorithmic management literature discusses the impacts of AI-based tools on determining what to do, where to monitor performances, and managerial decision-making. Research has shown that the trend in work design is moving towards work being forged by algorithm systems as they organize workflow, establish performance measurements and commodify the evaluation process (Mishra & Jadeja, 2025). Although these systems have the potential of improving the coordination and decreasing managerial workload, they can also increase the level of control and decrease the discretion of employees. Studies point out that algorithmic management tends to incorporate unspoken beliefs regarding efficiency and behavior, which may transform the job descriptions and authority lines (Zhao, 2025). Researchers claim that to avoid deskilling and disengagement, the work design applicable to AI-enabled situations should take into consideration interpretability, flexibility, and human supervision. The literature reiterates that results are very much affected by the organizational decisions on system integration and how much human judgment can be maintained in the algorithmic processes.

5.3 Meaning, Agency, and Trust

An increasing number of studies discusses the effects of digital technologies, such as AI, on perceptions of meaningful work, agency, trust, and fairness. Autonomy, competence, and perceived contribution are common traits of the meaningful work, and all of them may be mediated by algorithms (Tabata et al., 2025). Research indicates that lack of transparency in decision making processes can erode the sense of purpose and ownership among employees especially where the evaluation criteria are not clear or controllable. Agency is also influenced by the extent of control that employees have on tasks and decision-making. Relations such as trust and fairness become the mediating variables, and the study revealed that employees are more likely to agree with AI systems when they believe that the decision processes were fair and defendable (Rostamzadeh et al., 2025). The literature emphasizes the fact that the process of employee experience in digital environments is highly personal, as it is determined by the relationship between human values, organizational culture, and technology.

5.4 Transparent and Participatory AI

The literature on transparency, explainability and participatory AI emphasizes that they are relevant in promoting trust and empowerment in AI-driven organizations. Transparency is often recognized as the qualification of the meaningful human-AI interaction, as the employee should know how decisions are made and how they use data. Explainability facilitates the sense-making by conversing algorithmic outputs into rationales that are comprehensible. Engagement practices such as involvement of employees during system design and governance are demonstrated to increase the acceptance and perceived legitimacy of AI systems (Uzoamaka et al., 2025). Researchers believe that participatory AI is an alternative that changes power relations as it allows workers to have a say in the development of technological practices. This flow of literature supports the idea that ethical and human-focused AI is not only realized by the impact of technical protection but also by the process of inclusion within organizational structures that predict human experience and common values.

6. RESEARCH METHODOLOGY

This chapter uses a conceptual review and secondary case analysis approach. It does not gather primary data by interviews, surveys, experiments or field observations. Rather, it reviews the peer-reviewed literature, documents by organizations, policy documents, and published evidence drawn from case studies to explore the role of AI-based systems in shaping meaning, agency, autonomy, fairness, trust, and employee experiences in organizations (Morley et al., 2020). The methodology is appropriate as the emphasis of the chapter is to build conceptual understanding and not test statistical relationships. The strategy also facilitates a human-centred and socio-technical understanding of how to leverage AI to work (Porlezza & Schapals, 2024).

6.1 Research Design

The chapter follows a qualitative and interpretive research design. It focuses on the socio-technical nature of the introduction of AI, which is influenced by technology, governance, leadership, job design and employee involvement. The intent is not to make causal generalizations, but to describe the ways the AI systems might contribute to or detract from meaningful work, agency, fairness, trust, and engagement

(Hosseini et al., 2025). The chapter is theory oriented and conceptually oriented. It is based on a socio-technical systems and meaningful work theory, self-determination theory, organizational justice theory, work design and algorithmic management literature. The perspectives help to understand the variations in outcomes of AI in different organizational contexts (Dekker et al., 2022). The design is thus suitable for a book chapter which builds a conceptual model and uses secondary evidence to draw out practical implications.

6.2 Literature Selection

Journal articles, edited book chapters, academic databases, institutional reports, and reliable publications of the organizations were used as sources of relevant literature. Themes investigated in the search ranged from the role of AI in organisations, algorithmic management, human-AI collaboration, meaningful work, employee agency and autonomy, fairness, trust, work design and responsible governance of AI. Three criteria were used to determine the literature to be selected (Aizenberg & van den Hoven, 2020). The first criteria were to have the sources be relevant to the organizational work that can be facilitated by AI. Secondly, they were required to talk about employee experience, governance, ethics, or socio-technical aspects. Third, preference was given to the most recent and quality available sources, and where needed, some fundamental theories were added to make up the conceptual base. Unrelated sources to the main constructs in the chapter were deleted in revision.

6.3 Case Selection

The case evidence used in this chapter is secondary and illustrative. The cases chosen were from published cases, organizational reports and legitimate public papers. They were not used as the main data; they were auxiliary data. The aim of the cases is to show how the adoption of AI can result in various outcomes of employee experiences, depending on the transparency, governance, participation and job design. The cases were identified by the following criteria: relevance for AI in the work, verifiable information from the source, relevance for employee experience, and usefulness for various types of AI use (Uddin, 2023). Data sources for cases were not clear, statistics were not supported, and unverifiable cases were removed or adjusted. Percentage-based claims were included only when they could be traced to original and reliable sources. If not, these were identified as examples of trends but not as actual engagement, autonomy, trust or employee experience measures.

6.4 Coding and Analytical Procedure

Thematic and interpretive coding procedure was used in the analysis. The literature and cases were selected and reviewed to find common concepts related to the concept of AI-enabled work. Coding categories were: meaning, agency, autonomy, fairness, trust, engagement, transparency, governance, surveillance, participation, job redesign. There were three stages in the coding process. First, statements and findings from selected sources were extracted which are relevant for the research. Secondly, these findings were clustered within the key conceptual categories. Third, cross-case comparison was conducted to determine the similarities and differences between the utilization of AI as a decision support tool and AI for algorithmic management and/or monitoring. The coding was not set up to yield statistical outcome. It, on the contrary, facilitated conceptual interpretation, and assisted in linking secondary evidence with the suggested socio-technical, human-centred model.

6.5 Validity and Ethics

Validity was enhanced through multiple sources and concepts and careful linkage between claims and citations. To prevent a sole point of view, multiple sources of secondary information were used in the chapter. This was followed by the mapping of claims onto literature and on case evidence in relation to employee experience and autonomy, equity and trust. There are a few drawbacks to the chapter. It is a secondary source document, and therefore does not offer primary data from employees' interviews or from original surveys. The case examples should be considered illustrative, and not general. The results presented, therefore, can be interpreted as conceptual findings which can be used to inform future empirical research. Ethically, chapter adheres to the use of only publicly visible and published materials. Personal, confidential and organisation internal data was not collected. Secondary case material is not directly presented in the field of the discussion. The chapter also acknowledges that with respect to employee experience and AI it is essential to ensure that discussions and considerations are fair, transparent and conducted responsibly.

6.6 Generative-AI Use Disclosure

Only language refinement, grammar and structural editing were done using generative-AI tools. The conceptual framing, source selection, interpretations and analyses are the responsibility of the author only. The author has checked all factual statements, statistics, figures, tables and references in manuscript before submission.

7. CASE STUDIES

The cases in this section are presented as secondary and illustrative evidence. They are not considered as first-hand data. The intent of these cases is to illustrate the potential of AI-supported systems to impact employee autonomy, trust, fairness, surveillance, and the human experience in an organizational context. Published studies, reports and documented organizational examples are used to support the conceptual interpretation. The cases are not used to draw statistical inferences or generalizations (Bortolotti et al., 2023). Adoption rates are not directly considered as measures of employee engagement, autonomy, trust or workplace experience. Rather, the cases illustrate how various outcomes may be achieved in AI-enabled work systems through the design, governance, transparency, and participation of employees in the use of AI. This is in line with the conceptual review, and secondary case analysis design for this chapter. Table 5 presents the two illustrative case studies used in the chapter. Case I focuses on AI-supported decision-making and forecasting, where employee autonomy depends on explainability and human discretion. Case II focuses on algorithmic management and monitoring, where employee trust may decline when governance and transparency are weak. The table shows that the cases are based on secondary illustrative evidence, not primary data.

Table 5. Overview of Illustrative Cases

Case	AI Application Area	Evidence Status	Main Employee Experience Issue
Case I	Decision support and forecasting	Secondary illustrative evidence	Autonomy depends on explainability and human discretion
Case II	Algorithmic management and monitoring	Secondary illustrative evidence	Trust declines when governance and transparency are weak

7.1 Case Study I: AI Decision Support

Organizations increasingly rely on AI for making decisions in a variety of roles, including customer service, forecasting, data analysis, assisting in recruitment, and managerial decision making. Typically, AI systems are deployed in such environments to enhance the speed of decision making, alleviate information overload and ensure more uniform analysis. AI can serve as a decision support system, not a replacement for human decision making, to help humans make better decisions and increase the responsiveness of the organization (Ryan et al., 2022). The benefits of AI are, however, under the control of employees who understand and control it. AI recommendations that are not well-suited to the context can lead to confusion among employees, or when the reasoning behind the outputs from algorithms is unclear. Lack of transparency may lead to decreased trust in AI-driven decision-making and diminished sense of autonomy. If the AI system is not tailored to the specific tasks they perform, or if they are not adequately trained to use the outputs, they can also face difficulties in incorporating the AI-generated content (Pandey et al., 2024). This case shows how AI can be used as an augmentation, rather than a replacement, tool to allow employees to be autonomous. Employees should be empowered to question, interpret, and override AI recommendations when necessary. Explainability, training and human discretion come to play a significant role in meaningful AI-supported decision-making. The case also implies that leadership is at the core of facilitating the comprehension of the purpose of AI and its responsible application in the workplace. This case shows that decision-support AI improves employee experience when employees retain control over AI recommendations. It supports the view that explainability and human discretion strengthen autonomy, trust, and meaningful engagement.

7.2 Case Study II: Algorithmic Management

Algorithmic management is the application of AI-driven systems to track, allocate, evaluate, schedule and monitor employees. In organizations they are increasingly being implemented to enhance coordination, provide productivity measurement and aid managerial decision making. The introduction of algorithmic systems can, however, lead to employee concerns regarding surveillance, fairness and a loss of control if the systems are not introduced with clear communication and governance (Andrews, 2019). In some scenarios, using AI to gather information about an employee's work habit without adequate information can lead to discomfort, as revealed by published studies and organizational reports. There could be concerns if employees are unaware of the data being gathered, if performance scores are being derived in a certain way, or if the data gathered and presented by AI impacts managerial decisions. Under such circumstances, staff members might feel that AI is a way to manage them instead of assist them, thereby undermining the utility of AI. Under such circumstances, staff may think of AI as a control mechanism instead of a supportive mechanism, which will damage the utility of AI (Shehu et al., 2025). The case demonstrates how poor governance can impact trust in AI-based work systems. Lacking policies can lead to ambiguity regarding acceptable use of AI, privacy concerns, accountability measures, and evaluation standards for AI usage. This uncertainty can lead to an AI adoption and employee trust divide. Thus, algorithmic management must be transparent, accountable, involve staff and be ethically supervised. These protections can be absent and, in the absence of them, AI can undermine trust and foster an atmosphere of surveillance rather than engagement. This case shows that algorithmic management can weaken employee experience when monitoring systems lack transparency and employee participation. It supports the view that weak governance and limited employee voice reduce trust, fairness, and perceived autonomy.

7.3 Cross-Case Insights

The two case studies illustrate that while AI can be adopted, it isn't always a sign of employee experience improvement. Whether AI is designed and controlled as a means of augmenting humans or as a means of control makes all the difference. In decision support situations, AI can enhance autonomy by augmenting access to information, providing support for decision-making, and preserving autonomy for employees. However, in the field of algorithmic management, AI can foster mistrust during times of opacity, surveillance, and improper governance. An important lesson is that there isn't a direct relationship between using AI and engagement, trust, or work. Frequent AI use does not necessarily indicate trust, engagement, or inclusion (Albrecht et al., 2021). So, the adoption of AI should be analyzed together with the concepts of transparency, governance, participation and job design. In general, the value of AI in an organization depends on the human-centered design, ethical governance, voice and participation, fairness and privacy, and accountability. Table 6 compares the two cases and shows how AI affects meaning, control, trust, engagement, and governance. It highlights that AI can support employees when it is transparent, explainable, and participatory. However, AI may reduce trust and engagement when it is used mainly for monitoring or control.

Table 6. Cross-Case Insights

Theme	Case I: Decision Support	Case II: Algorithmic Management
Meaning	AI supports better decisions.	AI may reduce work meaning if used for control.
Control	Employees keep control when they can review AI suggestions.	Control reduces when AI decisions are unclear.
Trust	Trust improves with explainable AI.	Trust decreases with weak transparency.
Engagement	Engagement improves when AI supports work.	Engagement decreases when employees feel monitored.
Governance	Clear guidance supports responsible AI use.	Weak policy creates confusion and fear.

8. RESULTS AND DISCUSSION

The study reveals that AI implementation has a mixed impact on employee meaning, agency, and value to the organization, contingent on the design and governance of intelligent systems, as seen in the comparison of the two secondary case studies. AI looks like it can help with information accessibility, decision making and operational efficiency in both. But the results also indicate that the improvement in efficiency is not sufficient to create a positive employee experience (Chen, 2024). In an open decision-support system, workers will feel more involved, engaged, and confident in their work when using AI. On the other hand, if AI is employed in an opaque algorithmic management or with weak governance systems, it can diminish trust, promote concealed use, and foster a feeling of a lack of control. The findings show that the impact of AI on employee experience extends beyond just the adoption of the technology to the mix of automation, human decision making, transparency, and ethical review. This section explores the impact of AI on meaning and role identity, changes to notions of fairness and trust, and ongoing tensions between productivity and human dignity.

8.1 AI, Meaning, and Engagement

AI can shape the mindset of workers in relation to their work, role identity and contribution to the organization, as seen in the case studies. When AI is assisting humans in decision-making, workers might feel better about their work, as they are relieved from cognitive overload and better organized information, and take decisions faster. If employees have interpretive responsibilities, AI is likely to be perceived as a means to enhance their professional role, not take it over. When the AI systems are prescriptive, black-boxed or hard to question, however, employees may grow uncertain about the systems' value and contribution (Carter & Wynne, 2024). This can lead to identity tension, particularly if workers are concerned that their work will be negatively evaluated due to the implementation of AI or that it might diminish the importance of their skills. The results indicate that role identity can be reinforced through the use of AI as an augmentative, rather than substitutive force. Creating meaningful engagement depends on the employees' perception of AI as enhancing their capabilities, aiding their sense-making, and complementing their purpose rather than undermining it.

8.2 Agency, Fairness, and Trust

Across the cases, agency, fairness, and trust were closely related outcomes. If the employees are aware that the AI systems make recommendations but the final decision is theirs, they are more likely to feel an agency. In these cases, AI can be used to aid decision-making processes without taking away from employee discretion. However, even with high adoption rates of AI in organizational processes, poor transparency and weak governance can contribute to lower trust. Uncertainty of fairness, privacy and responsibility (Becker, 2018) due to unclear policies and accountability mechanisms. Algorithmic evaluation and monitoring practices can also raise concerns about surveillance, if the employees do not know how decisions are being made or how performance is being measured. Erosion of trust can happen when what employees expect from an organization and what the organization delivers are not in sync. These results suggest that fairness is not just about the results but also about the clarity of the procedure, the voice of the employees, and the explainability of the procedure. Responsibility, verifiable decisions, and traceable accountability of organizational leadership for the use of AI-integrated working systems are essential for building trust in AI.

8.3 Efficiency and Human Dignity

However, the cases illustrate that the combination of efficiency-driven AI use and respect for human rights and organizational sustainability is a significant challenge. While the benefits of AI can enhance productivity, speed decision-making and efficiency in information processing, they risk becoming fragile when it comes at the expense of employees' autonomy, trust and participation. Implementation without ethical safeguards and in an efficient way could lead to higher perceptions of control and dehumanization, thereby reducing long-term engagement. Organizations that integrate transparency, training, involvement, and responsible governance with AI adoption are more likely to enable them to connect performance outcomes with employee well-being (Kinowska & Sienkiewicz, 2023). The results indicate that the value creation in AI-supported environments is multi-faceted. It involves economic efficiency, but also social legitimacy, fairness, trust and human empowerment. When AI systems are respectful, promote professional identity and enable meaningful contribution, then they create sustainable value. These insights align with the chapter's thesis, which is that human-centric AI doesn't impede organizational performance. Instead, it's a prerequisite for value generation in AI-powered companies.

9. FUTURE RESEARCH DIRECTIONS

The results of the chapter demonstrate a number of research opportunities in the future that can be utilized to contribute to the state of knowledge of human experience and value creation within AI-facilitated organizations. With the increased integration of Artificial Intelligence into the work systems, the necessity to study this subject matter outside cross-sectional analysis emerges more and more. Future research must take up integrative approaches that would integrate organizational, psychological and ethical interests to reflect the changing relationship between intelligent systems and humans. Special focus is needed in order to learn more about how the meaning, identity, and agency are created and re-created with time as AI systems become more mature and organizational practices stabilize (Ezeilo & Green-McKenzie, 2024). Furthermore, the studies should have a closer connection with design and governance issues as well as examine the impact of participatory and human-centered design on the employee experience. The further development of the empirical scope to cover various cultural and sectoral settings will also enhance theory and practice. All these directions in research can help build stronger ethical, inclusive, and sustainable AI adoption models in organizations.

9.1 Longitudinal AI Work Studies

The next area of research should focus on longitudinal research studies to determine how the meaning of employees and role identity change as AI is normalized in organizational practices. Most of the short-term research focuses on the direct responses to the adoption of AI, without considering the adaptation, learning, and identity renegotiation changes with time. Longitudinal designs would help uncover whether the initial issues of autonomy and relevance continue to be, diminish or escalate with the workers acquiring new abilities and relations with intelligent systems (Alves et al., 2025). How career paths, professional self-conceived notions, and perceptions of contribution evolve in the long-term AI-mediated work systems can also be a topic of such studies. Monitoring the workers will go through many phases of AI integration, which will allow the researchers to better comprehend the dynamics of meaning-making and agency in a time-dependent manner. This is an especially significant method of determining whether AI eventually contributes to the enhancement and development or leads to the disengagement and erosion of identity.

9.2 Human-Centered AI Governance

Future studies should explore the effects of the human-centered design of AI and participatory form of governance on employee experience and organizational performance. Conceptual arguments on transparency and participation have been well developed but there is limited empirical evidence on its effectiveness. Future research would examine the role of employee engagement, whether during AI design, testing, and monitoring, working on trust, acceptance as well as perceived fairness (Ateeq et al., 2025). Comparative studies on various models of governance, including the aspects of centralized and decentralized AI management, might be of great help in terms of the best practices. Moreover, the study that examines the influence of leadership in instilling ethical principles to the development and application of AI should be conducted (Ravikumar & Aarthi, 2025b). Future research can be useful in determining the viable mechanisms through which organizations can integrate technological innovation with human dignity and empowerment by concentrating on participatory and value-based approaches.

9.3 Cross-Cultural AI Studies

Another important way to develop the knowledge of AI-enabled work is cross-cultural and sector-specific studies. The institutional frameworks, cultural norms, and labor regulations play a very important role in the perception and experience of AI among the employees. There may be differences related to trust, agency, and acceptance of intelligent systems as studies carried out in different national and cultural backgrounds may indicate. Equally, industry-specific studies may reveal the variations in the increase in AI adoption in diverse industries comprising health-care, manufacturing, education, and services, each of which has unique ethical and operational issues at hand (Jones & Asonye, 2023). The relative study can help in enlightening the contextual factors in determining the balance between automation and human judgment. Further diversification of studies outside of the well-researched spheres of dominance will improve the extrapolation of study results and facilitate the creation of situational frameworks of responsible Artificial Intelligence implementation (Ravikumar & Aarthi, 2025d).

10. MANAGERIAL IMPLICATIONS

The implications of the findings of this chapter are significant to managers who are charged with the responsibility of implementing and governing AI-enabled work systems. The role of managerial decision-making is critical to deciding between AI adoption improving the experience of employees and adding to disengagement and mistrust. Instead of addressing AI as a strictly technical investment, the managers need to consider it as a socio-technical intervention, which reforms roles, power, and organizational principles. The evidence provided in the case shows that effectiveness benefits cannot be maintained to generate long-term values in situations where employee agency and dignity are compromised (Butryn & Rudnicki, 2024). Managers must balance performance goals with ethical responsibility, transparency, and inclusion. Good AI leadership is strategic decisions made about the system design, governance, and workforce development. Ethical stewardship, augmentation, and continuous learning are three factors that allow organizations to capitalize on AI to enhance engagement and innovation. The implications below describe the practical recommendations to designing human-centered AI systems, fostering positive leadership and culture, and making adaptive skill building and job redesign in AI enabled organizations to happen.

10.1 AI for Augmentation

AI designs that present human capabilities as opposed to human judgment and expertise should be prioritized by managers. The findings of the case suggest that the engagement and receptiveness of the employees increase when AI systems are used as decision-support systems that will improve sense-making and alleviate cognitive load (Rathinavel et al., 2025). Augmentative design does not impose authority on employees, as it provides freedom of choice in the final decision and promotes critical thinking of AI outputs. Conversely, displacement-oriented implementations have the risk of undermining the role identity and creating resistance or using the system in a covert way. Managers should thus make sure that AI systems are clear, decipherable, and aligned to the current work processes (Buijsman et al., 2025). Engaging employees early, in terms of design and implementation, would be useful in finding areas where AI can be used to add value without reducing the human input. Placing AI in a collaborative context as opposed to replacing it will help organizations to support meaningful work and maintain employee commitment without sacrificing the achievement of productivity gains.

10.2 Ethical AI Leadership

The primary determinant of the perception and experience of AI in employees is leadership and organizational culture. Ethical stewardship demands that leaders define explicit values that drive the use of AI and they incorporate such values into the governance and the day-to-day practices. Due to the lack of formal AI policies and control systems as in the cases, the lack of trust and consequently unfairness and surveillance are promoted. Leaders should hence encourage openness, responsibility and discussion regarding the use of AI (Shneiderman & University of Maryland, 2020). This should be accompanied by the creation of a culture of openness so that employees are not afraid of using AI systems and get punished. Another feature of ethical leadership is constant thinking about the unforeseen consequences, e.g., the bias or over monitoring. Leaders can justify AI programs and make technological innovation solution-oriented to organizational direction and staff welfare by showing their commitment to human-centered values.

10.3 Skills and Job Redesign

The work environments powered by AI need an ongoing investment in the development of skills and flexible job design. The instances point out that workers tend to adopt AI tools without proper training and assistance readily. Continuous learning programs should be introduced by managers, who will cultivate technical skills, as well as critical knowledge of AI systems. They should focus on interpretive abilities, ethical consciousness, and team problem-solving as opposed to technical expertise developed in a narrow context. It is also vital that job redesign since AI also alters how tasks are laid out and how they are performed. Jobs will be redesigned to be more focused on human strengths that include judgment, creativity, and empathy with the help of AI-generated advice (Richardson et al., 2021). The lack of anxiety and enhancement of positive role identity can be achieved by providing clear channels of skill development and career advancement. By designing strategic learning plans and job redesign, organizations can empower their employees to learn to adjust to work facilitated by AI with confidence and remain engaged in the long term. Table 7 Provides practical managerial plans which are in line with augmentation, ethical stewardship and continuous learning.

Table 7. Managerial Actions for AI Adoption

Managerial Focus	Key Actions	Intended Impact
AI Design	Prioritize augmentation	Preserve role identity
Governance	Establish ethical AI policies	Build trust and fairness
Leadership	Communicate AI purpose	Reduce resistance
Skills	Continuous upskilling	Enable adaptation
Job Design	Redefine roles with AI	Sustain engagement

11. CONCLUSION

This chapter has explored how Artificial Intelligence can be incorporated into the organizational setting by looking at it through the prism of meaning, agency, and human experience versus prevailing efficiency-focused discourses. The discussion shows that AI-based systems have a profound impact on employees and their perception of their jobs, independence, and work meaning. Intelligent systems may be presented to the organization as the transparent and supportive decision aids, which subsequently may be used to improve the engagement, support the professional identity, and allow employees to play a more meaningful role in achieving the objectives of the organization. On the other hand, opaque algorithmic governance, inadequate governance, and practices which are surveillance-driven pose a threat to the erosion of trust, agency and undermine the human basis of work.

The results highlight the importance of the fact that AI is not a technological neutral phenomenon but a socio-technical actor that has its effects influenced by design decisions, leadership behaviors, and organizational culture. Restructuring AI as a collaborative companion, as opposed to a replacement of human judgment, will help organizations adopt technological intelligence as consistent with human values and moral commitments. When the benefits of productivity are offset by the regard of human dignity, equity, and empowerment, sustainable value creation in the AI-driven world becomes possible. Organizations can create an atmosphere where AI beneficial to meaningful work is incorporated into the work processes by incorporating transparency, participatory design, lifelong learning, and ethical stewardship into strategies of AI adoption. Finally, according to the chapter, the future of organization AI-enabled lies in the capacity of balancing technological progress with human-oriented values and making sure that innovation produces not only an economic effect but also a continuous level of employee involvement, confidence, and social welfare.

REFERENCES

Aarthi, S., Ravikumar, R. N., Khudayberganov, S., Ismailov, A., & Khujaniyozova, O. (2025). Using Intelligent Tutoring Systems to enhance student engagement. In *Advances in Computational Intelligence and Robotics* (pp. 155–188). IGI Global. DOI: 10.4018/979-8-3373-1827-1.ch008

Ahmad, A. R., Sapry, H. R. M., & Jameel, A. S. (2025). Reclaiming autonomy in the age of AI: A conceptual framework linking algorithmic management and job happiness. *International Journal of Research and Innovation in Social Science*, 7222–7228. DOI: 10.47772/IJRISS.2025.908000597

Aizenberg, E., & van den Hoven, J. (2020). Designing for human rights in AI. *Big Data & Society*, *7*(2), 205395172094956. DOI: 10.1177/2053951720949566

Akinnagbe, O. B. (2024). Human-AI collaboration: Enhancing productivity and decision-making. *International Journal of Education, Management, and Technology*, *2*(3), 387–417. DOI: 10.58578/ijemt.v2i3.4209

Albrecht, S. L., Green, C. R., & Marty, A. (2021). Meaningful work, job resources, and employee engagement. *Sustainability (Basel)*, *13*(7), 4045. DOI: 10.3390/su13074045

Alves, B., Alhussein, G., Riggare, S., Duncan, T. S., Saad, A., Lyreskog, D. M., Chatzichristos, C., Gerasimou, I., Hadjidimitriou, S., Hadjileontiadis, L. J., & Dias, B. (2025). Stakeholder perspectives on trustworthy AI for Parkinson disease management using a cocreation approach: Qualitative exploratory study. *Journal of Medical Internet Research*, *27*, e73710. DOI: 10.2196/73710 PMID: 40768261

Andrews, L. (2019). Public administration, public leadership and the construction of public value in the age of the algorithm and 'big data.'. *Public Administration*, *97*(2), 296–310. DOI: 10.1111/padm.12534

Anisha Estherita, S., & Vasantha, S. (2024). Fostering employee engagement and knowledge sharing through artificial intelligence. *Salud Ciencia y Tecnologia - Serie de Conferencias, 3*, 897. DOI: 10.56294/sctconf2024897

Ateeq, K., Oswal, N., Jawabri, A., Al Masaeid, T., Alquqa, E. K., Basha, S. E., & Alami, R. (2025). The transformative impact of artificial Intelligence (AI) on organisational behaviour (OB): A study of employee engagement, performance, and ethical implications. *Journal of Posthumanism*, *5*(4). Advance online publication. DOI: 10.63332/joph.v5i4.1221

Becker, A. (2018). An experimental study of voluntary nonprofit accountability and effects on public trust, reputation, perceived quality, and donation behavior. *Nonprofit and Voluntary Sector Quarterly*, *47*(3), 562–582. DOI: 10.1177/0899764018756200

Bortolotti, T., Boscari, S., Morton, E., & Powell, D. (2023). Integrating smart manufacturing to lean: A multiple-case study of the impact on shop-floor employees' autonomy and empowerment. In *IFIP Advances in Information and Communication Technology* (pp. 109–124). Springer Nature Switzerland., DOI: 10.1007/978-3-031-43662-8_9

Buijsman, S., Carter, S. E., & Bermúdez, J.-P. (2025). Autonomy by design: Preserving human autonomy in AI decision-support. *Philosophy & Technology*, *38*(3), 97. Advance online publication. DOI: 10.1007/s13347-025-00932-2

Butryn, B., & Rudnicki, P. (2024). The impact of artificial intelligence on managing the recruitment process in a company. *Informatyka Ekonomiczna*, *2024*(1–2), 1–12. DOI: 10.15611/ie.2024.1-2.01

Carter, W., & Wynne, K. T. (2024). Integrating artificial intelligence into team decision-making: Toward a theory of AI–human team effectiveness. *European Management Review, emre.12685*. DOI: 10.1111/emre.12685

Chen, H. (2024). The ethical challenges of educational Artificial Intelligence and coping measures: A discussion in the context of the 2024 World Digital Education Conference. *Science Insights Education Frontiers, 20*(2), 3263–3281. DOI: 10.15354/sief.24.re339

Dekker, R., Koot, P., Birbil, S. I., & van Embden Andres, M. (2022). Co-designing algorithms for governance: Ensuring responsible and accountable algorithmic management of refugee camp supplies. *Big Data & Society*, *9*(1), 205395172210878. DOI: 10.1177/20539517221087855

Dican, L. (2025). Human-AI collaboration and its impact on decision-making. *International Journal of Multidisciplinary Research and Growth Evaluation.*, *2*(2), 919–922. DOI: 10.54660/.IJMRGE.2025.6.2.919-922

Ezeilo, C. O., & Green-McKenzie, J. (2024). The covid-19 pandemic and the future of work. *Journal of Occupational and Environmental Medicine*, *66*(6), e245–e251. DOI: 10.1097/JOM.0000000000003107 PMID: 38531821

Familoni, B. T. (2024). Ethical frameworks for AI in healthcare entrepreneurship: A theoretical examination of challenges and approaches. *International Journal of Frontiers in Biology and Pharmacy Research, 5*(1), 057–065. DOI: 10.53294/ijfbpr.2024.5.1.0032

Herrmann, T., & Pfeiffer, S. (2022). Keeping the organization in the loop: A socio-technical extension of human-centered artificial intelligence. *AI & Society*. Advance online publication. DOI: 10.1007/s00146-022-01391-5

Hosseini, T., Bastami, M., & Sheikh Esmaili, S. (2025). Designing a comprehensive model for human resource transfer in the tax affairs organizations of Tehran. *Journal of Resource Management and Decision Engineering*, *4*(2), 1–10. DOI: 10.61838/kman.jrmde.4.2.14

Jarrahi, M. H., Lutz, C., Boyd, K., Oesterlund, C., & Willis, M. (2023). Artificial intelligence in the work context. *Journal of the Association for Information Science and Technology*, *74*(3), 303–310. DOI: 10.1002/asi.24730

Jones, M. A., & Asonye, B. O. (2023). The organizational cultural impact of the social use of AI and bots on remote employees returning to the workplace. *Journal of Management World*, *2023*(4), 154–162. DOI: 10.53935/jomw.v2024i4.1145

Khan, A. A., Akbar, M. A., Fahmideh, M., Liang, P., Waseem, M., Ahmad, A., Niazi, M., & Abrahamsson, P. (2023). AI ethics: An empirical study on the views of practitioners and lawmakers. *IEEE Transactions on Computational Social Systems*, *10*(6), 2971–2984. DOI: 10.1109/TCSS.2023.3251729

Kinowska, H., & Sienkiewicz, Ł. J. (2023). Influence of algorithmic management practices on workplace well-being – evidence from European organisations. *Information Technology & People*, *36*(8), 21–42. DOI: 10.1108/ITP-02-2022-0079

Kiverstein, J., Kirchhoff, M. D., & Froese, T. (2022). The problem of meaning: The Free Energy Principle and artificial agency. *Frontiers in Neurorobotics*, *16*, 844773. DOI: 10.3389/fnbot.2022.844773 PMID: 35812784

Ma, Y., Li, X., Hu, S., Liu, S., & Cheong, K. H. (2025). Trustworthy AI in education: Framework, cases, and governance strategies. *Innovation and Emerging Technologies*, *12*(2550026), 2550026. Advance online publication. DOI: 10.1142/S2737599425500264

Mabrouk, A. (2024). Human resouce management in the age of Artificial Intelligence: Concepts tools and steps. *Solo International Collaboration and Publication of Social Sciences and Humanities*, *3*(01), 1–12. DOI: 10.61455/sicopus.v3i01.216

Mishra, R., & Jadeja, D. (2025). A literature review on the impact of AI-enhanced HRIS on employee retention and engagement. In *Intersecting Natural Language Processing and FinTech Innovations in Service Marketing* (pp. 11–20). IGI Global Scientific Publishing., DOI: 10.4018/979-8-3693-9944-6.ch002

Morley, J., Floridi, L., Kinsey, L., & Elhalal, A. (2020). From what to how: An initial review of publicly available AI ethics tools, methods and research to translate principles into practices. *Science and Engineering Ethics*, *26*(4), 2141–2168. DOI: 10.1007/s11948-019-00165-5 PMID: 31828533

Pandey, J., Kumar, M., & Singh, S. (2024). Organizational ethical climate: Influence on employee meaning and well-being. *Management Decision*, *62*(10), 3235–3260. DOI: 10.1108/MD-10-2023-1823

Porlezza, C., & Schapals, A. K. (2024). AI ethics in journalism (studies): An evolving field between research and practice. *Emerging Media*, *2*(3), 356–370. DOI: 10.1177/27523543241288818

Prabagar, S., Mothkur, R., Swetha, C. B., Kurian, A., Pavithra, K., & Aarthi, S. (2025). Generative AI for inclusive special education. In *Advances in Computational Intelligence and Robotics* (pp. 205–236). IGI Global Scientific Publishing. DOI: 10.4018/979-8-3373-3745-6.ch008

Rathinavel, P., Ravikumar, R. N., Aarthi, S., Habib, M., Salaeva, N., & Pardaev, J. (2025). Augmenting human capabilities. In *Advances in Computational Intelligence and Robotics* (pp. 1–30). IGI Global Scientific Publishing. DOI: 10.4018/979-8-3373-2372-5.ch001

Ravikumar, R. N., & Aarthi, S. (2025a). AI-driven governance. In *Advances in Computational Intelligence and Robotics* (pp. 343–372). IGI Global Scientific Publishing. DOI: 10.4018/979-8-3373-3760-9.ch012

Ravikumar, R. N., & Aarthi, S. (2025b). Integrating machine learning with human decision making in HR. In *Empowering Human Resources Through Human-Computer Interaction* (pp. 115–146). IGI Global Scientific Publishing., DOI: 10.4018/979-8-3373-1676-5.ch005

Ravikumar, R. N., & Aarthi, S. (2025c). Mind meets machine. In *Advances in Computational Intelligence and Robotics* (pp. 143–172). IGI Global Scientific Publishing. DOI: 10.4018/979-8-3373-5747-8.ch006

Ravikumar, R. N., & Aarthi, S. (2025d). The role of educational developers in AI integration at scale. In *Advances in Computational Intelligence and Robotics* (pp. 289–322). IGI Global Scientific Publishing. DOI: 10.4018/979-8-3373-4129-3.ch011

Reinhardt, K. (2023). Trust and trustworthiness in AI ethics. *AI and Ethics*, *3*(3), 735–744. DOI: 10.1007/s43681-022-00200-5

Richardson, J. P., Smith, C., Curtis, S., Watson, S., Zhu, X., Barry, B., & Sharp, R. R. (2021). Patient apprehensions about the use of artificial intelligence in healthcare. *NPJ Digital Medicine*, *4*(1), 140. DOI: 10.1038/s41746-021-00509-1 PMID: 34548621

Riedl, M. O. (2019). Human-centered artificial intelligence and machine learning. *Human Behavior and Emerging Technologies*, *1*(1), 33–36. DOI: 10.1002/hbe2.117

Rostamzadeh, R., Alizadeh, F. K., Keivani, S., & Isavi, H. (2025). The role of artificial intelligence in improving organizational behavior: A systematic study. *Human Behavior and Emerging Technologies, 2025*(1). DOI: 10.1155/hbe2/8094428

Ryan, M., Christodoulou, E., Antoniou, J., & Iordanou, K. (2022). An AI ethics 'David and Goliath': Value conflicts between large tech companies and their employees. *AI & Society*. Advance online publication. DOI: 10.1007/s00146-022-01430-1

Sartori, L., & Theodorou, A. (2022). A sociotechnical perspective for the future of AI: Narratives, inequalities, and human control. *Ethics and Information Technology*, *24*(1), 4. Advance online publication. DOI: 10.1007/s10676-022-09624-3

Shehu, H., Ogunleye, E., Atilola, M. O., Eromosele, E. I., Lawal, A. B., & Chukwuma, T. T. (2025). Ethical and responsible AI in engineering and construction projects: Governance, trust, and human-centered design. *Scientific. Journal of Engineering Technology*, *2*(2), 53–62. DOI: 10.69739/sjet.v2i2.833

Shneiderman, B. (2020). Human-centered artificial intelligence: Three fresh ideas. *AIS Transactions on Human-Computer Interaction*, •••, 109–124. DOI: 10.17705/1thci.00131

Sigfrids, A., Leikas, J., Salo-Pöntinen, H., & Koskimies, E. (2023). Human-centricity in AI governance: A systemic approach. *Frontiers in Artificial Intelligence*, *6*, 976887. DOI: 10.3389/frai.2023.976887 PMID: 36872934

Sigfrids, A., Nieminen, M., Leikas, J., & Pikkuaho, P. (2022). How should public administrations foster the ethical development and use of artificial intelligence? A review of proposals for developing governance of AI. *Frontiers in Human Dynamics*, *4*, 858108. Advance online publication. DOI: 10.3389/fhumd.2022.858108

Tabata, M., Wildermuth, C., Bottomley, K., & Jenkins, D. (2025). Generative AI integration in leadership practice: Foundations, challenges, and opportunities. *Journal of Leadership Studies*, *18*(4), 41–54. DOI: 10.1002/jls.70005

Uddin, A. S. M. A. (2023). The era of AI: Upholding ethical leadership. *Open Journal of Leadership*, *12*(04), 400–417. DOI: 10.4236/ojl.2023.124019

Uzoamaka, N.-O. P., Amujiogu, A. A., & Blessing, E. O. (2025). Governance and ethical oversight of agentic artificial intelligence in business process management: Balancing human-autonomy, organizational accountability and algorithmic transparency. *Journal of Basic and Applied Research International, 31*(6), 121–133. DOI: 10.56557/jobari/2025/v31i610028

Xavier, D. F., Korunka, C., & Reiter-Palmon, R. (2025). AI integration and workforce development: Exploring job autonomy and creative self-efficacy in a global context. *PLoS One, 20*(6), e0319556. DOI: 10.1371/journal.pone.0319556 PMID: 40465594

Zhao, H. (2025). Artificial intelligence in social governance: Global insights from theoretical frameworks to practical applications using CiteSpace. *Global Review of Humanities, Arts, and Society, 1*(4), 26–37. DOI: 10.63802/grhas.v1.i4.74

KEY TERMS AND DEFINITIONS

AI-Enabled Organizations: Organizations that integrate AI systems into core processes such as management, operations, and decision-making.

Algorithmic Management: The use of algorithms to allocate tasks, monitor performance, and support managerial decisions.

Artificial Intelligence (AI): Computer-based systems designed to perform tasks that normally require human intelligence, such as learning, reasoning, and decision-making.

Autonomy: The degree of freedom employees have in deciding how tasks are performed in AI-mediated environments.

Employee Agency: The ability of employees to exercise choice, control, and influence over their work and decisions.

Employee Experience: Employees' overall perceptions, emotions, and responses to their work environment, including interactions with AI systems.

Ethical AI: The design and use of AI systems that respect fairness, accountability, privacy, and human dignity.

Explainability: The ability of AI systems to provide clear reasons for their outputs and recommendations.

Human–AI Collaboration: The interaction between employees and intelligent systems where both contribute to work outcomes.

Human-Centered AI: AI systems designed to augment human capabilities while prioritizing well-being, dignity, and engagement.

Intelligent Systems: AI-enabled technologies that can analyze data, adapt over time, and support or automate organizational decisions.

Meaningful Work: Work experienced as purposeful, valuable, and aligned with an individual's sense of contribution and identity.

Participatory AI Design: An approach that involves employees and stakeholders in the development and governance of AI systems.

Transparency: The extent to which AI system processes and decisions are understandable to users.

Trust in AI: Employees' confidence that AI systems are reliable, fair, and aligned with organizational values.

Chapter 6
Human-Centered AI and Value Co-Creation in FinTech:
Exploring Consumer Trust, Experience, and Perceived Value

Ashwarya Kapoor
http://orcid.org/0000-0003-3858-3945
School of Commerce and Economics, Manav Rachna International Institute of Research and Studies, Faridabad, India

ABSTRACT

The rapid integration of Artificial Intelligence (AI) in financial technology (FinTech) has transformed the way financial services are delivered, experienced and evaluated by consumers. AI-driven applications such as chatbots, robo-advisors, fraud detection systems and personalized financial recommendations are reshaping customer interactions while simultaneously redefining value creation. However, the increasing reliance on AI has also raised concerns regarding trust, transparency and the absence of human touch, leading to varying degrees of consumer skepticism. This study adopts an exploratory and descriptive research design using an interview-based approach to examine how users perceive AI-enabled FinTech services in terms of trust, experience and value co-creation. The findings reveal a dual perception among users while AI enhances convenience, efficiency and personalization, concerns regarding data privacy, algorithmic opacity and reduced human interaction influence trust levels.

DOI: 10.4018/979-8-3373-8282-1.ch006

1. INTRODUCTION

1.1 Background of the Study

The financial services industry has experienced a paradigm shift over the past decade with the rapid emergence of financial technology (FinTech), which integrates digital innovation with traditional financial systems to enhance efficiency, accessibility, and customer experience (Anifa et al., 2022; Papanikolaou et al., 2025). The evolution of FinTech has been further accelerated by the adoption of Artificial Intelligence (AI), which enables advanced data analytics, automation, and intelligent decision-making across financial processes such as credit scoring, fraud detection, investment advisory, and customer service (Keshari and Gautam, 2024; Sharma & Kapoor, 2026).

AI-driven FinTech systems are fundamentally transforming the way financial services are designed and delivered. These systems leverage machine learning algorithms, natural language processing, and predictive analytics to provide personalized, real-time, and scalable financial solutions (Zarifis & Cheng, 2023; Kapoor & Sindwani, 2025a). As a result, financial institutions are increasingly shifting from traditional, human-centric service models to technology-enabled ecosystems where AI acts as a central decision-making and interaction interface (Dodda, 2025; Shaikh et al., 2026).

At the same time, this transformation has redefined the concept of value creation. In contrast to conventional firm-driven models, value in AI-enabled environments is co-created through continuous interaction between users and intelligent systems (Chandra & Rahman, 2024). Consumers actively contribute data, feedback, and behavioral inputs, which in turn improve system performance and service personalization. This interactive process positions users not merely as passive recipients but as active participants in the value creation process (Lalicic & Weismayer, 2021).

1.2 Emerging Trends in AI-Driven FinTech

Recent literature highlights several key trends shaping the AI-driven FinTech landscape. First, there is a significant rise in the adoption of AI-powered financial services, including robo-advisors, conversational banking interfaces, and automated risk management systems (Akhtar et al., 2024). These technologies enhance operational efficiency, reduce costs, and improve decision accuracy, making them increasingly attractive for both service providers and users (Saiyed, 2025).

Second, personalization has emerged as a defining feature of AI-enabled financial services. AI systems analyze vast volumes of user data to deliver tailored financial recommendations, thereby enhancing customer experience and perceived value (Ramadugu & Doddipatla, 2022). However, such personalization also raises concerns regarding data privacy and ethical use of information.

Third, trust and transparency have become central issues in AI adoption. The "black-box" nature of many AI systems creates uncertainty among users, as they are often unable to understand how decisions are made. Studies indicate that transparency in algorithmic processes and data usage significantly enhances trust and adoption intentions (Balasubramaniam et al., 2023; Solberg et al., 2022).

Moreover, the growing emphasis on human-centered AI reflects a shift from purely technology-driven innovation to designing systems that align with human values, expectations, and ethical considerations (Kapoor & Sindwani, 2025b). Research suggests that trust in AI is influenced not only by technical performance but also by socio-ethical factors such as fairness, accountability, and user control (Bach et al., 2024).

1.3 Research Gap

Despite the extensive literature on FinTech adoption and AI integration, several critical gaps remain. First, a majority of existing studies focus on technology acceptance frameworks such as TAM and UTAUT, emphasizing perceived usefulness and ease of use, while comparatively less attention has been given to experiential and relational dimensions such as trust, perceived value, and user experience (Davis, 1989; Papanikolaou et al., 2025).

Second, although trust has been widely recognized as a key determinant of FinTech adoption, existing research often treats it as a static construct, without exploring how trust evolves through continuous interaction with AI systems or how it influences value co-creation (Jafri et al., 2024).

Third, there is a lack of qualitative, user-centric investigations that capture real consumer perceptions, experiences, and concerns regarding AI-driven financial services. Much of the literature relies heavily on quantitative approaches, thereby overlooking deeper behavioral insights.

Finally, while the concept of value co-creation has been widely studied in service marketing, its application in AI-driven FinTech contexts remains underexplored, particularly in understanding how human–AI interaction shapes perceived value and customer experience.

1.4 Research Questions and Objectives of the Study

1.4.1. Research Questions

In line with the objectives of the study, the following research questions have been formulated:

RQ1: What is the level of consumer awareness and perception regarding AI-driven FinTech services?

RQ2: What factors influence consumer trust and skepticism toward AI-enabled financial services?

RQ3: How does Artificial Intelligence influence customer experience and perceived value in FinTech services?

RQ4: How does human-centered AI facilitate value co-creation in AI-driven FinTech environments?

1.4.2 Objectives of the Study

- To analyze consumer awareness and perceptions of AI-driven FinTech services.
- To identify key factors influencing trust and skepticism toward AI in financial services.
- To examine the impact of AI on customer experience and perceived value.
- To explore the role of human-centered AI in facilitating value co-creation in FinTech environments.

1.5 Contribution of the Study

This study makes several important contributions to the existing body of knowledge.

First, it extends the understanding of FinTech adoption by integrating trust, transparency, and customer experience into the analysis, moving beyond traditional technology acceptance perspectives (Akhtar et al., 2024).

Second, it contributes to the emerging discourse on human-centered AI by highlighting the importance of aligning technological capabilities with user expectations, ethical considerations, and experiential value (Bach et al., 2024).

Third, the study introduces a value co-creation perspective in AI-driven financial services, emphasizing the interactive role of users in shaping service outcomes and perceived benefits.

Fourth, methodologically, the study adopts an interview-based exploratory approach, providing rich and contextual insights into consumer perceptions that are often overlooked in quantitative research (Jafri et al., 2024).

Finally, the findings offer practical implications for FinTech firms by underscoring the need for transparent, trustworthy, and hybrid (AI + human) service models to enhance user engagement and long-term value creation.

2. LITERATURE REVIEW

2.1 AI in FinTech and Service Transformation

The integration of Artificial Intelligence (AI) into financial technology (FinTech) has significantly transformed the structure and delivery of financial services (Mohsen et al., 2025). AI technologies such as machine learning, natural language processing, and predictive analytics have enabled financial institutions to automate processes, enhance decision-making, and deliver real-time services (Zarifis & Cheng, 2023). These innovations have led to the development of advanced applications including robo-advisors, fraud detection systems, algorithmic trading, and intelligent customer service platforms.

The adoption of AI in FinTech is primarily driven by its ability to improve operational efficiency and reduce costs while simultaneously enhancing service quality. According to Akhtar et al. (2024), AI enables financial institutions to process vast volumes of structured and unstructured data, leading to more accurate predictions and improved risk management. Furthermore, AI-driven automation minimizes human errors and enhances speed, thereby improving overall system reliability (Kapoor et al., 2026a, 2026b).

However, the transformation is not merely technological but also structural. Traditional financial service models, which were largely human-centric, are being replaced by hybrid or fully automated systems (Para et al., 2025). This shift has implications for customer interaction, as AI increasingly acts as the primary interface between financial institutions and users. While this enhances efficiency, it also raises concerns regarding the loss of human interaction and emotional engagement (Davenport et al., 2020).

2.2 Customer Experience in AI-Driven Financial Services

Customer experience has emerged as a critical determinant of success in AI-enabled FinTech environments. AI technologies facilitate personalized, seamless, and efficient service delivery by analyzing user behavior, preferences, and transaction patterns (Kapoor et al., 2026c). Personalization, in particular, has become a defining feature of AI-driven financial services, enabling tailored recommendations and proactive financial advice (Huang & Rust, 2021).

The ability of AI systems to provide 24/7 availability and instant responses significantly enhances convenience, which is a key component of customer experience (Vashishth et al., 2024). Chatbots and virtual assistants, for instance, offer immediate support and reduce waiting times, thereby improving user satisfaction (Marinova et al., 2017). Additionally, AI-driven interfaces enable frictionless transactions, contributing to a more streamlined and user-friendly experience.

Despite these advantages, the absence of human empathy and emotional intelligence in AI systems presents a limitation. Human interactions often involve emotional understanding, trust-building, and personalized engagement, which AI systems may not fully replicate (Geroimenko, 2025). As a result, while AI enhances functional aspects of experience, it may fall short in delivering relational or emotional value (Huang & Rust, 2021). This creates a need for hybrid service models that combine AI efficiency with human touch.

2.3 Trust and Transparency in AI Systems

Trust is widely recognized as a critical factor influencing the adoption and continued use of AI-driven financial services. In the context of FinTech, trust extends beyond the reliability of the service provider to include trust in the underlying technology and algorithms (Jafri et al., 2024). The complexity and opacity of AI systems often create uncertainty among users, leading to skepticism and reluctance to fully rely on automated decision-making.

One of the primary challenges in building trust in AI systems is the "black box" nature of machine learning algorithms (Alum et al., 2026). Users often lack an understanding of how decisions are made, particularly in areas such as credit scoring or investment recommendations. This lack of explainability can reduce confidence in AI systems and hinder adoption (Bach et al., 2024).

Transparency plays a crucial role in mitigating these concerns. Providing clear information about how AI systems function, how data is used, and how decisions are made can significantly enhance user trust (Balasubramaniam et al., 2023). Explainable AI (XAI) has emerged as an important area of research, focusing on making AI systems more interpretable and accountable. Studies suggest that when users perceive AI systems as transparent and fair, they are more likely to trust and adopt them (Solberg et al., 2022).

Additionally, data privacy concerns further complicate trust formation. Financial data is highly sensitive, and users are often apprehensive about how their data is collected, stored, and utilized (Kapoor et al., 2025a, 2025b). Ensuring robust data protection mechanisms and communicating these measures effectively is essential for building trust in AI-driven FinTech services (Akhtar et al., 2024).

2.4 Value Co-Creation in AI-Enabled Financial Ecosystems

The concept of value co-creation, rooted in Service-Dominant Logic, emphasizes the collaborative role of consumers and firms in creating value through interactions (Vargo & Lusch, 2008). In AI-driven environments, this concept takes on new dimensions, as technology becomes an active participant in the co-creation process.

AI systems continuously learn from user inputs, behaviors, and feedback, enabling them to improve service quality and personalization over time. This dynamic interaction creates a feedback loop where users contribute to the refinement of AI systems, and in turn, receive enhanced value (Prahalad & Ramaswamy, 2004). In this sense, value is not delivered unilaterally by the firm but is co-created through ongoing human–AI interaction.

In the context of FinTech, value co-creation manifests through personalized financial recommendations, adaptive user interfaces, and predictive services that anticipate user needs. However, the effectiveness of value co-creation depends on the level of user engagement and trust. If users are skeptical or unwilling to share data, the co-creation process may be hindered (Manser Payne et al., 2021).

Furthermore, the role of AI in value co-creation raises important ethical considerations. Issues such as algorithmic bias, fairness, and accountability can influence user perceptions and impact the overall value derived from AI systems. Therefore, ensuring ethical AI practices is essential for sustainable value co-creation (Lharti, 2026).

2.5 Consumer Skepticism and Adoption Challenges

Despite the numerous benefits of AI in FinTech, consumer skepticism remains a significant barrier to adoption. Skepticism arises from various factors, including lack of transparency, perceived risks, and uncertainty regarding the accuracy and fairness of AI-driven decisions (Jafri et al., 2024; Makker & Kapoor, 2026).

One of the key sources of skepticism is the perceived loss of control. Users may feel uncomfortable relying on automated systems for critical financial decisions, particularly when they do not fully understand how these systems operate. Additionally, concerns about data breaches and misuse of personal information further contribute to skepticism (Akhtar et al., 2024).

Another important factor is algorithmic bias. AI systems trained on biased data may produce discriminatory outcomes, which can undermine trust and lead to negative perceptions. Studies have shown that users are more likely to question and reject AI systems if they perceive them as unfair or biased (Bach et al., 2024).

Moreover, the absence of human interaction can also influence consumer attitudes. While AI systems offer efficiency and convenience, they may lack the relational aspects of service that are important for building long-term trust and loyalty. As a result, many users prefer a hybrid approach that combines AI capabilities with human support.

2.6 Human-Centered AI in FinTech

The concept of human-centered AI has gained prominence as a response to the challenges associated with AI adoption. Human-centered AI focuses on designing systems that prioritize user needs, values, and experiences, ensuring that technology serves as an enabler rather than a replacement for human capabilities (Huang & Rust, 2021).

In FinTech, human-centered AI involves creating systems that are transparent, explainable, and aligned with ethical principles. It also emphasizes the importance of maintaining a balance between automation and human interaction. By incorporating human oversight and intervention, financial institutions can enhance trust and provide a more holistic customer experience (Adedoyin et al., 2025).

Research indicates that users are more likely to adopt AI systems that are perceived as supportive and collaborative rather than autonomous and opaque (Bach et al., 2024). Therefore, integrating human-centered design principles into AI-driven FinTech services is essential for fostering trust, enhancing experience, and enabling effective value co-creation.

3. CONCEPTUAL FRAMEWORK

The rapid integration of Artificial Intelligence (AI) in FinTech has transformed traditional service delivery into an interactive, data-driven, and experience-centric ecosystem. In such an environment, value is no longer created solely by firms but emerges through continuous interaction between users and intelligent systems. This study proposes a conceptual framework that explains how key technological and relational factors influence customer experience and ultimately lead to value co-creation.

The framework is grounded in Service-Dominant Logic (Vargo & Lusch, 2008), which emphasizes value co-creation through interactions, and extends it to AI-enabled financial services by incorporating constructs relevant to human–AI interaction.

3.1 Key Constructs of the Framework

Perceived Intelligence

Perceived intelligence refers to the extent to which users believe that AI systems are capable, accurate, and effective in performing financial tasks (Zhao et al., 2024). AI systems that demonstrate high levels of predictive accuracy, responsiveness, and problem-solving ability are more likely to be perceived as intelligent (Huang & Rust, 2021). This perception enhances user confidence and contributes positively to overall experience. For example, when a robo-advisor consistently provides accurate investment suggestions aligned with users' financial goals, consumers are more likely to perceive the system as intelligent and reliable. Such perceptions enhance confidence in AI systems and positively influence customer experience.

Personalization

Personalization is a defining feature of AI-driven FinTech services, where systems tailor recommendations, financial advice, and user interfaces based on individual preferences and behavioral data (Pal et al., 2020). Personalized services enhance relevance and convenience, thereby improving customer satisfaction and perceived value (Akhtar et al., 2024). However, excessive personalization may also raise privacy concerns, making it a double-edged factor. For instance, AI-enabled mobile banking applications that recommend customized savings plans or spending insights based on transaction history may increase customer satisfaction and perceived value. However, if users feel that excessive personal information is being utilized without adequate consent, concerns regarding privacy may emerge.

Transparency

Transparency refers to the clarity with which AI systems communicate their processes, decision-making logic, and data usage (Felzmann et al., 2020). Due to the "black box" nature of AI, lack of transparency can lead to uncertainty and skepticism. Transparent systems that provide explainable outputs are more likely to build trust and encourage user engagement (Bach et al., 2024). As an illustration, when an AI-based lending platform clearly explains why a loan application has been approved or rejected, users are more likely to trust the decision-making process. In contrast, opaque decisions without explanations may increase skepticism and reduce trust.

Trust in AI

Trust in AI is a critical relational construct that reflects users' confidence in the reliability, fairness, and security of AI-driven systems (Regona et al., 2026). Trust is influenced by multiple factors including transparency, perceived intelligence, and past experiences (Jafri et al., 2024). In FinTech, where financial risk is involved, trust becomes a key determinant of adoption and continued usage.

Human Touch

Human touch refers to the presence of human interaction, empathy, and emotional support in service delivery (Solnet et al., 2019). While AI enhances efficiency, the absence of human elements may reduce emotional satisfaction and relational value. Hybrid models that integrate AI with human assistance are often preferred by users, as they balance efficiency with empathy (Davenport et al., 2020). For example, customers interacting with an AI chatbot for routine banking queries may appreciate instant responses, but they may still prefer escalation to a human advisor when dealing with complex investment or dispute-related issues. Such hybrid interactions can strengthen customer experience and trust.

Perceived Value

Perceived value represents the overall assessment of benefits derived from AI-driven services relative to costs and risks (Kim, 2020). It includes functional value (efficiency, convenience), emotional value (comfort, satisfaction), and social value (trust and credibility). Perceived value is a key outcome of customer experience and a precursor to value co-creation.

3.2 Customer Experience as a Mediating Construct

Customer experience acts as a central mechanism through which the above factors influence value creation. AI-driven FinTech services shape user experiences through interactions that are fast, personalized, and data-driven. However, the quality of this experience depends on how well technological efficiency is balanced with trust and human-centric design (Huang & Rust, 2021).

A positive customer experience enhances user engagement, satisfaction, and willingness to interact with AI systems, thereby facilitating value co-creation. For instance, when users experience seamless interactions, personalized recommendations, and transparent communication while using AI-enabled payment applications, they are more likely to engage actively with the platform by sharing feedback and continuously using its services. Such engagement subsequently contributes to value co-creation.

3.3 Value Co-Creation in AI-Driven FinTech

Value co-creation occurs when users actively participate in the service process by sharing data, providing feedback, and engaging with AI systems. These interactions enable continuous learning and improvement of AI models, resulting in enhanced service quality and personalized offerings (Prahalad & Ramaswamy, 2004).

In AI-driven FinTech, value co-creation is not a one-time outcome, but an ongoing process shaped by trust, experience, and user engagement. Therefore, the effectiveness of value co-creation depends on the alignment between technological capabilities and human expectations.

It is important to distinguish between perceived value and value co-creation in the context of AI-enabled FinTech services. While perceived value refers to users' evaluation of the benefits obtained from AI-driven services, such as convenience, efficiency, and personalization, value co-creation extends beyond benefit realization and involves users' active participation through continuous interaction, feedback, customization, and engagement with AI systems. Thus, value co-creation represents a collaborative process in which both users and service providers jointly contribute to service enhancement and improved outcomes.

Based on the literature and exploratory insights, the following propositions are advanced:

P1: Perceived intelligence positively influences customer experience in AI-driven FinTech services.

P2: Personalization positively influences customer experience and perceived value.

P3: Transparency positively influences trust in AI.

P4: Trust in AI positively influences perceived value and value co-creation.

P5: Human touch positively influences customer experience.

P6: Customer experience positively influences perceived value.

P7: Perceived value positively influences value co-creation.

Figure 1 illustrates the proposed conceptual framework guiding qualitative enquiry showing the influence of technological and relational factors on customer experience, perceived value, and value co-creation.

Figure 1. Proposed Conceptual Framework Guiding the Qualitative Inquiry

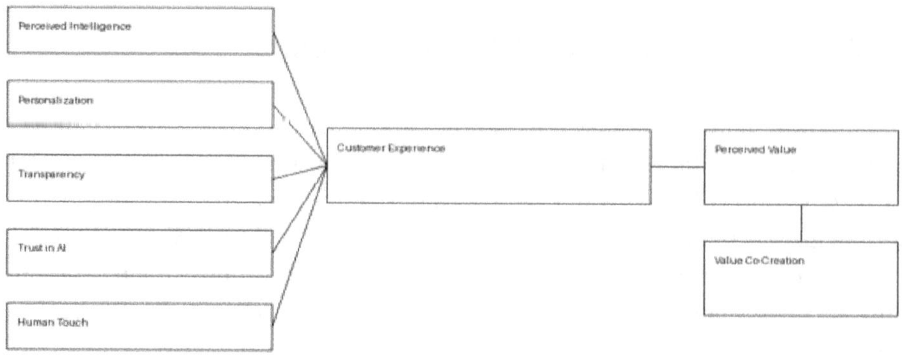

4. RESEARCH METHODOLOGY

4.1 Research Design

The present study adopts an exploratory and descriptive research design to gain a comprehensive understanding of consumer perceptions toward AI-enabled FinTech services. An exploratory approach is particularly suitable in contexts where the phenomenon is relatively new and evolving, such as the integration of Artificial Intelligence in financial services. It allows for deeper insights into user attitudes, perceptions, and experiences that are not yet fully established in existing literature.

Simultaneously, the descriptive aspect of the study enables the systematic presentation and interpretation of consumer responses, thereby providing a structured understanding of key factors influencing trust, experience, and value creation in AI-driven financial ecosystems.

4.2 Data Collection Method

The study relies on primary data collected through in-depth personal interviews, which serve as an effective qualitative tool for capturing rich, detailed, and context-specific insights. Interviews allow respondents to express their opinions, concerns, and experiences in their own words, thereby enabling a nuanced understanding of their interaction with AI-based financial services.

A semi-structured interview format was adopted to ensure flexibility while maintaining consistency across respondents. This approach allowed the researcher to probe deeper into specific areas of interest while also ensuring that all key themes relevant to the study objectives were adequately covered.

The interviews were conducted between January 2026 and March 2026. Depending on respondents' availability and convenience, interviews were conducted either face-to-face or through online communication platforms such as Google Meet and Microsoft Teams. Each interview lasted approximately 30 to 45 minutes.

Interviews were conducted primarily in English. However, respondents were also allowed to communicate in Hindi whenever they felt more comfortable expressing their opinions and experiences. This flexible approach facilitated richer and more authentic responses.

4.3 Sample Design and Respondent Profile

The sample for the study comprised 45 respondents from India who actively use AI-driven FinTech services such as mobile banking applications, digital payment platforms, robo-advisory services, and AI-enabled financial recommendation systems. The Indian context was considered particularly relevant due to the rapid digital transformation of the financial sector and the increasing adoption of AI-enabled financial services across the country.

Participants were recruited using purposive sampling through professional networks, academic contacts, and referrals. The purposive sampling approach ensured the inclusion of individuals possessing relevant experience with AI-enabled FinTech services.

To be eligible for participation, respondents were required to satisfy the following inclusion criteria: (1) be at least 18 years of age; (2) actively use one or more AI-enabled FinTech services, such as digital payment applications, mobile banking platforms, chatbots, robo-advisory services, or AI-based financial recommendation systems; and (3) possess prior experience of using such services for a minimum period of six months. Individuals with no prior experience of AI-enabled financial services were excluded from the study.

Table 1. Demographic and FinTech Usage Profile of Respondents

Characteristic	Category	Frequency (n=45)	Percentage (%)
Gender	Male	25	55.6
	Female	20	44.4
Age	18–25 years	12	26.7
	26–35 years	15	33.3

continued on following page

Table 1. Continued

Characteristic	Category	Frequency (n=45)	Percentage (%)
	36–45 years	10	22.2
	Above 45 years	8	17.8
Occupation	Student	8	17.8
	Salaried Employee	18	40.0
	Business/Self-employed	11	24.4
	Homemaker	3	6.7
	Others	5	11.1
Experience with AI-enabled FinTech Services	Less than 1 year	7	15.6
	1–3 years	20	44.4
	More than 3 years	18	40.0
Frequently Used FinTech Services*	Mobile Banking	38	84.4
	Digital Payment Platforms	41	91.1
	Chatbots/Virtual Assistants	27	60.0
	Robo-advisory Services	14	31.1
	AI-based Financial Recommendations	24	53.3

The demographic profile presented in Table 1indicates that the sample comprised respondents from diverse backgrounds in terms of gender, age, occupation, and experience with AI-enabled financial services. A majority of respondents were salaried employees and belonged to the 26–35 years age group, reflecting active users of digital financial services. Furthermore, digital payment platforms and mobile banking applications emerged as the most frequently utilized AI-enabled FinTech services, highlighting the increasing integration of intelligent technologies in routine financial activities. The diversity of the respondent profile ensured the inclusion of varied perspectives regarding trust, experience, and value creation in AI-driven FinTech ecosystems.

4.4 Interview Instrument and Key Themes

The interview schedule was carefully designed to align with the conceptual framework and research objectives of the study. It consisted of open-ended questions structured around the following key themes:

- **Awareness of AI Applications**

This section aimed to assess the extent to which respondents are familiar with AI-driven functionalities in FinTech, including automated recommendations, chatbots, and fraud detection systems.

- **Trust and Reliability Perceptions**

Questions in this domain explored the level of trust users place in AI systems, their perceptions of reliability, and concerns related to security, data privacy, and algorithmic decision-making.

- **Experience with AI Interactions**

This theme focused on understanding user experiences while interacting with AI-enabled platforms, including ease of use, responsiveness, personalization, and satisfaction levels.

- **Perceived Value and Concerns**

Respondents were asked to evaluate the overall value derived from AI-based services in terms of convenience, efficiency, and usefulness, along with any concerns such as lack of transparency, reduced human interaction, or fear of errors.

The semi-structured nature of the interview allowed respondents to elaborate on their experiences, thereby generating deeper insights into both positive perceptions and underlying skepticism.

4.5 Data Analysis Technique

The interview data were analyzed using thematic analysis, a widely accepted qualitative technique for identifying, analyzing, and reporting patterns within qualitative data. A hybrid thematic analysis approach, combining both deductive and inductive coding, was employed in the present study. Initially, a deductive coding process was undertaken wherein preliminary codes were developed based on the existing literature, study objectives, and the proposed conceptual framework. Subsequently, an inductive approach was adopted to identify additional themes and insights emerging directly from participants' narratives. This combination enabled the researchers to validate theoretically derived constructs while simultaneously capturing novel perspectives and contextual nuances associated with human-centered AI in FinTech services.

The analysis was conducted in multiple stages:

1. **Data Familiarization**

Interview responses were carefully reviewed and transcribed to ensure accuracy and completeness.

2. **Coding and Theme Identification**

Key statements and responses were categorized into meaningful codes based on recurring ideas and patterns. The coding process was undertaken by the authors of the study. Initially, the interview transcripts were independently reviewed and coded by two researchers to identify relevant themes and patterns. Subsequently, the researchers compared their coding outcomes and discussed any discrepancies until consensus was achieved. This iterative process facilitated refinement of the coding framework and ensured consistency in theme identification.

Several procedures were adopted to enhance coding credibility and trustworthiness. First, all transcripts were reviewed multiple times to ensure familiarity with the data and minimize interpretive bias. Second, peer debriefing sessions were conducted among the researchers to discuss emerging themes and validate interpretations. Third, an audit trail documenting coding decisions, theme development, and analytical reflections was maintained throughout the analysis process. These procedures contributed to enhancing the reliability, credibility, and transparency of the qualitative findings.

3. **Theme Development**

The codes were further grouped into broader themes such as trust, transparency, personalization, and perceived value, aligning with the conceptual framework. To provide an indication of the relative prominence of different themes, frequencies were calculated based on the number of participants referring to a particular issue or perception during the interviews. The frequency categories emerged during the coding and thematic development process; wherein similar responses were grouped under broader conceptual themes. Since participants frequently discussed multiple aspects of AI-enabled FinTech services within a single interview, the thematic categories were not mutually exclusive. Consequently, an individual respondent could contribute to more than one theme, and therefore the cumulative frequencies may exceed the total number of respondents.

4. **Interpretation and Analysis**

The identified themes were interpreted in relation to the research objectives and existing literature to derive meaningful insights.

In addition to thematic analysis, a frequency-based interpretation was employed to quantify the occurrence of specific responses. This hybrid approach enhances the robustness of the findings by combining qualitative depth with descriptive clarity.

4.6 Justification of Methodology

The use of an interview-based qualitative approach is particularly justified in this study due to the complex and evolving nature of AI-driven FinTech services. Consumer perceptions regarding trust, transparency, and value are inherently subjective and context-dependent, making them difficult to capture through purely quantitative methods.

By adopting a qualitative methodology, the study is able to uncover deeper behavioral insights, identify subtle patterns of skepticism and acceptance, and provide a holistic understanding of how users interact with AI systems in financial contexts.

4.7 Ethical Considerations

Respondents were informed about the purpose and objectives of the study prior to participation. Informed consent was obtained from all participants, and participation was entirely voluntary. Respondents were assured that they could withdraw from the study at any stage without any consequences. To ensure confidentiality and anonymity, participants' identities were not disclosed, and anonymised participant codes (e.g., P1, P2, P3) were used during data analysis and reporting. The information collected was used solely for academic purposes and was securely maintained throughout the research process.

The reporting of the study was guided by established qualitative research reporting principles, particularly the Consolidated Criteria for Reporting Qualitative Research (COREQ), to enhance methodological transparency and rigor.

5. ANALYSIS AND FINDINGS

To understand consumer perceptions of AI-enabled FinTech services, in-depth interviews were conducted with 45 respondents. The responses were analyzed thematically and supported with frequency-based representation to identify key patterns related to awareness, trust, experience, and value creation. The findings are presented below:

5.1 Thematic Analysis and Findings

5.1.1 Awareness of AI in FinTech

Table 2.

Response	Number of Respondents
Somewhat aware	18
Highly aware	12
Not very aware	15

The findings reveal that the majority of respondents fall within the "somewhat aware" category (18 respondents), indicating that while users are actively engaging with AI-enabled financial services, their understanding of the underlying technology remains limited. This suggests a gap between usage and technological awareness, where consumers benefit from AI functionalities without fully recognizing or comprehending them.

A notable proportion of respondents (15) reported being not very aware, highlighting that AI in FinTech often operates in the background, making it less visible to end users. Only 12 respondents demonstrated high awareness, reflecting a relatively smaller segment of informed users who understand AI applications such as automated recommendations, fraud detection, and chatbots.

This distribution indicates that although AI adoption in FinTech is widespread, consumer literacy regarding AI remains moderate, which may influence trust, perception, and engagement levels.

To further illustrate respondents' awareness regarding AI-enabled financial services, the following excerpts are presented:

"Initially, I was unaware that many financial applications used AI, but I gradually realized that features such as chatbots and spending insights are AI-driven." (P12)

5.1.2 Perception of AI-Based Financial Services

Table 3.

Response	Number of Respondents
Convenient and efficient	20
Useful but lacks human touch	17
Complex or confusing	8

The perception of AI-driven financial services is largely positive in terms of functional efficiency, with 20 respondents identifying these services as convenient and efficient. This reflects the ability of AI to streamline processes, reduce transaction time, and enhance accessibility.

However, a significant number of respondents (17) expressed that while AI is useful, it lacks human touch. This highlights an important limitation of AI systems—the absence of emotional intelligence, empathy, and personalized human interaction, which are critical components of service experience in financial contexts.

Additionally, 8 respondents perceived AI systems as complex or confusing, indicating that usability and interface design may act as barriers for certain user segments. These findings suggest that while AI enhances functional value, relational and experiential aspects require further improvement.

To further illustrate respondents' perception regarding AI-enabled financial services, the following excerpts are presented:

"I regularly use AI-enabled banking applications for personalized recommendations and instant support, which have significantly improved my banking experience." (P7)

5.1.3 Trust in AI Systems

Table 4.

Response	Number
Trust to some extent	19
Skeptical	16
Fully trust	10

Trust in AI systems appears to be moderate and conditional. The majority of respondents (19) indicated that they trust AI to some extent, suggesting cautious acceptance rather than complete reliance. This reflects a transitional phase where users are gradually adapting to AI technologies but still maintain a degree of uncertainty.

A substantial number of respondents (16) expressed skepticism, which can be attributed to concerns regarding transparency, data privacy, and algorithmic decision-making. Only 10 respondents reported complete trust, indicating that full confidence in AI systems is still limited.

These findings emphasize that trust is not yet fully established in AI-driven FinTech services and remains a critical factor influencing adoption and continued usage.

Participants expressed varying levels of trust toward AI-driven financial services:

"I trust AI applications for routine transactions, but I remain concerned about the security of my financial information." (P18)

"I feel more confident when AI systems clearly explain how decisions or recommendations are generated." (P24)

5.1.4 Concerns Regarding AI

Table 5.

Response	Number
Data privacy issues	21
Lack of transparency	14
Job replacement concerns	10

The analysis highlights several concerns associated with AI adoption, with data privacy emerging as the most significant issue (21 respondents). Given the sensitive nature of financial data, users are particularly cautious about how their information is collected, stored, and utilized.

The second major concern is the lack of transparency (14 respondents), which relates to the "black box" nature of AI systems. Users often find it difficult to understand how decisions are made, leading to uncertainty and reduced trust.

Additionally, 10 respondents expressed concerns regarding job displacement, reflecting broader societal apprehensions about automation and its impact on employment.

Overall, these findings indicate that risk perception plays a crucial role in shaping user attitudes toward AI in FinTech, particularly in areas involving security and accountability.

The concerns expressed by respondents are reflected in the following excerpts:

"Although AI-enabled financial services are convenient, I am concerned about the security of my personal and financial information." (P14)

"I sometimes hesitate to rely completely on AI systems because I do not fully understand how decisions and recommendations are generated." (P21)

5.1.5 Impact on Customer Experience

Table 6.

Response	Number
Enhances experience	22
Neutral	13
Negative impact	10

The majority of respondents (22) reported that AI enhances their overall experience, primarily due to improved efficiency, faster service delivery, and personalized interactions. This suggests that AI contributes positively to the functional dimension of customer experience.

However, 13 respondents indicated a neutral impact, implying that AI neither significantly enhances nor detracts from their experience. This may be due to limited awareness or minimal interaction with AI features.

Notably, 10 respondents perceived a negative impact, which can be linked to issues such as lack of human interaction, complexity, or trust-related concerns. These findings highlight that while AI improves operational aspects, it does not always translate into emotional satisfaction or engagement.

The following quotations further demonstrate participants' experiences:

"AI-powered banking applications save considerable time and provide recommendations that are highly relevant to my needs." (P9)

"Personalized notifications regarding expenses and savings opportunities have enhanced my overall financial management experience." (P31)

5.1.6 Role in Value Creation

Table 7.

Response	Number
Adds significant value	24
Limited value	14
No clear value	7

Participants also acknowledged their active role in creating value:

"By continuously using AI applications and providing feedback, users contribute to improving these services." (P5)

"The more I interact with AI-based financial platforms, the better they understand my preferences, which creates value for both users and providers." (P36)

5.2 Linking Findings with the Conceptual Framework

The findings of the study provide empirical support for the proposed conceptual framework presented in Figure 1. The interview responses indicate that perceived intelligence and personalization positively influence customer experience by enhancing convenience, efficiency, and relevance of financial services. A majority of respondents perceived AI-enabled services as convenient and efficient, suggesting that intelligent and personalized functionalities contribute significantly to favorable service experiences.

The findings further reveal that transparency and trust in AI are closely interconnected. Concerns regarding data privacy and the lack of transparency emerged as major barriers affecting users' trust in AI-driven financial services. These findings support the proposition that transparent AI systems are essential for fostering trust and encouraging continued engagement with AI-based platforms.

Moreover, the analysis highlights the importance of human touch in AI-enabled service environments. A substantial proportion of respondents reported that although AI services are useful, they often lack empathy and emotional support. This finding reinforces the framework's argument that human-centric design and hybrid service models are necessary to enhance customer experience.

The study also demonstrates that customer experience acts as a central mechanism linking technological and relational factors with perceived value. Positive experiences associated with convenience, responsiveness, and personalization were found to enhance users' perceptions of value. Finally, the findings suggest that value co-creation is facilitated when users trust AI systems, actively engage with them, and perceive meaningful benefits from their interactions. Thus, the empirical evidence largely supports the proposed conceptual framework and underscores the significance of balancing technological capabilities with human-centered considerations in AI-driven FinTech ecosystems.

5.3 Interrelationships Among Key Constructs

The thematic analysis reveals a strong interrelationship among the constructs proposed in the conceptual framework. The findings indicate that perceived intelligence and personalization positively influence customer experience by enhancing convenience, responsiveness, and relevance of financial services. Respondents who perceived AI systems as accurate and capable reported more favorable service experiences and greater satisfaction.

The analysis further suggests that transparency serves as an important antecedent of trust in AI. Respondents frequently expressed skepticism when they were unable to understand how AI systems arrived at financial decisions. Conversely, systems that communicated decisions clearly were perceived as more trustworthy. This indicates that transparency plays a crucial role in reducing uncertainty and fostering user confidence.

Trust in AI emerged as a central construct influencing both customer experience and perceived value. Users demonstrating higher levels of trust were more willing to engage with AI-enabled services, share information, and rely on automated recommendations. Such engagement enhanced their perceived benefits and overall service evaluations.

The findings also reveal that the presence of human touch strengthens customer experience by complementing AI efficiency with empathy and reassurance. Hybrid service models integrating AI with human assistance were perceived more positively than fully automated interactions.

Finally, positive customer experiences were found to contribute significantly to perceived value and facilitate value co-creation. Users experiencing seamless, personalized, and trustworthy interactions demonstrated greater willingness to continuously engage with AI platforms, provide feedback, and participate actively in service improvement processes. Therefore, the findings suggest that customer experience acts as an important mechanism linking technological and relational factors with value co-creation in AI-driven FinTech ecosystems.

6. DISCUSSION

The findings indicate that AI plays a significant role in value creation, with 24 respondents acknowledging that it adds substantial value to financial services. This value is primarily derived from convenience, speed, accuracy, and personalization, which enhance the overall utility of services.

However, 14 respondents perceived limited value, suggesting that the benefits of AI may not be fully realized or appreciated by all users. Additionally, 7 respondents reported no clear value, indicating a lack of awareness or dissatisfaction with AI-driven services.

These results suggest that while AI contributes to functional value, its impact on perceived value is influenced by factors such as trust, transparency, and user experience. Therefore, effective value creation in AI-driven FinTech requires not only technological efficiency but also user-centric design and trust-building mechanisms.

The findings of the study provide valuable insights into the role of Artificial Intelligence (AI) in shaping customer experience and value creation in FinTech services. The results indicate that AI-driven financial services significantly enhance the functional dimension of value, particularly in terms of efficiency, speed, accuracy, and personalization. A majority of respondents perceived AI-enabled services as convenient and effective, which reinforces the argument that AI contributes to improved service delivery and operational performance (Huang & Rust, 2021). The ability of AI systems to analyze large datasets and provide tailored recommendations enables users to make informed financial decisions, thereby enhancing perceived usefulness and overall satisfaction.

Despite these advantages, the study reveals that trust remains a critical concern influencing user acceptance and engagement with AI-driven FinTech services. While many respondents expressed partial trust, a considerable proportion exhibited skepticism toward AI systems. This finding aligns with prior research, which suggests that trust in AI is shaped not only by performance outcomes but also by perceptions of reliability, fairness, and data security (Jafri et al., 2024). The moderate level of trust observed in this study indicates that users are still in a transitional phase, where they acknowledge the benefits of AI but remain cautious about its implications.

A key factor contributing to this skepticism is the lack of transparency and explainability in AI systems. The "black-box" nature of algorithmic decision-making makes it difficult for users to understand how financial outcomes are generated, particularly in sensitive areas such as credit evaluation and investment recommendations. This lack of clarity can lead to uncertainty and reduced confidence in AI systems, thereby limiting their adoption (Bach et al., 2024). The findings suggest that transparency is not merely a technical attribute but a critical determinant of trust and user acceptance.

Furthermore, the study highlights that value co-creation in AI-enabled FinTech is contingent upon user trust and engagement. AI systems rely heavily on user data and interaction to improve their performance and deliver personalized services. However, if users are reluctant to trust these systems or share their data, the process of value co-creation may be hindered. This supports the perspective of Service-Dominant Logic, which emphasizes that value is co-created through active participation and interaction between the service provider and the consumer (Vargo & Lusch, 2008). In the context of AI, this interaction extends to human–machine collaboration, making trust a foundational element for effective value creation.

Another important finding of the study is the limited role of emotional and relational value in AI-driven services. While AI enhances functional efficiency, it often lacks the human touch required to build emotional connections with users. A significant number of respondents indicated that AI-based services, although useful, do not provide the same level of comfort, empathy, and reassurance as human interactions. This observation is consistent with existing literature, which suggests that AI systems are more effective in delivering cognitive and analytical tasks but fall short in addressing emotional and relational aspects of service (Davenport et al., 2020).

The absence of human touch creates a gap between functional value and experiential value, highlighting the need for a more balanced approach to service design. In this regard, the concept of human-centered AI becomes highly relevant, as it emphasizes the integration of technological capabilities with human values and expectations. The findings suggest that hybrid models, which combine AI-driven efficiency with human support, can enhance both trust and customer experience. Such models allow users to benefit from automation while retaining access to human assistance when required.

In conclusion, the study demonstrates that while AI-driven FinTech services excel in delivering efficiency and personalization, their effectiveness in fostering value co-creation depends on addressing challenges related to trust, transparency, and human interaction. A user-centric approach that prioritizes explainability, ethical considerations, and emotional engagement is essential for ensuring sustainable adoption and meaningful customer experiences in the AI-driven financial ecosystem.

7. IMPLICATIONS

7.1 Theoretical Implications

The present study makes significant contributions to the existing body of knowledge by extending the concept of value co-creation into the domain of AI-driven financial services. While traditional literature on value co-creation primarily focuses on human interactions within service ecosystems, this study incorporates the role of intelligent systems as active participants in the co-creation process. By doing so, it broadens the applicability of Service-Dominant Logic in technologically advanced contexts. Furthermore, the study integrates critical constructs such as trust and human centered AI, thereby enriching the theoretical understanding of how relational and technological factors jointly influence customer experience and value creation. The findings emphasize that in AI-enabled environments, value is not solely derived from technological efficiency but is also shaped by user perceptions of transparency, reliability, and emotional connection, thus offering a more holistic perspective on value co-creation in digital ecosystems.

7.2 Practical Implications

From a managerial perspective, the findings of the study offer valuable insights for FinTech firms aiming to enhance customer experience and foster sustainable adoption of AI-driven services. One of the key implications is the need to adopt explainable AI models, which can improve transparency and help users better understand how decisions are made, thereby strengthening trust. Additionally, the study highlights the importance of implementing hybrid service models that combine the efficiency of AI with the empathy and reassurance of human support. Such an approach can bridge the gap between functional and emotional value, leading to improved customer satisfaction and engagement. Moreover, FinTech firms should prioritize transparent communication strategies regarding data usage, security measures, and algorithmic processes, as these factors play a crucial role in reducing user skepticism and enhancing trust. By focusing on these aspects, organizations can create more user-centric, trustworthy, and value-driven financial services in an increasingly AI-powered environment.

8. CONCLUSION

The integration of Artificial Intelligence (AI) in FinTech has significantly transformed the delivery and experience of financial services, creating new opportunities for efficiency, personalization, and value creation. The findings of this study indicate that while AI-driven systems enhance functional value through speed, accuracy, and convenience, their effectiveness in fostering meaningful customer experiences is influenced by factors such as trust, transparency, and human interaction.

A key insight emerging from the study is that trust remains a critical determinant in the adoption and continued use of AI-enabled financial services. Concerns related to data privacy, lack of transparency, and algorithmic opacity contribute to user skepticism, thereby limiting the full potential of AI-driven innovations. Moreover, the absence of human touch in automated systems highlights the importance of balancing technological efficiency with emotional and relational aspects of service delivery.

The study further emphasizes that value co-creation in AI environments is conditional, relying heavily on user engagement and confidence in the system. Therefore, adopting a human-centered approach that integrates explainability, ethical considerations, and hybrid service models is essential. Such an approach will enable FinTech firms to build trust, enhance customer experience, and achieve sustainable value creation in an increasingly AI-driven world.

REFERENCES

Adedoyin, F., Dogan, H., Cetinkaya, D., & Jiang, N. (2025, May). Human-Centered AI in FinTech: A Conceptual Model and Strategic Research Agenda. In *2025 IEEE Conference on Artificial Intelligence (CAI)* (pp. 180-187). IEEE. DOI: 10.1109/CAI64502.2025.00036

Akhtar, M., Salman, A., Ghafoor, K. A., & Kamran, M. (2024). Artificial intelligence, financial services knowledge, government support, and user innovativeness: Exploring the moderated-mediated path to fintech adoption. *Heliyon, 10*(21), e39521. DOI: 10.1016/j.heliyon.2024.e39521 PMID: 39568835

Alum, E. U., Egwu, C. K., Manjula, V. S., Ekpang, P. O., Ekpang, J. E.II, Echegu, D. A., Alum, B. N., & Uti, D. E. (2026). Overcoming the Black Box Challenge: Building Trust in Artificial Intelligence Algorithms in Oncology. *Technology in Cancer Research & Treatment, 25*, 15330338261434649. DOI: 10.1177/15330338261434649 PMID: 41873493

Anifa, M., Ramakrishnan, S., Joghee, S., Kabiraj, S., & Bishnoi, M. M. (2022). Fintech innovations in the financial service industry. *Journal of Risk and Financial Management, 15*(7), 287. DOI: 10.3390/jrfm15070287

Bach, T. A., Khan, A., Hallock, H., Beltrão, G., & Sousa, S. (2024). A systematic literature review of user trust in AI-enabled systems: An HCI perspective. *International Journal of Human-Computer Interaction, 40*(5), 1251–1266. DOI: 10.1080/10447318.2022.2138826

Balasubramaniam, N., Kauppinen, M., Rannisto, A., Hiekkanen, K., & Kujala, S. (2023). Transparency and explainability of AI systems: From ethical guidelines to requirements. *Information and Software Technology, 159*, 107197. DOI: 10.1016/j.infsof.2023.107197

Chandra, B., & Rahman, Z. (2024). Artificial intelligence and value co-creation: A review, conceptual framework and directions for future research. *Journal of Service Theory and Practice, 34*(1), 7–32. DOI: 10.1108/JSTP-03-2023-0097

Davenport, T., Guha, A., Grewal, D., & Bressgott, T. (2020). How artificial intelligence will change the future of marketing. *Journal of the Academy of Marketing Science, 48*(1), 24–42. DOI: 10.1007/s11747-019-00696-0

Davis, F. D. (1989). Perceived usefulness, perceived ease of use, and user acceptance of information technology. *Management Information Systems Quarterly, 13*(3), 319–340. DOI: 10.2307/249008

Dodda, A. (2025). *Artificial intelligence and financial transformation: Unlocking the power of fintech, predictive analytics, and public governance in the next era of economic intelligence*. Deep Science Publishing.

Felzmann, H., Fosch-Villaronga, E., Lutz, C., & Tamò-Larrieux, A. (2020). Towards transparency by design for artificial intelligence. *Science and Engineering Ethics*, *26*(6), 3333–3361. DOI: 10.1007/s11948-020-00276-4 PMID: 33196975

Geroimenko, V. (2025). Emotional and Relational Aspects: Building Rapport and Human-Like Interaction with AI. In *Beyond and After Prompt Engineering: The Future of AI Communication* (pp. 289–316). Springer Nature Switzerland.

Huang, M. H., & Rust, R. T. (2021). A strategic framework for artificial intelligence in marketing. *Journal of the Academy of Marketing Science*, *49*(1), 30–50. DOI: 10.1007/s11747-020-00749-9

Jafri, J. A., Amin, S. I. M., Rahman, A. A., & Nor, S. M. (2024). A systematic literature review of the role of trust and security on Fintech adoption in banking. *Heliyon*, *10*(1), e22980. DOI: 10.1016/j.heliyon.2023.e22980 PMID: 38163181

Kapoor, A., Jaswal, A., & Sindwani, R. (2026b). Charting the roadmap to metaverse commerce adoption: A cause–effect perspective using fuzzy DEMATEL. *Journal of Modelling in Management*, •••, 1–29. DOI: 10.1108/JM2-07-2025-0352

Kapoor, A., Kapoor, S., & Sindwani, R. (2026c). Strategizing in Immersive Realities: Case-Based Insights Into Metaverse, Augment Reality, Virtual Reality, and Neuromarketing for Consumer Understanding. In *Reshaping Business at the Intersection of Neuromarketing and AI* (pp. 261-290). IGI Global Scientific Publishing.

Kapoor, A., & Sindwani, R. (2025a). Artificial Intelligence as a Catalyst for Advancing Contactless Payments: Unveiling Key Adoption Drivers. In *AI Marketing and Ethical Considerations in Consumer Engagement* (pp. 321–338). IGI Global Scientific Publishing. DOI: 10.4018/979-8-3373-3476-9.ch016

Kapoor, A., & Sindwani, R. (2025b). Navigating Inhibitors to Artificial Intelligence Adoption in Human Resource Management Practices: A Multi-criteria Decision-making Approach.

Kapoor, A., Sindwani, R., & Goel, M. (2025a). Unlocking India's mobile wallet potential: Identifying and prioritising key sustainable growth catalysts using best worst method. *International Journal of Process Management and Benchmarking*, *21*(2), 218–230. DOI: 10.1504/IJPMB.2025.148685

Kapoor, A., Sindwani, R., & Goel, M. (2025b). Assessing mobile wallet service quality using analytic hierarchy process and fuzzy evaluation method. *International Journal of Services and Operations Management, 50*(2), 246–266. DOI: 10.1504/IJSOM.2025.144481

Kapoor, A., Sindwani, R., Singh, A. K., & Kapoor, S. (2026a). Causal Modeling and Hierarchical Analysis of Critical Factors in Smart Voice Assistant Adoption: A Fuzzy DEMATEL Approach. *Journal of Global Marketing*, •••, 1–21. DOI: 10.1080/08911762.2026.2651270

Keshari, A., & Gautam, A. (2024). FinTech evolution and artificial intelligence: Opportunities and development. In *Applications of Artificial Intelligence in Business and Finance 5.0* (pp. 45–67). Apple Academic Press. DOI: 10.1201/9781003535133-3

Kim, J. (2020). The influence of perceived costs and perceived benefits on AI-driven interactive recommendation agent value. *Journal of Global Scholars of Marketing Science, 30*(3), 319–333. DOI: 10.1080/21639159.2020.1775491

Lalicic, L., & Weismayer, C. (2021). Consumers' reasons and perceived value co-creation of using artificial intelligence-enabled travel service agents. *Journal of Business Research, 129*, 891–901. DOI: 10.1016/j.jbusres.2020.11.005

Lharti, R. (2026). The Role of AI in Facilitating Value Co-Creation in Service Industries. In *Transforming Humanities and Social Sciences Through AI* (pp. 435–464). IGI Global Scientific Publishing.

Makker, R., & Kapoor, A. (2026). Decoding Greenwashing: Consumer Skepticism and Trust in Decathlon's Sustainability Claims. In *Futureproofed Sustainability Amidst Climate Change Polycrisis: Advancing SDGs and ESG for the Cities of Tomorrow* (pp. 73-96). IGI Global Scientific Publishing.

Manser Payne, E. H., Dahl, A. J., & Peltier, J. (2021). Digital servitization value co-creation framework for AI services: A research agenda for digital transformation in financial service ecosystems. *Journal of Research in Interactive Marketing, 15*(2), 200–222. DOI: 10.1108/JRIM-12-2020-0252

Marinova, D., de Ruyter, K., Huang, M. H., Meuter, M. L., & Challagalla, G. (2017). Getting smart: Learning from technology-empowered frontline interactions. *Journal of Service Research, 20*(1), 29–42. DOI: 10.1177/1094670516679273

Mohsen, S. E., Hamdan, A., & Shoaib, H. M. (2025). Digital transformation and integration of artificial intelligence in financial institutions. *Journal of Financial Reporting and Accounting, 23*(2), 680–699. DOI: 10.1108/JFRA-09-2023-0544

Pal, D., Arpnikanondt, C., & Razzaque, M. A. (2020). Personal information disclosure via voice assistants: The personalization–privacy paradox. *SN Computer Science*, *1*(5), 280. DOI: 10.1007/s42979-020-00287-9

Papanikolaou, N., Boufounou, P., & Eriotis, N. (2025). Determinants of Fintech Adoption: A Systematic Review Integrating Trust, Security, and User Perceptions within Technology Acceptance Frameworks.

Para, R., Bhatia, R., & Sandiri, S. (2025). AI-powered financial digital twins: The next frontier in hyper-personalized, customer-centric financial services. *Journal of Next-Generation Research 5.0.*

Prahalad, C. K., & Ramaswamy, V. (2004). Co-creation experiences: The next practice in value creation. *Journal of Interactive Marketing*, *18*(3), 5–14. DOI: 10.1002/dir.20015

Ramadugu, R., & Doddipatla, L. (2022). Emerging trends in fintech: How technology is reshaping the global financial landscape. *Journal of Computational Innovation*, *2*(1), 573–380. DOI: 10.53555/8fp9w410

Regona, M., Yigitcanlar, T., Hon, C., & Teo, M. (2026). Building Trust in Artificial Intelligence: A Systematic Review through the Lens of Trust Theory. *ACM Computing Surveys*, *58*(9), 1–39. DOI: 10.1145/3789256

Saiyed, A. (2025). AI-Driven Innovations in Fintech: Applications, challenges, and future trends. *International Journal of Electrical and Computer Engineering Research*, *5*(1), 8–15. DOI: 10.53375/ijecer.2025.437

Shaikh, M., Joseph, A., Zhao, H., Al Assadi, A., Bluemel, J. H., Diaz, D., & Zaki, M. (2026). AI agents in service experience: Towards autonomous and conscious agency. *Journal of Service Management*, *37*(3), 1–24. DOI: 10.1108/JOSM-04-2025-0187

Sharma, R., & Kapoor, A. (2026). From Automation to Innovation: The Transformative Impact of AI on Business Functions in India. *Management Dynamics*, *26*(1), 4. DOI: 10.57198/2583-4932.1366

Solberg, E., Kaarstad, M., Eitrheim, M. H. R., Bisio, R., Reegård, K., & Bloch, M. (2022). A conceptual model of trust, perceived risk, and reliance on AI decision aids. *Group & Organization Management*, *47*(2), 187–222. DOI: 10.1177/10596011221081238

Solnet, D., Subramony, M., Ford, R. C., Golubovskaya, M., Kang, H. J., & Hancer, M. (2019). Leveraging human touch in service interactions: Lessons from hospitality. *Journal of Service Management*, *30*(3), 392–409. DOI: 10.1108/JOSM-12-2018-0380

Vargo, S. L., & Lusch, R. F. (2008). Service-dominant logic: Continuing the evolution. *Journal of the Academy of Marketing Science, 36*(1), 1–10. DOI: 10.1007/s11747-007-0069-6

Vashishth, T. K., Sharma, V., Sharma, K. K., Kumar, B., Kumar, A., & Panwar, R. (2024). Artificial intelligence (AI)–powered chatbots: Providing instant support and personalized recommendations to guests 24/7. In *Technology and luxury hospitality* (pp. 211–236). Routledge. DOI: 10.4324/9781003488248-15

Zarifis, A., & Cheng, X. (2023). The five emerging business models of Fintech for AI adoption, growth and building trust. In *Business digital transformation: selected cases from industry leaders* (pp. 73–97). Springer International Publishing.

Zhao, Y., Chen, Y., Sun, Y., & Shen, X. L. (2024). Understanding users' voice assistant exploration intention: Unraveling the differential mechanisms of the multiple dimensions of perceived intelligence. *Internet Research, 34*(6), 2096–2122. DOI: 10.1108/INTR-10-2022-0807

Chapter 7
Scaling Personalization in Ecommerce Through Machine Learning for Hyper Relevant Customer Engagement

Sai Yellaiah Simhadri
Pampered Chef, USA

Mansi Kapoor
Swami Shraddhanand College, University of Delhi, India

Manika Garg
http://orcid.org/0009-0003-5680-3865
Maharaja Agrasen University, India

ABSTRACT

Ecommerce personalization has evolved into a strategic capability driven by machine learning, enabling firms to deliver adaptive and highly relevant customer experiences. Existing research remains fragmented, with limited integration of technological capabilities, organisational enablers, and customer privacy considerations. This conceptual chapter develops an integrated framework grounded in Dynamic Capabilities Theory and Information Boundary Theory to explain how machine learning enables personalization at scale and fosters hyper-relevant customer interactions. The framework highlights the roles of ethical AI, Explainable AI, data governance, organisational readiness, and customer trust in successful

DOI: 10.4018/979-8-3373-8282-1.ch007

implementation. The chapter offers theoretical insights and practical guidance for advancing responsible, scalable, and customer-centric personalization in digital commerce.

1. INTRODUCTION

The rapid growth of electronic commerce has fundamentally transformed the way organisations interact with consumers (Sharma et al., 2023). Increasing digitalisation, widespread smartphone adoption, and expanding online marketplaces have created an environment in which customers expect seamless, responsive, and highly personalised shopping experiences (Bilgihan et al., 2016).Traditional segmentation approaches based on demographic or geographic characteristics are no longer sufficient because contemporary consumers expect firms to recognise their individual preferences, anticipate their needs, and deliver relevant recommendations across multiple digital touchpoints. Consequently, personalization has evolved from a marketing tactic into a strategic capability that directly influences customer satisfaction, loyalty, retention, and long-term firm performance (Ledro et al., 2022).

The growing complexity of consumer behaviour and the exponential increase in digital data have accelerated the adoption of artificial intelligence (AI), particularly machine learning (ML), as the technological foundation for personalization (Riandhi et al., 2025). Unlike conventional rule-based systems, machine learning algorithms continuously learn from customer interactions, purchase histories, browsing patterns, contextual information, and behavioural signals to generate dynamic and adaptive recommendations (Ledro et al., 2022; Davenport et al., 2020). These capabilities allow ecommerce firms to provide highly relevant customer experiences at scale while simultaneously improving operational efficiency and marketing effectiveness. Recent industry evidence indicates that AI-driven personalization can increase revenues by 10% to 30% while significantly improving customer engagement and conversion rates (McKinsey & Company, 2023).

Major ecommerce platforms such as Amazon, Netflix, Alibaba, Walmart, Etsy, and Wayfair have demonstrated that machine learning has become a strategic organisational capability rather than merely a technological innovation (Daugherty and Wilson, 2022). Their recommendation engines integrate collaborative filtering, deep learning, natural language processing, image recognition, and predictive analytics to personalise product recommendations, optimise search results, forecast customer purchases, and deliver context-aware content in real time (Zhang et al., 2019). More recently, advances in Generative AI and Large Language Models (LLMs) have further transformed personalization by enabling conversational shopping assistants, AI-generated product descriptions, intelligent customer support, and real-time adaptive interactions (Dwivedi et al., 2023). These developments indicate that personalization is entering a new phase where predictive intelligence is complemented by generative capabilities, creating richer and more interactive customer experiences.

Despite these technological advances, implementing personalization at scale remains a complex organisational challenge. Existing conceptual studies primarily examine recommendation systems, predictive analytics, customer segmentation, or privacy management independently (Ledro et al., 2022; Davenport et al., 2020). Furthermore, emerging developments such as Generative AI and Explainable AI remain insufficiently incorporated into existing conceptual models (Dwivedi et al., 2023). Consequently, there remains a need for an integrated framework explaining how technological capabilities, organisational readiness, and customer trust collectively facilitate hyper-relevant customer engagement. Organisations must manage massive volumes of heterogeneous customer data while simultaneously addressing issues related to data quality, system integration, algorithmic bias, explainability, privacy protection, ethical AI, and regulatory compliance. Consumers increasingly demand personalised experiences, yet they also express growing concerns regarding surveillance, excessive data collection, algorithmic opacity, and misuse of personal information. This creates the well-documented personalization privacy paradox, where customers appreciate personalised services but remain reluctant to disclose personal information without adequate transparency and control (Awad & Krishnan, 2006; Petronio, 2002). Consequently, successful personalization depends not only on sophisticated algorithms but also on organisational capabilities that promote trust, transparency, ethical governance, and responsible AI deployment.

Although machine learning-based personalization has attracted substantial scholarly attention, existing research remains fragmented (Ledro et al., 2022). Much of the literature concentrates on individual machine learning techniques, including recommendation systems, sentiment analysis, purchase prediction, or customer segmentation, whereas other studies primarily examine technical algorithmic improvements. Comparatively limited attention has been devoted to understanding how these diverse machine learning capabilities collectively enable scalable personalization through organisational resources, customer journey management, ethical governance, and customer trust. Likewise, emerging technologies such as Generative AI, Explainable AI, and real-time adaptive personalization have received relatively limited conceptual integration within the broader personalization literature. This fragmentation restricts theoretical development and offers limited strategic guidance for organisations seeking to implement personalization at enterprise scale. Existing studies also rarely integrate technological capabilities with organisational enablers and behavioural perspectives within a unified conceptual framework. Understanding these relationships is important because organisations increasingly invest in AI-enabled personalization without clear guidance regarding the organisational capabilities, governance mechanisms, and customer trust required for successful implementation.

To address these gaps, this chapter develops a comprehensive conceptual framework that explains how machine learning techniques enable personalization at scale and facilitate hyper-relevant customer interactions while considering the organisational conditions necessary for successful implementation. Specifically, the objectives of this chapter are:

1. To examine the role of machine learning in enabling ecommerce personalization.
2. To explain how machine learning facilitates personalization at scale.
3. To develop a conceptual framework integrating technological capabilities, organisational enablers, and customer privacy.

This chapter makes several important contributions. First, it synthesises fragmented literature by integrating diverse machine learning applications into a unified conceptual model of scalable personalization. Second, it extends Dynamic Capabilities Theory by demonstrating how machine learning enables organisations to sense customer needs, seize personalization opportunities, and continuously transform digital capabilities in dynamic ecommerce environments. Third, it applies Information Boundary Theory to explain the personalization privacy paradox and the role of transparency, explainability, and ethical AI in fostering customer trust. Fourth, the chapter incorporates recent developments in Generative AI and Explainable AI to provide a contemporary perspective on the future of ecommerce personalization. Finally, it offers actionable managerial guidance for organisations seeking to implement responsible, scalable, and customer-centric personalization strategies.

The chapter is organised as follows. The next section presents the theoretical foundations underpinning the study, followed by a review of the relevant literature. The chapter then develops the proposed conceptual framework. The final sections present the discussion, conclusion, theoretical and practical implications, limitations, and directions for future research.

2. THEORETICAL FOUNDATIONS

Understanding machine learning driven personalization requires a theoretical perspective that captures both organisational capabilities and consumer responses. While machine learning provides the technological infrastructure for analysing customer data and generating personalised recommendations, successful personalization depends equally on an organisation's ability to continuously adapt its resources and on consumers' willingness to disclose personal information. Existing studies frequently examine either technological capabilities or privacy concerns independently, providing only a partial explanation of personalization success. This study therefore integrates Dynamic Capabilities Theory (DCT) (Teece et al., 1997) and Information Boundary Theory (IBT) (Petronio, 2002) to develop a comprehensive conceptual explanation of scalable personalization in ecommerce.

The two theories complement one another by addressing different but interconnected dimensions of personalization. Dynamic Capabilities Theory explains how organisations develop, deploy, and continuously reconfigure machine learning capabilities to create competitive advantage in rapidly changing digital markets. Information Boundary Theory explains how consumers regulate the disclosure of personal information and how privacy perceptions influence their acceptance of personalised services. Together, these theories provide a balanced perspective that considers both organisational capability development and customer privacy management. Integrating these perspectives enables the proposed conceptual framework to explain not only how firms implement machine learning driven personalization but also why customers may either embrace or resist these initiatives.

Dynamic Capabilities Theory

Dynamic Capabilities Theory, introduced by Teece, Pisano, and Shuen (1997), extends the Resource Based View by arguing that sustainable competitive advantage depends not only on possessing valuable organisational resources but also on continuously adapting those resources in response to rapidly changing environments. In highly dynamic digital markets, firms must continuously sense emerging customer needs, seize market opportunities, and transform organisational resources to remain competitive.

Machine learning driven personalization represents precisely this type of dynamic organisational capability. Rather than functioning as a standalone technological tool, machine learning enables firms to continuously analyse customer behaviour, learn from new information, and refine personalization strategies in real time. Ecommerce environments generate enormous volumes of behavioural, transactional, and contextual data that rapidly become obsolete unless organisations possess the capability to continuously update predictive models and adapt customer interactions.

The three dimensions of Dynamic Capabilities Theory directly correspond to personalization activities.

- Sensing refers to an organisation's capability to identify changes in customer preferences, emerging market trends, and new technological opportunities. Machine learning strengthens sensing capabilities through behavioural analytics, clickstream analysis, sentiment analysis, customer journey analytics, and predictive modelling. These technologies allow firms to identify latent customer needs before they become explicit.

- Seizing involves transforming identified opportunities into customer value. Machine learning enables organisations to deploy recommendation systems, personalised promotions, adaptive pricing, conversational AI, and personalised content delivery that respond dynamically to customer behaviour. These capabilities improve relevance, reduce decision complexity, and enhance customer engagement across multiple digital touchpoints.
- Transforming refers to continuously reconfiguring organisational resources to sustain competitive advantage. Machine learning models require ongoing retraining, integration of new data sources, algorithm optimisation, ethical governance, and cross-functional collaboration. Organisations capable of continuously improving these capabilities are better positioned to scale personalization while adapting to changing customer expectations, technological advances, and regulatory requirements.

Dynamic Capabilities Theory therefore provides the organisational foundation of this study by explaining how machine learning enables firms to build scalable personalization capabilities that continuously evolve in dynamic ecommerce environments.

Information Boundary Theory

Although machine learning enables increasingly sophisticated personalization, its effectiveness depends on consumers' willingness to share personal information. Information Boundary Theory, also known as Communication Privacy Management Theory, was developed by Petronio (2002) to explain how individuals establish, negotiate, and regulate the boundaries surrounding their personal information.

The theory proposes that individuals actively determine which information they disclose, to whom it is disclosed, and under what circumstances. These decisions depend upon perceived benefits, perceived risks, prior experiences, contextual factors, and individual privacy orientations. Consequently, consumers differ substantially in the permeability of their privacy boundaries.

This theoretical perspective is particularly relevant in machine learning driven personalization because recommendation systems, predictive analytics, behavioural targeting, and real time adaptive personalization require continuous collection and processing of personal data. Although consumers often appreciate highly relevant recommendations, they may simultaneously perceive behavioural tracking, algorithmic profiling, and predictive modelling as intrusive. This phenomenon has become increasingly important with the emergence of Generative AI and large language models that process large volumes of behavioural and conversational data.

Information Boundary Theory explains why identical personalization strategies may produce different customer responses. Consumers who perceive transparency, fairness, explainability, and adequate control over their personal information are more likely to permit greater information disclosure and accept personalised services. Conversely, consumers who perceive excessive surveillance, algorithmic opacity, or weak privacy protection are more likely to restrict information disclosure and resist personalization.

The theory therefore provides an important behavioural explanation for the personalization privacy paradox. Rather than viewing privacy solely as a trade-off between risks and benefits, Information Boundary Theory emphasises that privacy boundaries are continuously negotiated and influenced by organisational actions, including transparency, consent mechanisms, explainable AI, and ethical data governance.

Within the proposed conceptual framework, Information Boundary Theory explains why organisational enablers such as ethical AI, customer trust, transparency, privacy protection, and data governance strengthen the effectiveness of machine learning driven personalization.

The integration of Dynamic Capabilities Theory and Information Boundary Theory represents the primary theoretical contribution of this chapter. Individually, each theory explains only part of the personalization process. Dynamic Capabilities Theory explains how organisations develop and continuously improve machine learning capabilities, whereas Information Boundary Theory explains how customers evaluate and respond to personalised services through privacy boundary regulation. Together, these theories explain that successful personalization depends upon the simultaneous development of organisational capabilities and consumer trust. Machine learning algorithms alone cannot generate sustainable competitive advantage unless customers are willing to disclose accurate information. Likewise, transparent privacy policies and ethical governance create limited value unless organisations possess the technological capabilities required to transform customer data into meaningful personalised experiences. Accordingly, the proposed conceptual framework positions machine learning techniques as the technological drivers of personalization, personalization at scale and hyper-relevant customer interactions as the central organisational outcome, and organisational enablers including ethical AI, transparency, privacy management, customer trust, data quality, and system integration as the conditions that strengthen this relationship. The integration of these two theories therefore provides a holistic explanation of how organisations can develop scalable, responsible, and customer centric personalization strategies in contemporary ecommerce environments.

3. LITERATURE REVIEW

Personalization has become a defining characteristic of contemporary ecommerce, enabling firms to deliver tailored experiences that improve customer satisfaction, engagement, and long-term loyalty. Early personalization strategies primarily relied on demographic segmentation and rule-based recommendation systems that offered limited adaptability to changing customer preferences. The rapid growth of digital commerce, combined with advances in artificial intelligence and machine learning, has fundamentally transformed personalization into a dynamic, data-driven process capable of delivering highly relevant customer experiences across multiple digital touchpoints (Ledro et al., 2022; Grewal et al., (2017).

Existing research consistently demonstrates that personalization generates substantial benefits for both customers and organisations. From the customer perspective, personalised recommendations reduce information overload, simplify decision-making, and improve shopping convenience by presenting products that closely align with individual preferences and purchasing intentions (Ricci et al., 2015). For organisations, personalization improves customer acquisition, conversion rates, customer lifetime value, and retention while strengthening competitive advantage in increasingly saturated digital markets (Jaakkola & Terho, 2021).

The literature identifies customer data as the foundation of effective personalization. Contemporary ecommerce platforms collect behavioural, transactional, contextual, demographic, and interactional data that enable firms to develop detailed customer profiles and predict future purchasing behaviour (Köhn et al., 2020). Machine learning algorithms continuously analyse these data streams to generate recommendations, personalise content, optimise pricing, and automate customer interactions in real time. Unlike traditional personalization approaches, machine learning enables continuous learning from customer behaviour, allowing personalization strategies to evolve dynamically as customer preferences change (Köhn et al., 2020).

Researchers have proposed several approaches to ecommerce personalization. Recommendation systems remain the most widely studied application, employing collaborative filtering, content-based filtering, and hybrid algorithms to predict customer preferences (Bobadilla et al., 2013; Ricci et al., 2015). More recent studies have expanded personalization beyond product recommendations by incorporating behavioural prediction, sentiment analysis, dynamic content delivery, visual search, conversational interfaces, and predictive customer relationship management (Jannach et al., 2021; Dwivedi et al., 2023). These developments indicate that personalization has evolved into an integrated organisational capability rather than an isolated marketing function.

Recent advances in Generative AI have further expanded the scope of personalization. Large Language Models now enable conversational commerce, intelligent shopping assistants, AI-generated product descriptions, personalised marketing messages, and real-time customer support. Similarly, Explainable AI has emerged as an important mechanism for improving transparency by helping customers understand why particular recommendations are generated (Holzinger et al., 2023) These developments not only enhance personalization quality but also strengthen customer trust by reducing perceptions of algorithmic opacity and unfairnessAs a result, personalization is increasingly viewed as a combination of predictive intelligence, generative intelligence, and responsible AI governance. (Dwivedi et al., 2023; Davenport et al., 2020).

Despite these advances, the literature also highlights several challenges that limit the effectiveness of personalization. Heavy reliance on personal data raises concerns regarding privacy, algorithmic bias, transparency, fairness, and regulatory compliance. Excessive personalization may also create perceptions of surveillance, manipulation, and intrusiveness, reducing customer trust and increasing resistance to data sharing (Awad & Krishnan, 2006; Li 2012). Furthermore, many organisations continue to experience practical implementation barriers, including fragmented information systems, poor data quality, limited analytical expertise, and high implementation costs, particularly among small and medium-sized enterprises.

Although personalization has received considerable scholarly attention, existing research remains fragmented in several respects. First, many studies investigate individual personalization techniques, such as recommendation systems, customer segmentation, or purchase prediction, without considering how these technologies collectively contribute to scalable personalization. Second, the literature generally emphasises algorithmic performance while giving comparatively limited attention to organisational capabilities, ethical governance, and customer trust that determine successful implementation. Third, recent developments in Generative AI, Explainable AI, and adaptive personalization have not yet been fully integrated into existing conceptual models. Consequently, there remains limited understanding of how technological capabilities, organisational enablers, and consumer privacy considerations jointly influence personalization outcomes.

To address these limitations, this chapter conceptualises personalization as a multidimensional organisational capability supported by machine learning technologies and strengthened by organisational enablers, including ethical AI, data quality, system integration, customer trust, and transparency. Rather than examining isolated technologies, the proposed framework explains how machine learning capabilities collectively facilitate personalization at scale and create hyper-relevant customer interactions within increasingly complex digital commerce environments. This integrated perspective provides a stronger theoretical foundation for understanding personalization as a strategic organisational capability rather than simply a technological application.

4. CONCEPTUAL FRAMEWORK

The increasing adoption of machine learning has transformed personalization from a rule-based marketing practice into a dynamic organisational capability that enables firms to deliver highly relevant customer experiences at scale. Despite rapid technological advances, existing research remains fragmented. Most studies focus on individual machine learning techniques, recommendation systems, customer analytics, or privacy concerns independently, providing limited understanding of how these elements collectively contribute to scalable personalization. Furthermore, relatively few conceptual studies integrate technological capabilities, organisational readiness, and consumer privacy considerations within a unified theoretical framework. To address this limitation, this chapter proposes a comprehensive conceptual framework that explains how machine learning capabilities enable personalization at scale, leading to hyper-relevant customer interactions while being supported by critical organisational enablers. The framework is grounded in Dynamic Capabilities Theory (Teece et al.,, 1997) and Information Boundary Theory (Petronio, 2002). Dynamic Capabilities Theory explains how organisations continuously sense customer needs, seize personalization opportunities, and transform organisational resources to sustain competitive advantage in dynamic digital markets (Teece et al., 1997; Davenport et al., 2020). Information Boundary Theory complements this perspective by explaining how customers regulate information disclosure according to perceived benefits, privacy risks, transparency, and trust. Together, these theories provide a holistic explanation of both organisational capability development and consumer acceptance of AI-driven personalization.

The framework was developed through an extensive synthesis of literature on ecommerce personalization, artificial intelligence, machine learning, customer experience, digital marketing, and privacy management. Rather than viewing personalization as a single technological application, the framework conceptualises personalization as an organisational process supported by interconnected technological, behavioural, and managerial capabilities. The literature consistently identifies machine learning as the primary technological driver of personalization. However, successful implementation depends upon several organisational conditions, including ethical governance, data quality, technological infrastructure, organisational readiness, customer trust, and transparency. At the same time, customer acceptance depends on perceptions of privacy protection and organisational integrity. Accordingly, the framework integrates these complementary perspectives into a coherent explanation of how machine learning creates business value through personalization.

The framework consists of four principal constructs:

- Machine Learning Capabilities
- Personalization at Scale
- Hyper-Relevant Customer Interactions
- Organisational Enablers

These constructs collectively explain the transformation of technological capabilities into customer value.

Machine Learning Capabilities

Machine learning capabilities represent the technological foundation of the proposed framework. These capabilities enable organisations to collect, analyse, and interpret large volumes of customer data for generating predictive insights and adaptive personalization strategies. Unlike traditional analytical systems, machine learning continuously improves its predictive performance through iterative learning, allowing organisations to respond dynamically to evolving customer preferences and market conditions (Davenport et al., 2020; Ledro et al., 2022).

The framework conceptualises machine learning capabilities as a multidimensional construct comprising recommendation systems, customer purchase prediction, personalised content delivery, sentiment analysis (Cao et al. (2023), fake review detection, sales forecasting, product classification, computer vision, conversational artificial intelligence, and Generative AI applications (Ricci et al., 2015; Jannach et al., 2021; Dwivedi et al., 2023).

Machine learning algorithms further support customer purchase prediction by analysing behavioural, transactional, and contextual data to identify purchase intentions and future buying patterns with greater accuracy than traditional analytical approaches (Ma et al., 2022; Köhn et al., 2020).

These capabilities collectively enhance organisational sensing capabilities by continuously identifying behavioural patterns, customer preferences, contextual information, and emerging market opportunities. According to Dynamic Capabilities Theory, organisations possessing superior sensing capabilities are better positioned to identify customer needs and develop competitive personalization strategies (Teece et al.,, 1997; Davenport et al.,, 2020).

Accordingly, machine learning capabilities constitute the primary technological resource from which personalization capabilities emerge.

Personalization at Scale

Personalization at scale represents the central mechanism through which machine learning capabilities create customer value. Unlike conventional personalization, scalable personalization enables organisations to deliver consistent, adaptive, and highly relevant experiences simultaneously across millions of customers and multiple digital channels (Ledro et al., 2022).

This construct encompasses several interconnected organisational activities, including dynamic recommendation systems, adaptive content delivery, predictive customer engagement, omnichannel personalization, conversational commerce, and real-time decision support.

Machine learning transforms customer data into continuously evolving customer profiles, enabling organisations to personalise products, services, promotions, search results, and customer communications according to individual behavioural patterns (Lessmann et al., 2021).

Dynamic Capabilities Theory explains that organisations possessing advanced analytical capabilities are better able to seize customer opportunities through adaptive personalization strategies and continuously transform organisational processes in response to changing market conditions (Teece et al., 1997).

Thus, personalization at scale functions as the organisational capability that converts technological intelligence into meaningful customer experiences.

Hyper-Relevant Customer Interactions

Hyper-relevant customer interactions constitute the principal outcome of scalable personalization. These interactions occur when organisations anticipate customer needs and deliver contextually appropriate recommendations, products, content, promotions, and services throughout the customer journey.

Unlike traditional customer engagement approaches, hyper-relevant customer interactions are characterised by contextual awareness, predictive intelligence, continuous adaptation, and personalised communication. Such interactions improve customer satisfaction, perceived relevance, emotional engagement, purchase intention, customer retention, loyalty, and customer lifetime value (Jaakkola & Terho, 2021; Ledro et al., 2022).

However, the framework also recognises that hyper-relevant interactions may generate negative behavioural responses when personalization becomes excessively intrusive. Personalization fatigue, algorithmic bias, decision fatigue, privacy concerns, and perceptions of surveillance may reduce customer acceptance despite technological sophistication (Awad & Krishnan, 2006; Li, 2012; Holzinger et al., 2023).

Information Boundary Theory explains these behavioural differences by suggesting that customers continuously evaluate the benefits and risks associated with information disclosure before accepting personalised services (Petronio, 2002; Li, 2012). Consequently, successful hyper-relevant customer interactions require both technological precision and responsible organisational governance.

Organisational Enablers

The framework recognises that machine learning capabilities alone cannot guarantee successful personalization. Organisational enablers represent complementary capabilities that facilitate the effective implementation of machine learning-driven personalization (Ledro et al., 2022).

The proposed framework identifies seven major organisational enablers:

- Ethical Artificial Intelligence
- Explainable Artificial Intelligence
- Data Quality
- Integrated Digital Infrastructure
- Data Privacy and Security
- Organisational Readiness
- Customer Trust and Transparency

These enablers influence both technological implementation and customer acceptance.

Ethical AI ensures fairness, accountability, and responsible algorithmic decision-making. Explainable AI improves transparency by enabling customers and managers to understand how algorithmic recommendations are generated, thereby strengthening customer confidence and organisational accountability (Holzinger et al., 2023; Dwivedi et al., 2023).

High-quality data improve predictive accuracy, whereas integrated digital infrastructure enables consistent personalization across multiple customer touchpoints.

Organisational readiness facilitates successful implementation through skilled employees, leadership support, and digital transformation capabilities (Davenport et al., 2020).

Customer trust and transparent communication encourage consumers to disclose information required for effective personalization while reducing privacy concerns and perceived risks associated with AI-driven services (Cowan et al., 2021; Li, 2012).

Together, these organisational capabilities strengthen the effectiveness of personalization while reducing implementation risks.

Relationships Among the Constructs

Machine Learning Capabilities and Personalization at Scale

Machine learning capabilities positively influence personalization at scale by enabling organisations to analyse large volumes of behavioural, transactional, and contextual data and continuously generate adaptive recommendations. Advanced analytical capabilities improve customer understanding, automate decision-making, and enhance the organisation's ability to personalise customer experiences across multiple digital channels (Lessmann et al., 2021). This relationship is supported by Dynamic Capabilities Theory, which suggests that organisations possessing superior sensing capabilities develop stronger adaptive capabilities within dynamic environments (Teece et al., 1997).

Personalization at Scale and Hyper-Relevant Customer Interactions

Scalable personalization enables organisations to deliver timely, relevant, and context-aware customer experiences that strengthen customer engagement, satisfaction, loyalty, and long-term relationships (Jaakkola & Terho, 2021). Machine learning enables organisations to anticipate customer needs before they are explicitly expressed, thereby transforming reactive customer service into proactive customer engagement (Ledro et al., 2022). However, this relationship depends on customers perceiving personalization as valuable rather than intrusive (Awad & Krishnan, 2006; Li, 2012).

Organisational Enablers Strengthen the Relationship

The framework proposes that organisational enablers strengthen the relationship between machine learning capabilities, personalization at scale, and hyper-relevant customer interactions. Organisations possessing strong ethical governance, transparent AI systems, high-quality data, integrated technological infrastructure, organisational readiness, and effective privacy management are better positioned to transform machine learning capabilities into sustainable customer value (Holzinger et al., 2023; Davenport et al., 2020). Conversely, inadequate governance, poor data quality, fragmented information systems, limited organisational capabilities, and weak privacy protection reduce personalization effectiveness despite advanced technological investments (Ledro et al., 2022). Information Boundary Theory further explains that transparency and customer trust increase customers' willingness to disclose personal information, thereby improving the quality of personalization outcomes (Petronio, 2002; Cowan et al., 2021).

Figure 1. Proposed Conceptual Framework

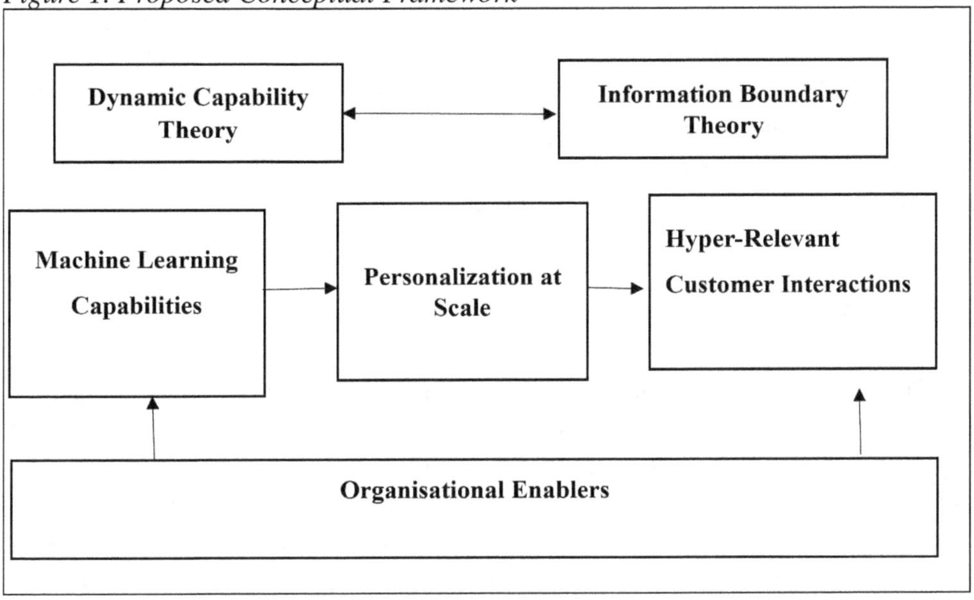

Source: Authors Own Work

Theoretical Contribution of the Framework

The proposed framework makes several theoretical contributions.

First, it integrates fragmented streams of literature on machine learning, ecommerce personalization, customer experience, and privacy management into a unified conceptual model. Previous studies have largely examined recommendation systems, predictive analytics, privacy concerns, or organisational capabilities independently. This framework demonstrates how these elements collectively interact to produce scalable personalization.

Second, the framework extends Dynamic Capabilities Theory by conceptualising machine learning as a strategic organisational capability that enables firms to continuously sense customer preferences, seize personalization opportunities, and transform organisational processes within rapidly evolving digital environments.

Third, the framework extends Information Boundary Theory by explaining how privacy boundaries, transparency, customer trust, and responsible AI governance influence the effectiveness of Machine learning driven personalization. Rather than treating privacy as a constraint, the framework positions responsible data governance as an organisational capability that strengthens personalization outcomes.

Finally, the framework provides an integrated socio-technical perspective by recognising that successful personalization depends not only on technological sophistication but also on organisational readiness, ethical governance, and customer acceptance. This holistic perspective advances current understanding of scalable personalization and provides a robust foundation for future empirical research examining the complex relationships among artificial intelligence, organisational capabilities, and customer engagement in digital commerce.

5. DISCUSSION

The present chapter contributes to the growing literature on artificial intelligence-enabled personalization by proposing an integrated conceptual framework that explains how machine learning capabilities facilitate personalization at scale and ultimately generate hyper-relevant customer interactions. Unlike previous studies that primarily examine isolated machine learning techniques or individual personalization applications, the proposed framework conceptualises personalization as a socio-technical capability that emerges through the interaction of technological resources, organisational capabilities, and consumer responses. This integrated perspective extends current understanding by demonstrating that successful personalization depends not solely on sophisticated algorithms but also on organisational readiness, ethical governance, data governance, and customer trust (Ledro et al., 2022; Davenport et al., 2020).

A key contribution of this framework is the integration of Dynamic Capabilities Theory with Information Boundary Theory. Existing research has largely employed Dynamic Capabilities Theory to explain organisational adaptation and competitive advantage in digital transformation (Teece et al., 1997), while Information Boundary Theory has primarily been used to explain information disclosure and privacy management in online environments (Petronio, 2002; Li, 2012). However, these theories have rarely been integrated within the context of AI-driven personalization. The proposed framework demonstrates that these perspectives are complementary rather than competing. Dynamic Capabilities Theory explains how organisations continuously sense customer needs, seize personalization opportunities, and transform organisational resources through machine learning, whereas Information Boundary Theory explains why customer acceptance depends on transparency, privacy protection, and responsible information management (Petronio, 2002; Li, 2012). Consequently, personalization should be understood as both an organisational capability and a customer-centred process.

The framework also advances the conceptualisation of machine learning within digital commerce. Much of the existing literature portrays machine learning primarily as a technological tool for improving recommendation accuracy or predicting purchasing behaviour (Ricci et al., 2015; Köhn et al., 2020). While these applications remain important, this chapter argues that machine learning should instead be viewed as a strategic organisational capability that supports continuous learning, adaptive decision-making, and long-term competitive advantage (Davenport et al., 2020). This perspective aligns with recent developments in artificial intelligence, where predictive models increasingly operate as core organisational assets rather than isolated analytical applications.

Another important contribution concerns the conceptualisation of personalization at scale. Previous studies have often associated scalability with the ability to process larger datasets or improve algorithmic efficiency. The proposed framework suggests that scalability extends beyond computational performance. Personalization at scale requires organisations to integrate customer data, digital infrastructure, organisational capabilities, and ethical governance into a coordinated system capable of delivering consistent experiences across multiple customer touchpoints. This broader conceptualisation reflects the reality that successful personalization depends on organisational coordination as much as technological sophistication.

The chapter further highlights the growing importance of Generative AI in reshaping personalization strategies. Traditional machine learning applications primarily focused on predicting customer preferences and recommending products. Recent advances in large language models and conversational artificial intelligence have significantly expanded these capabilities by enabling organisations to generate personalised content, provide intelligent customer assistance, automate customer communication, and create interactive shopping experiences in real time (Dwivedi et al., 2023; Jannach et al., 2021). Consequently, personalization is evolving from predictive recommendation towards adaptive customer engagement. Future personalization strategies are therefore likely to combine predictive analytics with generative intelligence, creating richer, more contextual, and highly personalised customer experiences.

The discussion also emphasises that technological sophistication alone does not guarantee successful personalization outcomes. Organisations continue to face substantial implementation challenges, including fragmented information systems, poor data quality, limited analytical expertise, organisational resistance to change, and increasing regulatory requirements. These findings reinforce previous research suggesting that digital transformation depends as much on organisational capabilities as on technological innovation (Davenport et al., 2020; Ledro et al., 2022). Investments in artificial intelligence therefore need to be accompanied by investments in organisational learning, employee capability development, integrated digital infrastructure, and cross-functional collaboration.

Customer trust emerges as another central theme within the proposed framework. Although consumers increasingly expect personalised experiences, they also demonstrate heightened awareness of privacy risks associated with behavioural tracking and algorithmic profiling. This tension reflects the personalization-privacy paradox identified in previous studies (Awad & Krishnan, 2006; Li, 2012). The framework suggests that transparency, explainability, ethical governance, and effective privacy management reduce perceived risks while encouraging greater customer participation in personalised services (Cowan et al., 2021). Rather than viewing privacy regulations as barriers to innovation, organisations should recognise responsible data governance as a strategic capability that strengthens long-term customer relationships and enhances the sustainability of personalization initiatives.

The proposed framework also contributes to the emerging discussion on Explainable AI as recommendation systems become increasingly complex through deep learning and transformer-based architectures, the transparency of algorithmic decision-making becomes increasingly important. Explainable AI enables organisations to provide understandable explanations for personalised recommendations, thereby increasing customer confidence, reducing perceptions of algorithmic bias, supporting regulatory compliance, and strengthening organisational accountability (Holzinger et al., 2023; Dwivedi et al., 2023). Integrating explainability into personalization strategies therefore represents an important step towards responsible artificial intelligence adoption.

From a managerial perspective, the framework suggests that organisations should avoid viewing personalization as an isolated marketing initiative. Instead, personalization should be embedded within broader digital transformation strategies that integrate technology, customer experience, organisational learning, and ethical governance (Ledro et al., 2022; Davenport et al., 2020). Managers should recognise that sustainable competitive advantage depends on continuously improving machine learning capabilities while simultaneously strengthening organisational enablers such as data governance, digital infrastructure, employee competencies, transparency, and customer trust.

Finally, the chapter identifies several opportunities for future research. Although the proposed framework provides a comprehensive conceptual explanation, empirical validation remains necessary. Future studies may examine the proposed relationships using structural equation modelling, longitudinal research designs, or experimental methods. Comparative investigations across industries, countries, and organisational contexts would improve understanding of how institutional environments influence personalization effectiveness. Future research should also examine the growing role of Generative AI, Explainable AI, multimodal artificial intelligence, and human-AI collaboration in shaping the next generation of personalised customer experiences (Dwivedi et al.,, 2023; Holzinger et al.,, 2023). Furthermore, investigating potential boundary conditions, including technology readiness, consumer privacy orientation, digital literacy, cultural differences, and organisational AI maturity, would extend the theoretical scope of the proposed framework and contribute to the responsible development of AI-enabled personalization in digital commerce.

6. CONCLUSION

The rapid evolution of artificial intelligence and machine learning has fundamentally transformed personalization from a conventional marketing practice into a strategic organisational capability that enables firms to deliver highly relevant, adaptive, and customer-centric experiences across digital commerce platforms. This chapter has demonstrated that achieving personalization at scale requires considerably more than sophisticated algorithms. It demands the integration of advanced machine learning capabilities with organisational readiness, ethical governance, customer trust, and effective data management to create sustainable value for both organisations and consumers.

Theoretical Implications

This chapter makes several important theoretical contributions to the literature on ecommerce personalization, artificial intelligence, and digital customer engagement. First, it advances existing knowledge by developing an integrated conceptual framework that synthesises fragmented research on machine learning, personalization at scale, organisational capabilities, and customer privacy. Previous studies have largely examined these domains independently, focusing either on algorithmic development, recommendation systems, customer analytics, or privacy concerns. By integrating these streams, the proposed framework provides a more comprehensive explanation of how machine learning creates value through scalable and customer-centric personalization.

Second, the chapter extends Dynamic Capabilities Theory by positioning machine learning as a strategic organisational capability rather than merely a technological resource. While Dynamic Capabilities Theory has traditionally been applied to explain organisational adaptation and competitive advantage, this chapter demonstrates how machine learning enables organisations to continuously sense customer preferences, seize personalization opportunities, and transform organisational processes in rapidly evolving digital environments. This perspective broadens the application of the theory within digital commerce and artificial intelligence research.

Third, the chapter contributes to Information Boundary Theory by extending its application to AI-enabled personalization. Existing applications of the theory have primarily focused on information disclosure and privacy management in online environments. This chapter demonstrates that Information Boundary Theory also provides an effective explanation for customers' responses to Machine learning driven personalization by highlighting the roles of transparency, explainability, trust, and ethical data governance in shaping customer acceptance.

Another important theoretical contribution lies in conceptualising personalization at scale as an organisational capability rather than a purely technological outcome. The framework proposes that scalable personalization emerges through the interaction of machine learning capabilities, organisational resources, and customer-centred governance mechanisms. This perspective shifts the focus of personalization research from algorithmic efficiency to organisational capability development and strategic value creation.

The chapter also contributes to the emerging literature on Generative AI and Explainable AI within digital commerce. While current research predominantly examines predictive machine learning applications, the framework incorporates recent advances in conversational AI, personalised content generation, and algorithmic transparency. By integrating these emerging technologies, the chapter provides a contemporary theoretical perspective that reflects the evolving nature of AI-enabled customer engagement.

Finally, the proposed framework establishes a foundation for future empirical research. The relationships among machine learning capabilities, personalization at scale, organisational enablers, and hyper-relevant customer interactions can be operationalised and empirically validated across different industries, organisational contexts, and cultural settings. This provides researchers with a robust theoretical model for advancing future studies on artificial intelligence, customer experience, and digital transformation.

Practical Implications

The proposed framework offers several practical implications for managers, digital marketers, technology leaders, and policymakers seeking to leverage machine learning for scalable personalization.

First, organisations should recognise that personalization is no longer a standalone marketing initiative but a strategic organisational capability that requires cross-functional integration. Managers should align marketing, information technology, analytics, customer relationship management, and operations to develop cohesive personalization strategies that deliver consistent customer experiences across multiple digital channels.

Second, firms should invest in robust data infrastructure and integrated customer data platforms. High-quality personalization depends on accurate, timely, and comprehensive customer information. Organisations should prioritise data quality management, system integration, cloud computing infrastructure, and real-time analytics to enable continuous learning and adaptive personalization. Investments in data governance should be viewed as strategic assets rather than operational costs.

Third, managers should strengthen organisational capabilities alongside technological investments. Implementing machine learning successfully requires skilled employees, leadership commitment, organisational learning, and effective change management. Continuous employee training in artificial intelligence, data analytics, ethical AI, and customer experience management is essential to maximise the value of personalization initiatives.

Fourth, organisations should adopt ethical AI governance as a core strategic priority. Managers should establish policies that promote fairness, accountability, transparency, and responsible data usage. Regular algorithm audits, bias detection, and compliance with privacy regulations should become standard organisational practices. These initiatives not only reduce regulatory risks but also enhance organisational credibility and customer confidence.

Fifth, the framework highlights the strategic importance of Explainable AI. Organisations should provide customers with understandable explanations for personalised recommendations, pricing decisions, and promotional offers. Transparent communication regarding data collection and algorithmic decision-making can reduce customer uncertainty, strengthen trust, and improve acceptance of AI-driven personalization.

Sixth, managers should carefully balance personalization with customer privacy. Excessive personalization may increase perceptions of surveillance, intrusiveness, and manipulation, potentially leading to personalization fatigue and reduced customer engagement. Providing customers with meaningful control over their data, privacy preferences, and personalization settings can strengthen long-term customer relationships while supporting regulatory compliance.

The framework also provides valuable guidance for small and medium-sized enterprises (SMEs). Although many SMEs face financial and technical resource constraints, cloud-based AI platforms, AI-as-a-Service solutions, and open-source machine learning tools provide cost-effective opportunities to implement advanced personalization capabilities. Rather than replicating the sophisticated systems of large multinational firms, SMEs should focus on targeted personalization strategies that align with their organisational capabilities and customer needs.

Finally, the chapter has implications for policymakers and regulators responsible for governing artificial intelligence in digital markets. The framework emphasises the importance of developing regulatory environments that encourage technological innovation while protecting consumer rights. Policies promoting transparency, accountability, ethical AI, and responsible data governance can foster greater public trust in AI-enabled personalization and support the sustainable development of digital commerce ecosystems.

Collectively, these implications demonstrate that successful Machine learning driven personalization requires a balanced approach that integrates technological innovation, organisational capability development, ethical governance, and customer trust. Organisations that effectively combine these elements will be better positioned to deliver scalable, responsible, and competitive personalization strategies in increasingly data-driven digital markets.

Limitations and Future Research Directions

This chapter provides a comprehensive conceptual framework explaining how machine learning capabilities enable personalization at scale and facilitate hyper-relevant customer interactions in ecommerce. While the framework integrates diverse streams of literature and offers important theoretical and managerial insights, several limitations should be acknowledged.

First, the chapter is conceptual in nature and does not empirically validate the proposed relationships among machine learning capabilities, personalization at scale, organisational enablers, and hyper-relevant customer interactions. The proposed framework is grounded in established theories and existing literature; however, its applicability across different organisational settings remains to be empirically examined. Future studies should operationalise the proposed constructs and test the framework using quantitative techniques such as structural equation modelling, partial least squares structural equation modelling, or covariance-based structural equation modelling. Such empirical investigations would provide evidence regarding the strength and significance of the proposed relationships.

Second, the framework has been developed primarily within the context of ecommerce. Although many of the proposed concepts may be relevant to other digital service industries, differences in customer behaviour, organisational processes, and regulatory environments may influence the effectiveness of Machine learning driven personalization. Future research should examine the applicability of the framework across industries such as banking, healthcare, tourism, education, retail, and digital entertainment to determine its generalisability.

Third, the framework presents a broad organisational perspective and does not explicitly consider differences between large organisations and small and medium-sized enterprises (SMEs). Resource availability, technological maturity, organisational capabilities, and implementation challenges differ substantially across firms of different sizes. Comparative studies investigating how SMEs and large organisations adopt and scale Machine learning driven personalization would provide valuable insights into context-specific implementation strategies.

Fourth, although the framework incorporates customer trust, privacy, and transparency through Information Boundary Theory, it does not explicitly examine the influence of individual consumer characteristics. Variables such as technology readiness, digital literacy, privacy orientation, perceived intrusiveness, trust propensity, age, cultural values, and prior experience with artificial intelligence may influence customer responses to personalized services. Future studies should investigate these variables as potential mediators or moderators to enhance understanding of consumer behaviour in AI-enabled personalization environments.

Fifth, artificial intelligence technologies continue to evolve rapidly. While this chapter incorporates emerging developments such as Generative AI and Explainable AI, future technological innovations, including autonomous AI agents, multimodal artificial intelligence, federated learning, edge AI, digital twins, and quantum machine learning, may significantly reshape personalization strategies. Continuous theoretical refinement will therefore be necessary to ensure that conceptual frameworks remain relevant within rapidly changing digital ecosystems.

Sixth, the present framework focuses primarily on positive organisational outcomes associated with personalization. Future research should examine potential unintended consequences, including algorithmic bias, personalization fatigue, filter bubbles, consumer manipulation, excessive behavioural surveillance, and ethical dilemmas arising from increasingly autonomous AI systems. Investigating these issues would contribute to the development of more balanced and responsible personalization strategies.

Future research should also adopt diverse methodological approaches to extend the proposed framework. Longitudinal studies could examine how machine learning capabilities and personalization strategies evolve over time as organisations progress through different stages of digital transformation. Experimental research could investigate customer reactions to varying levels of personalization, transparency, and explainability under different decision-making contexts. Qualitative studies involving managers, AI developers, and consumers could provide deeper insights into implementation challenges, organisational readiness, and ethical decision-making processes. Mixed-methods research would further enrich understanding by combining behavioural evidence with organisational perspectives.

Cross-cultural and cross-country comparative studies also represent an important avenue for future investigation. Consumer expectations regarding personalization, privacy, and artificial intelligence differ across institutional, legal, and cultural environments. Examining the proposed framework across developed and emerging economies would enhance understanding of how regulatory systems, cultural values, and digital maturity influence the effectiveness of Machine learning driven personalization.

Finally, future research should investigate the role of Explainable AI, responsible AI governance, and human-AI collaboration in strengthening customer trust and organisational performance. As organisations increasingly deploy conversational AI, intelligent virtual assistants, and Generative AI-based recommendation systems, understanding how transparency, accountability, and human oversight influence customer acceptance will become increasingly important. Such research will contribute to the development of ethical, trustworthy, and sustainable AI-enabled personalization strategies.

Despite these limitations, the proposed framework provides a robust foundation for future theoretical and empirical research. By integrating machine learning capabilities, organisational enablers, personalization at scale, and customer privacy considerations within a unified conceptual model, this chapter offers a comprehensive agenda for advancing research on AI-enabled personalization and digital customer engagement in increasingly intelligent and data-driven business environments.

REFERENCES

Awad, N. F., & Krishnan, M. S. (2006). The personalization privacy paradox: An empirical evaluation of information transparency and the willingness to be profiled online for personalization. *Management Information Systems Quarterly*, *30*(1), 13–28. DOI: 10.2307/25148715

Bilgihan, A., Kandampully, J., & Zhang, T. (2016). Towards a unified customer experience in online shopping environments: Antecedents and outcomes. *International Journal of Quality and Service Sciences*, *8*(1), 102–119. DOI: 10.1108/IJQSS-07-2015-0054

Bobadilla, J., Ortega, F., Hernando, A., & Gutiérrez, A. (2013). Recommender systems survey. *Knowledge-Based Systems*, *46*, 109–132. DOI: 10.1016/j.knosys.2013.03.012

Cao, J., Li, J., Yin, M., & Wang, Y. (2023). Online reviews sentiment analysis and product feature improvement with deep learning. *Transactions of the Association for Computational Linguistics*, *11*, 1–17.

Cowan, K., Javornik, A., & Jiang, P. (2021). Privacy concerns when using augmented reality face filters? Explaining why and when use avoidance occurs. *Psychology and Marketing*, *38*(10), 1799–1813. DOI: 10.1002/mar.21576

Daugherty, P., & Wilson, H. J. (2022). *Radically human: How new technology is transforming business and shaping our future*. Harvard Business Press.

Davenport, T. H., Guha, A., Grewal, D., & Bressgott, T. (2020). How artificial intelligence will change the future of marketing. *Journal of the Academy of Marketing Science*, *48*(1), 24–42. DOI: 10.1007/s11747-019-00696-0

Dwivedi, Y. K., Kshetri, N., Hughes, L., Slade, E. L., Jeyaraj, A., Kar, A. K., Baabdullah, A. M., Koohang, A., Raghavan, V., Ahuja, M., Albanna, H., Albashrawi, M. A., Al-Busaidi, A. S., Balakrishnan, J., Barlette, Y., Basu, S., Bose, I., Brooks, L., Buhalis, D., & Wright, R. (2023). So what if ChatGPT wrote it? Multidisciplinary perspectives on opportunities, challenges and implications of generative conversational AI for research, practice and policy. *International Journal of Information Management*, *71*, 102642. DOI: 10.1016/j.ijinfomgt.2023.102642

Grewal, D., Roggeveen, A. L., & Nordfält, J. (2017). The future of retailing. *Journal of Retailing*, *93*(1), 1–6. DOI: 10.1016/j.jretai.2016.12.008

Holzinger, A., Keiblinger, K., Holub, P., Zatloukal, K., & Müller, H. (2023). AI for life: Trends in artificial intelligence for biotechnology. *New Biotechnology*, *74*, 16–24. DOI: 10.1016/j.nbt.2023.02.001 PMID: 36754147

Jaakkola, E., & Terho, H. (2021). Service journey quality: Conceptualization, measurement and customer outcomes. *Journal of Service Management, 32*(6), 955–978. DOI: 10.1108/JOSM-06-2020-0233

Jannach, D., Manzoor, A., Cai, W., & Chen, L. (2021). A survey on conversational recommender systems. *ACM Computing Surveys, 54*(5), 1–36. DOI: 10.1145/3453154

Köhn, D., Lessmann, S., & Schaal, M. (2020). Predicting online shopping behaviour from clickstream data using deep learning. *Expert Systems with Applications, 150*, 113342. DOI: 10.1016/j.eswa.2020.113342

Ledro, C., Nosella, A., & Vinelli, A. (2022). Artificial intelligence in customer relationship management: Literature review and future research directions. *Journal of Business and Industrial Marketing, 37*(13), 48–63. DOI: 10.1108/JBIM-07-2021-0332

Lessmann, S., Haupt, J., Coussement, K., & De Bock, K. W. (2021). Targeting customers for profit: An ensemble learning framework to support marketing decision-making. *Information Sciences, 557*, 286–301. DOI: 10.1016/j.ins.2019.05.027

Li, Y. (2012). Theories in online information privacy research: A critical review and an integrated framework. *Decision Support Systems, 54*(1), 471–481. DOI: 10.1016/j.dss.2012.06.010

Ma, J., Guo, X., & Zhao, X. (2022). Identifying purchase intention through deep learning. *Annals of Operations Research, 314*, 1–20.

McKinsey & Company. (2023). What is personalization? https://www.mckinsey.com/featured-insights/mckinsey-explainers/what-is-personalization

Petronio, S. (2002). *Boundaries of privacy: Dialectics of disclosure*. State University of New York Press. DOI: 10.1353/book4588

Riandhi, A. N., Arviansyah, M. R., & Sondari, M. C. (2025). AI and consumer behavior: Trends, technologies, and future directions from a scopus-based systematic review. *Cogent Business & Management, 12*(1), 2544984. DOI: 10.1080/23311975.2025.2544984

Ricci, F., Rokach, L., & Shapira, B. (Eds.). (2015). *Recommender systems handbook* (2nd ed.). Springer. DOI: 10.1007/978-1-4899-7637-6

Sharma, R., Srivastva, S., & Fatima, S. (2023). E-commerce and digital transformation: Trends, challenges, and implications. *International Journal of Multidisciplinary Research, 5*(5).

Teece, D. J., Pisano, G., & Shuen, A. (1997). Dynamic capabilities and strategic management. *Strategic Management Journal, 18*(7), 509–533. DOI: 10.1002/(SICI)1097-0266(199708)18:7<509::AID-SMJ882>3.0.CO;2-Z

Zhang, S., Yao, L., Sun, A., & Tay, Y. (2019). Deep learning based recommender system: A survey and new perspectives. *ACM Computing Surveys, 52*(1), 1–38. DOI: 10.1145/3158369

Chapter 8
AI-Driven Immersive Technologies for Sustainable Consumer Experience and Value Creation in Retail and Tourism

Pranati Dash
http://orcid.org/0000-0002-3303-8705
Balaji Institute of Modern Management, Sri Balaji University, Pune, India

Saileja Mohanty
Symbiosis School of Banking and Finance, Symbiosis International (Deemed to be) University, India

Abinash Jena
http://orcid.org/0000-0001-7292-813X
Balaji Institute of Modern Management, Sri Balaji University, Pune, India

ABSTRACT

Drawing on interdisciplinary theoretical foundations and multi-case analysis, the study conceptualizes immersive systems as multi-layered value creation architectures that connect technological enablement, experiential constructs, behavioural outcomes, organizational and sustainability performance. The findings identify diagnosticity, presence, and personalization as key experiential mechanisms influencing consumer decision-making, engagement, and conversion. This chapter

DOI: 10.4018/979-8-3373-8282-1.ch008

develops an integrated framework for understanding how AI-enabled immersive technologies contribute to sustainable consumer experience and value creation in retail and tourism contexts. It positions sustainability as embedded outcome of improved experiential efficiency, while highlighting the critical role of human-centered AI governance in ensuring trust, ethical alignment, and long-term adoption. By integrating experience, technology, and sustainability within a unified model, the chapter offers both theoretical advancement and practical insights for organizations navigating AI-driven digital transformation.

1. INTRODUCTION

In the evolving digital landscape, the integration of Artificial Intelligence (AI) with immersive technologies like Augmented Reality (AR), Virtual Reality (VR) and Mixed Reality (MR) is bringing about phenomenal changes in the marketing strategy used by various sectors. Intelligent algorithms, automation tools, and decision-making infrastructure based on big data are gaining prominence in various industries. Yet besides operational benefits, AI opens up an innovative approach to the organizational-consumer experiential interface. Specifically, with AI becoming integrated into experience-centred industries including retail and tourism, new interaction models emerge in the context of augmented reality, virtual reality, mixed reality, which together make the category of extended reality (XR) (Dwivedi et al., 2021; Flavián et al., 2021).

Two of the most experiential industries in the world today are retail and tourism. Value generation in retail has increasingly become more focused on providing personalized and interactive experiences for consumers rather than merely selling the products themselves. Tourism, on the other hand, has an inherently experiential nature that involves planning, experiencing, and reflecting on past experiences (Lemon & Verhoef, 2016; Mehmetoglu & Engen, 2011). The emergence of immersive technologies supported by AI-enabled analytics has significantly expanded the scopes through which these types of experiences can be designed and delivered.

On a technological front, immersive systems exist within the spectrum known as the reality-virtuality continuum, whereby AR technology places digital objects into the real world, VR technology constructs a completely simulated environment, and MR technology allows for real-time interactions between both digital and real objects. Such technologies promote certain mental conditions like presence, telepresence, and immersion, thereby increasing engagement levels and the level of absorption (Guttentag, 2010; Wedel et al., 2020). When used in combination with AI-based personalization engines, immersive technologies become adaptive in nature.

Moreover, market trends regarding the uptake of such immersive solutions emphasize the growing strategic importance of immersive AI ecosystems. For instance, according to industry analysis, the global AR/VR ecosystem is forecast to exceed billions of dollars in revenue in the current decade, primarily due to visualization services in the retail sector, virtual commerce, and simulated tourism experiences (Statista, 2024). Furthermore, following the digital acceleration post-COVID-19 pandemic, organizations have increasingly invested in immersive interfaces to ensure resilience, contactless operations, and scalability in engaging with their target audiences (Pantano et al., 2020)

In this respect, AI serves an indispensable function by virtue of its ability to provide insights into consumers. AI-driven machine learning algorithms analyze consumer behaviour, purchase history, biometric factors, and contextual information to create customized product recommendations. In immersive environments, all of these insights inform the consumer's experience from virtual product try-on, destination discovery, service simulation, and digital store navigation. These so-called phygital systems facilitate a transition between online and offline consumption, enhancing diagnostic accuracy, mitigating purchasing risk, and consumer emotions (Hilken et al., 2017; Javornik, 2016; Javornik et al., 2021).

Along with the experience revolution, sustainability is also serving as a pivotal strategic consideration. The retail industry continues to grapple with problems around issues like overproduction, reverse logistics and wasteful packaging. Whereas tourism sector is facing issues of over-tourism, carbon emissions and ecological degradation. For most of these problems, AI-driven immersive solutions present tools that may help address these concerns through better demand forecasting, fewer product returns, product virtualization and environmentally conscious decision-making (Buhalis et al., 2019) .

Moreover, for example, virtual try-on technologies in the fashion industry or eyewear sector help to decrease return rates by providing customers with information on fit and appearance before purchasing a product. AI-powered inventory management ensures reduced overproduction and excess stock of goods. As for tourism, immersive destination experiences allow visitors to experience their heritage surroundings virtually and plan sustainable visits, thus limiting overcrowding in fragile ecosystems. This indicates that immersive digitalization creates added value in two ways, i.e. improved experience and enhanced sustainability.

Although modern technology is rapidly evolving, academic discussions still remain dispersed. Research in this area usually considers AI analytics, the impacts of immersive media, customer engagement results, or sustainability initiatives separately (Dwivedi et al., 2021, 2023). There is still a lack of an integrative approach which may link technological infrastructure, experiential psychology, sustainability advantages and holistic business value creation within a unified conceptual framework which constraints theoretical progress and practical implication.

Further various apprehensions related to the ethical management of AI powered technologies are becoming more prominent as these are getting involved in consumer processes. The willingness of consumers to trust AI and consistently engage with digital environments may be affected due to concerns like data privacy, transparency in algorithms, biases and informed control over consents (Floridi et al., 2018).

This chapter considers the aforementioned points and intends to fill a few gaps by exploring the holistic perspective of the interrelationships between AI enabled immersive technologies and creation of sustainable consumer experience as well as value generation in the experience heavy retail and tourism sectors. It has taken insight from various streams of literatures, then reviews sector specific application and provide an integrative framework based on technological enablers, experiential constructs, mechanisms of sustainability, and organizational benefits.

Key objectives of this chapters are to:

- Explore the theoretical foundation of AI-driven immersive experience design in the retail and tourism industry.
- Discuss the application of immersive technologies in sustainable marketing and responsible consumption.
- Develop an integrated framework incorporating technology, human experience and value creation.
- Propose strategic ways to engage in responsible organization of such initiatives.

We hereby seek to explore the way organizations can align technology and experience in a sustainable manner using a human centric approach. The primary focus is to illustrate the strategic significance of AI driven innovations specifically in retails and tourism sectors so that meaningful, ethical and sustainable experience can be facilitated. The following sections build on the identified gaps and tries to develop a theoretical foundation supporting AI enabled immersive technologies, while integrating diverse perspectives from theories revolving around experience economy, AI ecosystem, immersive presence, and sustainable marketing.

This chapter is guided by the following research questions in alignment with the identified gaps and objectives:

i. How do AI-driven immersive technologies influence consumer experience in retail and tourism sector.
ii. In what ways AI enabled immersive systems contribute towards sustainable value creation across environmental, social and economic dimensions?

iii. Which dimensions of experiential value are created through immersive technology the most and what are the behavioural outcomes.
iv. How does human centred AI governance shape the adoption, trust and long term legitimacy of immersive technologies in consumer facing environment?

The subsequent parts including literature review, sectoral analysis and framework development etc. revolve around these questions and collectively define the scope of this chapter's contribution.

2. METHODOLOGY

This chapter adopts a qualitative, integrative research design structured as a systematic literature review (SLR) along with a multi-case analysis. The conceptual and theoretical foundation was built based on the SLR, while the multi case component of the study grounded the proposed framework with documented real world applications.

Systematic Literature Review components: The SLR was done using three primary data bases; Scopus, Web-of-Science and Google Scholar. Search keywords included the terms like "AI in retail", "immersive technology AND consumer experience", "augmented reality AND tourism", "virtual reality AND value creation", "sustainability AND digital experience", "AI governance AND transparency" and "extended reality AND marketing". Inclusion criteria applied were; a. publications from the past ten years, especially post covid studies to show digital acceleration; b. articles from peer reviewed journals; c. relevance to at least one of the thematic pillars, i.e., AI, immersive technology, sustainability and value creation in retail or tourism. This study employs an analytical method wherein patterns across the literature were identified, coded and used to construct the integrated conceptual framework proposed in section 7.

Case Selection and Screening: Some cases were selected using the following criteria;

- Documented use of AI, immersive technology
- Alignment with sustainability objectives
- Relevance to retail or tourism sectors
- Availability of publicly verifiable data
- Recency

This process ensured each case provided meaningful insights related to both technological impact and sustainable marketing outcomes.

3. LITERATURE REVIEW

In this section we try to establish the theoretical background for AI-enabled immersive technologies and their role in sustained consumer experience and value creation. This suggests the intersection of various theories such as experience economy theory, intelligent ecosystem, immersive presence construct and sustainability driven marketing logic to help us understand how the technologically mediated environments generate experiential, organizational and societal value.

3.1 Experience Economy and Experiential Value

The conceptual foundation of immersive consumption can be traced back to the experience economy model. Services and experiences are different in a way that experiences are staged, memorable and emotionally resonant events which can engage the consumer on sensory, cognitive and relational dimensions (Mehmetoglu & Engen, 2011).

When consumers perceive interactions as personally meaningful not only functionally transactional, then they realise experiential value. In case of retail and tourism, experiential value is shaped through atmospherics, storytelling, symbolic engagement and participation. Tourism consumption has always been experiential as it encompasses anticipation, imagination, on-site immersion, and reflection. Gradually, retail environments are also relying more on interactive displays, experiential storescape, and digital augmentation to influence purchase behaviour and brand attachment (Lemon & Verhoef, 2016)

Immersive technologies amplify experiential value by intensifying sensory stimulation and participatory depth. Even before purchasing consumers can experience products using virtual simulation which transforms the evaluation process into digital, yet lived encounters. This pre consumption immersion improves the perceived authenticity, enjoyment and emotional connection, ultimately influences satisfaction and loyalty (Barta et al., 2023; Flavián et al., 2021)

3.2 Artificial Intelligence in Marketing and Service Ecosystems

Artificial intelligence represents the intelligence layer which can operationalize the delivery of immersive experience. It includes machine learning, natural language processing, computer vision and predictive analytics that enable automated cognition and adaptive decision-making.

In the marketing ecosystem AI enhances consumer engagement through:

- Hyper personalized recommendations

- o Predictive demand forecasting
- o Dynamic pricing optimization
- o Conversational service interfaces
- o Behavioural segmentation and targeting

Artificial Intelligence can actually transform traditional service delivery into intelligent service ecosystems, wherein human employees, digital interfaces and algorithmic agents co-create values. These ecosystems operate through continuous data capture and feedback loops, which allows real time adaptation of offerings and interactions (Huang et al., 2024; Huang & Rust, 2021). AI plays an instrumental part in immersive environments as it collates virtual content, fine-tunes simulation parameters, personalizes avatars and ultimately adapts experiential pathways based on the responses received from users. This way of adaptive immersion augments perceived relevance and reduces cognitive strain, also strengthens decision confidence and engagement intensity (Dwivedi et al., 2021, 2023; Koohang et al., 2023; Sreejesh et al., 2021)

3.3 Immersive Technologies: XR Continuum and Presence Constructs

Immersive technologies integrate physical and digital environments at different levels of simulation and interactivity. AR overlaps digital objects onto real world settings, improving environmental evidence without replacing physical context. VR creates fully simulated, computer-generated environments that users navigate through head-mounted displays and sensory interfaces. Mixed Reality blends physical and digital objects interactively to allow real-time manipulation across realities.

These technologies generate experiential effects through psychological constructs collectively described as presence.

Key presence dimensions include:

- Physical presence: Sense of 'being there' in a mediated environment
- Social presence: The perception of interacting with others
- Self-presence: Identifying with digital avatars
- Telepresence: Transportation into virtual space

Presence strengthens immersion, which in turn influences emotional arousal, enjoyment, trust and behavioural intention (Guttentag, 2010; Wedel et al., 2020). VR destination previews can create anticipation of being present that forms travel intention. In retail, AR product visualization enhances evaluation process and purchase confidence (Hilken et al., 2017). This way, the immersive technologies function not only as visualization tools but to amplify experiences that reshape perception, cognition and affective response.

3.4 Consumer Decision-Making in Immersive Environments

Decision making is usually based on some cues like images, text descriptions, peer reviews. Of late immersive environment introduced many progressive concepts such as interactive product manipulation, spatial navigation, scenario simulation and embodied cognition. Consumers can virtually compare different alternatives, usage contexts and visualize their outcomes. This experience reduces perceived risk and post-purchase dissonance. Research indicates that immersive product trials enhance perceived ownership and emotional attachment even prior to acquisition (Javornik, 2016; Javornik et al., 2021). From behavioural point of view, immersive environment activates hedonic motivations which combines utilitarian evaluation with entertainment values. This kind of dual processing mechanism strengthens the duration of engagement, brand recall and probability of conversion.

3.5 Sustainability and Responsible Consumption

Sustainable marketing is not only limited to eco-friendly products, it also covers responsible production, ethical communication, and it facilitates conscious consumption. Retail supply chains nowadays are facing many structural sustainability challenges including overstocking, wastage, reverse logistics for product returns, packaging intensity, etc. Similarly, for travel ecosystem, there are many constraints like destination overcrowding, carbon intensive travel, cultural site degradation, seasonal resource strain etc.

Immersive technologies can contribute to sustainability in many ways like digital substitution and optimization mechanisms. As we know, virtual product trial reduces return logistics. Similarly, AI demand forecasting can improve planning the production ahead. VR tourism previews also support informed visit and distribution of destinations. In fact, the smart itinerary system actually optimizes travel routes, which in turn lower resource intensity (Buhalis, 2020; Buhalis et al., 2023). From the perspective of a consumer, immersive storytelling may also promote sustainability awareness by visualizing the impact of environmental degradation, ethical sourcing journeys, and different narratives related to conservations. Thereby, they can influence responsible consumption behavior.

3.6 Human-Centered Value Integration

As we have been discussing, technological immersion improves experiential intensity, value creation, and it depends on human perception, trust, and acceptance. We must understand that human-centred design framework usually put focus on usability, transparency, inclusivity and psychological safety in the AI-mediated systems. Consumers evaluate different immersive platforms not only on the basis of functionality, but also to have assurance of data privacy, fairness of algorithm, emotional comfort, and cognitive accessibility. Presence of any ethical gaps, like manipulative nudge or non-transparent personalization, can negatively affect the trust and their adoption to these technologies. Therefore, responsible AI governance is really integral to sustain the experiential value creation (Floridi et al., 2018). In a way, all the aforementioned conceptual foundations converge into an integrated logical theme;

- Experiential economy theory provides due rationale as to why immersion matters.
- AI intelligence put light on the way experience is created.
- XR technologies explain where immersion occurs.
- Presence theory explains the psychological impact on users.
- Sustainability frameworks explain broader value outcomes.
- Human centred ethics explain the longterm legitimacy of these technologies.

Together, these perspectives establish the theoretical basis for examining AI-enabled immersive technologies as multi-dimensional value creation systems operating across experiential, organizational, and societal domains. While these theoretical perspectives explain why immersive technologies influence experience and value, it is equally important to understand how such systems are structurally organized. The following section therefore presents the architectural foundations of AI-enabled immersive systems.

3.7. AI-Enabled Immersive Experience Architecture

AI-enabled immersive systems represent an integrated architecture that combines artificial intelligence with immersive technologies such as AR, VR, and XR. It delivers interactive and adaptive user experiences. These systems operate through interconnected layers that collectively enable real-time data processing, intelligent decision-making and immersive interaction (Huang & Rust, 2021; Milgram, 1994a)

Instead of elaborating each component in isolation, the architecture can be understood as a structured set of layers that work in coordination to support experience creation. The key components of this architecture are summarized in Table-1.

Table 1. Layers of AI enabled immersive experience architecture

Layer	Key Components	Functional Role	Relevance to Experience Creation
Data Layer	User data, behavioral data, contextual inputs	Captures and processes real-time information	Enables understanding of user preferences and context (Huang & Rust, 2021)
AI Intelligence Layer	Machine learning, recommendation systems, predictive analytics	Processes data and generates insights	Drives personalization and adaptive decision-making (Huang & Rust, 2021)
Immersive Interface Layer	AR, VR, XR environments	Visualizes and delivers interactive experiences	Enhances realism, engagement, and presence (Milgram, 1994)
Interaction Layer	Gesture control, voice input, motion tracking	Facilitates user interaction with system	Enables intuitive and immersive engagement (Hilken et al., 2017)
Integration Layer	Cloud systems, edge computing, platforms	Connects all layers and ensures real-time operation	Supports scalability and seamless service delivery (Buhalis et al., 2019)

(Source: Authors' conceptualization)

As discussed AI-enabled immersive experience architecture transforms consumption from passive evaluation to active participation. In retail and tourism sectors such systems do not merely enhance engagement but reconfigure how value is perceived, co-created and sustained across digital and physical ecosystems.

This foundation enables practical deployment across experience-driven sectors, particularly retail and tourism, where immersive technologies are actively transforming consumer interaction and value creation.

4. SECTORAL APPLICATIONS: RETAIL & TOURISM

4.1 Immersive Retail Transformation

There has been a paradigm shift in retail environment after digital proliferation. It has evolved from transaction-oriented system to experience-centric engagement platforms because of AI-enabled immersive technology, which enables interactive product evaluation, real-time personalization, and seamless integration of digital and physical channels.

Virtual Trial and Product Visualization: Augmented reality applications help consumers to try different products like apparel, eyewear, and cosmetics through real-time visualization in virtual mode. AI-driven computer vision can improve accuracy by mapping facial and body features, thus improving product fit assessment. This technology enhances diagnosticity, which allows consumers to evaluate different product attributes in a better manner even before purchasing. All these result in enhancing the experience of consumers by improving decision confidence, which ultimately leads to improved conversion rate and reduced product return (Hilken et al., 2017).

Smart Fitting Rooms and Interactive Mirrors: In physical retail environments, smart fitting rooms and interactive mirrors enhance in-store engagement by integrating AI-driven assistance within trial spaces. Consumers can check alternative sizes, explore product variations, and receive personalized styling recommendations without leaving the fitting area. These systems strengthen personalization and real-time service responsiveness, thus improving engagement and perceived service quality. The integration of technologies like RFID, computer vision and recommendation systems enables a hybrid service model where human assistance is augmented by intelligent automation.

Virtual Stores and VR Showrooms: Virtual reality can create simulated retail environments where consumers can navigate between digital stores and interact with products in immersive settings. This is particularly relevant for certain categories of products like furniture, automobiles, and luxury goods where spatial evaluation is quite critical. All these things enhance presence and allow consumers to experience different products in the simulated context. This ultimately improves confidence in decision-making and reduces perceived risk, thereby influence the conversion outcome in a positive manner (Bonetti et al., 2018).

AI-Driven Personalization and Assisted Commerce: Consumer data including purchases, preferences and contextual needs are analysed by AI-powered systems to deliver personalized recommendations and product bundles. This can strengthen personalization within the immersive environment, thus reducing cognitive workload and enhancing engagement. As a result of this, consumers usually experience more relevant interactions, which leads to improved satisfaction and higher purchase likelihood (Huang & Rust, 2021).

Phygital Retail Integration: Immersive technologies can integrate seamlessly between online and offline retail environments and create a 'phygital' ecosystem. Different technological applications like AR-based navigation, mobile product scanning and digital twin store help in building continuity across various touchpoints.

This integration builds omni channel coherence and strengthens engagement. It also improves operational coordination and customer journey consistency.

4.2 Experiential Tourism Augmentation

Virtual destination previews: VR simulations allow potential tourists to experience destinations before travelling. These immersive previews enhance presence and emotional engagement and influence travel intention and decision confidence (Guttentag, 2010).

AI-Powered Travel Planning and Itinerary Design: AI systems also help in personalized travel planning by analysing preferences, constraints, and behavioral data of customers. These technologies optimize routes, predict crowd conditions, and recommend sustainable travel options. So, personalization is enhanced and decision confidence is strengthened.

Smart Tourism and Augmented Heritage Interpretation: Augmented reality enhances on-site experience by overlapping context-based information into physical environments. Application of this technology are used for historical reconstruction, interactive storytelling and real-time translation. This technology helps to strengthening presence for consumers and engagement towards the brand. It also depends on cultural understanding and enhances experiential richness (Wedel et al., 2020; Yadav & Sondhi, 2023).

Virtual substitution and remote tourism: There are many inaccessible or environmentally sensitive destinations in the world. Immersive technology has the ability to find virtual alternatives for these unique destinations. That is, it can provide experiential access to these while also reducing the ecological pressure. This technology ultimately contributes towards resource optimization and supports sustainable tourism by minimizing unrequired travel.

4.3. Emerging Market Applications: in the Context of India

Adoption of immersive technology is growing rapidly in emerging markets. Due to its increased digital infrastructure and mobile penetration. In one of the most crucial emerging markets like India, these applications include AR-based jewellery trial, facial mapping in eyewear retail, VR-enabled automotive showrooms, virtual tourism campaigns, etc. These kind of developments indicate that immersive technology enhances diagnosticity and personalization even in the ecosystems dominated by mobiles and contributes to increased engagement and adoption (Laria & Pantano, 2011; Siamagka et al., 2015).

These sectoral applications demonstrate the way immersive technology enhances experience value and influences consumer behaviour. They also reveal the implications of this technology for sustainability. The following part of the chapter tries to examine the mechanisms through which immersive systems may contribute to our sustainable value creation.

4.4. Sustainable Value Creation Mechanisms

AI-driven immersive technologies contribute to sustainability through a structured operational mechanism. These systems enable dematerialization, optimization of resources, and reduction of environmental impact, thus embedding sustainability within experiential value creation process. Now, let's discuss each point separately.

Digital substitution and dematerialization: Immersive technologies reduce dependence on physical processes by enabling virtual alternatives. In the case of retail sector, virtual product trials reduce physical sampling and reverse logistics. Similarly, in tourism, virtual destination preview helps in reduction of exploratory travel. These processes of dematerialization minimizes material consumption and contributes to environmental impact reduction (Buhalis, 2020; Buhalis et al., 2023).

Demand forecasting and inventory optimization: AI-driven analytics taken from immersive interactions provide deep insight into consumer preferences and behaviours. These insights improve demand forecasting accuracy, reduces overproduction, and reduces inventory. Such resource optimization process enhances operational efficiency and minimizes burden on environment (Davenport et al., 2020)

Infrastructure efficiency: These technologies made virtual showrooms and digital interfaces possible. while reducing dependence on resource-intensive physical infrastructure. Businesses can list and present their products digitally. Tourism organizations can now promote destinations without physical billboards or other instruments. These steps contribute towards improvement in resource efficiency (Bonetti et al., 2018).

Sustainable travel optimization: AI-enabled systems are optimizing travel routes, managing visitor flows, and recommending sustainable options to visitors. These capabilities help in reduction of congestion in popular location and promote less known places too (Gretzel et al., 2015).

Conservation through virtual access: Virtual tourism enables access to ecologically sensitive destinations without exploiting the physical presence, which in turn reduces ecological pressure and supports the conservation efforts by different governments and society. All these approaches ultimately contribute towards minimizing detrimental environmental impact (Beck et al., 2019).

Sustainability awareness: Awareness can also be created through immersive storytelling, wherein the negative environmental impact and sustainability practices can be visualized by the users. These experiences influence responsible consumption behavior and strengthen engagement with sustainability initiatives (Arantes, 2022).

Integrated sustainability outcomes: Through all the above discussions, we can understand the impact of immersive technologies and sustainability across three different dimensions:

1. Environmental, by reducing emission and resource consumption,
2. Operational, by improving efficiency and optimizing cost, and
3. Consumer centric, by enhancing awareness about the environmental causes and responsible decision-making.

A dual perspective in understanding the value generated by AI-driven immersive technologies in needed by examining both the 'consumer' and the 'producer' side value exchange. While the preceding sections focus mostly on experiential outcomes, the organizational dimension is equally significant as it works as a reinforcing cycle with consumer side value. From the consumers' perspective, immersive technology enables them to enhance experience quality, reduce perceived risk, better personalization and improved decision confidence. Even sustainability awareness may emerge as a consumer side benefit; as immersive storytelling can sensitize them about the consequences of their consumption decision. From the producers' point of view, value is created through measurable operational and financial outcomes; though improved conversion rates, reduced product returns, inventory management optimization, minimize dependence on physical infrastructure etc.

These two value streams are not independent, per say. When consumer experience improves, it leads to behavioural outcomes in terms of higher conversions, lower returns. And these outcomes directly benefit the organisational performance. Similarly, organisational investments in governance and ethical practices strengthens consumer trust and sustained adoption. This dual value logic is captured in the lower panel of the integrated framework. All these outcomes demonstrate that sustainability definitely emerges as an embedded outcome of immersive value creation. While the preceding sections provide conceptual and normative insights, it is essential to examine how these dynamics manifest in real-world contexts. The following section presents a multi-case analysis to empirically ground the proposed relationships.

5. MULTI-CASE ANALYSIS: AI-ENABLED IMMERSIVE EXPERIENCE IN RETAIL AND TOURISM

To empirically ground the conceptual exploration in earlier sections, this study adopts a multi-case analytical approach focusing on documented implementations of AI-enabled immersive technologies in the retail and tourism ecosystems. This approach aligns with case-based research methodology, where real-world applications are used to derive theoretically meaningful insights (Yin, 2018; Ying et al., 2022)

5.1 Retail Sector Cases

5.1.1 Shopify: AR-Enabled Commerce and Conversion Performance

Shopify is one of its kind cloud based commerce platform designed to facilitate businesses start, run & grow their stores. It centralizes the business operations by synchronising on line sales with in-person retail vide the POS system. It will not be an exaggeration to mention that shopify played a pivotal role in democratizing augmented reality (AR) adoption widely. It enables merchants to integrate 3D and AR-based product visualization directly in the digital storefronts. The Shopify product customizer allows customers to explore 3D models of products for an immersive shopping experience and an enhanced understanding of the product. Since Shopify AR is baked into the website, customers can just visit any Shopify merchant's website and interact with their products in real time using AR-enabled 3D models. Shopify has one AR-powered product customizer which has the potential to revolutionize the online shopping process for potential buyers, window shoppers, and loyal customers, everyone.

Key points:

Recent platform-level data indicates that immersive technologies significantly influence consumer behavior:

- Products with AR/3D visualization demonstrate up to 94% higher conversion rates compared to non-immersive listings
- AR interaction improves purchase confidence by enabling realistic product evaluation
- Industry analyses also report substantial reductions in return rates (up to ~40%) due to improved pre-purchase assessment

This case strongly supports the technology, experiential value & behavioral outcome pathway. AR enhances diagnosticity and perceived control which allows consumers to evaluate products more effectively. This directly translates into higher conversion rates (Hilken et al., 2017). From sustainability perspective, improved product understanding reduces return rates, thereby minimizing reverse logistics emissions and packaging waste. However, the system relies on extensive behavioural data tracking, raising concerns regarding algorithmic transparency and data privacy. This reinforces the importance of human-centred AI governance as a moderating layer (Floridi et al., 2018).

5.1.2 Wayfair / AR Furniture Visualization: Decision Accuracy and Return Reduction

Wayfair is a major American e-commerce platform which deals primarily with furniture and home goods. It is one of the world's largest online destinations for home furnishing with more than 30 million products from more than 20,000 suppliers throughout the globe. By nature, furniture retail is a high-uncertainty purchase category where spatial fit and contextual compatibility play a big role in decision making. However, the AR-enabled visualization platforms, widely adopted by Wayfair, allow consumers to place virtual furniture within their own environments.

Key points:

Recent industry and case-based analyses (Siu, 2026) provide quantifiable support;

- AR-based visualization has been associated with conversion rate improvements ranging from 40% to over 90% in furniture-related categories
- Return rates can decline by approximately 22%–40% due to improved product fit evaluation

Analytical Interpretation

This case illustrates the role of spatial presence and telepresence in enhancing experiential value. By enabling embodied interaction, AR reduces cognitive effort and perceived risk, leading to more confident decision-making (Flavián et al., 2019, 2021). This aligns with the transition from experiential value (presence) to behavioural outcomes, i.e. reduced uncertainty and likelihood of higher purchases. And from a sustainability standpoint, reduced return rates directly translate into lower transportation emissions and material waste, while decreased reliance on physical showrooms contributes to infrastructure dematerialization.

Albeit, in-home visualization systems involve environmental data capture, raising concerns regarding data ownership and user consent, and it must be addressed through transparent governance mechanisms.

5.2 Tourism Sector Cases

5.2.1 Kerala Tourism's AR-Based Virtual Tour Guide in Tourism

Kerala, a state in the southwestern part of India flanked on one side by Arabian sea & the Western ghat on the other side, is better referred to as the 'God's own country' because of its beautiful landscape, breathtaking views, & rich cultural heritages which creates an ethereal experience for the visitors to this place. It has a unique combination of pristine beaches, backwater, hill stations, exotic wild life, everything that a tourist may fall for. So, its tourism sector has continuously seen a substantial growth over a period of time. With the ever-changing technological landscape; Kerala Tourism embraced immersive technology through the introduction of an augmented reality based virtual tour guide. This aims not only to enhance tourist experience, but also to promote sustainable tourism.

Some of the key metrics derived from reliable sources show:

- In the year 2023 itself, Kerala recorded around 21 million domestic tourists, a significant increase from the 2022 number of appx.18 million (The Hindu Business Line, 2023).
- International Tourist Arrivals: International arrivals rose by 87.83%, from 345,549 in 2022 to 649,057 in 2023 (The Hindu Business Line, 2023).
- Kerala witnessed a substantial rise of around 87% in international tourist footfall from 2023 to 2022, reaching at the scorching number of 649,057 (The Hindu Business Line, 2023).

Analytical Interpretation

This case demonstrates the strong impact of presence and emotional immersion on consumer behavior. Immersive technology reduces the inherent intangibility of tourism products by allowing simulated pre-consumption experiences, thereby enhancing decision confidence (Guttentag, 2010). This reflects the pathway from experiential value, i.e 'presence' to 'behavioral transformation' meaning in this case, booking intention. From a sustainability perspective, VR previews enable more informed travel decisions and may reduce exploratory travel, thereby contributing to lower carbon-intensive behavior.

5.2.2 Marriott International: Immersive VR and Global Engagement Outcomes

Marriott International is the largest hotel company in the world considering the number of rooms available. As of 2026, they have 9,800 properties across the globe. They manage around 30 diverse brands based of different service level and lifestyles, from luxury to premium to staycation options. Only in 2025 Marriott added nearly 10,000 rooms to its system. They have been using virtual reality to shift the way guests experience their travel and also the way event planners design their spaces for some time now. It has implemented VR-based experiential marketing initiatives such as 'VRoom Service' enabling consumers to explore destinations and hotel environments virtually.

Empirical Evidence (Disztinger et al., 2017; Hospitality technology studies)

- VR campaigns generated approximately:
    - o Approximately 500 million social media impressions
    - o Approximately 300 million PR impressions
    - o Around 135% increase in online bookings, demonstrating the effectiveness of immersive visualization in influencing consumer decision-making (NextView Global, 2023)
- Significant increase in consumer engagement and destination awareness

Analytical Interpretation

This case highlights the role of immersive storytelling in enhancing emotional engagement and destination imagery, which are key drivers of travel intention (Buhalis, 2020; Buhalis et al., 2019).

Within the framework, this reflects the movement from experiential immersion (presence and emotional engagement) to behavioral outcomes (interest and intention). From a sustainability perspective, VR-based promotion reduces dependence on resource-intensive physical marketing events such as travel expos and site visits.

5.3 Cross-Case Comparative Analysis and Thematic Synthesis

The selected cases are synthesized across key analytical dimensions aligned with the proposed framework. Table 2 presents a structured comparison which links technological deployment, experiential constructs, behavioural outcomes, sustainability mechanisms, and ethical considerations.

Table 2. Mapping of essential constructs across cases

Layer	Shopify (Retail)	Wayfair (Retail)	Kerala Tourism	Marriott (Tourism)
Technology Enablement	AR & 3D product visualization	AR spatial placement tools	VR destination simulation	VR immersive storytelling
Experiential Value	Diagnosticity, product clarity	Spatial presence, fit visualization	Emotional immersion, telepresence	Narrative immersion, affective engagement
Quantifia ble Evidence	↑ Conversion up to almost 94% (Shopify, 2022)	↓ Returns around 22–40%, ↑ conversion up to 40%+ (Industry, 2024)	↑ Bookings around 80% (The Hindu Business Line, 2023)	~500M impressions, ~300M reach (Disztinger et al., 2017)
Behavioral Response	Higher purchase likelihood	Reduced uncertainty, higher confidence	Increased booking intention	Increased destination interest

continued on following page

Table 2. Continued

Layer	Shopify (Retail)	Wayfair (Retail)	Kerala Tourism	Marriott (Tourism)
Organizational Value	Revenue growth, conversion efficiency	Cost reduction (returns, logistics)	Revenue uplift, campaign ROI	Brand equity, customer engagement
Sustainability Pathway	Return reduction → lower emissions	Reduced logistics + showroom dematerialization	Reduced exploratory travel	Reduced physical marketing footprint
Ethical Dimension	Data tracking & personalization opacity	In-home data capture concerns	Persuasive influence in VR	Accessibility & inclusion gaps
Framework Flow	Tech → Diagnosticity → Conversion	Tech → Presence → Confidence	Presence → Intention → Booking	Presence → Engagement → Interest

(Source: Authors' conceptualization)

This comparative mapping reveals that despite sectoral differences, all cases exhibit a consistent structural logic of immersive value creation. Each case reveals how AI-enabled immersive technologies operate through identifiable experiential mechanisms that influence consumer behaviour and organizational outcomes. Building on this comparative analysis, four dominant and interrelated themes come out in both retail and tourism contexts.

i. Experiential Enhancement as the Primary Value Driver

Across all cases, immersive technologies enhance consumer experience through three core constructs: diagnosticity, presence, and personalization.

- In retail contexts (Shopify, Wayfair), AR enables realistic product interaction, improving evaluation accuracy and perceived control.
- In tourism contexts (Kerala Tourism, Marriott), VR enhances emotional immersion and anticipatory experience formation.

These findings reinforce that immersive technologies function as experience amplifiers, transforming abstract evaluation into simulated, interactive engagement (Flavián et al., 2021; Hilken et al., 2017).

ii. Behavioral Transformation Through Immersive Interaction

A consistent empirical outcome across cases is the transformation of consumer behavior. Enhanced experiential value leads to measurable behavioral responses, including:

- Increased conversion rates in retail
- Reduced purchase uncertainty and higher confidence
- Increased travel intention and booking behavior
- Greater engagement and destination interest

This demonstrates that immersive technologies act as behavioral enablers, bridging the gap between evaluation and action by reducing perceived risk and enhancing emotional engagement.

iii. Sustainability as an Embedded Outcome of Experiential Efficiency

Sustainability outcomes emerge as a secondary but structurally embedded effect of improved experiential design. Three key mechanisms are observed:

- Return Reduction and efficient Resource use
- Improved product visualization reduces return rates and associated logistics emissions (Shopify, Wayfair).
- Avoidance of Physical Infrastructure:

Virtual showrooms and immersive interfaces reduce reliance on physical retail space and promotional infrastructure.

- Travel Optimization and Digital Substitution:

VR-based destination previews reduce exploratory travel and support informed decision-making (Kerala tousism, Marriott).

These findings indicate that sustainability is not an isolated objective but an integrated outcome of immersive value creation processes. However, these examples also highlight the importance of AI governance in a human-centred manner. Sustainability outcomes must be supported by transparent, ethical and responsible data-driven practices. Beyond the sustainability outcomes, there is an increase in reliance on data-driven immersive systems, which raises serious ethical and governance concerns. This consensus of dimensions are examined in the following sections.

iv. Emergence of Human-Centered AI Governance as a Critical Moderator

Across all cases, ethical and governance considerations emerge as a critical dimension influencing adoption and long-term viability. Key concerns include:

- Data privacy and behavioral tracking (retail AR systems)
- Biometric and interaction data usage
- Persuasive influence in immersive environments (VR tourism)
- Accessibility and inclusion challenges (VR adoption)

These issues highlight the necessity of embedding human-centered AI governance within immersive systems to ensure trust, transparency, and ethical alignment (Floridi et al., 2018).

6. HUMAN-CENTRED AND ETHICAL VALUE DIMENSIONS

AI-enabled immersive technologies enhance personalization, engagement and operational efficiency. They also intensify concerns related to privacy, autonomy, algorithmic bias, and psychological influence. In experience-intensive sectors such as retail and tourism where immersive interfaces shape consumers' perception and decision-making, ethical planning of AI systems becomes crucial to sustaining legitimacy and long-term adoption. This section examines the human-centred and governance dimensions that must accompany AI-enabled immersive transformation.

6.1 Human-Centred AI: Conceptual Orientation

Human-centred AI refers to the design and arrangement of intelligent systems that supplement human well-being, preserve agency and align technological outcomes with societal values. Instead of replacing human judgment, these systems aim to support decision making, experiential comfort and service inclusivity.

Within immersive environments, human-centred design stresses on:

- Usability and accessibility
- Cognitive comfort
- Emotional safety
- Cultural sensitivity
- Transparency of system functioning

Consumers evaluate immersive platforms not only on the basis of functional efficiency but also on how intuitively, respectfully, and ethically they interact with human users. Human-centered system design emphasizes augmentation over replacement, i.e. by aligning AI with human well-being (Floridi et al., 2018).

Data Privacy and Informed Consent

AI systems continuously collect detailed information about consumers, which includes facial geometric and biometric identifiers, eyeball movement patterns, spatial navigation patterns, emotional response indicators, as well as voice and gesture inputs. Although these kinds of data enable hyper-personalization, but this also raises the risk of privacy. Unauthorized data storage, lack of transparency and surveillance practices, or third-party data sharing can affect the trust of consumer in a negative way. As we all know, most immersive platforms collect biometric and behavioral data by default, raises governance concerns (Chaturvedi et al., 2023; Dwivedi et al., 2021).

Therefore, it is the need of hour to interpret ethical governance covering different tenets of immersive technology, like explicit informed consent protocols. Disclosure of transparent data usage, opt-in personalization framework, secure storage and encryption system, etc. Assurance of privacy is very critical in AR trial systems and VR behavioural simulators, where sensitivity of biometric data is critically at a higher level.

Algorithmic Transparency and Explainability: AI-driven immersive platform operate for curating recommendations, unfolding virtual environments, and guiding decision pathways through complex machine learning models. But when algorithms and process are not transparent, consumers may develop a perception of manipulation or hidden persuasion. So these platforms must always highlight the transparency of their algorithmic system. They may think of disclosing the logic of personalization and focus on explainable recommendation systems. Sponsored product placement should also be visible to the customer, and proper clarification of AI and human assistance should be given. AI frameworks, which can be explained properly, perceive more fairness and strengthen the confidence of users in e-commerce platforms. There is a positive correlation between trust in automatic recommendation with explainable AI (Rai, 2020).

Bias, Fairness, and Inclusivity

The scope of algorithmic bias emerge when the AI system is built on non-representative datasets. In these cases, this may come to effect in form of limited availability of body-type diversity, lack of accuracy in skin tone, cultural stereotyping, and even exclusion of specific languages in virtual assistants. These types of algorithmic biases, weaken inclusivity, and may isolate the consumer groups who are unrepresented or underrepresented. Dataset diversity, fairness audit, and inclusive visualization may be the ground base for ethical immersive design, and percolate immersive representation and personalization fairness (Mehrabi et al., 2022).

Psychological Influence and Manipulative Design

The next major concern about immersive environment is the way the intrinsic sensory engagement allows immersion and enhanced cognitive absorption. This kind of influence raises ethical questions regarding behavioural manipulation and persuasive nudging. This can also simulate artificial scarcity by overstimulating impulsive urges and even gamified addiction loops (Susser et al., 2019). Hence, responsible immersive algorithms must ensure that the software design is within ethical boundaries to preserve the consumer's autonomy and rational decision making abilities.

Trust Architecture in Immersive Ecosystems

Trust functions as the central mediating construct in AI-enabled experience adoption. Many a times trust mediates AI adoption and technology acceptance (Gursoy et al., 2019). And by trust we mean consumers trust towards data protection mechanisms, system accuracy, intentions of the brands and more importantly transaction security.

There are few measure through which trust architecture can be strengthened:

- Certification labels for ethical AI
- Transparent governance disclosures
- Third-party audits
- Secure payment integration
- Authenticity verification of virtual products and destinations

particularly in tourism, trust is crucial where immersive previews greatly influence high-investment travel decisions.

6.2 Regulatory and Governance Frameworks

Global policy ecosystems are evolving to regulate AI deployment and immersive data governance. Some key regulatory directions include:

- Data protection laws (e.g., GDPR-type frameworks)
- Biometric data governance policies
- AI ethics guidelines
- Platform accountability mandates

All the organizations which deploy immersive AI systems must align with emerging digital governance standards to ensure compliance and reputational security. More importantly governance of ethical dimensions of AI enabled immersive technologies requires translation into concrete, implementable mechanisms which organizations can actually implement as illustrated in Table 3.

Table 3. Implementable AI Governance Mechanism

Ethical concern	Sector relevance	Actionable mechanism
Data Privacy	Retail AR (biometric capture), VR tourism (behavioral profiling)	Privacy-by-design architecture; explicit opt-in consent; compliance with GDPR and India's DPDPA; data minimization principles ; collect only what is necessary for the experience
Algorithmic Transparency	AI recommendation engines in retail; AI-driven itinerary personalization in tourism	Explainable AI (XAI) frameworks (e.g., LIME, SHAP); plain-language disclosure of recommendation logic to consumers; audit trails for algorithmic decision-making
Bias, Fairness, and Inclusivity	Personalization engines that may disadvantage under-represented consumer groups	Regular third-party audits using fairness metrics (demographic parity, equalized odds); diverse and representative training datasets; ongoing model monitoring
Psychological Influence and Manipulative Design	Emotionally immersive VR environments in tourism that may unduly influence decisions	Ethical UX guidelines prohibiting dark patterns; alignment with EU AI Act high-risk system classification; mandatory cooling-off disclosures in high-commitment decisions
Digital inclusion	Mobile-first emerging markets (India, Southeast Asia) where device access varies	Accessibility-first immersive design; mobile-optimized lightweight AR for low-bandwidth contexts; affordability considerations in hardware-dependent deployments

Source: Authors' conceptualization. GDPR = General Data Protection Regulation; DPDPA = Digital Personal Data Protection Act (India, 2023); XAI = Explainable Artificial Intelligence.

Ethical governance is more effective when it is embedded within the immersive system architecture, not just a compliance layer.

6.3 Digital Well-Being and Experiential Balance

The extended duration of immersion in the virtual environment may cause a threat for users physical & mental wellbeing. It may produce psychological fatigue, disorientation or dependence on distraction. So companies must design ethical experience by incorporating various safeguards for user wellbeing like time use reminders, sensory moderation controls, filtering the content based on age etc. Possibly such measures can ensure immersive engagement remain enriching rather than being overwhelming.

6.4 Responsible AI as Strategic Differentiator

Ethical governance should not be treated as a compliance obligation but a tool for strategic differentiator. Organisations that demonstrate transparent, inclusive, and privacy-respecting immersive ecosystems reinforce the consumers' trust on brand. They also develop relational equity and long-term loyalty. Thus responsible AI deployment aligns primarily with:

- Purpose-driven brand positioning
- ESG commitments
- Stakeholder accountability
- Societal value creation

Human-centered and ethical AI dimensions form the normative foundation upon which immersive experience architectures must operate. Privacy protection, algorithmic fairness, transparency, and psychological responsibility are essential to sustaining trust and adoption in AI-mediated environments. In retail and tourism, where immersive technologies influence perception, preference, and behaviour, ethical governance can never be distinguished from experiential value creation.

7. MAPPING THEORETICAL & EMPIRICAL PATTERNS TO FRAMEWORK CONSTRUCTS

The literature discussed thus far and the cross-case analysis enables mapping between different observations and the core constructs of the proposed framework:

- Technology Enablement: AR/VR systems provide the infrastructural basis for immersive interaction
- Experiential Value Layer: Diagnosticity, presence, and personalization emerge as key mediating constructs
- Behavioral Response Layer: Conversion, confidence, engagement, and intention represent measurable outcomes
- Organizational Value Layer: Revenue growth, efficiency gains, and brand enhancement are observed

- Sustainability Layer: Resource optimization, dematerialization, and reduced environmental impact
- Governance Layer: Ethical AI considerations moderate all stages of value creation

This mapping demonstrates that the cases are not isolated examples but collectively reflect a generalizable, multi-layered value creation logic. Earlier sections established the foundational role of AI-enabled immersive technologies in transforming customer experience and value creation. But the case synthesis revealed consistent and replicable patterns linking experiential constructs, behavioural outcomes, sustainability mechanisms, and ethical considerations across retail and tourism contexts. Rather than treating these elements independently, the framework presented in *Figure-1* integrates them into a coherent structure that explains how immersive systems generate both immediate and long-term value.

Figure 1.

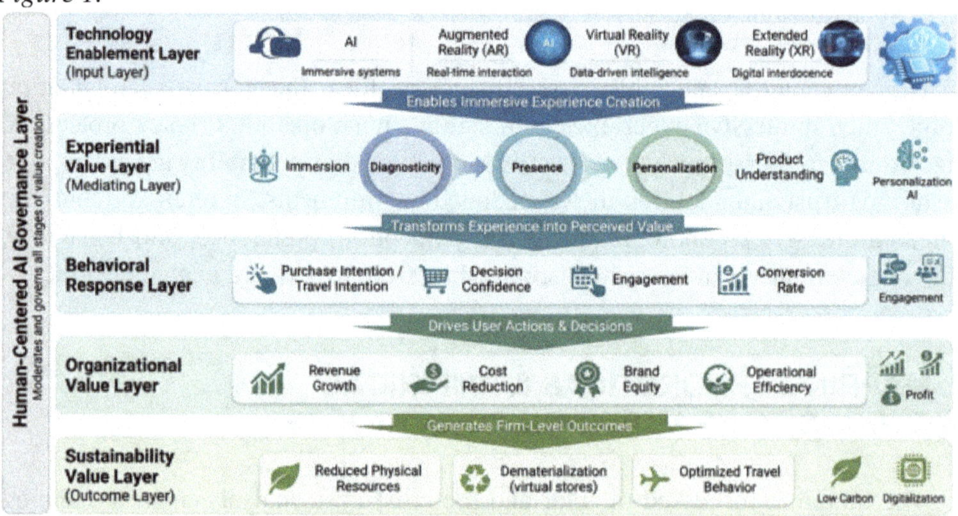

(Source: Authors' conceptualization)

The framework illustrates the multi-layered process through which AI-enabled immersive technologies generate experiential, behavioral, organizational, and sustainability value, moderated by human-centered AI governance.

Technology Enablement Layer

The foundation of this framework is built through the technology enablement layer, which comprises of AI-enabled immersive systems such as augmented reality, virtual reality, and extended reality. These technologies form the backbone of interactive, real-time and context-aware consumer experience creation. These technologies integrate data-driven intelligence with immersive interfaces and facilitate adaptive and personalized user engagement. In alliance with reality-virtuality continuum (Milgram, 1994). These systems operate in a spectrum ranging from physical augmentation to virtual environment, which expands the scope of experiential interaction.

Experiential Value Layer

Building upon the technological foundation, this framework identifies experiential value as the central mediating mechanism through which emerging technology influences the consumer behavior. This layer is conceptualized through three different core constructs.

- **Diagnosticity** is the extent to which immersive systems enhance product understanding and evaluation accuracy.
- **Presence** means the degree of perceived immersion and sense of 'being there' within virtual or augmented environments.
- **Personalization** is the ability of AI system to create experience based on the preferences and behavioral data of user.

Evidence from the cases substantiates these constructs. For example, Shopify's AR-enabled interface enhances diagnosticity, which allows realistic product interaction. Wayfair's 3D visualization tool improves presence through embedded product evaluation. Similarly, in the context of tourism, VR-based experiences used by Kerala tourism and Marriott enhance emotional immersion and anticipation of experience formation. These findings align well with the prior research indicating the impact of immersive technology on experiential richness and engagement, while also reducing abstraction and increasing interactivity (Flavián et al., 2021; Hilken et al., 2017).

Behavioral Response Layer

The experience garnered through immersive technology translates into behavioural responses by users. It represents the immediate outcome of value perception and influences conversion, decision confidence, engagement, interest or intention in the context of retail and tourism. The case analysis provides strong support for this linkage. Shopify demonstrated significant improvement in conversion rate associated with AR interaction, while Wayfair's immersive tools reduce uncertainty and enhance purchase confidence. In the case of tourism, the Marriott's VR campaign illustrated the influence of presence and booking behaviour, which emphasizes increased engagement and destination interest. This layer reflects the transition from experience value to actionable behaviour and it is consistent with established consumer behaviour theories stressing the role of perceived value in decision-making.

Organizational Value Layer

Behavioral responses subsequently generate organizational value, reflected in performance and efficiency outcomes. These include:

- Revenue growth and conversion efficiency
- Reduced operational costs (e.g., return logistics)
- Enhanced brand equity and customer engagement

Across all the cases, immersive technologies contribute to measurable organizational benefits. For example, increased conversion rate in retail and improved booking performance in tourism directly impact revenue generation, and reduced return rate improves operational efficiency. Thus, these layers demonstrate that immersive technologies are not merely experiential tools, but are strategic assets which influence the competitiveness and performance of firm.

Sustainability Value Layer

The key contribution of the framework lies in its integration of sustainability as an embedded outcome of immersive value creation. Point to be noted here is that in all these cases, sustainability was not the direct intent of the organizations. However, it is coming up as a by-product of AI-enabled immersive system and value creation for consumers. We can reveal three primary sustainability mechanisms.

- One is reduction in physical resource usage, for example, AR-based visualization reduces product return, minimizes logistics emission, and packaging wastage.
- Dematerialization of infrastructure, that is virtual showrooms and digital interfaces reduce reliance on physical retail and promotional spaces
- Optimization of travel behavior:

VR-enabled preview of destination helps users make informed decisions and reduce exploratory travel.

All these findings suggest that sustainability is not an external objective, but an intrinsic and indirect outcome of improved experiential efficiency, which aligns with emerging perspective on digital sustainability in service ecosystems.

Human-Centered AI Governance Layer

This framework incorporates human-centered AI governance as a moderating layer which influences all stages of value creation. Immersive technology raises very critical ethical concerns like data privacy, behavioral tracking, transparency of algorithms, fairness, accessibility, digital inclusion and the potential for persuasive or manipulative design. For example, AR system in retail involves extensive data capture related to user interaction and preferences. Similarly, in VR environment in tourism, it may influence decision-making through emotionally immersive simulations. These issues highlight the importance of ethical principles within the system design and deployment (Floridi et al., 2018). This layer ensures that value creation is aligned with broader societal and ethical considerations, which will reinforce the need for responsible innovation.

8. THEORETICAL CONTRIBUTIONS

This study helps in developing an integrated perspective on experience and value creation across retail and tourism sectors, thereby advancing the understanding of AI enabled immersive technologies. Considering conceptual foundation and cross case evidences, it informs the role of immersive technology in the holistic value creation process. It aligns technology, human experience, consumer behaviour and organisational & social outcomes.

This study takes AI personalization and immersive interfaces as independent mechanisms to shape experiential value. It also identified different constructs like diagnosticity, presence and personalization which play foundational role in experience creation for consumers. The proposed framework explains how immersive learning changes the process of evaluation and engagement patterns.

Primarily it shifts focus from technology centric perspective to experience driven value creation, which leads to behavioural patterns like decision confidence, engagement and purchase intention. This study puts focus on the dual perspective of value creation, as the organization also benefits from revenue growth, operational efficiency, reduced product return, low load on physical infrastructure etc., other than the consumers' enhance experience. Thus, it reinforces the strategic role of AI enabled immersive technologies in the business ecosystem.

This chapter also highlights the conceptualization of sustainability as an embedded outcome of immersive service creation process. The proposed framework shows that improved experiential accuracy and organizational efficiency can reduce product returns, dematerialization of physical infrastructure and optimization of decision making process. This can naturally help the organizations in resources optimization and environmental benefits, thus contributing towards sustainability. This perspective extends sustainability study by integrating it within the experiential and behavioural paths driven by digital technologies.

Another contribution of this study is the positioning of human centred AI governance as a crucial moderating dimension. Ethical considerations like data privacy, transparency, inclusivity and responsible design while creating value, underlines the critical role of governance to legitimize the emerging systems and shape effectiveness. Ethics is not just superficial concern, it plays a central role to influence adoption, growth and sustainable use of AI.

In spite of differences between retail and tourism sector in terms of tangibility and other attributes, the analysis shows consistent patterns which links technological enablement, experiential values, behavioural outcome and ultimately sustainability outcomes. This revelation of generalizability enhances the robustness of the proposed framework and supports its relevance for diverse sectors. Basically the chapter offers a comprehensive and integrative theoretical perspective which attaches immersive technology, organizational performance, sustainability and ethical governance in a coherent model with the help of conceptual reasoning and real world examples.

9. MANAGERIAL IMPLICATIONS

The study has many important implications for managers using digital transformation and AI enabled ecosystem. They should recognize that immersive technology can create value by enhancing the quality of experience, not only technological novelty. While investing in technologies like AR and VR systems, elements like dignosticity, presence and personalization must be given priority, as these constructs influences consumers experience and decisional making process. Supporting realistic product visualization or immersive destination preview could drastically reduce uncertainty, decision fatigue and improve consumer confidence. All these will lead to higher conversion and better engagement outcomes.

Organizations should align their immersive technology with measurable business outcomes and integrate in the value creation process. Thus a shift from digital initiative to data driven performance oriented immersive strategy is the key to success.

Managers can use different immersive technology to support sustainability objectives which comes as a by-product. Usage of these AR/VR technologies help reduce product return, lower dependence of physical resources, ensure informed decisions. In case of tourism, immersive travel tech optimizes planning and reduce unnecessary exploratory visits. Many such practices discussed in this chapter in fact demonstrate how sustainability can be achieved within the digital experience, instead of being treated as separate strategic function.

The findings also emphasize the need of a responsible and human centred AI governance and policy formulation. Since the immersive systems depend to a great extent on user data collection, analysis and algorithmic decision making process, ensuring transparency and privacy is of utmost importance. Organizations can build consumer trust and long term adoption, by articulating clear policies, consent and ethical design. They must also consider the concerns of accessibility and inclusivity to have a holistic approach towards this paradigm shift in doing business.

The integration of physical and digital interfaces can enhance continuity across the customer journey and improve their overall experience. This becomes more relevant in omni channel retail and digitally enabled tourism ecosystems where seamless interaction across different platforms is non-negotiable. The cross sectoral analysis provide insights on the way immersive technology follows generalizable value creation. Hence managers can transfer best proctices across diverse sectors and industries.

Managers should adopt AI enabled immersive technologies as strategic tools for integrated value creation while balancing enhance consumer experience, improved organizational efficiency, sustainability and ethical practices to achieve sustainable competitive advantage.

10. LIMITATIONS & FUTURE RESEARCH DIRECTION

This study is subject to certain limitations. Conceptual chapters having case based evidence, the findings are shaped by a few specific cases selected for this study. The situations discussed here like Shopify, Wayfair, Kerala Tourism, Marriot, are well resourced, technologically advanced and institutionally supported organisations. However, the interrelated and contextual nature of the retail and tourism sector means that cultural norms, administrative structures and geography, economic conditions may significantly affect the applicability of this framework in different settings.

The framework is conceptual in nature and needs empirical validation for different contexts and user groups. Future research can extend this study in many directions. Empirical studies using quantitative methods may be done to test the relationship proposed in the framework to examine the relative impact of experiential constructs like diagnosticity, presence, and personalization. Research may also be done to explore sector-specific changes or variations, especially in emerging markets, where technological adoption and user behaviour may be significantly different. There is also a scope to investigate the evolving role of governance mechanisms, including ethical practices, regulatory framework, and user trust in immersive environments. Overall, this study provides a foundation to advance research at the intersection of immersive technology, experience design, sustainability, and responsible AI.

11. CONCLUSION

This chapter develops an integrative understanding of how AI-enabled immersive technologies reshape experience and value creation across retail and tourism contexts. By combining conceptual foundation with empirical case analysis, this demonstrated that immersive system offerings help in technological enablement, improves experiential value. This leads to favourable responses which can generate organizational and sustainability outcomes. These findings highlight that value creation is dependent on the effective integration of human-centred AI governance.

This chapter presents a coherent framework that connects experience, autonomous system development, and depth within a single model. It emphasizes that emerging technologies should not be viewed as mere investment tools or just strategic infrastructure to influence the whole organization design interaction.

DISCLOSURE

Images in the chapter are created with the support of AI.

REFERENCES

Arantes, L. (2022). Digital marketing and sustainability: A study on consumer perceptions. *ICIEMC Proceedings, 3*, 40-49.

Barta, S., Gurrea, R., & Flavián, C. (2023). How Augmented Reality Increases Engagement Through Its Impact on Risk and the Decision Process. *Cyberpsychology, Behavior, and Social Networking*, *26*(3), 177–187. DOI: 10.1089/cyber.2022.0087 PMID: 36706429

Beck, J., Rainoldi, M., & Egger, R. (2019). Virtual reality in tourism: a state-of-the-art review. In *Tourism Review* (Vol. 74, Number 3, pp. 586–612). Emerald Group Holdings Ltd. DOI: 10.1108/TR-03-2017-0049

Bonetti, F., Warnaby, G., & Quinn, L. (2018). Augmented Reality and Virtual Reality in Physical and Online Retailing: A Review, Synthesis and Research Agenda. In T. Jung & M. tom Dieck (Eds.), *Augmented reality and virtual reality: Progress in IS*. Springer. DOI: 10.1007/978-3-319-64027-3_9

Buhalis, D. (2020). Technology in tourism-from information communication technologies to eTourism and smart tourism towards ambient intelligence tourism: A perspective article. *Tourism Review*, *75*(1), 267–272. DOI: 10.1108/TR-06-2019-0258

Buhalis, D., Harwood, T., Bogicevic, V., Viglia, G., Beldona, S., & Hofacker, C. (2019). Technological disruptions in services: Lessons from tourism and hospitality. *Journal of Service Management*, *30*(4), 484–506. DOI: 10.1108/JOSM-12-2018-0398

Buhalis, D., Leung, D., & Lin, M. (2023). Metaverse as a disruptive technology revolutionising tourism management and marketing. *Tourism Management*, *97*, 104724. Advance online publication. DOI: 10.1016/j.tourman.2023.104724

Chaturvedi, R., Verma, S., Das, R., & Dwivedi, Y. K. (2023). Social companionship with artificial intelligence: Recent trends and future avenues. *Technological Forecasting and Social Change*, *193*, 122634. DOI: 10.1016/j.techfore.2023.122634

Davenport, T., Guha, A., Grewal, D., & Bressgott, T. (2020). How artificial intelligence will change the future of marketing. *Journal of the Academy of Marketing Science*, *48*(1), 24–42. DOI: 10.1007/s11747-019-00696-0

Disztinger, P., Schlögl, S., & Groth, A. (2017, Jan.). Technology acceptance of virtual reality for travel planning. In *Information and Communication Technologies in Tourism 2017: Proceedings of the International Conference in Rome, Italy, January 24-26, 2017* (pp. 255-268). Springer International Publishing.

Dwivedi, Y. K., Hughes, L., Ismagilova, E., Aarts, G., Coombs, C., Crick, T., Duan, Y., Dwivedi, R., Edwards, J., Eirug, A., Galanos, V., Ilavarasan, P. V., Janssen, M., Jones, P., Kar, A. K., Kizgin, H., Kronemann, B., Lal, B., Lucini, B., & Williams, M. D. (2021). Artificial Intelligence (AI): Multidisciplinary perspectives on emerging challenges, opportunities, and agenda for research, practice and policy. *International Journal of Information Management*, *57*, 101994. Advance online publication. DOI: 10.1016/j.ijinfomgt.2019.08.002

Dwivedi, Y. K., Kshetri, N., Hughes, L., Slade, E. L., Jeyaraj, A., Kar, A. K., Baabdullah, A. M., Koohang, A., Raghavan, V., Ahuja, M., Albanna, H., Albashrawi, M. A., Al-Busaidi, A. S., Balakrishnan, J., Barlette, Y., Basu, S., Bose, I., Brooks, L., Buhalis, D., & Wright, R. (2023). "So what if ChatGPT wrote it?" Multidisciplinary perspectives on opportunities, challenges and implications of generative conversational AI for research, practice and policy. *International Journal of Information Management*, *71*, 102642. Advance online publication. DOI: 10.1016/j.ijinfomgt.2023.102642

Flavián, C., Ibáñez-Sánchez, S., & Orús, C. (2019). Integrating virtual reality devices into the body: Effects of technological embodiment on customer engagement and behavioral intentions toward the destination. *Journal of Travel & Tourism Marketing*, *36*(7), 847–863. DOI: 10.1080/10548408.2019.1618781

Flavián, C., Ibáñez-Sánchez, S., & Orús, C. (2021). Impacts of technological embodiment through virtual reality on potential guests' emotions and engagement. *Journal of Hospitality Marketing & Management*, *30*(1), 1–20. DOI: 10.1080/19368623.2020.1770146

Floridi, L., Cowls, J., Beltrametti, M., Chatila, R., Chazerand, P., Dignum, V., Luetge, C., Madelin, R., Pagallo, U., Rossi, F., Schafer, B., Valcke, P., & Vayena, E. (2018). AI4People—An Ethical Framework for a Good AI Society: Opportunities, Risks, Principles, and Recommendations. *Minds and Machines*, *28*(4), 689–707. DOI: 10.1007/s11023-018-9482-5 PMID: 30930541

Gretzel, U., Sigala, M., Xiang, Z., & Koo, C. (2015). Smart tourism: Foundations and developments. *Electronic Markets*, *25*(3), 179–188. DOI: 10.1007/s12525-015-0196-8

Gursoy, D., Chi, O. H., Lu, L., & Nunkoo, R. (2019). Consumers acceptance of artificially intelligent (AI) device use in service delivery. *International Journal of Information Management*, *49*, 157–169. DOI: 10.1016/j.ijinfomgt.2019.03.008

Guttentag, D. A. (2010). Virtual reality: Applications and implications for tourism. *Tourism Management*, *31*(5), 637–651. DOI: 10.1016/j.tourman.2009.07.003

Hilken, T., de Ruyter, K., Chylinski, M., Mahr, D., & Keeling, D. I. (2017). Augmenting the eye of the beholder: Exploring the strategic potential of augmented reality to enhance online service experiences. *Journal of the Academy of Marketing Science, 45*(6), 884–905. DOI: 10.1007/s11747-017-0541-x

Huang, L., Solangi, Y. A., Magazzino, C., & Solangi, S. A. (2024). Evaluating the efficiency of green innovation and marketing strategies for long-term sustainability in the context of Environmental labeling. *Journal of Cleaner Production, 450*, 141870. Advance online publication. DOI: 10.1016/j.jclepro.2024.141870

Huang, M.-H., & Rust, R. T. (2021). *A strategic framework for artificial intelligence in marketing*. DOI: 10.1007/s11747-020-00749-9/Published

Javornik, A. (2016). 'It's an illusion, but it looks real!' Consumer affective, cognitive and behavioural responses to augmented reality applications. *Journal of Marketing Management, 32*(9–10), 987–1011. DOI: 10.1080/0267257X.2016.1174726

Javornik, A., Duffy, K., Rokka, J., Scholz, J., Nobbs, K., Motala, A., & Goldenberg, A. (2021). Strategic approaches to augmented reality deployment by luxury brands. *Journal of Business Research, 136*, 284–292. DOI: 10.1016/j.jbusres.2021.07.040

Koohang, A., Nord, J. H., Ooi, K.-B., Tan, G. W.-H., Al-Emran, M., Aw, E. C.-X., Baabdullah, A. M., Buhalis, D., Cham, T.-H., Dennis, C., Dutot, V., Dwivedi, Y. K., Hughes, L., Mogaji, E., Pandey, N., Phau, I., Raman, R., Sharma, A., Sigala, M., & Wong, L.-W. (2023). Shaping the Metaverse into Reality: A Holistic Multidisciplinary Understanding of Opportunities, Challenges, and Avenues for Future Investigation. *Journal of Computer Information Systems, 63*(3), 735–765. DOI: 10.1080/08874417.2023.2165197

Laria, G., & Pantano, E. (2011). Immersive environments for an advanced technology-based store. In *The 7th International Conference on Networked Computing and Advanced Information Management* (pp. 218-221). IEEE.

Lemon, K. N., & Verhoef, P. C. (2016). Understanding customer experience throughout the customer journey. *Journal of Marketing, 80*(6), 69–96. DOI: 10.1509/jm.15.0420

Mehmetoglu, M., & Engen, M. (2011). Pine and Gilmore's Concept of Experience Economy and Its Dimensions: An Empirical Examination in Tourism. *Journal of Quality Assurance in Hospitality & Tourism, 12*(4), 237–255. DOI: 10.1080/1528008X.2011.541847

Mehrabi, N., Morstatter, F., Saxena, N., Lerman, K., & Galstyan, A. (2022). A Survey on Bias and Fairness in Machine Learning. In *ACM Computing Surveys* (Vol. 54, Number 6). Association for Computing Machinery. DOI: 10.1145/3457607

Milgram, P. (1994). A taxonomy of mixed reality visual displays. In *IEICE Transactions on Information Systems* (Number 12). http://vered.rose.utoronto.ca/people/paul_dir/IEICE94/ieice.html

Pantano, E., Pizzi, G., Scarpi, D., & Dennis, C. (2020). Competing during a pandemic? Retailers' ups and downs during the COVID-19 outbreak. *Journal of Business Research, 116*, 209–213. DOI: 10.1016/j.jbusres.2020.05.036 PMID: 32501307

Rai, A. (2020). Explainable AI: from black box to glass box. In *Journal of the Academy of Marketing Science* (Vol. 48, Number 1, pp. 137–141). Springer. DOI: 10.1007/s11747-019-00710-5

Shopify. (2022, Apr. 29). *The ROI on AR: How augmented reality is boosting ecommerce sales*. https://www.shopify.com/blog/ar-shopping

Siamagka, N. T., Christodoulides, G., Michaelidou, N., & Valvi, A. (2015). Determinants of social media adoption by B2B organizations. *Industrial Marketing Management, 51*, 89–99. DOI: 10.1016/j.indmarman.2015.05.005

Siu, E. (2026, Feb. 23). AR experiences that boosted conversion rates by 189%. *Single Grain*. https://www.singlegrain.com/digital-marketing/ar-experiences-that-boosted-conversion-rates-by-189/

Sreejesh, S., Ghosh, T., & Dwivedi, Y. K. (2021). Moving beyond the content: The role of contextual cues in the effectiveness of gamification of advertising. *Journal of Business Research, 132*, 88–101. DOI: 10.1016/j.jbusres.2021.04.007

Statista. (2024). *Statistics & facts on augmented reality (AR)*. https://www.statista.com/topics/3286/augmented-reality-ar

Susser, D., Roessler, B., & Nissenbaum, H. (2019). Technology, autonomy, and manipulation. *Internet Policy Review, 8*(2). Advance online publication. DOI: 10.14763/2019.2.1410

The Hindu Business Line. (2023). *Kerala's domestic tourist arrivals at record 21.87 crore in 2023: Minister Riyas*. https://www.thehindubusinessline.com/news/keralas-domestic-tourist-arrivals-at-record-218-crore-in-2023-minister-riyas/article67912764.ece

Wedel, M., Bigné, E., & Zhang, J. (2020). Virtual and augmented reality: Advancing research in consumer marketing. *International Journal of Research in Marketing, 37*(3), 443–465. DOI: 10.1016/j.ijresmar.2020.04.004

Yadav, A., & Sondhi, H. (2023). Systematic Literature Review on Sustainable Marketing and Artificial Intelligence. *Proceedings of the 17th INDIACom; 2023 10th International Conference on Computing for Sustainable Global Development, INDIACom 2023*, 583–588.

Yin, R. K. (2018). *Case study research and applications* (vol. 6). Sage.

Ying, T., Tang, J., Ye, S., Tan, X., & Wei, W. (2022). Virtual Reality in Destination Marketing: Telepresence, Social Presence, and Tourists' Visit Intentions. *Journal of Travel Research*, *61*(8), 1738–1756. DOI: 10.1177/00472875211047273

Chapter 9
Human-Centered AI Transformation in Emerging Markets:
Integrating Institutional Conditions, Organizational Purpose, and Employee Experience

Okechukwu Ethelbert Amah
http://orcid.org/0000-0002-6574-6941
Lagos Business School, Pan-Atlantic University, Nigeria

Daniel Omolola Rufai
http://orcid.org/0009-0005-1575-9663
Lagos Business School, Pan-Atlantic University, Nigeria

ABSTRACT

The impacts of AI on organizations cut across every sector, but there are contextual factors (institutional conditions, organizational purpose, and employee experience) that may create challenges in emerging markets for optimal utilization of AI tools. The theoretical foundation of this chapter relies on institutional theory and stakeholder theory. A conceptual framework was developed to explain the relationships and interactions of institutional conditions on organizational purpose and employee experience in building human-centered AI transformation. The chapter's outcomes showed that AI deployment succeeds when supported by institutional conditions, which enhance organizational purpose alignment and create positive employee experiences within the workplace. The chapter expands theoretical knowledge on

DOI: 10.4018/979-8-3373-8282-1.ch009

human-centered AI transformation and provides HR managers and organizations with guidance on how to be resilient amidst institutional conditions to utilize AI technology effectively and prioritize employee well-being.

1.0 INTRODUCTION

The adoption of artificial intelligence (AI) varies across developed and emerging markets, which influence organizational performance, purpose, work structures, and how people are managed within the workplace. By using AI, organizations can improve operational efficiency and serve their customers better through informed decision-making and increased work automation (Ghobakhloo et al., 2023). Various studies have been conducted on AI technologies productivity and operational efficiency across various sectors, with a substantial body of literature in developed economies. This highlights the importance of AI technologies in enhancing work efficiency, reducing errors, increasing job satisfaction, and enhancing manpower development. These impacts underscore the need to introduce AI technologies in emerging markets.

This represents a positive transition in organizations within emerging markets from a traditional work model to an AI-enabled work model. This shift enhances work efficiency and enables organizations to expand their business operations in emerging markets. For example, in Nigeria, the implementation of AI technologies in the banking sector enables banks to upgrade their databases to connect with customers in rural areas and increase organizational efficiency (Ezeocha, 2024). Additionally, the integration of AI tools like chatbots enables customers to make enquiries or complain about products and services online, while customer representatives are available to attend to complex problems in the organization (Anand et al., 2023). These demonstrate the importance of AI technologies to organizations in emerging markets.

Irrespective of the benefits of AI technologies, the transition to an AI-enabled work model has introduced several challenges, such as digital isolation, technostress, job insecurity, reduced employee autonomy, and erosion of human judgment on their tasks and decision-making in the organization. These challenges are more pronounced in emerging markets due to institutional constraints, such as weak regulatory frameworks, unequal access to digital infrastructure, high cost of training, and a shortage of skilled manpower, which affect AI adoption within organizations. As a result, organizations without a clear purpose for AI integrations face difficulties in effectively deploying and utilising AI technologies, thereby creating negative experiences for employees. The emerging markets are confronted with tensions between modernisation and maintaining traditional values, which makes organizational purpose essential in determining how AI usage impacts employee flourishing.

These challenges highlight the importance of designing AI technologies in alignment with human needs within emerging markets. Existing approaches to addressing these challenges have focused on operational efficiency and automation, with limited impact on employee well-being. Thus, this necessitates the need for human-centered AI transformation in emerging markets to ensure effective deployment and optimal utilization of AI technologies.

Human-centered AI transformation focuses on how AI technologies can be redesigned to support human needs and well-being in the organization (Usmani et al., 2023; Fenwick et al., 2024). This is crucial for enhancing human collaboration with AI and promoting transparency and accountability in management decisions that affect employees' jobs. Human-centered AI transformation can be referred to as a purposeful plan to re-strategize AI tools to enhance human skills and capabilities rather than displacing them from their duties (Fenwick et al., 2024). This is important to encourage meaningful human oversight and promote employees' psychological well-being amidst AI integration in organizational systems.

Existing studies have shown that integrating AI technologies has positive impacts on employees, such as enabling greater autonomy at work, increasing task performance and employee engagement, and providing opportunities to learn new skills (Afroogh et al., 2024; Drakul, 2025). However, AI technologies create negative impacts on employees' well-being when they are not properly implemented with a clear purpose in the organization, such as increased burnout, a lack of trust in management decisions, reduced work autonomy, and uncertainty about job security. These implementation failures will undermine employees' self-efficacy in performing their tasks and reduce job satisfaction. Hence, how AI technologies are implemented in strategic alignment with core organizational purpose determines the positive or negative impacts on employee experience and overall well-being in the organization.

Despite the rapid adoption of artificial intelligence in developed markets, the effective utilization of AI in emerging markets remains uneven, hindered by contextual factors such as institutional conditions, unclear organizational purpose, and differences in employee experience. Previous studies have examined institutional constraints, organizational purpose, and employee experience independently without explaining their interdependence mechanisms in building a human centered AI transformation (Madanchian & Taherdoost, 2025; Zirar et al., 2023). Existing research on institutional constraints focuses on regulatory policies and quality governance, yet fails to identify their effects on AI integration (Dieleman et al., 2022; Lawrence et al., 2023). Similarly, there are studies on organizational purpose that examine its impact on productivity and performance, but there is no clarity on how organizational purpose drives AI adoption within emerging markets. (Gartenberg et al., 2019; George et al., 2021). Furthermore, most existing studies on AI deployment are conducted in developed markets, with limited focus on emerging markets, thereby overlooking the institutional constraints in this context (Brougham & Haar, 2020; Malik et al., 2022). Hence, the relationships and interactions between institutional conditions, organizational purpose, and employee experience are not integrated, as they are interconnected rather than independent mechanisms that reinforce AI integration in building human-centered AI transformations. This justifies the need to understand how institutional conditions, organizational purpose, and employee experience promote or hinder the deployment of AI technologies in emerging markets.

To address these gaps, this chapter adopts a conceptual review, given the limited literature on AI technology in emerging markets. Previous studies on institutional conditions, organizational purpose and employee experience were synthesized to develop an integrated model that connects these three constructs to build a sustainable human-centered AI transformation in emerging markets. The chapter identifies variations in contextual factors that affect AI transformation across emerging and developed markets. The outcome of this chapter advances theoretical knowledge and provides recommendations for HR managers, policymakers, and stakeholders on utilizing AI technologies and prioritizing employee well-being within the organization.

2.0 REVIEW METHODOLOGY

This chapter adopts a conceptual review by synthesizing existing literature on artificial intelligence, institutional conditions, organizational purpose, employee experience, institutional theory and stakeholder theory to identify key theoretical linkages relevant to AI transformation. The theories (institutional theory and stakeholder theory) were carefully selected for their importance in explaining the interactions and relationships among the concepts. The chapter relies on secondary data, and the studies reviewed were selected based on their relevance to AI transformation, institutional conditions, organizational purpose, and employee experience. The essence of the review is to develop a human-centered framework for AI transformation in emerging markets. The conceptual framework explains how institutional conditions, organizational purpose, and employee experience interact to facilitate human-centered AI transformation in digital work environments.

2.1 Human-Centered AI Transformation

The ideology behind human-centered AI (HCAI) is based on ensuring humans have some level of control and intervention over how AI technologies operate and generate outputs in specific tasks within the organization. Also, AI technologies change how work and people are managed, often with a positive or negative impact on their well-being in flexible work arrangements. These necessitate a human-centered AI to protect employees' interests, safety, and well-being as AI technologies are introduced into organizational systems. This shift represents a transformative change in the development and integration of AI technologies in work operations to embrace human values and ethics in the implementation processes to ensure there is a balance between employee well-being and organizational performance.

Human-centered AI can be described as the transformative process in AI systems by ensuring AI algorithms are blended with human needs and values in the development of AI technologies to enhance operational efficiency and the overall well-being of employees in the workplace (Schmager et al., 2025; Xu, 2026). HCAI enhances human-AI collaboration, thereby creating hybrid intelligence in the workplace, where humans can use their knowledge alongside AI competencies to generate meaningful outcomes compared to outcomes generated by either alone (Dellermann et al., 2019; Venigandla et al., 2024). These may remain abstract without human-centered AI practices embedded into organizational work processes and day-to-day activities.

2.2 Human-Centered AI Practices

Human-centered AI practices refer to as organizational policies that ensure the deployment of AI systems prioritize human values and overall well-being within the workplace. The HCAI practices are crucial to ensure that technologies are used responsibly, augmenting employees' tasks rather than displacing them from their jobs. Organizations that are HCAI conscious institutionalized these practices into daily organizational activities to promote human flourishing within AI-mediated work environments. The HCAI practices include transparency, human oversight, ethical implementation, and AI literacy.

***Transparency*:** This is when employees understand and can explain how the AI system generates outputs and the impact these outputs have on their work with the organization. Transparency in AI-generated outcomes enables employees to understand their capabilities and limitations, thereby influencing their trust in AI decision-making.

***Human Oversight*:** This is ensuring employees have the capacity to influence, monitor and question outputs produced by AI technologies in alignment with organizational systems. Meaningful human oversight enhances employees' confidence to interact and collaborate with the AI system for quality decision-making within the organization.

Ethical Implementation: This refers to the deployment of AI systems in a way that upholds ethical principles (transparency, fairness, accountability, and reliability) and responsible use of AI in organizational systems. This is important to ensure AI technologies are monitored to prevent abusive use that may cause harm to employees or other stakeholders in the organization.

***AI Literacy*:** This refers to the knowledge, skills, abilities, and competencies possessed by employees that can enable them to interact and use an AI system effectively to actualize organizational goals. This is achievable through organizational support in the form of skill acquisition and training programs that can increase employee performance and work engagement. Hence, institutional conditions such as regulatory governance, digital infrastructure, and cultural beliefs play a crucial role in translating HCAI practices into organizational practices that can enhance ethical use of AI systems, while promoting employee well-being.

2.3 Theoretical Foundation

2.3.1 Institutional Theory

This study relies on institutional theory and stakeholder theory to explain the mechanisms and the pathway that connect the three constructs (institutional constraints, organizational purpose, and employee experience) to achieve a human-centered AI transformation in emerging markets. Institutional theory was developed by Meyer and Rowan (1977) and focuses on the influences of the external work environment on how organizations are shaped. They posited that institutional norms shape how organizations operate within an environment, influence their access to required resources, and determine the legitimacy they need to operate, which is achieved by complying with the rules and regulations of their operating environment (Meyer & Rowan, 1977). These norms are categorized into regulatory, normative, and cognitive dimensions, which influence organizational behaviors and decision-making within a specific work environment (Scott, 2014). The regulatory represents government policies, and the normative represents the ethical standards of an organization, while the cognitive explains the perception or cultural beliefs of an organization about certain conditions.

In applying this theory to human-centered AI transformation in emerging markets, institutional theory positions regulatory dimensions as rules and regulations, digital infrastructure, and governance control within an organization operating environment. These factors are critical to an organization's adoption of AI technology in emerging markets because they determine the success or failure of AI implementation in operational systems. The normative dimension expects organizations to comply with the ethical and professional standards of their association or industry when integrating AI technologies into their work processes and to consider the impact on employees' well-being. However, when organizations do not comply with ethical standards, AI integration becomes mere automation rather than the augmentation necessary to enhance human flourishing and organizational productivity. The cognitive dimension explains the cultural beliefs regarding AI technology arising from the uncertainty that AI create job insecurity and erodes human oversight, which influences organizational trust in AI and the implementation process. Collectively, these conditions put pressure on organizations to respond to the pressure of the external environment. Hence, institutional theory is not sufficient for organization to capture the totality of the pressures arising from external forces, which necessitates the need for stakeholder theory.

2.3.2 Stakeholder Theory

Stakeholder theory was first introduced by Freeman (1984) and emphasised that organizations should prioritise all stakeholders (employees, customers, and other groups of individuals) and ensure they benefit from the value created, rather than focusing solely on shareholders' interests. Organizational success depends on creating multiple values that benefit stakeholders regardless of their status or positions (Freeman, 2010). Organizations that are driven by purpose prioritise stakeholders' values and demonstrate social responsibility to their immediate and external customers to achieve sustainable success. The theory was expanded, and three major attributes were identified that can enhance the management of all stakeholders. These include power, legitimacy, and urgency, which serve as a means of determining when and how to ensure that every service rendered creates meaningful value for all stakeholders (Mitchell et al., 1997).

In applying this theory to AI transformation in emerging markets, stakeholder theory emphasised the importance of organizations prioritising stakeholders' needs through long-term value creation that is sustainable. This explains the importance of organizational purpose in the deployment of AI technologies and the impact on every stakeholder's well-being and the attainment of organizational goals. Purpose-driven organizations ensure AI implementation is fair and transparent in a way that enhances human capacity and inclusiveness, while helping organizations to achieve operational efficiency. In emerging markets, organizations face multiple demands and pressures from stakeholders, necessitating the definition of AI purpose during implementation to ensure value creation for all stakeholders.

The theory explains the importance of employee experience beyond the implementation stage of AI systems and identifies the employee as the most relevant stakeholder, requiring attention and whose actions affect other stakeholders. This is because employees possess a certain level of power through collective action as legitimate contributors, and it requires urgency because AI technologies have a direct impact on their work experience and engagement in the organization. Hence, organizations that do not pay attention to how AI technologies affect employees' experience face a high risk of labour turnover and low productivity, regardless of their investment in technological advancements (Tasleem & Gangadharan, 2022; Saini et al., 2025). Conversely, organizations that implement AI systems and prioritize employee needs and well-being, along with organizational productivity achieve sustainable outcomes (Valtonen et al., 2025).

The integration of the two enhances theoretical knowledge for explaining human-centered AI transformations in emerging markets. Institutional theory and stakeholder theory were carefully selected because both play complementary roles in addressing gaps in emerging markets and provide organizations with the knowledge to navigate the challenges in their businesses. Institutional theory highlighted the dual roles of institutional conditions that affect organizations in the implementation of AI technologies. Institutional conditions become a burden on organizations when government policies, digital infrastructure, and skills gaps disrupt organizations' readiness to implement AI technologies. However, organizations in enabling institutional conditions find it easier to implement AI technologies into their systems for work augmentation and improving the overall well-being of the organization. Stakeholder theory emphasises that organizations with a purpose should consider employees as primary stakeholders when designing and implementing AI technologies to meet their needs, augment assigned tasks and make decisions that improve their well-being.

3.0 CORE CONSTRUCTS

3.1 Institutional Conditions and AI Transformation

Institutional conditions are one of the major determinants that shape how organizations adopt and implement AI systems into their operational systems, within emerging and developed markets. Institutional conditions consist of external factors within an AI-enabled work environment that shape organizational perceptions, integrations, implementation, and decision-making processes, and behavioural compliance with AI technologies in actualizing their goals. Institutional theory categorized these conditions into three main dimensions, which include regulative, normative, and cognitive and together shape how organizations adopt AI technologies into their operational systems. The regulative conditions are critical and provide the policies and legal framework for AI deployment (Cazzaniga et al., 2024), while the normative conditions define professional practices and ethical standards that guide AI implementation (Maleki, 2026). The cognitive conditions are cultural beliefs and perceptions of organizations about the uncertainties around AI replacing human tasks and work relationships in the organizations (Jussupow et al., 2022).

From a different perspective, Cazzaniga et al. (2024) classified these conditions as quality of digital infrastructure, government regulatory policies, ecosystems and economic conditions influence the feasibility of AI adoption and implementation sustainability within the organization. For instance, in an AI-enabled work environment, inadequate digital infrastructure increases workplace stress and workloads, while weak regulatory policies create uncertainty about employees' job security amid the introduction of AI technologies markets (Vanu et al., 2024). Hence, when this occurs, AI adoption becomes a burden on organizational productivity and employees' overall well-being. Institutional conditions play dual roles, either as an enabler or a constraint to AI integration, depending on how organizations adopt digital technologies to be innovative within a specific context to achieve organizational goals (Hassan et al., 2024). Institutional conditions are positive when they enhance the effective deployment of AI technologies, whereas negative when they disrupt an organization's optimal deployment and utilization of AI technologies.

Institutional conditions vary across regions and countries, demonstrating that emerging and developed markets can be affected by unstable government regulations, limited digital infrastructure, and economic conditions (Al-Assaf, Abdel-Halim, & Shehadeh, 2025). For instance, some emerging markets possess advanced digital infrastructure and stable regulatory governance (Staley & Amankwa, 2025), whereas some developed markets may face regulatory uncertainty, skills gaps, surveillance concerns, and unequal access to digital infrastructure (van Kessel et al., 2022; Oyeyemi et al., 2025). Hence, institutional conditions such as quality infrastructure, digital readiness, stable regulatory governance, and ethical standards enhance the effective integration of AI technologies into organizational systems. However, institutional conditions like strict government policies, low-quality digital infrastructure, economic conditions, cultural beliefs, and unethical standards often limit organizations in the successful adoption and implementation of digital technologies (Khanna & Palepu, 2010; Puffer et al., 2016; Benbya et al., 2021).

Thus, this can be referred to as an institutional void, which occurs when institutions (regulatory policies, economic systems, ethical standards, and cultural beliefs) are absent or lack support, thereby hindering organizational success and the integration of emerging technologies (Dieleman et al., 2022). Institutional void creates uncertainty problems for organizations in adopting digital technologies, which has implications on employee experience and engagement as well as organizational capabilities within an AI-enabled work environment (Khanna & Palepu, 2010; Benbya et al., 2021). As a result, organizations operating in emerging and developed markets may experience reduced innovations, slow implementation, and low organizational capability, thereby disrupting organizational efficiency and productivity. Thus, institutional conditions may affect AI transformation in emerging markets and organizations' adoption of AI, which include digital infrastructure readiness, governance capacity and regulatory policies, human capital development, and institutional quality.

3.1.1 Digital Infrastructure Readiness

Digital infrastructure readiness refers to the technical support within an economy or organization that enhances the effective deployment of AI technologies. This technical support includes technology, connectivity, and a stable network, which determines how organizations deploy AI technologies to manage people, make decisions, and transform their work processes to achieve a specific goal (Khasawneh & Dweiri, 2025). Digital infrastructure readiness is a major determinant of organizational capacity to integrate and maximise the advantage of AI technology in emerging markets.

Organizations must provide adequate and sustainable technological systems to ensure effective deployment and optimal use of AI technologies in enhancing organizational productivity and operational efficiency (Holmström, 2022). However, insufficient digital infrastructure may impede the organizational integration of AI and limit its impact on organizational performance, thereby increasing workplace stress and disrupting the organization's overall well-being (Marsh et al., 2022). The effect of digital infrastructure readiness is not limited to organizations; it shapes employee experiences, including poor optimal use of AI technologies, digital fatigue, and isolation, which affect employees' well-being (Supriyadi et al., 2025). This signifies the importance of digital infrastructure readiness in shaping AI adoption and how it affects everyday work, organizational decisions to invest in AI, and employees' trust in using AI.

3.1.2 Regulatory and Governance Capacity

Government capacity and regulatory policies constitute another dimension of institutional conditions affecting AI adoption in emerging markets. They reflect government policies governing AI adoption and deployment in organizations, as well as their capacity to monitor and ensure compliance with those policies. The AI strategy framework sets the standards organizations are expected to meet for data privacy, transparency, and algorithmic accountability, in line with established procedures (Fatima et al., 2020).

Organizations are confronted with unstable government regulations and policies, which may affect compliance, implementation planning and investment in AI technology. This creates uncertainty for organizations planning a human-centered AI transformation in their work processes and limits organizational performance in the long run. Similarly, when governments' capacity to monitor and enforce AI policies is ineffective, it may lead organizations to undermine the credibility of the regulatory policies, thereby disrupting their implementation processes (Walter, 2024). This affects the rate of AI integration and advancement among organizations in emerging markets.

3.1.3 Human Capital Development

Human capital development is the process by which individuals make efforts to acquire the skills, knowledge, and competencies that make them relevant and meaningful to organizations and society at large. Human capital development plays a crucial role in the sustainability of AI technologies within organizations and is greatly influenced by institutional constraints that shape employees' skills and competencies acquired over time within an economy (Wang et al., 2026). Regardless of an organization's investment in ensuring employees acquire the relevant skills and exposure to AI literacy to do their work, the environmental conditions determine how effective and efficient employees become over time. In an AI-enabled work environment, employees require AI skills such as programming, machine learning, and digital literacy to use and collaborate with AI technologies for effective performance (Chowdhury et al., 2022).

As a result, employees are seeking opportunities beyond their current environment to learn and acquire relevant skills to make a meaningful impact within and beyond their community (Balavadze & Zhgenti, 2018). This may affects organizations' ability to attract skilled, competent employees needed to function effectively in AI-enabled work environments. Similarly, organizations sought expertise and competent, skilled workers outside their work environment to fill AI-specific roles due to a knowledge gap among their employees. Hence, it is important to establish clarity on how institutional conditions differ from institutional voids, organizational readiness and internal capability to enable them to adopt strategic plans that are sustainable towards AI transformation.

3.1.4 Distinction Between Institutional Conditions, Institutional Voids, Organizational Readiness and Internal Capabilities

***Institutional Conditions*:** External environmental factors that influence AI adoption within organizations. These include regulatory policies, digital infrastructure, and cultural beliefs that may enable or constrain AI transformation across emerging and developed markets.

***Institutional Voids*:** This represents gaps in the institutional environments such as unstable regulatory policies, inadequate digital infrastructure, and limited government support and human capital that may disrupt the effective implementation of AI systems within organizations.

***Organizational Readiness*:** This indicates the extent to which organizations possess enabling structures. leadership commitment, and organizational culture that can enhance the effective adoption of emerging technologies.

***Internal Capabilities*:** It represents internal resources and competencies within organizations that can enhance the successful deployment of AI systems. These include employee competencies, AI literacy, and managerial expertise.

3.2 Organizational Purpose in AI Transformation

Organizational purpose defines the core values and fundamental reasons for the existence of an organization beyond making profits and providing values that contribute meaningfully to societal development. This shapes an organization's values and priorities, influences leadership engagement with stakeholders, and shapes the organization's overall decision-making process. In AI transformation, Organizations driven by purpose move from seeing AI solely as a productivity and operational efficiency tool to a mechanism that supports employees' work and provides sustainable value to their stakeholders (Holmström & Magnusson, 2025). This influences employees' experience and increases their work engagement and performance, which aligns with organizational values (Gartenberg et al., 2019). In this chapter, organizational purpose is conceptualized as a strategic implementation orientation that enables organizations to achieve human-centered AI transformations rather than ethical aspiration within the workplace.

These transformations are relevant in an AI-enabled work environment, where organizations with purpose balance AI-enhanced operational efficiency with employees' job security and overall well-being. Organizational purpose serves as a guiding framework for ensuring transparency, reducing bias, and preventing erosion of human oversight in the deployment and implementation of AI technologies. This requires organizations to invest in AI literacy training, provide moral and digital infrastructure support, and ensure AI technologies are designed to meet the needs of the employees in alignment with the overall goals of the organization. Organizations with purpose must be equipped with training investment, moral and digital infrastructure to be intentional in AI-systems integration rather than reactive to AI adoption. Hence, this demonstrates organizations' AI readiness and increases employees' trust in AI, enabling them to use AI systems effectively to achieve organizational goals.

Organizational purpose shapes an organization's AI readiness and the extent of what AI technologies are required to do within organizational systems. For instance, some organizations use AI to increase their productivity and work processes, while others integrate AI technologies as core competencies and value propositions, and without which organizational systems cannot function. Organizations that rely on AI for higher productivity and operational efficiency still maintain their traditional purpose but use AI technology to enhance the work processes and minimize costs (Yaşar, 2024). Conversely, organizations that use AI primarily as their core competency rely heavily on technological advancement and cannot do anything without AI (Benbya et al., 2020). Organizational purpose in AI transformation is more feasible by how organizations define AI roles in their operational systems.

3.2.1 Augmentation vs Automation Orientation

Organizational purpose enables organizations to clearly identify the role of AI technologies in organizational systems, either as augmentation or automation, before the implementation process. The use of AI technology as an augmentation positions it as a human partner required to enhance employee performance, increase focus, and enable meaningful oversight of AI-generated outcomes in the actualization of organizational goals (Westover, 2025). AI technology as an augmentation increases employee trust, job satisfaction, and work engagement, which increases organizational productivity and employee well-being (Sadeghi, 2024). In this situation, AI technology acts as an enabler, and it fosters human-AI collaboration and work relationship.

AI is used for automation when organizations prioritize and rely heavily on AI technologies to automate routine human tasks, thereby reducing labour costs and human involvement in organizational work processes (Kamal et al., 2024). Despite these benefits, AI automation increases the threat to job security, increases workplace stress, and exacerbates workplace inequality (Malik et al., 2022; Soulami et al., 2024). This reduces employees' trust in AI technologies due to a lack of meaningful human oversight over AI-generated outputs and their impact on overall well-being. This demonstrates that AI as augmentation and automation have different impacts on employees' performance and their perception of the utilization of AI technologies in doing their work. For instance, when organizations introduce AI automation to employees for creative and non-routine tasks, it limits their capacity and performance, creating division among employees who perceive AI as an enabler or a threat to their work (Dan et al., 2024; Jia et al., 2024).

3.2.2 Strategic Alignment and Purpose Clarity

AI technologies are not deployed into organizational systems in a vacuum; they are strategically positioned to align with the organization's mission and values. This clearly identifies the role of AI technology during the adoption process as a productivity tool, an enabler, or a means to gain a competitive advantage in the labour market (Gans, 2023; Szenftner et al., 2024; Polisetty et al., 2024). This understanding provides clear communication to stakeholders and employees on how AI technologies impact their job roles and what to expect, enabling leaders to allocate resources in line with the AI organizational purpose.

Purpose clarity enables employees to understand the AI organizational purpose, reduces uncertainty about AI adoption in the workplace, supports investment and decision-making, and ensures adequate AI literacy training for employees to actualize organizational goals (Trunk et al., 2020; Bankins et al., 2024). However, when employees lack clarity about AI adoption, it increases fear that AI technologies will displace them from their roles, thereby increasing the intention to quit and reducing work engagement (Presbitero & Teng-Calleja, 2023). Studies show that purpose ambiguity creates confusion among stakeholders and delays implementation, thereby undermining the sustainability of AI adoption in the organization. This highlights the importance of clarity about organizational purpose for stakeholders in AI adoption and changes as technology evolves.

3.3 Employee Experience in AI Transformation

Employee experience is a multidimensional construct that represents employees' overall perceptions and responses within an AI-enabled work environment. The introduction of AI technologies into organizational systems has transformed employees' experience, moving from traditional to digital work settings, where they interact with and collaborate with AI agents to achieve expected tasks. In AI transformation, employees' experience is the perception of an employee that is built over time, arising from their engagement and interaction with AI technologies, and the overall systems of the organization throughout their stay in the workplace. These experiences vary across emerging and developed markets, influencing employees' perceptions and interactions with AI technologies, which differ and change depending on job characteristics and how AI technologies are designed and implemented.

The extent of these experiences depends on the availability of organizational support, digital infrastructure, and employees' ability to use AI technology effectively and responsibly. Hence, when AI technologies are designed and implemented with employees' well-being in mind, they create positive experiences, such as enhancing job performance, job autonomy, and work relationships, reducing stress, thereby increasing motivation and engagement (Sadeghi, 2024). However, employees' experience becomes negative when AI technologies are designed without human oversight (Malik et al., 2022). They create uncertainty about job security, increase job monitoring, reduce autonomy, and humanise routine tasks, thereby reducing employee performance and increasing stress, affecting employees' trust in AI and future emerging technologies (Malik et al., 2022; Chung et al., 2025). Nevertheless, organizations can leverage AI technology to provide adequate support, ensuring it enhances employee performance and well-being rather than creating anxiety about displacing them from their roles.

Employees' experience with AI technology is multidimensional and shaped by factors beyond technological characteristics, including organizational support and managerial practices (Bankins et al., 2024). Organizational support and managerial practices such as communication patterns, leadership behaviors, feedback on AI usage and transparency in the implementation process influence employee experience of AI technology. Organizations that institutionalize a learning culture, ensure feedback and transparency in how AI technologies are implemented, and encourage employees' trust in AI, which affects their job satisfaction and work engagement (Shen & Hong, 2025). Conversely, when employees perceive a lack of support from their managers or superiors in using AI, it reduces their trust and confidence in management decisions generated by AI and organizational practices (Li & Bitterly, 2024; Bankins et al., 2024). These often increase workplace isolation, stress, and reduce work relationships between employees and AI, which leads to a negative impact on employee well-being and reduce organizational performance.

In this chapter, employee experience comprises five interrelated dimensions: trust in AI, skills development, adaptation capacity, employee agency, and well-being. These dimensions interdependently shape employee experience within an AI-mediated work environment and determine the effectiveness and sustainability of human-centered AI transformation in emerging markets.

3.3.1 Trust in AI

Trust is crucial to employees' acceptance and use of AI technology. Trust in AI technology is the personal perception and willingness of an employee to use AI technology, based on reliability, transparency, and consistency in achieving specific tasks repeatedly. Trust in AI increases employees' engagement, job satisfaction, and overall workplace performance. Through engagement, employees interact and learn how AI technologies impact their work, which encourages them to maximize the potential of AI for career advancement and future opportunities (Kong et al. 2023; Valtonen et al., 2025). This underscores the importance of trust as a dimension of employee experience that is essential for AI transformation, which requires organizations to be clear about the purpose of AI technologies and to provide the necessary support to encourage employees to continue using AI.

3.3.2 Skills Development

Skill development refers to employees' acquisition and enhancement of knowledge and relevant competencies through training that is essential for AI-enabled work environments. The adoption of AI technologies changes how work is done; there is a need for skill development and adaptation capabilities to ensure effective utilization of AI technologies in the workplace. Organizations demonstrate commitment to their employees through continuous training and development programs in AI literacy to enhance employees' skills and abilities to effectively use AI technologies in their roles (Benlian & Pinski, 2023). Inadequate training in AI skills reduces employees' adaptability, creating stress and mixed feelings about AI displacing them from their roles (Putri & Werdini, 2025).

3.3.3 *Adaptation Capacity*

Adaptation capacity reflects employees' ability to adjust effectively to new work processes arising from organizational changes associated with AI implementation within the workplace. As a result, employees often face challenges related to changes in work roles, work relationships, skill acquisition, and decision-making (Greenhaus & Callalan, 2020). Leadership and organizational support, including encouragement, psychological safety, and enabling resources that facilitate smooth transitions, may enhance employee adaptation (Lee, 2021). Supporting employees' adaptation capacity is essential for organizations to actualize the purpose of AI implementation. Research demonstrates that employees with high adaptation capacity are more likely to navigate evolving work demands, embrace work processes, and engage in human-AI collaboration, while maintaining positive performance, compared to employees with low adaptation capacity (Farrow, 2021). Thus, adaptation capacity enhances positive employee experiences during organizational change and AI transformation.

3.3.4 *Employee Agency*

Employee agency is employees' capacity to exercise autonomy, participate in decision-making, and provide meaningful human oversight to influence their work processes, regardless of AI integration. Employees feel comfortable using AI technologies when they guarantee workplace autonomy and meaningful human oversight, thereby encouraging creativity and human-AI collaboration (Kong et al., 2023). This highlights the importance of employee agency in AI transformation that ensures technologies are designed to create a balance between employees' needs and organizational goals. Organizations that implement AI technology without human intervention often create diverse problems for employees, including workplace stress, reduced job satisfaction, threats to job security, and reduced work engagement (Ranjan et al., 2026). However, organizations that implement AI technologies to augment work processes give employees the ability to control how AI operates and make meaningful decisions about the recommendations it generates, thereby increasing employee well-being (Sadeghi, 2024).

3.3.5 *Well-being*

Well-being is a key dimension of employee experience. It reflects employees' physical, psychological, emotional conditions and work-related outcomes in relation to the deployment of AI systems within the workplace. Employee well-being goes beyond the absence of stress or burnout; it indicates whether employees have autonomy, meaningful work, and enabling resources that can enable them to engage effectively in AI-mediated work environments (Zhang et al., 2026). This underscores the importance of human-centered AI transformation that ensures AI systems are designed to augment employees' job performance, rather than undermine their well-being through job demands, technostress, and unethical use of AI. Human-centered AI practices such as transparent communication, ethical implementation, human oversight and AI literacy are essential to promote employee well-being in the age of AI transformation.

4.0 CONCEPTUAL FRAMEWORK AND PREPOSITIONS

Existing studies have developed conceptual frameworks for AI governance, AI-readiness, employee-AI collaboration, and human-centered AI placing much emphasis on regulatory compliance, ethical principles, and technical perspectives (Papagiannidis et al., 2025; Misra et al., 2025). These frameworks have examined each of the components separately with limited focus on how institutional conditions shape organizational purpose and employee experience. This chapter developed a proposed framework that addresses these gaps by integrating institutional conditions, organizational purpose, and employee experience together, thereby extending existing knowledge on AI transformation literature. The framework conceptualizes employee experience as a multidimensional construct that comprises trust in AI, skills development, adaptation capacity, employee agency, and well-being. Furthermore, it posited that institutional conditions can either enable or constrain AI transformation in emerging and developed markets. Five propositions are developed from the conceptual framework to explain the interdependence and relationships among the contextual conditions (among institutional conditions, organizational purpose, and employee experience) in building practical and sustainable human-centered AI transformation.

Figure 1. Conceptual Framework of Human-centered AI Transformation in Emerging Markets

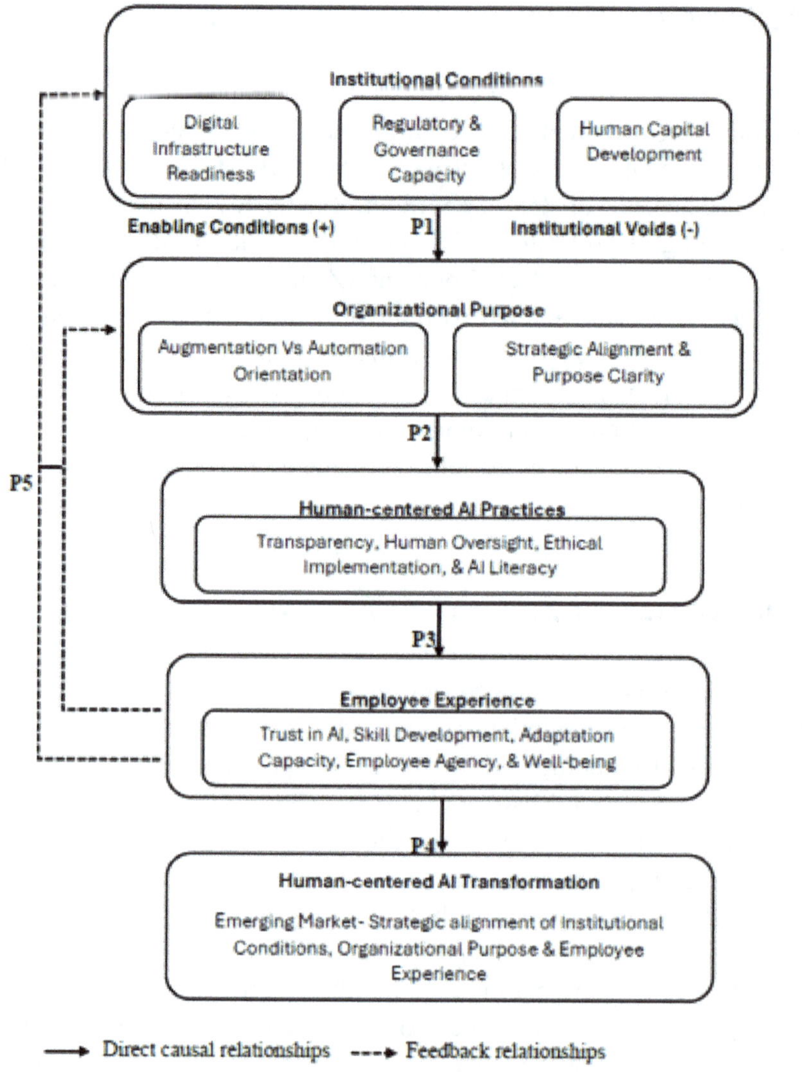

4.1 Description of the Proposed Conceptual Framework and Propositions

The conceptual framework presented in Figure 1 advances the conceptualization of human-centered AI transformation in the emerging market through the integration of institutional conditions, organizational purpose, and employee experience. The framework consists of five core theoretical propositions (P1-P5) with feedback relationships that make the model dynamic and mutually reinforcing. Collectively, the propositions demonstrated that the conditions under which AI systems are deployed, the organizational purpose, and employee experience determine whether human-centered AI transformation is achievable in emerging markets.

4.1.1 Institutional Conditions: The Foundational Layer

Institutional conditions influence human-centered AI through multiple mechanisms (organizational purpose, human-centered AI practices and employee experience). The institutional conditions can either constrain or enable organization's readiness to adopt human-centered AI systems. The constraints represent institutional voids that may hinder organizational adoption of AI systems, while the enabler conditions enhance effective deployment of AI systems. They are operationalized through interdependent dimensions such as the digital infrastructure readiness, regulatory and governance capacity, and human capital development. Hence, AI-readiness in emerging markets is not dependent solely on technological access, but rather on the integration of digital infrastructure, regulatory governance, and human capital conditions. The proposition developed based on this explanation is as follows:

P1: Enabling institutional conditions positively influence organizational readiness to adopt human-centered AI, whereas institutional voids weaken such readiness.

4.1.2 Organizational Purpose Influence on Human-centered AI Practices

Organizational purpose is a strategic alignment by which organizations respond to institutional conditions and define the roles of technology either as a core value proposition (augmentation) or as a mechanism for operational efficiency (automation). Organizations that prioritise AI augmentation preserve human oversight and ensure AI skill-up training and development programs, thereby creating a meaningful experience for the employees and strengthening human-centered AI practices in the organization. Conversely, organizations that focus on AI automation prioritize higher productivity and overhead cost reduction, thereby disrupting employee well-being (Valtonen et al., 2026), thereby weakening human-centered AI practices. The following proposition was developed based on this illustration.

P2: A clear organizational AI purpose oriented toward augmentation strengthens the adoption of human-centered AI practices.

4.1.3 Human-centered AI Practices on Employee Experience

Human-centered AI practices serve as the mediating construct between organizational purpose and employee experience. These practices comprise transparency in AI decision-making, meaningful human oversight, ethical implementation, and AI literacy. This operationalized the principles of human-centered AI that can enhance employee experience. Drawing from this description, the chapter presents the proposition below:

P3: Human-centered AI practices positively influence employee trust, autonomy, engagement, adaptability, and well-being.

4.1.4 Employee Experience and Human-centered AI Transformation

Employee experience is a multidimensional construct comprising five distinct yet interrelated dimensions that influence employee experience and interaction with AI systems. These constructs encompass trust in AI, skill development, adaptation capacity, employee agency, and overall well-being. Hence, these constructs shape employees' response to AI technologies, which influence how organizations sustain and invest in the deployment of AI for optimal utilization, preserving employees' well-being towards the attainment of organizational goals, especially human-centered AI transformation. Arising from the above is the proposition below:

P4: Positive employee experiences reinforce organizational commitment to human-centerd-AI through learning and implementation feedback.

4.1.5 Feedback Effect of Employee Experience on Organizational Purpose and Institutional Conditions

There are two main feedback loops from the framework: one starting with employee experience and returning to organizational AI purpose, and the other starting with employee experience and returning to institutional conditions.

4.1.5.1 Employee Experience Feedback to Organizational Purpose

Employees' experience with AI technology on the job determines its sustainability and organizations' continued investment in deploying emerging technologies into their operational systems. For instance, when there are strategic adaptations, implementation learning, and positive feedback on employees' usage of AI technology, it encourages work engagement and organizations' commitment to a human-centered AI purpose (Jasinenko & Steuber, 2022). While resistance, poor performance, and increased stress from AI technology encourage organizations to re-strategize their purpose (Jasinenko & Steuber, 2023).

4.1.5.2 Employee Experience Feedback to Institutional Conditions

Employee experience drives transformation in institutional conditions through institutional learning and collective voice, encouraging the government to re-strategize on favourable policies and invest in digital technologies that support effective deployment of AI in organizations. A persistent increase in the negative consequences of AI technologies on employee well-being and quality of work-life heightens collective agitation and public pressure to protect workers through stable regulatory governance (Bailey, 2022). Positive feedback on institutional conditions increases sustainable investment in digital readiness and adequate deployment of AI technologies for emerging markets (Adeniyi et al., 2024; Fahim et al., 2025). The proposition developed based on this explanation is as follows:

P5: Employee experience has a feedback effect on organizational purpose and institutional conditions.

4.2 Human-Centered AI Transformation

Human-centered AI transformation refers to the successful integration of AI systems into organizational processes that are ethical, equitable, and adaptive across the organization and its workforce. This demonstrates that when institutional conditions, organizational purpose, human-centered AI practices, and employee experience are mutually reinforcing, they enhance human-centered AI transformation in emerging markets. However, when any component of the framework is misaligned, whether due to institutional voids, unclear organizational purpose, poor human-centered AI practices, or diminished employee experience, it may undermine human-centered AI transformation across organizational contexts.

5.0 THEORETICAL CONTRIBUTIONS

The chapter advances theoretical knowledge by developing a unified framework that explains AI transformation in emerging markets through institutional conditions, organizational purpose, and employee experience. While previous studies have examined these constructs, they were conducted independently (Madanchian & Taherdoost, 2025; Zirar et al., 2023), underscoring the importance of the proposed framework. Furthermore, the chapter conceptualizes organizational purpose as a strategic approach that can enable organizations to adopt responsible AI rather than merely pursue ethical aspirations. It emphasizes that organizational purpose has the tendency to shape how organizations integrate technologies without undermining human values and employee well-being, while advancing organizational long-term sustainability within AI-mediated work environments.

6.0 PRACTICAL AND POLICY IMPLICATIONS

The proposed framework provides practical and policy implications for governments, regulators, organizational leaders, HR managers, and technology teams, given their crucial roles in AI transformation. For governments and regulators, the framework outlines how they can establish enabling institutional conditions by implementing AI governance, investing in digital infrastructure, and adopting ethical regulatory systems to enhance the effective and responsible deployment of AI systems. Organizational leaders can ensure AI implementation is consistent with the organization's purpose by prioritizing the enhancement of employees' capabilities together with organizational performance. Purpose-driven AI implementation may help HR managers to promote positive employee experience with AI systems through skill development, AI literacy, employee agency, and overall well-being in organizational contexts. Similarly, technology teams can design AI systems that adhere to ethical principles (transparent, reliable, and accountable), thereby enhancing employees' trust in AI technologies, meaningful human oversight, and effective human-AI collaboration. Taken together, their proactive actions can enhance sustainable human-centered AI transformation.

7.0 LIMITATIONS AND FUTURE RESEARCH

The study had several limitations due to its conceptual review approach, which relied on synthesising existing literature to build an integrated model without empirical findings. The findings were based on theoretical integration rather than empirical studies, which limits their general acceptability across organizations in emerging markets. The study identified five major contextual factors which are relevant but may not capture the disparities in AI transformation across emerging and developed markets.

These limitations justify further studies to adopt empirical approaches on how institutional conditions, organizational purpose, and employee experience within a specific context are analyzed. Specifically, future studies should examine how institutional dimensions (regulative, normative, and cognitive) interact and influence employees' AI experience in both developed and emerging markets. Hence, attention should be focused on employee experience with AI systems' influence on organizational commitment to human-centered AI. There is a need for cross-sectional studies across regions and industries to clarify differences in AI adoption and transformation processes. This will generate robust findings on how institutional environments affect organizations' deployment of AI technologies and their impact on employee well-being, with the goal of building a human-centered AI transformation.

8.0 CONCLUSION

This study examined how institutional conditions, organizational purpose, and employee experience shape human-centered AI transformation in emerging markets. Institutional theory was used to understand how institutional conditions, through regulatory policies, digital infrastructure, and cultural beliefs, influence the organizational deployment of AI technologies within organizations, thereby affecting organizational purpose and employee experience. While stakeholder theory was used to understand how the organizational purpose of AI technologies (Automation versus augmentation) impacts employee experience, which in turn shapes their trust in AI technologies, skill development, adaptation capacity, employee agency, and overall well-being.

Institutional conditions play a dual role by either enabling or constraining organizations' capacity to integrate AI systems in advancing human-centered AI transformation. Hence, these conditions are dynamic and context-dependent across regions. This chapter argues that enabling and constraining conditions may coexist in emerging and developed markets, thereby shaping AI transformation in distinct ways. Thus, institutional conditions influence organizations' responses to technological changes within geographical environments. This implies that human-centered AI transformation is not determined only by technological integration but contingent upon institutional alignment within emerging and developed markets.

DECLARATION OF GENERATIVE AI USE

The chapter used generative AI tools to refine language and improve the clarity and readability of the manuscript. The authors carefully reviewed and verified all intellectual content, thereby taking full responsibility for the manuscript's originality and interpretation.

REFERENCES

Adeniyi, A., Akashaba, B., Aiyenuro, O., & Abiola, O. (2024). Framework for strategic investments in technology to enhance sustainable economic development in emerging markets. *International Journal of Innovative Science and Research Technology*, *9*(10), 1458–1468. DOI: 10.38124/ijisrt/IJISRT24OCT598

Afroogh, S., Akbari, A., Malone, E., Kargar, M., & Alambeigi, H. (2024). Trust in AI: Progress, challenges, and future directions. *Humanities & Social Sciences Communications*, *11*(1), 4044. Advance online publication. DOI: 10.1057/s41599-024-04044-8

Al-Assaf, G., Abdel-Halim, M., & Shehadeh, M. (2025). The macroeconomic drivers of fintech development in emerging markets: An empirical investigation. *Discover Sustainability*, *6*(1), 863. DOI: 10.1007/s43621-025-01597-9

Anand, S., Karthikeya, M., Sai, A. A., & Balamurali, O. (2023, January). Multilingual hybrid chatbot for empowering rural women self-help groups in india. In *2023 International Conference for Advancement in Technology (ICONAT)* (pp. 1-6). IEEE. DOI: 10.1109/ICONAT57137.2023.10080347

Bailey, D. E. (2022). Emerging technologies at work: Policy ideas to address negative consequences for work, workers, and society. *Industrial & Labor Relations Review*, *75*(3), 527–551. DOI: 10.1177/00197939221076747

Balavadze, T., & Zhgenti, T. (2018). The Bank of Georgia Learning Hub. *International Journal of Advanced Corporate Learning*, *11*(1), 5–9. DOI: 10.3991/ijac.v11i1.9367

Bankins, S., Ocampo, A. C., Marrone, M., Restubog, S. L. D., & Woo, S. E. (2024). A multilevel review of artificial intelligence in organizations: Implications for organizational behavior research and practice. *Journal of Organizational Behavior*, *45*(2), 159–182. DOI: 10.1002/job.2735

Benbya, H., Davenport, T. H., & Pachidi, S. (2020). Artificial intelligence in organizations: Current state and future opportunities. *MIS Quarterly Executive*, *19*(4).

Benbya, H., Pachidi, S., & Jarvenpaa, S. (2021). Special issue editorial: Artificial intelligence in organizations: Implications for information systems research. *Journal of the Association for Information Systems*, *22*(2), 10. DOI: 10.17705/1jais.00662

Benlian, A., & Pinski, M. (2025). The AI literacy development canvas: Assessing and building AI literacy in organizations. *Business Horizons*. Advance online publication. DOI: 10.1016/j.bushor.2025.10.001

Brougham, D., & Haar, J. (2020). Technological disruption and employment: The influence on job insecurity and turnover intentions: A multi-country study. *Technological Forecasting and Social Change*, *161*, 120276. DOI: 10.1016/j.techfore.2020.120276

Cazzaniga, M., Jaumotte, M. F., Li, L., Melina, M. G., Panton, A. J., Pizzinelli, C., & Tavares, M. M. M. (2024). *Gen-AI: Artificial intelligence and the future of work*. International Monetary Fund. DOI: 10.5089/9798400262548.006

Chowdhury, S., Budhwar, P., Dey, P. K., Joel-Edgar, S., & Abadie, A. (2022). AI-employee collaboration and business performance: Integrating knowledge-based view, socio-technical systems and organisational socialisation framework. *Journal of Business Research*, *144*, 31–49. DOI: 10.1016/j.jbusres.2022.01.069

Chung, Y. W., Im, S., Kim, J. E., & Yun, J. K. (2025). Artificial intelligence awareness, career resilience, job insecurity and behavioural outcomes. *Australian Journal of Psychology*, *77*(1), 2559910. DOI: 10.1080/00049530.2025.2559910 PMID: 41036316

Dan, Z., Tang, N., & Hai, S. (2024). Dual effects of AI-enabled job non-routinization on proactive and responsive creativity. In *Academy of Management Proceedings* (Vol. 2024, No. 1, Article 15016). Academy of Management. DOI: 10.5465/AMPROC.2024.15016abstract

Dellermann, D., Ebel, P., Söllner, M., & Leimeister, J. M. (2019). Hybrid intelligence. *Business & Information Systems Engineering*, *61*(5), 637–643. DOI: 10.1007/s12599-019-00595-2

Dieleman, M., Markus, S., Rajwani, T., & White, G. O.III. (2022). Revisiting institutional voids: Advancing the international business literature by leveraging social sciences. *Journal of International Management*, *28*(3), 100935. DOI: 10.1016/j.intman.2022.100935

Drakul, S. (2025). Application and economic effects of integrating artificial intelligence technologies in modern business. *Global Journal of Economic and Finance Research*, *2*(4), 201–204. DOI: 10.55677/GJEFR/04-2025-Vol02E4

Ezeocha, C. M. (2024). Financial Technology as a Tool for Promoting Financial Inclusion in Nigeria: A Theoretical Review. *African Journal of Management and Business Research*, *15*(1), 166–181. DOI: 10.62154/qqr2sy50

Fahim, M., Mostafa, N. A., & Grida, M. (2025). Using Generative AI in Supply Chain Management: How and How not? *Procedia Computer Science*, *274*, 87–96. DOI: 10.1016/j.procs.2025.12.009

Farrow, E. (2021). Mindset matters: How mindset affects the ability of staff to anticipate and adapt to Artificial Intelligence (AI) future scenarios in organisational settings. *AI & Society*, *36*(3), 895–909. DOI: 10.1007/s00146-020-01101-z PMID: 33223620

Fatima, S., Desouza, K. C., & Dawson, G. S. (2020). National strategic artificial intelligence plans: A multi-dimensional analysis. *Economic Analysis and Policy*, *67*, 178–194. DOI: 10.1016/j.eap.2020.07.008

Fenwick, A., Molnar, G., & Frangos, P. (2024). The critical role of HRM in AI-driven digital transformation: A paradigm shift to enable firms to move from AI implementation to human-centric adoption. *Discover Artificial Intelligence*, *4*(1), 34. DOI: 10.1007/s44163-024-00125-4

Freeman, R. E. (1984). *Strategic management: A stakeholder approach*. Pitman.

Freeman, R. E. (2010). *Strategic management: A stakeholder approach*. Cambridge University Press. DOI: 10.1017/CBO9781139192675

Gans, J. S. (2023). Artificial intelligence adoption in a competitive market. *Economica*, *90*(358), 690–705. DOI: 10.1111/ecca.12458

Gartenberg, C., Prat, A., & Serafeim, G. (2019). Corporate purpose and financial performance. *Organization Science*, *30*(1), 1–18. DOI: 10.1287/orsc.2018.1230

George, G., Merrill, R. K., & Schillebeeckx, S. J. (2021). Digital sustainability and entrepreneurship: How digital innovations are helping tackle climate change and sustainable development. *Entrepreneurship Theory and Practice*, *45*(5), 999–1027. DOI: 10.1177/1042258719899425

Greenhaus, J. H., & Callalan, G. A. (2020). Implications of the changing nature of work for the interface between work and nonwork roles. In *The Cambridge handbook of the changing nature of work* (pp. 467–488). Cambridge University Press. DOI: 10.1017/9781108278034.022

Hassan, M., Kushniruk, A., & Borycki, E. (2024). Barriers to and facilitators of artificial intelligence adoption in health care: Scoping review. *JMIR Human Factors*, *11*, e48633. DOI: 10.2196/48633 PMID: 39207831

Holmström, J. (2022). From AI to digital transformation: The AI readiness framework. *Business Horizons*, *65*(3), 329–339. DOI: 10.1016/j.bushor.2021.03.006

Holmström, J., & Magnusson, J. (2025). Navigating the organizational AI journey: The AI transformation framework. *Business Horizons*, *69*(1), 89–100. DOI: 10.1016/j.bushor.2025.01.002

Jasinenko, A., & Steuber, J. (2022). Organizational Purpose: Definition, Measurement and the Ambivalent Effect on Employee Wellbeing. In *Academy of Management Proceedings* (Vol. 2022, No. 1, p. 17387). Briarcliff Manor, NY 10510: Academy of Management.

Jasinenko, A., & Steuber, J. (2023). Perceived organizational purpose: Systematic literature review, construct definition, measurement and potential employee outcomes. *Journal of Management Studies*, *60*(6), 1415–1447. DOI: 10.1111/joms.12852

Jia, N., Luo, X., Fang, Z., & Liao, C. (2024). When and how artificial intelligence augments employee creativity. *Academy of Management Journal*, *67*(1), 5–32. DOI: 10.5465/amj.2022.0426

Jussupow, E., Spohrer, K., & Heinzl, A. (2022). Identity threats as a reason for resistance to artificial intelligence: Survey study with medical students and professionals. *JMIR Formative Research*, *6*(3), e28750. DOI: 10.2196/28750 PMID: 35319465

Kamal, O. A. A., Chikezie, P. M. E., Abbey, N. I., & Onyeka, C. O. (2024). AI-driven end-to-end workflow optimization and automation system for SMEs. *International Journal of Management & Entrepreneurship*, *6*(11), 3666–3684.

Khanna, T., & Palepu, K. G. (2010). *Winning in emerging markets: A road map for strategy and execution*. Harvard Business Press.

Khasawneh, M. A., & Dweiri, F. (2025). Influence of digital infrastructure on project management success: Readiness, fitness, and tools as moderators. *Emerging Science Journal*, *9*(6), 3319–3348. DOI: 10.28991/ESJ-2025-09-06-024

Kong, H., Yin, Z., Baruch, Y., & Yuan, Y. (2023). The impact of trust in AI on career sustainability: The role of employee–AI collaboration and protean career orientation. *Journal of Vocational Behavior*, *146*, 103928. DOI: 10.1016/j.jvb.2023.103928

Lawrence, C., Cui, I., & Ho, D. (2023). The bureaucratic challenge to AI governance: An empirical assessment of implementation at US federal agencies. In *Proceedings of the 2023 AAAI/ACM Conference on AI, Ethics, and Society* (pp. 606-652). DOI: 10.1145/3600211.3604701

Lee, H. (2021). Changes in workplace practices during the COVID-19 pandemic: The roles of emotion, psychological safety and organisation support. *Journal of Organizational Effectiveness: People and Performance*, *8*(1), 97–128. DOI: 10.1108/JOEPP-06-2020-0104

Li, M., & Bitterly, T. B. (2024). How perceived lack of benevolence harms trust of artificial intelligence management. *The Journal of Applied Psychology*, *109*(11), 1794–1816. DOI: 10.1037/apl0001200 PMID: 38815093

Madanchian, M., & Taherdoost, H. (2025). Ethical theories, governance models, and strategic frameworks for responsible AI adoption and organizational success. *Frontiers in Artificial Intelligence, 8*, 1619029. DOI: 10.3389/frai.2025.1619029 PMID: 40741285

Maleki, A. (2026). Rethinking ethical academic integrity ecosystems in higher education in the age of artificial intelligence. *Discover Artificial Intelligence*, *6*(1), 145. DOI: 10.1007/s44163-026-00887-z

Malik, N., Tripathi, S. N., Kar, A. K., & Gupta, S. (2022). Impact of artificial intelligence on employees working in industry 4.0 led organizations. *International Journal of Manpower*, *43*(2), 334–354. DOI: 10.1108/IJM-03-2021-0173

Marsh, E., Vallejos, E. P., & Spence, A. (2022). The digital workplace and its dark side: An integrative review. *Computers in Human Behavior, 128*, 107118. DOI: 10.1016/j.chb.2021.107118

Meyer, J. W., & Rowan, B. (1977). Institutionalized organizations: Formal structure as myth and ceremony. *American Journal of Sociology*, *83*(2), 340–363. DOI: 10.1086/226550

Misra, S., Barik, K., & Kvalvik, P. (2025). A Comprehensive Review of Human-Centric AI, Regulatory Frameworks, and Their Role in Shaping Industry 5.0. *Procedia Computer Science*, *259*, 1672–1681. DOI: 10.1016/j.procs.2025.04.122

Mitchell, R. K., Agle, B. R., & Wood, D. J. (1997). Toward a theory of stakeholder identification and salience: Defining the principle of who and what really counts. *Academy of Management Review*, *22*(4), 853–886. DOI: 10.2307/259247

Oyeyemi, B. B., John, A. O., & Awodola, M. (2025). Infrastructure and regulatory barriers to AI supply chain systems in Nigeria vs. the US. *Engineering Science and Technology*, *6*(4), 155–172. DOI: 10.51594/estj.v6i4.1912

Papagiannidis, E., Mikalef, P., & Conboy, K. (2025). Responsible artificial intelligence governance: A review and research framework. *The Journal of Strategic Information Systems*, *34*(2), 101885. DOI: 10.1016/j.jsis.2024.101885

Polisetty, A., Chakraborty, D. G. S., Kar, A. K., & Pahari, S. (2024). What determines AI adoption in companies? Mixed-method evidence. *Journal of Computer Information Systems*, *64*(3), 370–387. DOI: 10.1080/08874417.2023.2219668

Presbitero, A., & Teng-Calleja, M. (2023). Job attitudes and career behaviors relating to employees' perceived incorporation of artificial intelligence in the workplace: A career self-management perspective. *Personnel Review*, *52*(4), 1169–1187. DOI: 10.1108/PR-02-2021-0103

Puffer, S. M., McCarthy, D. J., & Jaeger, A. M. (2016). Institution building and institutional voids: Can Poland's experience inform Russia and Brazil? *International Journal of Emerging Markets*, *11*(1), 18–41. DOI: 10.1108/IJoEM-02-2015-0027

Putri, K. M. H., & Werdini, Y. E. (2025). Artificial intelligence adoption, job insecurity, and psychological resilience: Challenges for employee adaptation in future work environments. *International Journal of Issue Science*, *1*(5).

Ranjan, B., Sivanesan, I., & Bernie, S. B. (2026). Artificial intelligence and anxiety: The human price of adapting to a smarter workplace. *Inspire Intelligence Journal (ISSN: 3110-942X), 1*(1), 52-67.

Sadeghi, S. (2024). Employee well-being in the age of AI: Perceptions, concerns, behaviors, and outcomes. *arXiv preprint arXiv:2412.04796.*

Saini, M., Singh, D., Kataria, A., & Singh, R. (2025). Digital transformation and environmental sustainability: Reviewing the role of human capital. *Journal of Organizational Change Management*, •••, 1–24. DOI: 10.1108/JOCM-03-2025-0289

Schmager, S., Pappas, I. O., & Vassilakopoulou, P. (2025). Understanding Human-Centred AI: A review of its defining elements and a research agenda. *Behaviour & Information Technology*, *44*(15), 3771–3810. DOI: 10.1080/0144929X.2024.2448719

Shen, S. Y., & Hong, Y. (2025). Bridging the Trust Gap: Exploring the Role of Trust in AI Integration Within the Workplace. In *Academy of Management Proceedings* (Vol. 2025, No. 1, p. 18789). Academy of Management.

Soulami, M., Benchekroun, S., & Galiulina, A. (2024). Exploring how AI adoption in the workplace affects employees: A bibliometric and systematic review. *Frontiers in Artificial Intelligence*, *7*, 1473872. DOI: 10.3389/frai.2024.1473872 PMID: 39610851

Staley, I., & Amankwa, E. (2025). Bridging blockchain and digital asset gaps: A comparative policy analysis of regulatory practices in emerging markets. *The Institution of Engineering and Technology (IET). IET Blockchain*, *5*(1), e70019. DOI: 10.1049/blc2.70019

Supriyadi, T., Sulistiasih, S., Rahmi, K. H., Pramono, B., & Fahrudin, A. (2025). The impact of digital fatigue on employee productivity and well-being: A scoping literature review. *Environment and Social Psychology*, *10*(2), 1–13. DOI: 10.59429/esp.v10i2.3420

Szenftner, A., Stumpp, S., & Knopf, T. (2024). Exploring the potential of AI to increase productivity in small marketing teams. In *European Conference on Innovation and Entrepreneurship* (Vol. 19, No. 1, pp. 970–977). Academic Conferences International Limited. DOI: 10.34190/ecie.19.1.2468

Tasleem, N., & Gangadharan, S. (2022). Navigating stakeholder dynamics in large-scale transformations. *Journal of Advance Multidisciplinary Research*, *1*(2), 48–56. DOI: 10.54660/.JAMR.2022.1.2.48-56

Trunk, A., Birkel, H., & Hartmann, E. (2020). On the current state of combining human and artificial intelligence for strategic organizational decision making. *Business Research*, *13*(3), 875–919. DOI: 10.1007/s40685-020-00133-x

Usmani, A., Happonen, A., & Watada, J. (2023). Human-centered artificial intelligence: Designing for user empowerment and ethical considerations. In *2023 5th International Congress on Human-Computer Interaction, Optimization and Robotic Applications (HORA)* (pp. 1–7). IEEE. DOI: 10.1109/HORA58378.2023.10156761

Valtonen, A., Kimpimäki, J. P., & Savela, N. (2026). Employee wellbeing: A computational review on the consequences of workplace automation. *Technovation*, *152*, 103424. DOI: 10.1016/j.technovation.2025.103424

Valtonen, A., Saunila, M., Ukko, J., Treves, L., & Ritala, P. (2025). AI and employee wellbeing in the workplace: An empirical study. *Journal of Business Research*, *199*, 115584. DOI: 10.1016/j.jbusres.2025.115584

van Kessel, R., Wong, B. L. H., Rubinić, I., O'Nuallain, E., & Czabanowska, K. (2022). Is Europe prepared to go digital? Making the case for developing digital capacity: An exploratory analysis of Eurostat survey data. *PLOS Digital Health*, *1*(2), e0000013. DOI: 10.1371/journal.pdig.0000013 PMID: 36812527

Vanu, N., Farouk, M. O., Samiun, M., Sharmin, S., Billah, M., & Hossain, S. (2024). The Innovations and Trends of Information Technology with AI: Weapons to Reassemble the Future World. *Journal of Computer and Communications*, *12*(12), 34–54. DOI: 10.4236/jcc.2024.1212003

Venigandla, K., Vemuri, N., & Vemuri, N. (2024). Hybrid intelligence systems combining human expertise and AI/RPA for complex problem solving. [IJISRT]. *International Journal of Innovative Science and Research Technology*, *9*(3), 2066–2075. DOI: 10.38124/ijisrt/IJISRT24MAR2039

Walter, Y. (2024). Managing the race to the moon: Global policy and governance in Artificial Intelligence regulation: A contemporary overview and an analysis of socioeconomic consequences. *Discover Artificial Intelligence*, *4*(1), 14. DOI: 10.1007/s44163-024-00109-4

Wang, Q., Qi, Y., & Li, R. (2026). Artificial intelligence and corporate sustainability: Shaping the future of ESG in the age of industry 5.0. *Sustainable Development (Bradford)*, *34*(1), 1–26. DOI: 10.1002/sd.70200

Westover, J. H. (2025). How to become an effective AI-augmented leader. *Human Capital Leadership Review*, *20*(4), 2–10. DOI: 10.70175/hclreview.2020.20.4.2

Xu, W. (2026). Human-centered artificial intelligence (HCAI): Foundations and approaches. *arXiv preprint arXiv:2601.01247.*

Yaşar, T. (2024). Artificial intelligence in business operations: Exploring how AI technologies are reshaping processes, enhancing decision-making, and driving efficiency across various industries. *Human-Computer Interaction.*

Zhang, C., Chen, S., Zhang, D., & Zhang, Q. (2026). The Impact of Artificial Intelligence Usage on Affective Work Well-Being: A Self-Determination Theory Perspective. *Behavioral Sciences (Basel, Switzerland)*, *16*(5), 670. DOI: 10.3390/bs16050670 PMID: 42193549

Zirar, A., Ali, S. I., & Islam, N. (2023). Worker and workplace Artificial Intelligence (AI) coexistence: Emerging themes and research agenda. *Technovation*, *124*, 102747. Advance online publication. DOI: 10.1016/j.technovation.2023.102747

Chapter 10
Human Experience in AI-Enabled Workplace:
An AI-Enabled Communication and Diagnostic Support Case Study Within Veterinary Clinics in Ukraine

Nataliia Klietsova
http://orcid.org/0000-0003-4910-8912
University of Hertfordshire, UK

Andrii Klietsov
Sumy National Agrarian Universtiy, Ukraine

Somayeh Pouransari
http://orcid.org/0009-0001-8076-0768
University of Hertfordshire, UK

Reza Naji
http://orcid.org/0009-0001-9301-5599
University of Hertfordshire, UK

ABSTRACT

Artificial intelligence (AI) within veterinary workplaces supports client communication, clinical documentation, diagnostic preparation, and team records. However, the significance of these tools cannot be reduced to technical efficiency alone. This chapter examines that human dimension through a qualitative embedded case study of VetDopomoga, a Ukrainian veterinary clinic network. Using semi-structured

DOI: 10.4018/979-8-3373-8282-1.ch010

interview data, the study shows that AI-enabled tools can produce structured records, reduce repetitive work, improve case preparation, support handovers, and strengthen communication with animal owners. Participants identified routine human correction, uneven adoption across roles and branches, governance and privacy concerns, training gaps, technical vulnerability during outages, and risks of overreliance on AI-generated outputs by less experienced staff as key implementation tensions. The chapter provides insights for AI implementation in veterinary clinics in similar contexts.

INTRODUCTION

AI has been rapidly moving from the margins of organisational experimentation into the everyday routines of professional work. In many sectors, AI-enabled systems are already used to structure information, automate repetitive tasks, generate summaries, support triage, classify images, and assist decision preparation. As a result, the practical question is no longer whether AI will affect work, but how it changes the experience, organisation, and meaning of work for people who remain professionally and ethically accountable for outcomes. This issue is especially important in settings where work is relational, emotionally demanding, and safety-critical. Veterinary medicine is one such setting.

Veterinary clinics are often discussed as sites of clinical expertise, service provision, and small-business management at the same time. They sit at the intersection of professional judgement, client communication, record-keeping, diagnostic interpretation, teamwork, and emotional labour. Unlike many other professional contexts, veterinary work also involves mediated care, where clinicians make decisions for animal patients while communicating with human owners who may be distressed, uncertain, or unable to describe symptoms accurately. This creates a distinctive environment in which information quality, explanation, empathy, and trust are central to good practice. It also means that the introduction of AI into veterinary workflows can reshape much more than documentation speed or technical efficiency. It may affect the quality of clinical preparation, the perceived authority of professional judgement, the balance between screen-based work and patient interaction, as well as the everyday burden of emotionally demanding communication.

Existing discussions of AI adoption often emphasise performance improvement, cost reduction, or task automation (Davenport & Ronanki, 2018; Brynjolfsson & McAfee, 2017). These perspectives are useful, but they are insufficient in workplaces where ethical responsibility remains human and where professional autonomy is central to safe practice. Human-centred AI scholarship has therefore argued that the value of AI can be by computational capability, but more importantly, by whether it strengthens human agency, trust, responsibility, and meaningful participation in decision-making (Shneiderman, 2020; Floridi & Cowls, 2019). Work design scholars have made a complementary argument; In a digital environment, technologies do not simply improve pre-existing jobs, instead they reconfigure tasks, skills, interdependencies, and pressures in ways that can either support or erode job quality (Parker & Grote, 2022). For veterinary clinics, these questions are particularly important because the profession is already characterised by high workload, emotional intensity, and growing demands for efficiency and consistency.

The Ukrainian context adds another important layer. In a turbulent environment in Ukraine shaped by the invasion of Ukraine by Russia, the adoption of digital tools can be deemed as a strategy of organisational continuity and operational resilience. Clinics may need to maintain service quality despite staff shortages, emotional strain, disrupted routines, and communication difficulties. Under such conditions, AI-enabled systems may help structure intake, preserve records, support coordination, and reduce some forms of cognitive and administrative overload. At the same time, they may generate new risks and new demands, particularly around verification, training, system dependency, and governance. This makes the Ukrainian veterinary context especially valuable for examining AI not as a situated organisational practice with real constraints and real human responsibilities.

This chapter examines this context through an empirical case study of VetDopomoga, a veterinary clinic network in Ukraine that has introduced AI-enabled tools for communication, documentation, workflow support, and diagnostic assistance. The chapter focuses on the human experience and dimension, and asks how veterinary professionals experience AI-enabled work in practice, how they interpret the role of AI in relation to their own judgement and autonomy, what kinds of benefits and tensions they perceive, and what this means for responsible implementation. The study is based on semi-structured interviews with 20 veterinary-trained professionals across three branches of the clinic, which represent different roles within the clinic's career development pathway, from senior clinicians to veterinary-trained intake and support staff.

The chapter makes three contributions. First, it extends the literature on AI-enabled workplaces by bringing veterinary medicine into a conversation that has been dominated by corporate, industrial, and human healthcare settings. Second, it offers an HRM-oriented and 'One Health'-informed account of how AI reshapes work design, autonomy, wellbeing, and organisational resilience in a veterinary SME context. Third, it develops a model of human-centred AI adoption in veterinary SMEs, showing how responsible implementation depends on human oversight, role-sensitive training, workflow redesign, ethical governance, and explicit protection of professional judgement and empathy.

The rest of the chapter is structured as follows; The next section reviews literature on AI-enabled work, veterinary digitalisation, professional judgement, and workplace experience. The chapter then develops a theoretical framework built around human-centred AI, sociotechnical systems, and work design/job redesign. After introducing the VetDopomoga case, it presents the study methodology. The findings are then presented in the subsequent section. The chapter concludes with a discussion of implications for theory, veterinary management, HRM, and responsible AI adoption in small and medium-sized clinical organisations.

LITERATURE REVIEW

AI and the Transformation of Professional Work

In organisational practice, AI is increasingly used to sort and structure information, produce summaries, recommend actions, monitor performance, and support prediction (Mosaku et al., 2025). These capabilities may improve speed and consistency, but they also redistribute tasks between people and technologies and alter the boundaries between judgement, automation, and accountability (Davenport & Ronanki, 2018; Parker & Grote, 2022). Parker and Grote (2022) argue that automation, algorithms, and other digital systems redesign jobs by changing autonomy, skill use, task interdependence, and the nature of monitoring and coordination.

Wilson et al. (2017) suggest that AI is often most effective when used to augment rather than replace human capabilities. Nevertheless, augmentation is not automatically benign. The quality of human–AI collaboration depends on whether professionals understand the system's limits, whether they retain control over final decisions, and whether organisational arrangements support critical engagement rather than passive acceptance of machine outputs. In practice, this may mean that AI-enabled work is always also a training, workflow, and governance issue.

The concept of technostress further complicates the picture. Tarafdar et al. (2019) show that digital systems can produce both "techno-eustress" and "techno-distress". The same technology may reduce burden for some users while creating anxiety, surveillance pressure, or dependency for others. Whether AI is experienced as support or strain depends on design, implementation, role expectations, and the user's level of confidence and preparation. For clinicians and other professionals working under time pressure, AI may simultaneously reduce repetitive labour and create new expectations of constant checking, screen attention, or system responsiveness. All in all, questions of trust, autonomy, role clarity, and human responsibility remain central.

AI in Veterinary Medicine: From Technical Promise to Workplace Reality

Veterinary medicine has begun to adopt AI in a variety of domains, especially in diagnostic imaging, pattern recognition, administrative processing, and communication workflows. Hennessey et al. (2022) show that artificial intelligence has gained visibility in veterinary diagnostic imaging, where algorithmic tools may support image classification, anomaly detection, and consistency of interpretation. More recent veterinary studies suggest that this landscape is widening beyond imaging to include clinical pathology, workflow automation, documentation support, and quality assurance for model deployment and validation (Akinsulie et al., 2024; Akbarein et al., 2025; Neal et al., 2025; Pacholec et al., 2025a, 2025b). Accordingly, AI may enhance the speed and structure of imaging-related work and may serve as a useful "second reader" in cases where clinicians face time pressure or information overload. However, the existing veterinary AI literature remains strongly weighted toward technical capability and performance-oriented questions. Much less attention has been paid to how AI is incorporated into everyday veterinary work or how clinicians experience these systems as part of their workflow. A diagnostic-support system may be technically accurate in controlled settings, but its organisational effects depend on how it is embedded in documentation routines, interpreted by users, and balanced against professional judgement. In practice, veterinary work and diagnotics (Gereiner & Gardner, 2000) rarely consists of isolated diagnostic acts; it includes case intake, history gathering, interaction with owners, record maintenance, handovers between staff, discharge communication, and follow-up advice. AI that enters this environment becomes part of a broader workplace ecology.

Cloud-based and AI-driven data infrastructures further extend this issue. Hähnel (2025) notes that contemporary AI-driven medical data management raises both organisational opportunities and ethical concerns, especially around distributed data, responsibility, and governance. In veterinary settings, where records, phone calls, imaging data, and care histories may all need to interact across staff roles and locations, such infrastructures may help clinics maintain continuity and standardisation. However, they also raise questions about ownership of data, quality of inputs, privacy, human oversight, and what happens when AI-generated summaries are inaccurate or insufficiently nuanced.

Veterinary work is also distinguished by the importance of the veterinarian-client relationship. Unlike many automated administrative systems in other sectors, AI tools in veterinary clinics inevitably touch communication with animal owners. These owners are often anxious, emotional, or uncertain about symptoms and may provide information in non-medical language. Any AI system used for intake, summarisation, or communication support therefore enters a relational space, not just an informational one. The ability to structure information may be helpful, but the risk of flattening nuance or losing emotional detail is equally important. Recent healthcare literature on patient-facing AI similarly emphasises transparency, human oversight, and the relational acceptability of AI-supported communication (Osnat, 2025; Laranjo et al., 2025).

Professional Judgement, Autonomy, and Meaningful Work

The literature on AI-enabled workplaces increasingly stresses that professional judgement remains central even when decision support is available. In safety-critical settings, Cummings (2021) warns against inflated assumptions about AI maturity and argues that systems may appear more authoritative than their actual reliability warrants. This concern resonates strongly in veterinary medicine, where clinicians remain legally and ethically responsible for patient care even if AI contributes to record structuring or diagnostic preparation. If AI is presented or experienced as "confident", less experienced staff may be tempted to overtrust outputs that still require professional interpretation. Work design research suggests that digital systems may either strengthen professional work by removing low-value tasks or undermine it by narrowing discretion and increasing monitoring or dependence (Parker & Grote, 2022). For professionals, meaningful work is often tied to judgement, craft, relational responsibility, and the ability to make context-sensitive decisions.

Communication, Emotional Labour, and Client-Facing Work

Veterinary practice includes substantial emotional labour (Gardner & Hini, 2006). Staff must manage owner anxiety, grief, urgency, and uncertainty while maintaining clarity and professionalism. This applies to veterinarians, as well as veterinary-trained intake staff and assistants who play important roles in call handling, triage support, case preparation, and continuity of communication. The ability to communicate accurately and empathetically is therefore not peripheral; it is central to clinical quality and trust.

Kogan and Rishniw (2023) highlight that veterinary workplace conditions shape perceptions and satisfaction, emphasising that organisational context matters for professional experience. In AI-enabled clinics, communication tools may help structure client histories, standardise explanations, and improve continuity across interactions. However, such tools may also create new concerns. Participants may feel pressure to follow AI-mediated scripts too rigidly. Owners may worry that "a machine" rather than a human is listening. Clinicians may fear loss of nuance or reduced emotional presence if they become too screen-focused during consultations.

Recent Developments: Generative AI (GenAI), Explainability, and Implementation Governance

Recent literature makes it clear that the AI landscape is moving beyond narrow predictive models toward generative, conversational, and multimodal systems that influence documentation, communication, and professional reasoning more directly (Hosseinian-Far et al., 2025). In veterinary medicine, recent reviews and professional discussions show growing interest in image-analysis tools, administrative support, voice-to-text systems, owner communication support, and workflow automation (Burti et al., 2024; Sobkowich, 2025; Albergante et al., 2025). Survey evidence also suggests veterinary professionals who have practical exposure to AI tend to express greater optimism and higher willingness to adopt it, although this optimism remains conditional on support, governance, and usability (Gabor et al., 2025). These developments are important because they shift the problem from "Can AI perform a task?" to "How should organisations govern AI that now participates in communication, records, and workflow decisions?". This shift has two implications for the present chapter. First, GenAI creates new opportunities for structuring histories, summarising interactions, and reducing writing burden, which are directly relevant to the selected case study organisation. Second, it highlights longstanding concerns about hallucination, overconfident language, opacity, automation bias, as well as GenAI's sycophancy that may elevate risks within critical organisational contexts. Recent healthcare literature increasingly emphasises explainability, calibrated trust, structured implementation governance, and sociotechnical evaluation rather than simple adoption enthusiasm (McCradden et al., 2023; Glover et al., 2025; Owoyemi et al., 2025; Olawade et al., 2025). Mesinovic et al. (2025) argue that large language models (LLMs) in healthcare require stronger explainability if clinicians and patients are to evaluate outputs critically. Coiera and Fraile Navarro (2024) similarly warn that GenAI should be treated as an ecosystem problem, in which safety depends on model quality as well as on monitoring, organisational oversight, and the interaction between tools, people, and infrastructures. Wells et al. (2025) make a related implementation argument by showing that responsible AI adoption in healthcare requires risk review, human-in-the-loop safeguards, transparency, end-user education, and post-implementation monitoring.

The Turbulent Environment in Ukraine and the One Health Context

Existing work by Klietsova and Klietsov (2023a, 2023b) and Klietsova et al. (2024, 2025) shows that digitalisation, human capital preservation, and organisational adaptation have become particularly important in a turbulent environment in

Ukraine and under war-related disruption. In this context, veterinary clinics face pressures linked to staffing, continuity of care, emotional strain, and operational instability. AI-enabled systems may help clinics preserve structure and coordination under pressure, but they do so within conditions of uncertainty that can intensify both the benefits and the risks of digital dependence.

A 'One Health' perspective also strengthens the relevance of the case. The notion of One Health denotes that veterinary care is connected to broader issues of public health, animal welfare, professional wellbeing, and community resilience. If AI reshapes veterinary work, it may also influence how clinical teams sustain quality of care, maintain communication, and protect the wellbeing of staff operating under difficult conditions.

Research Gap

Despite rapid discussion of AI across many sectors, several gaps remain. First, veterinary AI research is still heavily oriented toward technical performance rather than the lived workplace experience of professionals. Second, the literature rarely examines AI in veterinary SMEs as an organisational and HRM issue involving role differentiation, training, workflow redesign, supervision capacity, and staff wellbeing. Third, little is known about how AI is experienced across different stages of professional progression within veterinary practice, especially when staff share veterinary education but perform different practical roles. Fourth, recent debates on GenAI, explainability, and responsible implementation have only begun to enter veterinary scholarship, which leaves unresolved questions about how conversational and documentation-support tools affect judgement, communication, and professional confidence in practice. Finally, the turbulent environment in Ukraine has not been meaningfully integrated into debates about AI-enabled clinical work.

This chapter aims to examine these gaps by evaluating AI-enabled communication and diagnostic support as part of a real veterinary workplace rather than as an isolated technology. Its empirical focus on professional judgement, autonomy, communication, workload, wellbeing, and responsibility makes it possible to move beyond an "AI efficiency" narrative and toward a richer understanding of how human work is being reshaped in a veterinary SME context.

Theoretical Framework

This chapter is primarily underpinned by three theoretical foundations: human-centred AI, sociotechnical systems theory, and work design/job redesign.

Human-centred AI provides the normative core of the chapter. Shneiderman (2020) argues that AI should be designed and implemented in ways that enhance human control, support accountability, and improve human outcomes rather than reducing users to passive operators of opaque systems. Floridi and Cowls (2019) similarly emphasise principles such as beneficence, non-maleficence, autonomy, justice, and explicability. These principles are especially important in professional contexts where AI can influence decisions without bearing the final ethical burden of those decisions. Within the veterinary medicine context, human-centred AI is particularly relevant because the veterinarian remains the morally and professionally accountable actor. This argument is consistent with recent sociotechnical healthcare literature, which emphasises that AI tools should be evaluated as part of a broader intervention ensemble rather than as stand-alone technical artefacts (McCradden et al., 2023). A system may generate summaries, suggest structures, or support interpretation, but it cannot assume responsibility for treatment decisions, client communication, or the consequences of error. Human-centred AI therefore requires more than functional usefulness. It requires that users understand what AI is doing, retain meaningful oversight, know when to question outputs, and remain able to prioritise empathy and context over rigid machine-generated phrasing. This is useful for the present study in three ways. First, it centres the analysis on the experience and agency of veterinary professionals rather than on the performance of the tool. Second, it provides a normative basis for interpreting concerns about overreliance, false confidence, privacy, and the need for verification. Third, it frames a core finding that participants did not reject AI but saw its legitimacy as dependent on professional judgement and human responsibility.

Sociotechnical systems theory shifts the analytic lens from the individual user to the broader system in which technologies are embedded. Rather than treating AI as a standalone object, sociotechnical thinking understands organisational outcomes as emerging from the interaction between social elements (people, roles, skills, norms, communication patterns) and technical elements (tools, data structures, interfaces, infrastructures, procedures), highlighting the emergent behaviour of a system (Checkland, 1999). The point is not simply that "people use technology," but that technologies and work arrangements co-shape each other. This is especially important in veterinary clinics. AI-enabled communication and documentation tools do not operate in a vacuum. They influence intake, consultation preparation, inter-staff handovers, records, follow-up advice, and sometimes diagnostic support. Their value depends on whether information flows are reliable, whether different branches and teams use tools consistently, whether client narratives are captured accurately, and whether roles are aligned around human verification and escalation. A poor-quality voice transcript, an unclear owner description, or uneven branch-level adoption can alter the effectiveness of the entire workflow. Similarly, a well-designed process can make even a modest AI function valuable by improving coordination and continuity. The VetDopomoga case study organisation is therefore best understood as a sociotechnical system rather than a simple technology adoption story. The three veterinary practice branches operate as embedded units within one organisational case, and AI-enabled tools appear at multiple points of interaction i.e., client-facing intake, record generation, clinical preparation, handover, and management oversight. Participants' accounts show that the usefulness of AI often depended not on the tool alone but on whether the social system around it - training, shared procedures, role expectations, and communication - was sufficiently coherent.

The third core theoretical foundation comes from work design and job redesign scholarship. Parker and Grote (2022) argue that digital systems can reshape the nature of work by redistributing tasks, altering autonomy, changing interdependence, and creating new forms of burden or support. This is particularly valuable for the present chapter because it provides a direct HRM-oriented lens. It allows analysis of how AI changes the content, rhythm, and meaning of professional work.

In the veterinary context, AI tools can create new tasks such as checking outputs, correcting vocabulary, validating chronology, monitoring the quality of inputs, and managing uncertainty when systems failed or when AI produced overly confident wording. These changes in business processes are thus classic examples of job redesign, where work extends beyond automation, and enters the real of reallocation. Some low-value labour is reduced, but supervisory and interpretive labour increases. For senior clinicians, this may reinforce a role as final arbiter and mentor. For junior clinicians, AI may support learning while also creating new dependency risks. For assistants and intake staff, AI may strengthen contribution to workflow coordination but increase responsibility for information quality and escalation. Work design theory also illuminates autonomy and meaningful work. If AI becomes too directive or if staff begin to trust outputs uncritically, autonomy may narrow even while efficiency improves. Conversely, if AI removes low-value repetition and supports preparation, professionals may experience greater capacity for judgement, explanation, and care.

Supporting Analytical Lenses

Although the chapter is anchored in the three frameworks above, several additional concepts support the interpretation of findings. The first is trust in AI (Glikson & Wooley, 2020). Trust matters because AI is only useful when professionals consider its outputs credible enough to engage with, but not so authoritative that they stop questioning them. In the present study, trust was neither absent nor unconditional. It was calibrated, role-sensitive, and deeply linked to explainability and prior experience of correction. Trust therefore functions as an analytical lens nested within the broader human-centred AI framework.

The second supporting lens is technostress (Issa et al., 2024). Participants' accounts suggest that AI can relieve pressure associated with repetitive documentation and information fragmentation but can also generate new forms of strain linked to checking, learning, screen attention, and system dependency. This reflects Tarafdar et al.'s (2019) distinction between techno-eustress and techno-distress. The same tool may be experienced as burden-reducing and burden-generating at once, depending on workflow design, role position, and the stability of surrounding systems.

The third supporting lens is professional identity and emotional labour (Edward et al., 2017). These concepts help interpret participants' concerns about overreliance on AI, the need to preserve a "human voice" with anxious owners, and the tension between screen-based efficiency and relational presence.

Table 1 maps the three core theories and the pertinent discussions above onto the empirical concerns and analytical expectations of the study.

Table 1. Conceptual framework used in the chapter (source: authors)

Framework	Core question	What it highlights in this study	Indicative empirical markers
Human-centred AI (Shneiderman, 2020)	Under what conditions does AI remain supportive rather than substitutive?	Human oversight, explainability, calibrated trust, responsibility, ethical accountability, empathy	Verification practices, correction of outputs, reluctance to delegate final judgement, concern about overreliance
Sociotechnical systems theory (McCradden et al., 2023)	How do people, tools, workflows, and organisational routines interact to shape outcomes?	Branch-level consistency, handovers, communication flows, infrastructure reliability, governance, data quality	Uneven adoption across branches, dependence on input quality, workflow bottlenecks, fallback routines
Work design / job redesign (Parker and Grote, 2022)	How does AI redistribute tasks, autonomy, skills, and burden?	Documentation relief, checking work, role progression, training needs, meaningful work, wellbeing	Reduced repetitive writing, new verification labour, role-sensitive learning needs, shifts in autonomy and workload

Case Study Context: VetDopomoga as an AI-Enabled Veterinary Workplace

VetDopomoga is a Ukrainian veterinary clinic network that provides a useful case study for examining AI-enabled work under real operational conditions. The organisation was selected because it offers an analytically rich example of how AI becomes embedded in everyday veterinary routines. The clinic has three branches operating within a single organisational system, which makes it possible to observe both shared practices and variation across local teams. This multi-branch structure also allows AI to be studied not as a single workstation tool, but as part of a broader workflow environment involving intake, records, communication, handover, and diagnostic support.

The clinics have introduced a set of AI-enabled functions that are used in different parts of the care pathway. These include voice-based support for structuring intake and consultation information, call-related tools that organise incoming client communication, medical scribe functions that help generate structured records and summaries, and AI-assisted imaging support intended to aid interpretation and preparation. A knowledge core function is still under development at the time of preparing this chapter. The relevance of these tools intersect with multiple human roles, including senior and junior clinicians, assistants, and veterinary-trained staff who occupy client-facing and coordination roles. The case study also reflects practical constraints common to veterinary SMEs, such as limited time for training, the need to integrate new tools into busy routines, the burden of validating outputs, and the organisational cost of maintaining both digital and manual fallback pathways (Glover et al., 2025; Owoyemi et al., 2025; Wells et al., 2025). These implementation realities are central to the chapter's argument that AI adoption is inseparable from managerial design and workflow governance.

The context of war and the broader turbulent environment in Ukraine also shapes the organisational significance of AI in this case. In Ukraine, veterinary clinics have had to maintain continuity of care under conditions marked by emotional strain, disruption, infrastructural instability, and the need for resilience. This does not mean that AI should be romanticised as a solution to pressures associated with the turbulent environment in Ukraine. Instead, it denotes digital tools may acquire heightened organisational importance when teams must preserve clarity, coordination, and documentation quality under stress.

The case is also relevant to One Health thinking. Veterinary practice does not exist in isolation from broader social and public-health systems. It involves animal welfare, owner wellbeing, community trust, and the resilience of care infrastructures. From the One Health perspective, supporting veterinary professionals through better workflow, safer communication, and reduced cognitive fragmentation may have significance beyond the individual clinic. At the same time, if AI is poorly designed or poorly governed, it may create new risks for care quality, data protection, or staff wellbeing. This makes the human experience of AI-enabled work in veterinary clinics a legitimate subject not only for management scholarship but also for broader interdisciplinary debate.

The value of the VetDopomoga case therefore lies in its combination of attributes: a real veterinary SME setting, a multi-branch embedded structure, an existing AI-enabled workflow, role differentiation within a common veterinary educational base, and a turbulent environment in Ukraine that turns digital adaptation into both a resilience strategy and a source of new organisational demands. These attributes make the case highly suitable for an in-depth qualitative analysis of how AI is experienced, interpreted, and governed in veterinary work.

METHODOLOGY

The methodology was designed to align closely with the conceptual framework set out in Table 1. The study was therefore not intended simply to capture whether staff liked or disliked AI tools. It was structured to investigate how human oversight, sociotechnical coordination, and work redesign were experienced in practice across professional roles and branches within one veterinary organisation.

Research Design

The chapter adopts a qualitative single-case study design with embedded units, following Yin's (2018) logic of case study research. The broader case is VetDopomoga as an AI-enabled veterinary workplace. The embedded units are the organisation's three branches, which operate within one clinic network but display variation in everyday workflow, team composition, and exposure to AI-enabled practices. This design is appropriate because the study seeks to understand not whether AI "works" in abstract, but how it is experienced, interpreted, and negotiated by veterinary professionals within a real organisational setting.

A qualitative case approach is especially suitable here as it examines lived professional experience rather than testing pre-defined variables. It also treats AI use as a contextual and organisational phenomenon shaped by workflow, role progression, and local conditions. Moreover, it allows close attention to the tensions of adoption e.g., ambiguity, trust, caution, learning, correction, responsibility, that are often flattened in quantitative or purely technical studies.

Participants' Profiles

Participants included 20 veterinary professionals with full veterinary education, positioned at different stages of professional and organisational role progression within the clinic, and employed across three VetDopomoga branches, with some participants working across more than one branch as part of their clinical and organisational duties. Although all participants possessed the educational qualifications required for veterinary practice, they occupied different positions within the clinic's professional and organisational role progression pathway. The sample comprised senior veterinary doctors and a clinic manager (n = 4), veterinary doctors (n = 6), junior veterinary doctors (n = 2), veterinary-trained clinical assistants (n = 4), and veterinary-trained professionals in client-facing intake or reception roles (n = 4). Participants' professional experience ranged from 1.5 to 22 years, which enabled the study to capture perspectives from both early-career and highly experienced professionals.

This participant structure was intentionally kept broad, since AI-enabled tools are embedded across multiple points of the veterinary workflow rather than being used only by senior clinicians. Staff involved in client communication, intake, documentation, workflow coordination, and clinical support also interact with AI-enabled systems in ways that shape everyday work. Including participants across these stages and roles therefore made it possible to generate a fuller account of how AI influenced professional judgement, autonomy, workload, documentation, client communication, training needs, and wellbeing.

Sampling Strategy

The study used a criterion-based purposive sampling strategy with maximum variation. The core inclusion criterion was full veterinary education combined with direct experience of working with, or alongside, AI-enabled communication, documentation, or diagnostic-support tools within the clinic. Within this criterion-based sample, maximum variation was sought by including participants from different branches, with different levels of professional experience, and across different points in the clinic's internal career pathway.

This strategy was appropriate because it enabled the analysis to explore how AI was experienced by veterinary-trained professionals who shared a common educational foundation but undertook different practical, organisational, and client-facing functions within the same workplace. As a result, the study could identify both common patterns and role-specific differences in how AI reshaped work.

Data Collection

Semi-structured interviews were conducted with the 20 participants. The interview guide explored participants' experiences of AI-enabled tools in relation to eight broad domains: professional judgement; autonomy; documentation burden; client communication; trust in AI; training needs; wellbeing and burnout; and ethical responsibility. Because the chapter focuses on workplace experience rather than technical system evaluation, questions encouraged participants to reflect on routine practices, role-specific interactions with AI, examples of correction or doubt, changes in workload, and the relational consequences of AI-supported communication.

Interviews were conducted in Ukrainian and subsequently translated into English for analysis and reporting. The translation was checked by two authors fluent on both languages to avoid any bias during the translation process. This approach allowed participants to express professional experience in the language of their everyday clinical work while enabling chapter writing in English for an international audience. Selected internal case materials were used as supplementary evidence for triangulation, including call transcripts, voice-agent transcripts, AI-generated clinical summaries, screenshots of AI-enabled workflows, internal instructions, training materials, and examples of corrected AI outputs where these were ethically appropriate and relevant to interpretation. These materials were not treated as replacements for interviews, but as contextual and triangulating sources.

Data Analysis

The interview data were organised into a structured analytical matrix and then analysed using reflexive thematic analysis, following Braun and Clarke (2006). This method was chosen because the study aimed to explore the lived professional experiences of veterinary staff working with AI-enabled communication and diagnostic-support tools. Rather than counting responses or testing predetermined hypotheses, the analysis focused on patterns of meaning across participants' accounts, especially in relation to judgement, trust, workload, autonomy, communication, wellbeing, and responsibility.

NVivo 14 was used as an assisting tool to organise transcripts, manage codes, and compare emerging patterns across interviews. However, NVivo 14 was not treated as a substitute for researcher interpretation. The development of codes, subthemes, and final themes remained a reflexive and interpretative process led by the researchers. The analysis moved iteratively between individual accounts, role comparisons, and broader cross-case patterns. Attentiowas paid both to shared meanings and to differences between senior clinicians, doctors, junior staff, assistants, and client-facing participants.

The interview matrix also enabled the researchers to note structured variations across participants, including role, branch, years of experience, AI tools used, trust orientation, perceived benefits, perceived difficulties, training needs, and illustrative anonymised quotes. This was particularly valuable because it supported a disciplined comparison of findings without reducing the qualitative material to mere counts.

Ethical Transparency, Reflexivity, and Positionality

Participation was completely voluntary and an author who was affiliated with the case study organisation was excluded from tasks involving participants' recruitment, data collection and analyses. Participants' profiles and pertinent data were kept anonymous, and their relevant right to withdraw from the study was two months from the date of interview. Ethics approval was sought from Sumy National Agrarian University and VetDopomoga (application number 03-v). These protocols regulated participant recruitment, informed consent, anonymisation, confidentiality, data protection, and the responsible use of internal clinic-based materials. Participants were informed about the purpose of the study, the voluntary nature of participation, their right to withdraw, and the anonymised use of their responses in the chapter. No identifiable personal, clinical, client-related, or commercially sensitive information is disclosed in the chapter.

Table 2. Participants' Profiles (source: authors)

Role category	n	Typical interaction with AI-enabled workflow
Senior veterinary doctors/clinic manager	4	Final clinical responsibility, governance, oversight, mentoring
Veterinary doctors	6	Consultation preparation, records, discharge and follow-up communication
Junior veterinary doctors	2	Learning support, differential thinking, supervised use of AI outputs
Veterinary-trained clinical assistants	4	Handover, workflow coordination, support for clinical routines
Veterinary-trained client-facing intake/reception roles	4	Triage support, call structuring, intake preparation and continuity

FINDINGS

The analysis generated five interrelated themes: (1) AI as structured support for professional judgement, but not a substitute for responsibility; (2) reduced documentation burden alongside new checking work; (3) changing autonomy, professional identity, and the meaning of expertise; (4) clearer client communication with risks to emotional presence; and (5) training, wellbeing, and resilient implementation under strain. These themes were shared across the sample, but they were experienced differently depending on role, experience, and branch-level consistency of use.

AI as Support for Judgement, not a Substitute for Responsibility

The strongest and most consistent finding across the interviews was that participants did not regard AI as an autonomous decision-maker. Instead, they described it as a support tool that could assist preparation, structure information, or suggest useful directions, but that could not carry final professional responsibility. This position was shared across the sample and was articulated most clearly by senior clinicians and the clinic manager. As one senior participant put it, "AI can support the clinic, but it cannot carry ethical responsibility" (Senior veterinary doctor, P11). Another stated even more directly: "AI reduces cognitive load, not human responsibility" (Senior vet / clinic manager, P20).

This theme reflects a disciplined hierarchy of authority, rather than an outright rejection of AI. Participants repeatedly described AI as a "second opinion," a preparatory tool, or a way of making information more manageable. A senior veterinary doctor explained: "AI is useful as a second opinion, not as the final answer" (P06). This wording is important because it shows how participants calibrated the role of AI. The system's usefulness was real, but it remained conditional on the clinician's ability to verify, interpret, and, where necessary, override the output. Such conditional trust was especially strong in matters involving diagnostic interpretation, trauma cases, chronology of symptoms, and situations in which AI language appeared too broad or too confident.

The structured matrix of interviews shows that trust in AI was predominantly moderate rather than unconditional. Nine participants described their trust as moderate, five as moderate-high, three as cautious-moderate, two as cautious, and one as low-moderate.No participant positioned trust as complete or unqualified. Even those who were relatively positive linked trust to human oversight, input quality, and the need for experience-based judgement. This pattern suggests that trust in the case was not a matter of faith in technology but a form of bounded professional confidence. AI was acceptable when used critically, checked carefully, and placed within a framework of human responsibility.

Differences by role were visible. Senior clinicians tended to frame AI in terms of subordination to professional judgement and responsibility. For them, the central issue was governance: the clinic needed clear rules that prevented AI from slipping into an authority role. Junior doctors described AI more as a learning and structuring support but also showed more anxiety about the possibility of being influenced by confident wording. One junior doctor said, "AI helps me learn, but I still need professional confirmation" (P03). Another observed, "Sometimes AI sounds confident, but I know I must check" (P08). These accounts suggest that junior staff may benefit substantially from AI-supported structuring but also face a stronger risk of overestimating output quality when experience is limited.

Veterinary-trained assistants and intake staff interpreted the issue somewhat differently. They were less concerned with diagnostic judgement and more with whether AI helped them contribute safely and effectively to workflow. AI supported triage, continuity, and handover, but it did not replace escalation to clinical decision-makers. Participants in client-facing roles were especially clear that AI could support triage preparation but could never replace clinical judgement. One intake participant summarised this succinctly: "AI helps with structure, but anxious clients still need a human voice" (P05). Here, the limit of AI did not seem to be only diagnostic but relational.

Evidence of correction and override reinforced this theme. The matrix included multiple cases where participants corrected AI overgeneralisation, amended symptom chronology, changed urgency categories, restored clinical nuance, corrected medication timing, or escalated uncertain outputs to a senior veterinarian. These were not rare exceptions; they were part of how the system was used responsibly. In other words, human correction was not evidence of system failure alone. It was evidence of the organisational reality that AI-generated outputs still required interpretation. The findings therefore support a strong conclusion: in this case, AI was incorporated into veterinary work as a support to judgement, but legitimacy depended on preserving explicit human accountability.

Documentation Relief and the Creation of New Checking Work

A second major theme concerned workload, especially documentation burden. Across roles, participants identified improvements in the structure and consistency of records. They reported that AI-enabled tools helped create clearer case notes, more complete discharge instructions, better case histories before consultations, and more standardised records across branches. For clinical assistants and intake staff, AI also supported better handover and continuity, helping staff avoid losing details during busy shifts or when a client called back later. One participant noted that "the main benefit is structure, not just speed" (Veterinary doctor, P07). Participants valued time-saving and also the cognitive relief of having information organised more clearly.

The emotional and practical relevance of structured documentation was particularly visible in overload conditions. One veterinary-trained assistant observed, "It helps when the clinic is overloaded and everyone is tired" (P09). Another senior clinician linked AI to "less documentation fatigue" while emphasising that stress associated with the turbulent environment in Ukraine itself remained unchanged. These comments suggest that AI did not reduce the burden of clinical responsibility or the emotional reality of difficult work; instead.it did reduce some of the fragmentation and repetition associated with record keeping and information transfer. Several participants connected AI directly to better preparation before consultation, noting that more structured histories allowed them to enter consultations with greater clarity and less information-searching.

However, documentation relief came with a compensatory burden i.e., 'checking'. Participants repeatedly said that AI outputs needed to be reviewed before saving, sharing, or acting on them. This was the case for note generation, symptom chronology, procedure labels, discharge advice, imaging-related suggestions, and voice transcripts. In effect, AI reduced one type of labour while creating another. Time saved through automatic structuring could be partially offset by time spent editing poor output or restoring nuance. One veterinary doctor remarked that editing weak AI output "can take time" (P07). Another participant opined that additional checking became a normal part of work rather than an exception. The burden of checking had several dimensions. The first was linguistic and semantic correction, where AI-generated text sometimes required vocabulary adjustment or more precise wording. The second was contextual correction, where participants had to ensure that owner narratives, symptom sequences, and urgent concerns had been represented accurately. The third was workflow correction, where staff had to decide when an output was sufficient, when it should be escalated, and when manual fallback was safer than digital dependence. This checking work tended to fall unevenly across roles. Senior doctors often carried the final validation burden, while assistants and intake staff were responsible for catching inconsistencies earlier in the process. Junior doctors sometimes experienced checking as a source of pressure because it required both reliance on and independence from the system.

A subtheme within this area was input quality. Participants working across branches were especially likely to note that the value of AI depended heavily on the quality of data entering the system. One doctor rotating between branches commented, "Bad input gives bad output... we still control quality" (P17). This is a crucial sociotechnical insight. AI did not automatically make the workflow better; it amplified the consequences of poor-quality or inconsistent input. In practical terms, documentation support depended on disciplined use, consistent language, and staff awareness of what kinds of information needed to be captured accurately.

Thus, the documentation theme cannot be interpreted as a simple efficiency story. AI eased repetitive writing and improved structure, but it also redistributed labour toward verification, editing, and quality control. The findings therefore support a more nuanced interpretation: AI changed the composition of documentation work. It made some tasks lighter, but it made responsible checking more visible and more central.

Professional Autonomy, Role Progression, and the Meaning of Expertise

The third theme concerned autonomy and professional identity. Participants did not report a straightforward loss of autonomy, but neither did they depict AI as neutral. Instead, they described a subtle reconfiguration of what autonomy meant in AI-enabled practice. For senior clinicians, autonomy became linked to the ability to use AI critically without becoming governed by it. Their concern was not that AI would directly replace them, but that it might reshape the expectations of less experienced staff or narrow the space for nuanced judgement if used uncritically. A senior doctor stated that autonomy was protected “only if AI is used critically” (P06), while another insisted that AI “must remain subordinate to professional judgement” (P11).

For veterinary doctors, AI tended to be described as a support that could strengthen preparation and consistency, particularly before consultations or in follow-up communication. However, several participants also reported tension between screen-based workflow and clinical presence. The most explicit articulation came from a veterinary doctor who said, “The danger is becoming too focused on the screen” (P13). This quote captures an important dimension of autonomy, not just for making decisions, but more importantly the freedom to offer sufficient attention to tasks where required. If AI produces more structured information but also increases the need to watch, check, and monitor digital output during consultations, professionals may experience a subtle shift in how their attention is organised.

Junior doctors experienced autonomy differently again. For them, AI often functioned as a scaffold for clinical thinking and communication. It helped organise differential reasoning and reduced anxiety in routine cases. Although the same support could create dependency or self-doubt if the output was unclear or overly authoritative. Their accounts suggest that AI may support professional progression when embedded within supervision but may undermine confidence if used in isolation. This is especially visible in quotes such as “AI helps me learn, but I still need professional confirmation” (P03). AI was therefore neither purely empowering nor purely constraining; its effect on autonomy depended on whether organisational support and mentoring remained strong.

The theme of meaningful work also emerged. Participants did not suggest that AI diminished the importance of veterinary expertise. On the contrary, the findings indicate that AI made the human dimensions of expertise more explicit. Where AI handled routine structure, clinicians became more conscious that their unique value lay in interpreting ambiguity, recognising when output was inadequate, and responding ethically and empathetically. The most meaningful parts of work were repeatedly associated with judgement, responsibility, and communication rather than with the production of formatted notes. Accordingly, AI sometimes clarified rather than diminished professional identity by making obvious which parts of work could be structured and which remained deeply human.

At the same time, role progression mattered. Veterinary-trained assistants described AI as supporting their development within the clinical workflow. It helped them contribute to handovers, preparation steps, and continuity while also increasing their responsibility for catching errors and understanding structured information. Their comments suggest that AI can act as a developmental scaffold within the organisation, but only if role expectations are clear. If assistants are expected to trust outputs without sufficient training, AI may increase vulnerability rather than support progression.

Overall, the theme of autonomy and professional identity shows that AI did not simply replace or preserve existing job boundaries. It redefined parts of what expertise looked like in practice. Autonomy shifted from "doing everything manually" toward "using technology critically while retaining interpretive and ethical control" (P06; P11; P20). This finding is strongly aligned with a work redesign perspective: technology did not eliminate expertise, but it changed where expertise was expressed.

Client Communication, Empathy, and the Relation Boundary of AI

A fourth theme concerned communication with animal owners. Participants across roles consistently said that AI-enabled tools improved the structure of client communication. Better case histories before appointments, more complete intake information, clearer discharge notes, and more consistent explanations all contributed to a sense that communication had become more organised. Staff in client-facing roles emphasised that AI-supported call structuring helped prepare clinicians before the visit, reducing the likelihood of missing important details and improving continuity when clients called repeatedly. One client-facing participant said the system helped create "more complete information for doctors" (P10), while another described "better prioritisation of client calls" (P15).

For clinicians, these improvements often translated into clearer explanations during consultations. Structured notes and summaries could help them explain findings or home-care instructions more coherently. Participants also noted that AI-supported wording sometimes made medical information easier to translate into owner-facing language. This is particularly significant in veterinary care because owners often communicate symptoms emotionally rather than medically. As one veterinary doctor put it, "Owners speak emotionally, not medically, so AI needs human interpretation" (P12). That statement captures both the strength and the limit of AI in communication, i.e., it can help organise information, but it cannot fully interpret emotional context without human mediation.

Participants repeatedly stressed that communication is not just a transfer of information, but also a relational and emotional task. Intake staff were especially attentive to this issue. They recognised the usefulness of structured questions and triage guidance; however, they also described situations in which anxious, crying, or distrustful owners required a distinctly human response. One participant commented, "Some clients need reassurance that a real person is still involved" (P15). Another warned that "AI-mediated scripts were difficult when owners were highly distressed" (P05). These accounts suggest that AI may strengthen the informational side of communication while leaving the emotional burden firmly with staff.

Clinicians also raised concerns about presence. The danger, as some described it, was not that AI would speak directly to clients in place of the veterinarian, but that the clinician might become too oriented toward the screen and less attentive to the owner and patient in front of them. This risk was not universal, but it is theoretically significant. Communication quality depends not only on what is said but on how attention, eye contact, reassurance, and responsiveness are enacted. If AI use increases the need to monitor, edit, or consult screen-based output during conversations, the relational quality of care may be affected even when informational accuracy improves.

Role-based contrasts are particularly important here. Client-facing veterinary-trained staff often perceived AI as a support for triage, call handling, and preparation. Doctors deemed it as a support for explanation and continuity. Senior clinicians, however, were more likely to frame communication in terms of consistency and organisational standardisation. This suggests that AI may influence communication differently at different points in the care pathway, e.g., as tools for structuring at intake, preparation prior to a consultation, and/or standardising in follow-up and discharge.

These findings suggest that AI can improve the structure and continuity of communication, but it cannot remove the need for human empathy, reassurance, and contextual interpretation. Communication was one of the clearest areas in which AI's supportive potential and human limitations appeared side by side.

Training, Wellbeing, and Resilient Implementation

The final theme concerns implementation conditions: training, adaptation, wellbeing, and resilience. Training needs were raised across the dataset. Participants asked for clearer standard operating procedures, role-specific instructions, emergency fallback rules, AI literacy, editing guidance, and mentoring for junior staff. Senior participants focused on governance and clinic-wide rules, while junior and support staff focused on onboarding, supervision, and practical clarity about how to work with outputs. One participant working across branches stated, "The tool helps only when everyone uses it in the same way" (P16). This reflects a central insight from the case study where inconsistent implementation weakens both trust and efficiency.

Several participants described adaptation as a process rather than a one-time event. A clinical assistant stated, "At first it was stressful; later it became part of the routine" (P14). This indicates that some forms of technostress may decline as users gain familiarity and as the organisation develops supportive routines. However, adaptation was not automatic. It depended on role-sensitive training and on whether staff understood not only how to use the system, but how to interpret its limits. In other words, learning to use AI responsibly was part of professional socialisation within the clinic.

Wellbeing findings were similarly nuanced. Participants frequently described reduced documentation fatigue, less frustration during overload, or lower anxiety in routine cases. AI seemed to support a sense of order and reduce repetitive burden, especially in relation to note generation, intake structure, and handover continuity. Participants articulated that AI did not remove the emotional intensity of veterinary work or the wider pressures of life and practice in a turbulent environment in Ukraine. Several explicitly distinguished between relief from administrative or cognitive burden and the persistence of war-related stress, trauma, or emotional strain. AI could make work more manageable; it could not neutralise the environment in which that work occurred.

Resilience concerns added another layer. Participants in client-facing and cross-branch roles were especially attentive to technical disruption and the need for fallback procedures. Outages, alarms, or internet interruptions could quickly expose overdependence on digital systems. One intake participant stated, "In frontline work, AI is helpful, but we always need Plan B" (P10). Another stressed that the system only helped "if there is a backup" during disruptions (P19). These comments show that resilient implementation depends on AI availability, as well as maintaining manual or alternative procedures when AI is temporarily unavailable.

Data governance and privacy also emerged within this theme, particularly through statements from senior accounts. Participants recognised that standardisation and centralisation can improve workflow but also worried about the responsibilities attached to data handling and the consequences of inaccurate or insufficiently governed outputs. This concern was framed as an argument for more formal governance, rather than constraining AI use. The clinic manager and senior doctors consistently linked responsible implementation to clear rules, validation procedures, and structured training pathways.

In summary, the implementation theme reveals that the success of AI in this case depended on technical usefulness, as well as organisational discipline. Training, consistency, fallback planning, emotional realism, and governance all shaped whether AI was experienced as support or risk. This theme also connects all the others: judgement requires training, documentation support requires consistent input, autonomy depends on critical literacy, communication requires human sensitivity, and resilience requires backup and governance.

Thematic Structure of the Findings

The above-mentioned five themes show that AI adoption in veterinary practice was experienced as a multidimensional organisational change rather than as a single technical intervention. The findings indicate that the effects of AI were interconnected across judgement, documentation, communication, autonomy, training, and wellbeing, and that these effects varied according to role, responsibility, and degree of exposure to AI-enabled workflows. Table 3 summarises the thematic structure of the findings.

Table 3. Thematic Structure of the Findings (source: authors)

Main theme	Subthemes	Meaning	Illustrative anonymous quote
Trust in AI-supported decisions	Transparency; bounded trust; human verification; ethical accountability	Participants valued AI as a second reader or structuring support but insisted that final clinical responsibility must remain human.	"AI is useful as a second opinion, not as the final answer." (Senior veterinary doctor, P06)
Cognitive workload and documentation	Structured notes; reduced repetition; checking burden; input quality	AI reduced repetitive writing and documentation fatigue, while also creating new work in reviewing, editing, and validating outputs.	"The main benefit is structure, not just speed." (Veterinary doctor, P07)
Professional autonomy and identity	Critical use; learning support; dependency risk; meaningful work	AI reshaped autonomy by shifting expertise toward interpretation, override, and contextual judgement rather than manual record production.	"AI helps me learn, but I still need professional confirmation." (Junior veterinary doctor, P03)
Client communication and empathy	Structured intake; clearer explanations; emotional nuance; human voice	AI improved the clarity and continuity of owner communication but did not replace empathy or context-sensitive reassurance.	"Some clients need reassurance that a real person is still involved." (Client-facing veterinary-trained professional, P15)
Training, wellbeing, and resilient implementation	Role-sensitive training; SOPs; fallback procedures; disruption associated with war and the broader turbulent environment	Successful use depended on training, shared procedures, and backup plans; AI reduced some cognitive load but did not remove strain associated with the turbulent environment in Ukraine.	"In frontline work, AI is helpful, but we always need Plan B." (Client-facing veterinary-trained professional, P10)

To make the findings more concrete, two brief examples from the interview matrix are worth highlighting. The first concerns documentation and case preparation. Several doctors described situations in which AI-generated summaries improved the clarity of case histories before consultation, particularly when appointments were busy and owner narratives were fragmented. However, this benefit depended on review: one participant described correcting an incomplete symptom chronology before using the summary in clinical discussion, while another stated that the value of the record lay in its structured starting point rather than in its presumed correctness. The practical lesson is that AI created better first drafts, not finished clinical artefacts.

The second example concerns client communication. Veterinary-trained intake staff reported that AI-supported call structuring made it easier to capture essential information and maintain continuity when owners phoned back or when care had to be transferred across staff. However, these same participants warned that anxious clients still required reassurance, contextual explanation, and a recognisably human voice. In this sense, AI improved informational consistency while leaving the emotional and relational burden of care decisively human. These two examples encapsulate the broader pattern of the chapter: support was real, but so were the limits.

DISCUSSION

The findings support the central argument of the chapter: AI in veterinary clinics is experienced as a reconfiguration of human work, and beyond just its technical dimension. Across roles, participants valued AI for structuring information, supporting preparation, reducing repetitive documentation, and improving continuity. Nevertheless, participants emphasised that these advantages did not reduce the importance of human interpretation, ethical accountability, or relational care. In this respect, the data move beyond an efficiency narrative and support a more theoretically informed understanding of AI-enabled veterinary work. They also speak directly to current debates on generative AI and explainability: the usefulness of AI in documentation and communication was shaped by staff awareness of verification, risk, and the organisational conditions under which outputs can be trusted.

AI as Augmentation Under Conditions of Bounded Trust

From the perspective of human-centred AI, the most significant result is that participants overwhelmingly framed AI as support rather than replacement. This aligns with Shneiderman's (2020) argument that effective AI should enhance human capability without undermining human control. It also speaks to Floridi and Cowls' (2019) emphasis on autonomy and explicability. Trust in the present case was real but bounded. Even the most positive participants described trust as conditional on review, correction, and professional experience. This is important because it shows that responsible AI adoption depends on calibrating trust appropriately, and not necessarily maiming trust.

The distinction matters particularly in safety- and care-critical work. Cummings (2021) reports that AI systems can seem more mature or authoritative than they really are. The junior doctors in this study offered a vivid example of that problem. They often experienced AI as helpful for learning and structuring clinical thinking but also recognised the danger of outputs that sounded confident without being sufficiently contextualised. The data therefore support a nuanced reading of augmentation. AI can genuinely extend human capability, but only when implementation preserves critical distance, role-appropriate oversight, and the authority of human expertise. This is consistent with recent veterinary quality-assurance work, which emphasises that trustworthy deployment depends on validation and review procedures rather than on model performance alone (Pacholec et al., 2025a, 2025b).

A Sociotechnical Reading of Variation Across Roles and Branches

The findings also strongly support a sociotechnical interpretation. The value of AI in the case was not inherent in the tool itself; it depended on the quality of inputs, consistency of use, clarity of roles, branch-level coordination, and the availability of backup procedures. Participants who worked across branches were particularly revealing in this respect. They showed that the same tool could be more or less useful depending on whether teams used it consistently and whether organisational norms supported shared workflows.

From a sociotechnical perspective, where branch practices were aligned, AI helped produce continuity and standardisation. Yet, where adoption was uneven, the same system generated friction or inconsistency. Similarly, input quality was a sociotechnical issue. "Bad input gives bad output" was not just a complaint about the software. It was a reminder that the technical system depends on disciplined human use. In other words, AI did not sit outside the organisation. It became part of the organisation's coordination logic, and its value rose or fell with the quality of the surrounding work system.

Work Redesign Rather than Simple Automation

The chapter's contribution to human resource management (HRM) is clearest when the findings are interpreted through work design and job redesign. AI reduced some work yet not work as such. It reduced duplicated writing, supported structured histories, facilitated handovers, and lowered some forms of documentation fatigue. At the same time, it created or intensified checking work, screen attention, editing responsibility, and the need for AI literacy. This pattern reflects Parker and Grote's (2022) argument that digital technologies reshape jobs rather than simply removing labour.

The redistribution of work differed by role. Senior clinicians took on more responsibility for validation and governance. Junior doctors benefited from structured support but faced new risks of dependency. Assistants gained stronger participation in workflow coordination but also greater responsibility for information quality. Intake staff were supported in triage and communication preparation; however, they remained responsible for managing anxious owners and recognising when structured questioning was not enough. AI thus redesigned the work system asymmetrically. It did not create one "AI experience" for the whole clinic. It produced role-dependent gains and burdens.

This is highly relevant to HRM debates because it shows that responsible AI adoption requires more than tool deployment. It requires role-sensitive redesign of tasks, expectations, supervision, and training. Without that redesign, organisations may inadvertently transfer hidden burdens to particular staff groups or confuse the boundary between support and responsibility.

Professional Identity and the Persistence of Human Value

Another important contribution concerns professional identity and meaningful work. A common fear in public discourse is that AI erodes professional expertise by taking over the cognitive core of work. The findings here do not support a simple version of that narrative. Participants did not describe their expertise as being displaced. Instead, AI tended to make the human core of expertise more visible. The more that structure and repetition could be delegated to AI, the more participants defined their own distinctive value in terms of judgement, contextual interpretation, ethical responsibility, empathy, and the ability to decide when the machine was wrong or incomplete.

At the same time, the chapter does not claim that identity is untouched. Participants noted risks of screen dependency, overconfidence in outputs, and subtle shifts in how attention is allocated during consultations. These findings suggest that identity is not threatened through direct replacement so much as through gradual changes in what professionals spend their time doing. If checking screens, editing templates, and monitoring digital systems expand too far, then the relational and interpretive dimensions of work may be crowded out. The challenge is therefore not to "protect old work" from new tools, but to redesign work so that AI removes low-value friction without displacing the high-value human dimensions of practice.

Communication, Empathy, and One Health Relevance

The communication findings add an important veterinary and One Health dimension to the broader AI-at-work literature. Much AI research focuses on tasks that are informational, analytic, or administrative. Veterinary communication is different. It involves emotionally charged interpretation between clinicians and owners on behalf of animal patients. The findings show that AI can help structure this communication, improve continuity, and make explanations clearer. But they also show that structured communication is not equivalent to empathetic communication. Owners may still be distressed, distrustful, or unable to articulate symptoms clearly. In such situations, the "human voice" remains essential.

This matters for One Health because veterinary communication has effects that extend beyond the immediate transaction. Clear and trustworthy communication supports adherence, continuity of care, animal welfare, owner confidence, and organisational legitimacy. Poorly managed communication may compromise all of these. The chapter therefore suggests that AI in veterinary settings should be assessed not only by internal clinic efficiency, but also by its impact on the relational quality of care.

Strain Associated with the Turbulent Environment in Ukraine, Resilience, and the Limits of Technological Solutionism

The turbulent environment in Ukraine sharpens the analysis without displacing the main topic. Participants' accounts indicate that AI was valuable partly because it created order under strain: better handover, more consistent records, clearer intake, and reduced documentation fatigue in overloaded conditions. Nevertheless, the findings challenge technological solutionism by showing that AI did not remove emotional trauma, war-related stress, or infrastructural fragility. Participants insisted on backup procedures and pointed to outages, alarms, and disruptions as reminders that digital dependency has limits. This suggests that in crisis-affected settings, the value of AI lies in supporting resilient organisation while preserving human judgement, and not just reducing complexity through automation. AI can help clinics cope, but it can also introduce new points of fragility if governance, training, or fallback procedures are weak. The chapter therefore contributes to discussions of digital resilience by showing that resilience is not only about adopting advanced tools; it is about adopting them in ways that are organisationally robust and ethically disciplined.

A further point deserves emphasis: in SME clinics, AI adoption carries hidden organisational costs even when software promises efficiency. Participants in this study spoke more about time, supervision, and workflow discipline than about financial accounting, but these are themselves forms of cost. Time spent training new users, validating records, standardising use across branches, and maintaining manual backup procedures represents real organisational investment. This is particularly relevant for smaller clinics, where the margin for failed implementation is narrow. The implication is that managerial evaluation of AI should include integration effort, supervision load, and infrastructural resilience rather than focusing only on headline productivity gains. Recent implementation and governance literature points in the same direction, emphasising practical checklists, sociotechnical readiness, and governance capacity as conditions of successful adoption (Owoyemi et al., 2025; Glover et al., 2025; Olawade et al., 2025).

Theoretical and Practical Contributions

Theoretically, the chapter extends human-centred AI scholarship into veterinary practice, showing how professional accountability shapes trust and acceptable use. The findings also enrich sociotechnical understandings of AI by demonstrating how branch consistency, role differentiation, and input quality determine real workplace outcomes. This work also strengthens HRM and work design debates by showing that AI adoption in veterinary SMEs is fundamentally a job redesign issue involving autonomy, training, workload, and meaning.

Practically, the findings imply that clinics should not ask only whether AI improves speed or structure. They should ask: Who checks outputs? Who needs different kinds of training? How are fallback procedures maintained? How is empathy protected in client communication? How is responsibility kept visible? These questions provide the basis for the practical model developed in the next section.

Overall, the discussion confirms that the human experience of AI in veterinary clinics is neither utopian nor purely resistant. It is conditional, negotiated, and deeply organisational. AI was welcomed when it reduced fragmentation and supported continuity but accepted only on the condition that people remained responsible, visible, and in control.

A Model of Human-Centred AI Adoption in Veterinary SMEs

Building on the findings, this chapter proposes a model of human-centred AI adoption in veterinary SMEs. The model is intended as an integrated practical output rather than a purely conceptual add-on. Covering six dimensions, it adopts a responsible adoption framework, outlining pertinent implementation roadmap, HRM recommendations, and an ethical considerations. Its purpose is to help clinics adopt AI in ways that support professional judgement, communication quality, staff wellbeing, and organisational resilience:

Dimension 1 - Human oversight and Final Responsibility: AI outputs should be used to support, structure, and prepare work, but final clinical and communicative responsibility must remain with qualified professionals. In practice, this means that every AI-supported note, recommendation, or structured summary should be understood as reviewable rather than final. Clinics should formalise validation rules, escalation pathways, and role boundaries so that less experienced staff are not left to interpret ambiguous outputs without support.

Dimension 2 - Trust Through Explainability and Calibrated Use: The findings show that staff do not need blind confidence in AI; they need justified confidence rooted in experience, transparency, and explainability. Clinics should therefore train staff on how to use AI tools, as well as in how to recognise limitations, poor inputs, overconfident language, and situations that require override. Explainability does not need to be purely technical. It can also be procedural where staff understand what the tool is for, what it is not for, and when human judgement takes priority.

Dimension 3 - Workflow Redesign Rather Than Tool Insertion: AI should not simply be "added" to an existing clinic routine with the expectation that benefits will emerge automatically. The case shows that AI changes documentation, intake, handover, and communication tasks. Clinics therefore need to redesign workflows deliberately: clarify who captures information, who checks it, who edits it, how outputs move between roles, and how cross-branch consistency is maintained. Without workflow redesign, hidden burdens of correction and monitoring may accumulate.

Dimension 4- Role-Sensitive Training and Professional Development: Senior clinicians, veterinary doctors, junior doctors, assistants, and client-facing staff interact with AI differently. Training should therefore differ accordingly. Junior professionals may need mentoring on critical use and confidence calibration; assistants may need guidance on information quality and escalation; client-facing staff may need scripts, fallback procedures, and communication training for emotionally difficult interactions. AI literacy should be treated as part of professional development rather than as a one-off technical induction.

Dimension 5 - Wellbeing Protection and Realistic Expectations: AI can reduce documentation fatigue and cognitive fragmentation, but it cannot remove emotional labour, burnout risk, or the strain associated with war and the broader turbulent environment in Ukraine. Organisations should therefore avoid presenting AI as a cure for deeper structural strain. Instead, they should use AI strategically to reduce repetitive overload while monitoring whether it creates new burdens of checking, screen dependency, or perceived surveillance. The goal is to improve work quality, not simply to demand more output.

Dimension 6 - Ethical Governance and Resilient Fallback: Governance includes data protection, privacy, validation requirements, role clarity, and procedures for handling AI error or ambiguity. In line with recent sociotechnical implementation literature, governance should be treated as an ongoing organisational capability rather than a one-off compliance exercise (McCradden et al., 2023; Owoyemi et al., 2025). Resilience requires manual or alternative procedures when systems fail, power is interrupted, or connectivity is unstable. In high-pressure settings, backup processes are not signs of technological weakness; they are signs of responsible implementation.

Implications for Clinic Managers, Veterinary Educators, and AI Developers

For clinic managers, the central implication is that AI governance cannot be delegated entirely to the tool vendor or to enthusiastic early adopters. Managers need to define validation responsibilities, role boundaries, documentation standards, and fallback procedures from the outset. They also need to recognise that uneven adoption across branches can itself become a source of risk if handovers and communication standards diverge.

For veterinary educators and internal trainers, the findings suggest that AI literacy should be treated as a professional capability rather than as optional technical curiosity. Junior clinicians may need guidance on critical reading of AI-generated language; assistants may need escalation protocols and information-quality training; client-facing staff may need practice in combining structured intake with empathy and reassurance.

For AI developers, the chapter highlights that usability in veterinary settings depends on more than model accuracy. Tools need interfaces that make review easy, encourage correction rather than conceal uncertainty, and fit the rhythms of busy clinic work. In practice, the most useful tools were not those that appeared most autonomous, but those that allowed staff to preserve oversight while reducing fragmentation.

An Implementation Roadmap

A practical implementation roadmap for veterinary SMEs can be summarised in five steps:

1. Map the workflow before introducing AI. Identify where communication, documentation, handover, and diagnostic preparation currently create friction.

2. Define role boundaries and validation rules. Decide who can use which tools, who must review outputs, and when escalation is required.
3. Provide staged, role-sensitive training. Treat AI literacy, critical use, and communication skills as developmental needs.
4. Pilot, review, and adjust. Collect staff feedback, track correction points, and refine workflows before full standardisation.
5. Maintain backup and governance. Ensure that privacy, data quality, manual fallback, and ethical accountability are not sacrificed for convenience.

This model reflects the central lesson of the case where veterinary AI adoption succeeds when the organisation clearly protects human judgement, empathy, and responsibility.

Limitations and Future Research Pathways

This chapter should be read with the limits of qualitative single-case evidence in mind. The study offers context-rich insight into one veterinary clinic network operating under distinctive organisational conditions and a turbulent environment in Ukraine shaped by the continuing effects of war. The study does not claim statistical generalisability across all veterinary settings. The sample was intentionally structured to capture role variation within one organisation, which is analytically useful but also means that broader sectoral comparisons remain to be made. In addition, the study focuses on staff experience rather than direct measurement of patient outcomes, owner satisfaction, or long-term financial impact.

These limitations do not weaken the chapter's contribution, but they shape how it should be interpreted. The value of the case lies in showing mechanisms and tensions that may travel to other settings, not in claiming universal prevalence. Future research could therefore compare AI-enabled work across privately owned clinics, hospital systems, and educational veterinary settings; examine owner perceptions of AI-mediated communication; track how trust and dependency evolve over time; and investigate how explainability, governance, and training affect adoption in larger multi-site organisations. Comparative research across countries would also be valuable, particularly in contexts where regulatory expectations, staffing pressures, and digital infrastructures differ.

CONCLUSIONS

This chapter has examined the human experience of AI-enabled work in a Ukrainian veterinary clinic network. It has shown that AI-enabled communication, documentation, and diagnostic-support tools can improve structure, continuity, preparation, and aspects of workload management. However, their significance is not exhausted by efficiency. They reshape professional judgement, the distribution of work, patterns of communication, training needs, and the boundaries of ethical responsibility.

The findings show that veterinary professionals were generally receptive to AI when it reduced fragmentation and supported workflow, but they were equally clear that AI could not replace clinical judgement, empathy, or accountability. Trust was conditional. Benefits were real but uneven. Although documentation burden declined, the need for checking and validation increased. Similarly, communication became more structured, while the need for a human voice remained. The context of war and the broader turbulent environment in Ukraine intensified both the value of standardisation and the need for resilient fallback procedures. The chapter contributes to scholarship on AI-enabled workplaces by bringing veterinary medicine into a conversation often dominated by other sectors. It also contributes to HRM and One Health debates by showing how AI adoption in veterinary SMEs is inseparable from work design, professional development, wellbeing, and organisational resilience. The proposed model of human-centred AI adoption offers a practical framework for clinics seeking to implement AI responsibly.

Ultimately, the chapter argues for a simple but consequential principle: in veterinary practice, AI should reduce cognitive load, not human responsibility. Responsible implementation begins where that principle is made operational.

REFERENCES

Akbarein, H., Taaghi, M. H., Mohebbi, M., & Soufizadeh, P. (2025). Applications and considerations of artificial intelligence in veterinary sciences: A narrative review. *Veterinary Medicine and Science, 11*(3), e70315. Advance online publication. DOI: 10.1002/vms3.70315 PMID: 40173266

Akinsulie, O. C., Idris, I., Aliyu, V. A., Shahzad, S., Banwo, O. G., Ogunleye, S. C., Olorunshola, M., Okedoyin, D. O., Ugwu, C., Oladapo, I. P., Gbadegoye, J. O., Akande, Q. A., Babawale, P., Rostami, S., & Soetan, K. O. (2024). The potential application of artificial intelligence in veterinary clinical practice and biomedical research. *Frontiers in Veterinary Science, 11*, 1347550. Advance online publication. DOI: 10.3389/fvets.2024.1347550 PMID: 38356661

Albergante, L., O'Flynn, C., & O'Donnell, K. (2025). Artificial intelligence is beginning to create value for selected small animal veterinary applications while remaining immature for others. *Journal of the American Veterinary Medical Association, 263*(3), 280–287. DOI: 10.2460/javma.24.09.0617 PMID: 39746305

Braun, V., & Clarke, V. (2006). Using thematic analysis in psychology. *Qualitative Research in Psychology, 3*(2), 77–101. DOI: 10.1191/1478088706qp063oa

Brynjolfsson, E., & McAfee, A. (2017). Machine, platform, crowd: Harnessing our digital future. W. W. Norton. https://wwnorton.com/books/Machine-Platform-Crowd/

Burti, S., Benigni, L., & Gutierrez-Quintana, R. (2024). Artificial intelligence in veterinary diagnostic imaging: Perspectives and limitations. *Research in Veterinary Science, 175*, 105317. Advance online publication. DOI: 10.1016/j.rvsc.2024.105317 PMID: 38843690

Checkland, P. (1999). Systems thinking. In Rethinking management information systems (pp. 45–56). DOI: 10.1093/oso/9780198775331.003.0004

Coiera, E., & Fraile Navarro, D. (2024). AI as an ecosystem: Ensuring generative AI is safe and effective. *NEJM AI, 1*(9), AIp2400611. DOI: 10.1056/AIp2400611

Cummings, M. L. (2021). Rethinking the maturity of artificial intelligence in safety-critical settings. *AI Magazine, 42*(1), 37–47. DOI: 10.1002/j.2371-9621.2021.tb00005.x

Davenport, T. H., & Ronanki, R. (2018). Artificial intelligence for the real world. *Harvard Business Review, 96*(1), 108–116. https://hbr.org/2018/01/artificial-intelligence-for-the-real-world

Edward, K. L., Hercelinskyj, G., & Giandinoto, J. A. (2017). Emotional labour in mental health nursing: An integrative systematic review. *International Journal of Mental Health Nursing*, *26*(3), 215–225. DOI: 10.1111/inm.12330 PMID: 28374961

Floridi, L., & Cowls, J. (2019). A unified framework of five principles for AI in society. *Harvard Data Science Review*, *1*(1). Advance online publication. DOI: 10.1162/99608f92.8cd550d1

Gabor, S., Danylenko, G., & Basran, P. S. (2025). Familiarity with artificial intelligence drives optimism and adoption among veterinary professionals: 2024 survey. *American Journal of Veterinary Research*, *86*(S1), S63–S69. DOI: 10.2460/ajvr.24.10.0293 PMID: 39933254

Gardner, D. H., & Hini, D. (2006). Work-related stress in the veterinary profession in New Zealand. *New Zealand Veterinary Journal*, *54*(3), 119–124. DOI: 10.1080/00480169.2006.36623 PMID: 16751842

Glikson, E., & Woolley, A. W. (2020). Human trust in artificial intelligence: Review of empirical research. *The Academy of Management Annals*, *14*(2), 627–660. DOI: 10.5465/annals.2018.0057

Glover, W., Renton, M., Minaye, H., & Dabiri, O. (2025). Assessing equitable development and implementation of artificial intelligence-enabled patient engagement technologies: A sociotechnical systems approach. *Mayo Clinic Proceedings. Digital Health*, *3*(1), 100192. Advance online publication. DOI: 10.1016/j.mcpdig.2024.100192 PMID: 40206991

Hähnel, M. (2025). Ethical challenges and solutions in AI-driven medical data management: A focus on distributed machine learning. *Discover Artificial Intelligence*, *5*(1), 53. Advance online publication. DOI: 10.1007/s44163-025-00266-0

Hennessey, E., DiFazio, M., Hennessey, R., & Cassel, N. (2022). Artificial intelligence in veterinary diagnostic imaging: A literature review. *Veterinary Radiology & Ultrasound*, *63*(S1), 851–870. DOI: 10.1111/vru.13163 PMID: 36468206

Hosseinian-Far, A., Farsi, M., Gharehbaghi, K., Jahankhani, H., & Daneshkhah, A. (2025). Reimagining Industry 5.0: Generative artificial intelligence as the enabling technology. In Symbiotic intelligence (pp. 128–146). CRC Press. DOI: 10.1201/9781003540373-7

Issa, H., Jaber, J., & Lakkis, H. (2024). Navigating AI unpredictability: Exploring technostress in AI-powered healthcare systems. *Technological Forecasting and Social Change*, *202*, 123311. Advance online publication. DOI: 10.1016/j.techfore.2024.123311

Klietsova, N., Batsenko, L., Klietsov, A., Halenin, R., Kravchenko, I., Ksenofontova, M., & Dorozhko, Y. (2024). International experience of personnel selection in the conditions of the digital environment, war and sustainable development: Social and corporate responsibility of employers for the non-transparent hiring process. *Evolutionary Studies in Imaginative Culture*, *8*(1), 26–38. DOI. 10.70082/esiculture.vi.766

Klietsova, N., Halenin, R., Mostova, A., Sclyar, I., & Krasovska, A. (2025). Digital transformation of Ukrainian SMEs during wartime: Resilience, adaptation, and management strategies. In *Sustainable development: Modern theories and best practices* (pp. 26–30). Teadmus OÜ., https://api.teadmus.org/storage/published_books/monthly_thesis_book_06_2025/book.pdf

Klietsova, N., & Klietsov, A. (2023a). Реформування галузі ветеринарної медицини України щодо ідентифікації тварин-компаньйонів у контексті сталого розвитку, 'One Health' і діджиталізації [Reforming the veterinary medicine sector of Ukraine regarding the identification of companion animals in the context of sustainable development, 'One Health' and digitalization]. Bulletin of Sumy National Agrarian University. The Series. *Veterinary Medicine*, *63*(4), 68–75. DOI: 10.32782/bsnau.vet.2023.4.11

Klietsova, N., & Klietsov, A. (2023b). Social protection of economic and legal rights of emigrants in the context of reforming veterinary legislation of Ukraine and preservation of human capital under conditions of war and digitalization. In *Modern paradigm of public and private law amidst sustainable development* (Vol. 1, pp. 286–332). Baltija Publishing., DOI: 10.30525/978-9934-26-331-6-14

Kogan, L. R., & Rishniw, M. (2023). Differences in perceptions and satisfaction exist among veterinarians employed at corporate versus privately owned veterinary clinics. *Journal of the American Veterinary Medical Association*, *261*(12), 1838–1846. DOI: 10.2460/javma.23.06.0326 PMID: 37607680

Laranjo, L., Tudor Car, L., Payne, R. E., Neves, A. L., Kidd, M., & Miranda, J. J. (2025). Artificial intelligence in primary care: Innovation at a crossroads. *The Lancet Primary Care*, *100078*. Advance online publication. DOI: 10.1016/j.lanprc.2025.100078 PMID: 41969643

McCradden, M. D., Joshi, S., Anderson, J. A., & London, A. J. (2023). A normative framework for artificial intelligence as a sociotechnical system in healthcare. *Patterns (New York, N.Y.)*, *4*(11), 100864. Advance online publication. DOI: 10.1016/j.patter.2023.100864 PMID: 38035190

Mesinovic, M., Watkinson, P., & Zhu, T. (2025). Explainability in the age of large language models for healthcare. *Communications Engineering*, *4*(1), 128. Advance online publication. DOI: 10.1038/s44172-025-00453-y PMID: 40676176

Mosaku, I., Ajewole, O., Adegoke, S., & Hosseinian-Far, A. (2025). Data-driven future: A review of technologies and applications in the era of industry 5.0. In *Symbiotic intelligence: Advancing forecasting through human-AI collaboration*. CRC Press., DOI: 10.1201/9781003540373-8

Neal, S. V., Rudmann, D. G., & Corps, K. N. (2025). Artificial intelligence in veterinary clinical pathology – An introduction and review. *Veterinary Clinical Pathology*, *54*(S2), S13–S29. DOI: 10.1111/vcp.70012 PMID: 40462415

Olawade, D. B., Weerasinghe, K., Teke, J., Msiska, M., Boussios, S., & Hatzidimitriadou, E. (2025). Evaluating AI adoption in healthcare: Insights from information governance professionals in the United Kingdom. *International Journal of Medical Informatics*, *194*, 105909. Advance online publication. DOI: 10.1016/j.ijmedinf.2025.105909 PMID: 40198930

Osnat, B. (2025). Patient perspectives on artificial intelligence in healthcare: A global scoping review of benefits, ethical concerns, and implementation strategies. *International Journal of Medical Informatics*, *196*, 106007. Advance online publication. DOI: 10.1016/j.ijmedinf.2025.106007 PMID: 40494217

Owoyemi, A., Osuchukwu, J., Salwei, M. E., & Boyd, A. (2025). Checklist approach to developing and implementing AI in clinical settings: Instrument development study. *JMIRx Med*, *6*, e65565. Advance online publication. DOI: 10.2196/65565 PMID: 39977249

Pacholec, C., Flatland, B., Xie, H., & Zimmerman, K. (2025a). Harnessing artificial intelligence for enhanced veterinary diagnostics: A look to quality assurance, Part I – Model development. *Veterinary Clinical Pathology*, *54*(S2), S30. DOI: 10.1111/vcp.13401 PMID: 39638756

Pacholec, C., Flatland, B., Xie, H., & Zimmerman, K. (2025b). Harnessing artificial intelligence for enhanced veterinary diagnostics: A look to quality assurance, Part II – External validation. *Veterinary Clinical Pathology*, *54*(S2), S43. DOI: 10.1111/vcp.13407 PMID: 39843399

Parker, S. K., & Grote, G. (2022). Automation, algorithms, and beyond: Why work design matters more than ever in a digital world. *Applied Psychology*, *71*(4), 1171–1204. DOI: 10.1111/apps.12241

Shneiderman, B. (2020). Human-centered artificial intelligence: Reliable, safe and trustworthy. *International Journal of Human-Computer Interaction*, *36*(6), 495–504. DOI: 10.1080/10447318.2020.1741118

Sobkowich, K. E. (2025). Demystifying artificial intelligence for veterinary professionals: Practical applications and future potential. *American Journal of Veterinary Research*, *86*(S1), S6–S15. DOI: 10.2460/ajvr.24.09.0275 PMID: 39842402

Tarafdar, M., Cooper, C. L., & Stich, J. F. (2019). The technostress trifecta – Techno eustress, techno distress and design: Theoretical directions and an agenda for research. *Information Systems Journal*, *29*(1), 6–42. DOI: 10.1111/isj.12169

Wells, B. J., Saef, J., & Green-Saxena, A.. (2025). A practical framework for appropriate implementation and review of artificial intelligence (FAIR-AI) in healthcare. npj. *Digital Medicine*, *8*(1), 514. Advance online publication. DOI: 10.1038/s41746-025-01900-y PMID: 40790350

Wilson, H. J., Daugherty, P. R., & Morini-Bianzino, N. (2017). The jobs that artificial intelligence will create. *MIT Sloan Management Review*, *58*(4), 14–16. https://sloanreview.mit.edu/article/will-ai-create-as-many-jobs-as-it-eliminates/

Yin, R. K. (2018). *Case study research and applications: Design and methods* (6th ed.). Sage., https://uk.sagepub.com/en-gb/eur/case-study-research-and-applications/book250150

Compilation of References

Aarthi, S., Ravikumar, R. N., Khudayberganov, S., Ismailov, A., & Khujaniyozova, O. (2025). Using Intelligent Tutoring Systems to enhance student engagement. In *Advances in Computational Intelligence and Robotics* (pp. 155–188). IGI Global. DOI: 10.4018/979-8-3373-1827-1.ch008

Adedoyin, F., Dogan, H., Cetinkaya, D., & Jiang, N. (2025, May). Human-Centered AI in FinTech: A Conceptual Model and Strategic Research Agenda. In *2025 IEEE Conference on Artificial Intelligence (CAI)* (pp. 180-187). IEEE. DOI: 10.1109/CAI64502.2025.00036

Adeniyi, A., Akashaba, B., Aiyenuro, O., & Abiola, O. (2024). Framework for strategic investments in technology to enhance sustainable economic development in emerging markets. *International Journal of Innovative Science and Research Technology*, *9*(10), 1458–1468. DOI: 10.38124/ijisrt/IJISRT24OCT598

Afroogh, S., Akbari, A., Malone, E., Kargar, M., & Alambeigi, H. (2024). Trust in AI: Progress, challenges, and future directions. *Humanities & Social Sciences Communications*, *11*(1), 4044. Advance online publication. DOI: 10.1057/s41599-024-04044-8

Ahmad, A. R., Sapry, H. R. M., & Jameel, A. S. (2025). Reclaiming autonomy in the age of AI: A conceptual framework linking algorithmic management and job happiness. *International Journal of Research and Innovation in Social Science*, 7222–7228. DOI: 10.47772/IJRISS.2025.908000597

Aitken, J., Böhme, T., & McAsh, E. (2025). Co-Creation of Societal Benefits Through Human-Centered Design and Management of Dynamic Capabilities in Oyster Farm Communities. *Strategic Change*, *34*(1), 93–101. DOI: 10.1002/jsc.2611

Aizenberg, E., & van den Hoven, J. (2020). Designing for human rights in AI. *Big Data & Society*, *7*(2), 205395172094956. DOI: 10.1177/2053951720949566

Akbarein, H., Taaghi, M. H., Mohebbi, M., & Soufizadeh, P. (2025). Applications and considerations of artificial intelligence in veterinary sciences: A narrative review. *Veterinary Medicine and Science, 11*(3), e70315. Advance online publication. DOI: 10.1002/vms3.70315 PMID: 40173266

Akhtar, M., Salman, A., Ghafoor, K. A., & Kamran, M. (2024). Artificial intelligence, financial services knowledge, government support, and user innovativeness: Exploring the moderated-mediated path to fintech adoption. *Heliyon, 10*(21), e39521. DOI: 10.1016/j.heliyon.2024.e39521 PMID: 39568835

Akinnagbe, O. B. (2024). Human-AI collaboration: Enhancing productivity and decision-making. *International Journal of Education, Management, and Technology, 2*(3), 387–417. DOI: 10.58578/ijemt.v2i3.4209

Akinsulie, O. C., Idris, I., Aliyu, V. A., Shahzad, S., Banwo, O. G., Ogunleye, S. C., Olorunshola, M., Okedoyin, D. O., Ugwu, C., Oladapo, I. P., Gbadegoye, J. O., Akande, Q. A., Babawale, P., Rostami, S., & Soetan, K. O. (2024). The potential application of artificial intelligence in veterinary clinical practice and biomedical research. *Frontiers in Veterinary Science, 11*, 1347550. Advance online publication. DOI: 10.3389/fvets.2024.1347550 PMID: 38356661

Alamelu, R., & Motha, C. S. (2026). A causal evaluation framework for aligning employee experience with organisational resilience: Insights from fuzzy DEMATEL and MICMAC. In *Employee experience management for organizational resilience* (pp. 423–446). IGI Global Scientific Publishing.

Al-Assaf, G., Abdel-Halim, M., & Shehadeh, M. (2025). The macroeconomic drivers of fintech development in emerging markets: An empirical investigation. *Discover Sustainability, 6*(1), 863. DOI: 10.1007/s43621-025-01597-9

Albasrie, A. D. A., Himawan, I. S., & Sharipudin, C. (2024). Sustainable wellness tourism in Indonesia (Case study on health tourism development at Hanara Wellbeing Center Bandung). *Media Konservasi, 2S*(3), 435–435. DOI: 10.29244/medkon.29.3.435

Albergante, L., O'Flynn, C., & O'Donnell, K. (2025). Artificial intelligence is beginning to create value for selected small animal veterinary applications while remaining immature for others. *Journal of the American Veterinary Medical Association, 263*(3), 280–287. DOI: 10.2460/javma.24.09.0617 PMID: 39746305

Albrecht, S. L., Green, C. R., & Marty, A. (2021). Meaningful work, job resources, and employee engagement. *Sustainability (Basel), 13*(7), 4045. DOI: 10.3390/su13074045

Alsaif, A., & Sabih Aksoy, M. (2023). AI-HRM: artificial intelligence in human resource management: a literature review. *Journal of Computing and Communication, 2*(2), 1–7. DOI: 10.21608/jocc.2023.307053

Alum, E. U., Egwu, C. K., Manjula, V. S., Ekpang, P. O., Ekpang, J. E.II, Echegu, D. A., Alum, B. N., & Uti, D. E. (2026). Overcoming the Black Box Challenge: Building Trust in Artificial Intelligence Algorithms in Oncology. *Technology in Cancer Research & Treatment, 25*, 15330338261434649. DOI: 10.1177/15330338261434649 PMID: 41873493

Alves, B., Alhussein, G., Riggare, S., Duncan, T. S., Saad, A., Lyreskog, D. M., Chatzichristos, C., Gerasimou, I., Hadjidimitriou, S., Hadjileontiadis, L. J., & Dias, B. (2025). Stakeholder perspectives on trustworthy AI for Parkinson disease management using a cocreation approach: Qualitative exploratory study. *Journal of Medical Internet Research, 27*, e73710. DOI: 10.2196/73710 PMID: 40768261

Anand, S., Karthikeya, M., Sai, A. A., & Balamurali, O. (2023, January). Multilingual hybrid chatbot for empowering rural women self-help groups in india. In *2023 International Conference for Advancement in Technology (ICONAT)* (pp. 1-6). IEEE. DOI: 10.1109/ICONAT57137.2023.10080347

Andrews, L. (2019). Public administration, public leadership and the construction of public value in the age of the algorithm and 'big data.'. *Public Administration, 97*(2), 296–310. DOI: 10.1111/padm.12534

Andriani, A. D. C., & Siripipatthanakul, S. (2026). Technology-Driven Organization Policies: E-Waste Governance Framework. In Technology Policy and Its Impact on Green Governance and Sustainability (pp. 31-62). IGI Global Scientific Publishing.

Andriani, A. D., C Siripipatthanakul, S. (2025). Strategic Governance Communication and Green Indicators for Digital Business Sustainability.

Andriani, A. D. (2025). The future of digital content: AI-generated texts, images, videos, and real-time production. In *Impacts of AI-Generated Content on Brand Reputation* (pp. 149–176). IGI Global Scientific Publishing. DOI: 10.4018/979-8-3373-4327-3.ch006

Andriani, A. D., Mulyana, D., Dida, S. C., & Wahyudin, U. (2021). The role of healing environment in reducing the stress of patients with non-communicable disease. *Journal of Natural Science, Biology, and Medicine, 12*(3), 300–306. DOI: 10.4103/jnsbm.JNSBM_12_3_7

Anifa, M., Ramakrishnan, S., Joghee, S., Kabiraj, S., & Bishnoi, M. M. (2022). Fintech innovations in the financial service industry. *Journal of Risk and Financial Management*, *15*(7), 287. DOI: 10.3390/jrfm15070287

Anisha Estherita, S., & Vasantha, S. (2024). Fostering employee engagement and knowledge sharing through artificial intelligence. *Salud Ciencia y Tecnologia - Serie de Conferencias*, *3*, 897. DOI: 10.56294/sctconf2024897

Anitha, K., Amala, J., & El Gareh, F. (2026). AI-enhanced organisational culture and its effect on employee engagement: Building proficiencies for sustainable decision making. In *Building AI-driven decision making competencies for sustainability* (pp. 1–28). IGI Global Scientific Publishing.

Appelbaum, E., Bailey, T., Berg, P., & Kalleberg, A. L. (2000). *Manufacturing advantage: Why high-performance work systems pay off*. Cornell University Press.

Arantes, L. (2022). Digital marketing and sustainability: A study on consumer perceptions. *ICIEMC Proceedings*, *3*, 40-49.

Ateeq, K., Oswal, N., Jawabri, A., Al Masaeid, T., Alquqa, E. K., Basha, S. E., & Alami, R. (2025). The transformative impact of artificial Intelligence (AI) on organisational behaviour (OB): A study of employee engagement, performance, and ethical implications. *Journal of Posthumanism*, *5*(4). Advance online publication. DOI: 10.63332/joph.v5i4.1221

Autor, D. H. (2015). Why are there still so many jobs? The history and future of workplace automation. *The Journal of Economic Perspectives*, *29*(3), 3–30. DOI: 10.1257/jep.29.3.3

Awad, N. F., & Krishnan, M. S. (2006). The personalization privacy paradox: An empirical evaluation of information transparency and the willingness to be profiled online for personalization. *Management Information Systems Quarterly*, *30*(1), 13–28. DOI: 10.2307/25148715

Babashahi, L., Barbosa, C. E., Lima, Y., Lyra, A., Salazar, H., Argôlo, M., Almeida, M. A., & Souza, J. M. (2024). AI in the workplace: A systematic review of skill transformation in the industry. *Administrative Sciences*, *14*(6), 127. DOI: 10.3390/admsci14060127

Bach, T. A., Khan, A., Hallock, H., Beltrão, G., & Sousa, S. (2024). A systematic literature review of user trust in AI-enabled systems: An HCI perspective. *International Journal of Human-Computer Interaction*, *40*(5), 1251–1266. DOI: 10.1080/10447318.2022.2138826

Bailey, D. E. (2022). Emerging technologies at work: Policy ideas to address negative consequences for work, workers, and society. *Industrial & Labor Relations Review*, *75*(3), 527–551. DOI: 10.1177/00197939221076747

Bakker, A. B., & Demerouti, E. (2017). Job demands–resources theory: Taking stock and looking forward. *Journal of Occupational Health Psychology*, *22*(3), 273–285. DOI: 10.1037/ocp0000056 PMID: 27732008

Balaji, K. (2025). Human-centric innovation: Building sustainable organizations for Industry 5.0. In *Human-centric, sustainable, and resilient organizations in the digital age* (pp. 101–124). IGI Global Scientific Publishing. DOI: 10.4018/979-8-3693-8181-6.ch005

Balasubramaniam, N., Kauppinen, M., Rannisto, A., Hiekkanen, K., & Kujala, S. (2023). Transparency and explainability of AI systems: From ethical guidelines to requirements. *Information and Software Technology*, *159*, 107197. DOI: 10.1016/j.infsof.2023.107197

Balavadze, T., & Zhgenti, T. (2018). The Bank of Georgia Learning Hub. *International Journal of Advanced Corporate Learning*, *11*(1), 5–9. DOI: 10.3991/ijac.v11i1.9367

Bankins, S., Formosa, P., Griep, Y., & Richards, D. (2022). AI decision making with dignity? Contrasting workers' justice perceptions of human and AI decision making in a human resource management context. *Information Systems Frontiers*, *24*(3), 857–875. DOI: 10.1007/s10796-021-10223-8

Bankins, S., Ocampo, A. C., Marrone, M., Restubog, S. L. D., & Woo, S. E. (2024). A multilevel review of artificial intelligence in organizations: Implications for organizational behavior research and practice. *Journal of Organizational Behavior*, *45*(2), 159–182. DOI: 10.1002/job.2735

Barta, S., Gurrea, R., & Flavián, C. (2023). How Augmented Reality Increases Engagement Through Its Impact on Risk and the Decision Process. *Cyberpsychology, Behavior, and Social Networking*, *26*(3), 177–187. DOI: 10.1089/cyber.2022.0087 PMID: 36706429

Beck, J., Rainoldi, M., & Egger, R. (2019). Virtual reality in tourism: a state-of-the-art review. In *Tourism Review* (Vol. 74, Number 3, pp. 586–612). Emerald Group Holdings Ltd. DOI: 10.1108/TR-03-2017-0049

Becker, A. (2018). An experimental study of voluntary nonprofit accountability and effects on public trust, reputation, perceived quality, and donation behavior. *Nonprofit and Voluntary Sector Quarterly*, *47*(3), 562–582. DOI: 10.1177/0899764018756200

Benbya, H., Davenport, T. H., & Pachidi, S. (2020). Artificial intelligence in organizations: Current state and future opportunities. *MIS Quarterly Executive*, *19*(4).

Benbya, H., Pachidi, S., & Jarvenpaa, S. (2021). Special issue editorial: Artificial intelligence in organizations: Implications for information systems research. *Journal of the Association for Information Systems*, *22*(2), 10. DOI: 10.17705/1jais.00662

Benlian, A., & Pinski, M. (2025). The AI literacy development canvas: Assessing and building AI literacy in organizations. *Business Horizons*. Advance online publication. DOI: 10.1016/j.bushor.2025.10.001

Bersin, J. (2019). HR technology disruption: AI and the future of work. Deloitte Insights. https://www2.deloitte.com/us/en/insights/focus/human-capital-trends/2019/ai-in-hr.html

Bienefeld, N., Keller, E., & Grote, G. (2025). AI interventions to alleviate healthcare shortages and enhance work conditions in critical care: Qualitative analysis. *Journal of Medical Internet Research*, *27*, e50852. DOI: 10.2196/50852 PMID: 39805110

Bilgihan, A., Kandampully, J., & Zhang, T. (2016). Towards a unified customer experience in online shopping environments: Antecedents and outcomes. *International Journal of Quality and Service Sciences*, *8*(1), 102–119. DOI: 10.1108/IJQSS-07-2015-0054

Bobadilla, J., Ortega, F., Hernando, A., & Gutiérrez, A. (2013). Recommender systems survey. *Knowledge-Based Systems*, *46*, 109–132. DOI: 10.1016/j.knosys.2013.03.012

Bohr, A. C., & Memarzadeh, K. (2020). *Artificial Intelligence in Healthcare*. Academic Press.

Bonetti, F., Warnaby, G., & Quinn, L. (2018). Augmented Reality and Virtual Reality in Physical and Online Retailing: A Review, Synthesis and Research Agenda. In T. Jung & M. tom Dieck (Eds.), *Augmented reality and virtual reality: Progress in IS*. Springer. DOI: 10.1007/978-3-319-64027-3_9

Bortolotti, T., Boscari, S., Morton, E., & Powell, D. (2023). Integrating smart manufacturing to lean: A multiple-case study of the impact on shop-floor employees' autonomy and empowerment. In *IFIP Advances in Information and Communication Technology* (pp. 109–124). Springer Nature Switzerland., DOI: 10.1007/978-3-031-43662-8_9

Boyd, R. L., & Markowitz, D. M. (2026). Artificial Intelligence and the Psychology of Human Connection. Perspectives on psychological science: a journal of the Association for Psychological Science, 21(2), 192–220. https://doi.org/DOI: 10.1177/17456916251404394

Braun, V., & Clarke, V. (2006). Using thematic analysis in psychology. *Qualitative Research in Psychology, 3*(2), 77–101. DOI: 10.1191/1478088706qp063oa

Brougham, D., & Haar, J. (2020). Technological disruption and employment: The influence on job insecurity and turnover intentions: A multi-country study. *Technological Forecasting and Social Change, 161*, 120276. DOI: 10.1016/j.techfore.2020.120276

Brynjolfsson, E., & McAfee, A. (2017). Machine, platform, crowd: Harnessing our digital future. W. W. Norton. https://wwnorton.com/books/Machine-Platform-Crowd/

Brynjolfsson, E., & McAfee, A. (2014). *The second machine age: Work, progress, and prosperity in a time of brilliant technologies*. W. W. Norton & Company.

Brynjolfsson, E., & McAfee, A. (2017). *Machine, platform, crowd: Harnessing our digital future*. W. W. Norton & Company.

Brynjolfsson, E., Rock, D. C., & Syverson, C. (2021). The productivity J-curve: How intangible capital signals errors in future efficiency statistics. *Science, 371*(6525), 161–164.

Buhalis, D. (2020). Technology in tourism-from information communication technologies to eTourism and smart tourism towards ambient intelligence tourism: A perspective article. *Tourism Review, 75*(1), 267–272. DOI: 10.1108/TR-06-2019-0258

Buhalis, D., Harwood, T., Bogicevic, V., Viglia, G., Beldona, S., & Hofacker, C. (2019). Technological disruptions in services: Lessons from tourism and hospitality. *Journal of Service Management, 30*(4), 484–506. DOI: 10.1108/JOSM-12-2018-0398

Buhalis, D., Leung, D., & Lin, M. (2023). Metaverse as a disruptive technology revolutionising tourism management and marketing. *Tourism Management, 97*, 104724. Advance online publication. DOI: 10.1016/j.tourman.2023.104724

Buijsman, S., Carter, S. E., & Bermúdez, J.-P. (2025). Autonomy by design: Preserving human autonomy in AI decision-support. *Philosophy & Technology, 38*(3), 97. Advance online publication. DOI: 10.1007/s13347-025-00932-2

Burti, S., Benigni, L., & Gutierrez-Quintana, R. (2024). Artificial intelligence in veterinary diagnostic imaging: Perspectives and limitations. *Research in Veterinary Science, 175*, 105317. Advance online publication. DOI: 10.1016/j.rvsc.2024.105317 PMID: 38843690

Butryn, B., & Rudnicki, P. (2024). The impact of artificial intelligence on managing the recruitment process in a company. *Informatyka Ekonomiczna, 2024*(1–2), 1–12. DOI: 10.15611/ie.2024.1-2.01

Cao, J., Li, J., Yin, M., & Wang, Y. (2023). Online reviews sentiment analysis and product feature improvement with deep learning. *Transactions of the Association for Computational Linguistics*, *11*, 1–17.

Carter, W., & Wynne, K. T. (2024). Integrating artificial intelligence into team decision-making: Toward a theory of AI–human team effectiveness. *European Management Review, emre.12685*. DOI: 10.1111/emre.12685

Cazzaniga, M., Jaumotte, M. F., Li, L., Melina, M. G., Panton, A. J., Pizzinelli, C., & Tavares, M. M. M. (2024). *Gen-AI: Artificial intelligence and the future of work*. International Monetary Fund. DOI: 10.5089/9798400262548.006

Chandra, B., & Rahman, Z. (2024). Artificial intelligence and value co-creation: A review, conceptual framework and directions for future research. *Journal of Service Theory and Practice*, *34*(1), 7–32. DOI: 10.1108/JSTP-03-2023-0097

Chaturvedi, R., Verma, S., Das, R., & Dwivedi, Y. K. (2023). Social companionship with artificial intelligence: Recent trends and future avenues. *Technological Forecasting and Social Change*, *193*, 122634. DOI: 10.1016/j.techfore.2023.122634

Checkland, P. (1999). Systems thinking. In Rethinking management information systems (pp. 45–56). DOI: 10.1093/oso/9780198775331.003.0004

Chen, H. (2024). The ethical challenges of educational Artificial Intelligence and coping measures: A discussion in the context of the 2024 World Digital Education Conference. *Science Insights Education Frontiers, 20*(2), 3263–3281. DOI: 10.15354/sief.24.re339

Cherns, A. (1976). The principles of sociotechnical design. *Human Relations*, *29*(8), 783–792. DOI: 10.1177/001872677602900806

Chowdhury, S., Budhwar, P., Dey, P. K., Joel-Edgar, S., & Abadie, A. (2022). AI-employee collaboration and business performance: Integrating knowledge-based view, socio-technical systems and organisational socialisation framework. *Journal of Business Research*, *144*, 31–49. DOI: 10.1016/j.jbusres.2022.01.069

Chui, M., Hazan, E., Roberts, R., Singla, A., Smaje, K., Sukharevsky, A., Kwakye, J. C., & Wright, G. (2023). *The economic potential of generative AI: The next productivity frontier*. McKinsey Global Institute.

Chung, Y. W., Im, S., Kim, J. E., & Yun, J. K. (2025). Artificial intelligence awareness, career resilience, job insecurity and behavioural outcomes. *Australian Journal of Psychology*, *77*(1), 2559910. DOI: 10.1080/00049530.2025.2559910 PMID: 41036316

Coiera, E., & Fraile Navarro, D. (2024). AI as an ecosystem: Ensuring generative AI is safe and effective. *NEJM AI, 1*(9), AIp2400611. DOI: 10.1056/AIp2400611

Cowan, K., Javornik, A., & Jiang, P. (2021). Privacy concerns when using augmented reality face filters? Explaining why and when use avoidance occurs. *Psychology and Marketing*, *38*(10), 1799–1813. DOI: 10.1002/mar.21576

Cummings, M. L. (2021). Rethinking the maturity of artificial intelligence in safety-critical settings. *AI Magazine*, *42*(1), 37–47. DOI: 10.1002/j.2371-9621.2021.tb00005.x

Dan, Z., Tang, N., & Hai, S. (2024). Dual effects of AI-enabled job non-routinization on proactive and responsive creativity. In *Academy of Management Proceedings* (Vol. 2024, No. 1, Article 15016). Academy of Management. DOI: 10.5465/AMPROC.2024.15016abstract

Daugherty, P., & Wilson, H. J. (2022). *Radically human: How new technology is transforming business and shaping our future*. Harvard Business Press.

Davenport, T. H. C., & Mittal, N. (2022). *All-in on AI: How smart companies win big with artificial intelligence*. Harvard Business Review Press.

Davenport, T. H., Guha, A., Grewal, D., & Bressgott, T. (2020). How artificial intelligence will change the future of marketing. *Journal of the Academy of Marketing Science*, *48*(1), 24–42. DOI: 10.1007/s11747-019-00696-0

Davenport, T. H., & Kirby, J. (2016). Just how smart are smart machines? *MIT Sloan Management Review*, *57*(3), 21–25.

Davenport, T. H., & Ronanki, R. (2018). Artificial intelligence for the real world. *Harvard Business Review*, *96*(1), 108–116.

Davis, F. D. (1989). Perceived usefulness, perceived ease of use, and user acceptance of information technology. *Management Information Systems Quarterly*, *13*(3), 319–340. DOI: 10.2307/249008

Dawadi, S., Shrestha, S. C., & Giri, R. A. (2021). Mixed-methods research: A discussion on its types, challenges, and ethics. *Journal of Practical Studies in Education*, *2*(2), 25–36. DOI: 10.46809/jpse.v2i2.20

Deci, E. L., & Ryan, R. M. (2000). The "what" and "why" of goal pursuits: Human needs and the self-determination of behavior. *Psychological Inquiry*, *11*(4), 227–268. DOI: 10.1207/S15327965PLI1104_01

Dekker, R., Koot, P., Birbil, S. I., & van Embden Andres, M. (2022). Co-designing algorithms for governance: Ensuring responsible and accountable algorithmic management of refugee camp supplies. *Big Data & Society*, *9*(1), 205395172210878. DOI: 10.1177/20539517221087855

Dellermann, D., Ebel, P., Söllner, M., & Leimeister, J. M. (2019). Hybrid intelligence. *Business & Information Systems Engineering*, *61*(5), 637–643. DOI: 10.1007/s12599-019-00595-2

Dican, L. (2025). Human-AI collaboration and its impact on decision-making. *International Journal of Multidisciplinary Research and Growth Evaluation.*, *2*(2), 919–922. DOI: 10.54660/.IJMRGE.2025.6.2.919-922

Dieleman, M., Markus, S., Rajwani, T., & White, G. O.III. (2022). Revisiting institutional voids: Advancing the international business literature by leveraging social sciences. *Journal of International Management*, *28*(3), 100935. DOI: 10.1016/j.intman.2022.100935

Dima, J., Gilbert, M.-H., Dextras-Gauthier, J., & Giraud, L. (2024). The effects of artificial intelligence on human resource activities and the roles of the human resource triad: Opportunities and challenges. *Frontiers in Psychology*, *15*, 1360401. Advance online publication. DOI: 10.3389/fpsyg.2024.1360401 PMID: 38903456

Disztinger, P., Schlögl, S., & Groth, A. (2017, Jan.). Technology acceptance of virtual reality for travel planning. In *Information and Communication Technologies in Tourism 2017: Proceedings of the International Conference in Rome, Italy, January 24-26, 2017* (pp. 255-268). Springer International Publishing.

Dodda, A. (2025). *Artificial intelligence and financial transformation: Unlocking the power of fintech, predictive analytics, and public governance in the next era of economic intelligence*. Deep Science Publishing.

Drakul, S. (2025). Application and economic effects of integrating artificial intelligence technologies in modern business. *Global Journal of Economic and Finance Research*, *2*(4), 201–204. DOI: 10.55677/GJEFR/04-2025-Vol02E4

Duggan, J., Carbery, R., McDonnell, A., & Sherman, U. (2023). Algorithmic HRM control in the gig economy: The app-worker perspective. *Human Resource Management*, *62*(6), 883–899. DOI: 10.1002/hrm.22168

Dwivedi, Y. K., Hughes, L., Ismagilova, E., Aarts, G., Coombs, C., Crick, T., Duan, Y., Dwivedi, R., Edwards, J., Eirug, A., Galanos, V., Ilavarasan, P. V., Janssen, M., Jones, P., Kar, A. K., Kizgin, H., Kronemann, B., Lal, B., Lucini, B., & Williams, M. D. (2021). Artificial Intelligence (AI): Multidisciplinary perspectives on emerging challenges, opportunities, and agenda for research, practice and policy. *International Journal of Information Management*, *57*, 101994. Advance online publication. DOI: 10.1016/j.ijinfomgt.2019.08.002

Dwivedi, Y. K., Kshetri, N., Hughes, L., Slade, E. L., Jeyaraj, A., Kar, A. K., Baabdullah, A. M., Koohang, A., Raghavan, V., Ahuja, M., Albanna, H., Albashrawi, M. A., Al-Busaidi, A. S., Balakrishnan, J., Barlette, Y., Basu, S., Bose, I., Brooks, L., Buhalis, D., & Wright, R. (2023). So what if ChatGPT wrote it? Multidisciplinary perspectives on opportunities, challenges and implications of generative conversational AI for research, practice and policy. *International Journal of Information Management, 71*, 102642. DOI: 10.1016/j.ijinfomgt.2023.102642

Economic Survey of India. (2024–2025). *Harnessing AI for India's workforce development.* Government of India, Ministry of Finance. https://www.pib.gov.in/PressReleasePage.aspx?PRID=2097907

Edward, K. L., Hercelinskyj, G., & Giandinoto, J. A. (2017). Emotional labour in mental health nursing: An integrative systematic review. *International Journal of Mental Health Nursing*, *26*(3), 215–225. DOI: 10.1111/inm.12330 PMID: 28374961

Espinosa Gámez, M. (2026). Emotional intelligence: A human-centred AI perspective. In *Handbook of human-centered artificial intelligence* (pp. 1–65). Springer Nature Singapore.

Ezeilo, C. O., & Green-McKenzie, J. (2024). The covid-19 pandemic and the future of work. *Journal of Occupational and Environmental Medicine*, *66*(6), e245–e251. DOI: 10.1097/JOM.0000000000003107 PMID: 38531821

Ezeocha, C. M. (2024). Financial Technology as a Tool for Promoting Financial Inclusion in Nigeria: A Theoretical Review. *African Journal of Management and Business Research, 15*(1), 166–181. DOI: 10.62154/qqr2sy50

Fahim, M., Mostafa, N. A., & Grida, M. (2025). Using Generative AI in Supply Chain Management: How and How not? *Procedia Computer Science*, *274*, 87–96. DOI: 10.1016/j.procs.2025.12.009

Familoni, B. T. (2024). Ethical frameworks for AI in healthcare entrepreneurship: A theoretical examination of challenges and approaches. *International Journal of Frontiers in Biology and Pharmacy Research, 5*(1), 057–065. DOI: 10.53294/ijfbpr.2024.5.1.0032

Farrow, E. (2021). Mindset matters: How mindset affects the ability of staff to anticipate and adapt to Artificial Intelligence (AI) future scenarios in organisational settings. *AI & Society*, *36*(3), 895–909. DOI: 10.1007/s00146-020-01101-z PMID: 33223620

Fatima, S., Desouza, K. C., & Dawson, G. S. (2020). National strategic artificial intelligence plans: A multi-dimensional analysis. *Economic Analysis and Policy*, *67*, 178–194. DOI: 10.1016/j.eap.2020.07.008

Felzmann, H., Fosch-Villaronga, E., Lutz, C., & Tamò-Larrieux, A. (2020). Towards transparency by design for artificial intelligence. *Science and Engineering Ethics*, *26*(6), 3333–3361. DOI: 10.1007/s11948-020-00276-4 PMID: 33196975

Fenwick, A., Molnar, G., & Frangos, P. (2024). Revisiting the role of HR in the age of AI: Bringing humans and machines closer together in the workplace. *Frontiers in Artificial Intelligence*, *6*, 1272823. Advance online publication. DOI: 10.3389/frai.2023.1272823 PMID: 38288334

Fenwick, A., Molnar, G., & Frangos, P. (2024). The critical role of HRM in AI-driven digital transformation: A paradigm shift to enable firms to move from AI implementation to human-centric adoption. *Discover Artificial Intelligence*, *4*(1), 34. DOI: 10.1007/s44163-024-00125-4

Fischer, M., Imgrund, F., Janina, C. C., & Winkelmann, A. (2020). Strategy followed by structure: Antecedents of business model adaptability in the digital age. *International Journal of Information Management*, *52*, 102095.

Flavián, C., Ibáñez-Sánchez, S., & Orús, C. (2019). Integrating virtual reality devices into the body: Effects of technological embodiment on customer engagement and behavioral intentions toward the destination. *Journal of Travel & Tourism Marketing*, *36*(7), 847–863. DOI: 10.1080/10548408.2019.1618781

Flavián, C., Ibáñez-Sánchez, S., & Orús, C. (2021). Impacts of technological embodiment through virtual reality on potential guests' emotions and engagement. *Journal of Hospitality Marketing & Management*, *30*(1), 1–20. DOI: 10.1080/19368623.2020.1770146

Floridi, L., & Cowls, J. (2019). A unified framework of five principles for AI in society. *Harvard Data Science Review*, *1*(1). Advance online publication. DOI: 10.1162/99608f92.8cd550d1

Floridi, L., Cowls, J., Beltrametti, M., Chatila, R., Chazerand, P., Dignum, V., Luetge, C., Madelin, R., Pagallo, U., Rossi, F., Schafer, B., Valcke, P., & Vayena, E. (2018). AI4People—An ethical framework for a good AI society: Opportunities, risks, principles, and recommendations. *Minds and Machines, 28*(4), 689–707. DOI: 10.1007/s11023-018-9482-5 PMID: 30930541

Ford, D., Storey, M.-A., Zimmermann, T., Bird, C., Jaffe, S., Maddila, C., Butler, J., Houck, B., & Nagappan, N. (2021). A tale of two cities: Software developers working from home during the COVID-19 pandemic. *Empirical Software Engineering, 26*(4), 70. Advance online publication. DOI: 10.1007/s10664-021-09984-3

Freeman, R. E. (1984). *Strategic management: A stakeholder approach*. Pitman.

Gabor, S., Danylenko, G., & Basran, P. S. (2025). Familiarity with artificial intelligence drives optimism and adoption among veterinary professionals: 2024 survey. *American Journal of Veterinary Research, 86*(S1), S63–S69. DOI: 10.2460/ajvr.24.10.0293 PMID: 39933254

Gans, J. S. (2023). Artificial intelligence adoption in a competitive market. *Economica, 90*(358), 690–705. DOI: 10.1111/ecca.12458

Gardner, D. H., & Hini, D. (2006). Work-related stress in the veterinary profession in New Zealand. *New Zealand Veterinary Journal, 54*(3), 119–124. DOI: 10.1080/00480169.2006.36623 PMID: 16751842

Gartenberg, C., Prat, A., & Serafeim, G. (2019). Corporate purpose and financial performance. *Organization Science, 30*(1), 1–18. DOI: 10.1287/orsc.2018.1230

George, G., Merrill, R. K., & Schillebeeckx, S. J. (2021). Digital sustainability and entrepreneurship: How digital innovations are helping tackle climate change and sustainable development. *Entrepreneurship Theory and Practice, 45*(5), 999–1027. DOI: 10.1177/1042258719899425

Geroimenko, V. (2025). Emotional and Relational Aspects: Building Rapport and Human-Like Interaction with AI. In *Beyond and After Prompt Engineering: The Future of AI Communication* (pp. 289–316). Springer Nature Switzerland.

Glikson, E., & Woolley, A. W. (2020). Human trust in artificial intelligence: Review of empirical research. *The Academy of Management Annals, 14*(2), 627–660. DOI: 10.5465/annals.2018.0057

Glover, W., Renton, M., Minaye, H., & Dabiri, O. (2025). Assessing equitable development and implementation of artificial intelligence-enabled patient engagement technologies: A sociotechnical systems approach. *Mayo Clinic Proceedings. Digital Health, 3*(1), 100192. Advance online publication. DOI: 10.1016/j.mcpdig.2024.100192 PMID: 40206991

Greenhaus, J. H., & Callalan, G. A. (2020). Implications of the changing nature of work for the interface between work and nonwork roles. In *The Cambridge handbook of the changing nature of work* (pp. 467–488). Cambridge University Press. DOI: 10.1017/9781108278034.022

Gretzel, U., Sigala, M., Xiang, Z., & Koo, C. (2015). Smart tourism: Foundations and developments. *Electronic Markets, 25*(3), 179–188. DOI: 10.1007/s12525-015-0196-8

Grewal, D., Roggeveen, A. L., & Nordfält, J. (2017). The future of retailing. *Journal of Retailing, 93*(1), 1–6. DOI: 10.1016/j.jretai.2016.12.008

Guest, D. E. (2017). Human resource management and employee well-being: Towards a new analytic framework. *Human Resource Management Journal, 27*(1), 22–38. DOI: 10.1111/1748-8583.12139

Gunning, D. (2017). Explainable artificial intelligence (XAI). Defense Advanced Research Projects Agency (DARPA). https://www.darpa.mil/program/explainable-artificial-intelligence

Gursoy, D., Chi, O. H., Lu, L., & Nunkoo, R. (2019). Consumers acceptance of artificially intelligent (AI) device use in service delivery. *International Journal of Information Management, 49*, 157–169. DOI: 10.1016/j.ijinfomgt.2019.03.008

Gustafsson, J. (2020). Single case studies vs. multiple case studies: A comparative study. Academy of Business. *Engineering and Science*, •••, 1–15.

Guttentag, D. A. (2010). Virtual reality: Applications and implications for tourism. *Tourism Management, 31*(5), 637–651. DOI: 10.1016/j.tourman.2009.07.003

Hackman, J. R., & Oldham, G. R. (1976). Motivation through the design of work: Test of a theory. *Organizational Behavior and Human Performance, 16*(2), 250–279. DOI: 10.1016/0030-5073(76)90016-7

Hähnel, M. (2025). Ethical challenges and solutions in AI-driven medical data management: A focus on distributed machine learning. *Discover Artificial Intelligence, 5*(1), 53. Advance online publication. DOI: 10.1007/s44163-025-00266-0

Hasani, N., Hosseini, A., Ashjazadeh, Y., Diederichs, V., Ghotb, S., Riggio, M., Hansen, E., & Nasir, V. (2025). Outlook on human-centred design in Industry 5.0: Towards mass customisation, personalisation, co-creation, and co-production. *International Journal of Sustainable Engineering*, *18*(1), 2486343. DOI: 10.1080/19397038.2025.2486343

Hassan, M., Kushniruk, A., & Borycki, E. (2024). Barriers to and facilitators of artificial intelligence adoption in health care: Scoping review. *JMIR Human Factors*, *11*, e48633. DOI: 10.2196/48633 PMID: 39207831

Hennessey, E., DiFazio, M., Hennessey, R., & Cassel, N. (2022). Artificial intelligence in veterinary diagnostic imaging: A literature review. *Veterinary Radiology & Ultrasound*, *63*(S1), 851–870. DOI: 10.1111/vru.13163 PMID: 36468206

Herrmann, T., & Pfeiffer, S. (2022). Keeping the organization in the loop: A socio-technical extension of human-centered artificial intelligence. *AI & Society*. Advance online publication. DOI: 10.1007/s00146-022-01391-5

Heskett, J. L., Sasser, W. E.Jr, & Schlesinger, L. A. (1997). *The service profit chain: How leading companies link profit and growth to loyalty, satisfaction, and value*. Free Press.

Hilken, T., de Ruyter, K., Chylinski, M., Mahr, D., & Keeling, D. I. (2017). Augmenting the eye of the beholder: Exploring the strategic potential of augmented reality to enhance online service experiences. *Journal of the Academy of Marketing Science*, *45*(6), 884–905. DOI: 10.1007/s11747-017-0541-x

Hochschild, A. R. (1983). *The managed heart: Commercialization of human feeling*. University of California Press.

Holmström, J. (2022). From AI to digital transformation: The AI readiness framework. *Business Horizons*, *65*(3), 329–339. DOI: 10.1016/j.bushor.2021.03.006

Holmström, J., & Magnusson, J. (2025). Navigating the organizational AI journey: The AI transformation framework. *Business Horizons*, *69*(1), 89–100. DOI: 10.1016/j.bushor.2025.01.002

Holzinger, A., Keiblinger, K., Holub, P., Zatloukal, K., & Müller, H. (2023). AI for life: Trends in artificial intelligence for biotechnology. *New Biotechnology*, *74*, 16–24. DOI: 10.1016/j.nbt.2023.02.001 PMID: 36754147

Hosseinian-Far, A., Farsi, M., Gharehbaghi, K., Jahankhani, H., & Daneshkhah, A. (2025). Reimagining Industry 5.0: Generative artificial intelligence as the enabling technology. In Symbiotic intelligence (pp. 128–146). CRC Press. DOI: 10.1201/9781003540373-7

Hosseini, T., Bastami, M., & Sheikh Esmaili, S. (2025). Designing a comprehensive model for human resource transfer in the tax affairs organizations of Tehran. *Journal of Resource Management and Decision Engineering*, *4*(2), 1–10. DOI: 10.61838/kman.jrmde.4.2.14

Huang, M.-H., & Rust, R. T. (2021). *A strategic framework for artificial intelligence in marketing*. DOI: 10.1007/s11747-020-00749-9/Published

Huang, L., Solangi, Y. A., Magazzino, C., & Solangi, S. A. (2024). Evaluating the efficiency of green innovation and marketing strategies for long-term sustainability in the context of Environmental labeling. *Journal of Cleaner Production*, *450*, 141870. Advance online publication. DOI: 10.1016/j.jclepro.2024.141870

Huang, M. H., & Rust, R. T. (2021). A strategic framework for artificial intelligence in marketing. *Journal of the Academy of Marketing Science*, *49*(1), 30–50. DOI: 10.1007/s11747-020-00749-9

Hwang, B. N., Puntha, P., & Jitanugoon, S. (2026). Human-centric AI: Transforming service ecosystems for inclusivity and excellence in resource-constrained contexts. *Journal of Service Theory and Practice*, *36*(3), 1–55. DOI: 10.1108/JSTP-01-2025-0017

International Labour Organization. (2025). *Governing AI in the world of work: A review of global ethics guidelines*. International Labour Organization. https://www.ilo.org/resource/article/governing-ai-world-work-review-global-ethics-guidelines

Issa, H., Jaber, J., & Lakkis, H. (2024). Navigating AI unpredictability: Exploring technostress in AI-powered healthcare systems. *Technological Forecasting and Social Change*, *202*, 123311. Advance online publication. DOI: 10.1016/j.techfore.2024.123311

Jaakkola, E. (2020). Designing conceptual articles: Four approaches. *AMS Review*, *10*(1–2), 18–26. DOI: 10.1007/s13162-020-00161-0

Jaakkola, E., & Terho, H. (2021). Service journey quality: Conceptualization, measurement and customer outcomes. *Journal of Service Management*, *32*(6), 955–978. DOI: 10.1108/JOSM-06-2020-0233

Jafri, J. A., Amin, S. I. M., Rahman, A. A., & Nor, S. M. (2024). A systematic literature review of the role of trust and security on Fintech adoption in banking. *Heliyon*, *10*(1), e22980. DOI: 10.1016/j.heliyon.2023.e22980 PMID: 38163181

Jannach, D., Manzoor, A., Cai, W., & Chen, L. (2021). A survey on conversational recommender systems. *ACM Computing Surveys*, *54*(5), 1–36. DOI: 10.1145/3453154

Jarrahi, M. H. (2018). Artificial intelligence and the future of work: Human–AI symbiosis in organizational decision making. *Business Horizons*, *61*(4), 577–586. DOI: 10.1016/j.bushor.2018.03.007

Jarrahi, M. H. (2025). *Research on human–AI collaboration and the future of work (profile)*. Wikipedia.

Jarrahi, M. H., Lutz, C., Boyd, K., Oesterlund, C., & Willis, M. (2023). Artificial intelligence in the work context. *Journal of the Association for Information Science and Technology*, *74*(3), 303–310. DOI: 10.1002/asi.24730

Jasinenko, A., & Steuber, J. (2022). Organizational Purpose: Definition, Measurement and the Ambivalent Effect on Employee Wellbeing. In *Academy of Management Proceedings* (Vol. 2022, No. 1, p. 17387). Briarcliff Manor, NY 10510: Academy of Management.

Jasinenko, A., & Steuber, J. (2023). Perceived organizational purpose: Systematic literature review, construct definition, measurement and potential employee outcomes. *Journal of Management Studies*, *60*(6), 1415–1447. DOI: 10.1111/joms.12852

Javornik, A. (2016). 'It's an illusion, but it looks real!' Consumer affective, cognitive and behavioural responses to augmented reality applications. *Journal of Marketing Management*, *32*(9–10), 987–1011. DOI: 10.1080/0267257X.2016.1174726

Javornik, A., Duffy, K., Rokka, J., Scholz, J., Nobbs, K., Motala, A., & Goldenberg, A. (2021). Strategic approaches to augmented reality deployment by luxury brands. *Journal of Business Research*, *136*, 284–292. DOI: 10.1016/j.jbusres.2021.07.040

Jia, N., Luo, X., Fang, Z., & Liao, C. (2024). When and how artificial intelligence augments employee creativity. *Academy of Management Journal*, *67*(1), 5–32. DOI: 10.5465/amj.2022.0426

Jones, M. A., & Asonye, B. O. (2023). The organizational cultural impact of the social use of AI and bots on remote employees returning to the workplace. *Journal of Management World*, *2023*(4), 154–162. DOI: 10.53935/jomw.v2024i4.1145

Jussupow, E., Spohrer, K., & Heinzl, A. (2022). Identity threats as a reason for resistance to artificial intelligence: Survey study with medical students and professionals. *JMIR Formative Research*, *6*(3), e28750. DOI: 10.2196/28750 PMID: 35319465

Kahn, W. A. (1990). Psychological conditions of personal engagement and disengagement at work. *Academy of Management Journal*, *33*(4), 692–724. DOI: 10.2307/256287

Kamal, O. A. A., Chikezie, P. M. E., Abbey, N. I., & Onyeka, C. O. (2024). AI-driven end-to-end workflow optimization and automation system for SMEs. *International Journal of Management & Entrepreneurship*, *6*(11), 3666–3684.

Kapoor, A., & Sindwani, R. (2025b). Navigating Inhibitors to Artificial Intelligence Adoption in Human Resource Management Practices: A Multi-criteria Decision making Approach.

Kapoor, A., Kapoor, S., & Sindwani, R. (2026c). Strategizing in Immersive Realities: Case-Based Insights Into Metaverse, Augment Reality, Virtual Reality, and Neuromarketing for Consumer Understanding. In *Reshaping Business at the Intersection of Neuromarketing and AI* (pp. 261-290). IGI Global Scientific Publishing.

Kapoor, A., Jaswal, A., & Sindwani, R. (2026b). Charting the roadmap to metaverse commerce adoption: A cause–effect perspective using fuzzy DEMATEL. *Journal of Modelling in Management*, •••, 1–29. DOI: 10.1108/JM2-07-2025-0352

Kapoor, A., & Sindwani, R. (2025a). Artificial Intelligence as a Catalyst for Advancing Contactless Payments: Unveiling Key Adoption Drivers. In *AI Marketing and Ethical Considerations in Consumer Engagement* (pp. 321–338). IGI Global Scientific Publishing. DOI: 10.4018/979-8-3373-3476-9.ch016

Kapoor, A., Sindwani, R., & Goel, M. (2025a). Unlocking India's mobile wallet potential: Identifying and prioritising key sustainable growth catalysts using best worst method. *International Journal of Process Management and Benchmarking*, *21*(2), 218–230. DOI: 10.1504/IJPMB.2025.148685

Kapoor, A., Sindwani, R., & Goel, M. (2025b). Assessing mobile wallet service quality using analytic hierarchy process and fuzzy evaluation method. *International Journal of Services and Operations Management*, *50*(2), 246–266. DOI: 10.1504/IJSOM.2025.144481

Kapoor, A., Sindwani, R., Singh, A. K., & Kapoor, S. (2026a). Causal Modeling and Hierarchical Analysis of Critical Factors in Smart Voice Assistant Adoption: A Fuzzy DEMATEL Approach. *Journal of Global Marketing*, •••, 1–21. DOI: 10.1080/08911762.2026.2651270

Kaufman, B. E. (2020). The future of HRM: A systems perspective. *Human Resource Management Review*, *30*(4), 100685. DOI: 10.1016/j.hrmr.2019.100685

Kellogg, K. C., Valentine, M. A., & Christin, A. (2020). Algorithms at work: The new contested terrain of control. *The Academy of Management Annals*, *14*(1), 366–410. DOI: 10.5465/annals.2018.0174

Keshari, A., & Gautam, A. (2024). FinTech evolution and artificial intelligence: Opportunities and development. In *Applications of Artificial Intelligence in Business and Finance 5.0* (pp. 45–67). Apple Academic Press. DOI: 10.1201/9781003535133-3

Khan, A. A., Akbar, M. A., Fahmideh, M., Liang, P., Waseem, M., Ahmad, A., Niazi, M., & Abrahamsson, P. (2023). AI ethics: An empirical study on the views of practitioners and lawmakers. *IEEE Transactions on Computational Social Systems*, *10*(6), 2971–2984. DOI: 10.1109/TCSS.2023.3251729

Khanna, T., & Palepu, K. G. (2010). *Winning in emerging markets: A road map for strategy and execution*. Harvard Business Press.

Khasawneh, M. A., & Dweiri, F. (2025). Influence of digital infrastructure on project management success: Readiness, fitness, and tools as moderators. *Emerging Science Journal*, *9*(6), 3319–3348. DOI: 10.28991/ESJ-2025-09-06-024

Khullar, S., Baghel, R. S., & Swami, P. (2026). Human-AI collaboration: Balancing trust, emotion, and productivity. In *AI hallucination management in the enterprise metaverse*. IGI Global Scientific Publishing., DOI: 10.4018/979-8-3373-7534-2.ch003

Khullar, S., Kate, C., Rao, A. S., Sharrif, U. H., Gupta, A., & Kaliappan, S. (2026). Explainable intelligence for ethical human-centric AI: Trust modeling using gradient boosting. In *Proceedings of the 2026 5th International Conference on Innovative Practices in Technology and Management (ICIPTM)* (pp. 1–9). IEEE. DOI: 10.1109/ICIPTM69057.2026.11465350

Khullar, S., Sobhan, A., Tank, N., & Swami, P. (2026). From personalization to responsibility: AI-driven adaptive learning environments. In *Ethical leadership and pedagogical transformation in AI-driven education*. IGI Global Scientific Publishing., DOI: 10.4018/979-8-2600-1840-8.ch010

Khullar, S., & Tank, N. (2026). Integrating AI inference with IoT and big data for smart city solutions. In *Harnessing AI inference for intelligent decision-making in real-time dataflows*. IGI Global Scientific Publishing., DOI: 10.4018/979-8-3373-7046-0.ch009

Kim, J. (2020). The influence of perceived costs and perceived benefits on AI-driven interactive recommendation agent value. *Journal of Global Scholars of Marketing Science*, *30*(3), 319–333. DOI: 10.1080/21639159.2020.1775491

Kim, S., Khoreva, V., & Vaiman, V. (2025). Strategic human resource management in the era of algorithmic technologies: Key insights and future research agenda. *Human Resource Management*, *64*(2), 447–464. DOI: 10.1002/hrm.22268

Kinowska, H., & Sienkiewicz, Ł. J. (2023). Influence of algorithmic management practices on workplace well-being – evidence from European organisations. *Information Technology & People*, *36*(8), 21–42. DOI: 10.1108/ITP-02-2022-0079

Kiverstein, J., Kirchhoff, M. D., & Froese, T. (2022). The problem of meaning: The Free Energy Principle and artificial agency. *Frontiers in Neurorobotics*, *16*, 844773. DOI: 10.3389/fnbot.2022.844773 PMID: 35812784

Klietsova, N., Batsenko, L., Klietsov, A., Halenin, R., Kravchenko, I., Ksenofontova, M., & Dorozhko, Y. (2024). International experience of personnel selection in the conditions of the digital environment, war and sustainable development: Social and corporate responsibility of employers for the non-transparent hiring process. *Evolutionary Studies in Imaginative Culture*, *8*(1), 26–38. DOI: 10.70082/esiculture.vi.766

Klietsova, N., Halenin, R., Mostova, A., Sclyar, I., & Krasovska, A. (2025). Digital transformation of Ukrainian SMEs during wartime: Resilience, adaptation, and management strategies. In *Sustainable development: Modern theories and best practices* (pp. 26–30). Teadmus OÜ., https://api.teadmus.org/storage/published_books/monthly_thesis_book_06_2025/book.pdf

Klietsova, N., & Klietsov, A. (2023a). Реформування галузі ветеринарної медицини України щодо ідентифікації тварин-компаньйонів у контексті сталого розвитку, 'One Health' і діджиталізації [Reforming the veterinary medicine sector of Ukraine regarding the identification of companion animals in the context of sustainable development, 'One Health' and digitalization]. Bulletin of Sumy National Agrarian University. The Series. *Veterinary Medicine*, *63*(4), 68–75. DOI: 10.32782/bsnau.vet.2023.4.11

Klietsova, N., & Klietsov, A. (2023b). Social protection of economic and legal rights of emigrants in the context of reforming veterinary legislation of Ukraine and preservation of human capital under conditions of war and digitalization. In *Modern paradigm of public and private law amidst sustainable development* (Vol. 1, pp. 286–332). Baltija Publishing., DOI: 10.30525/978-9934-26-331-6-14

Kogan, L. R., & Rishniw, M. (2023). Differences in perceptions and satisfaction exist among veterinarians employed at corporate versus privately owned veterinary clinics. *Journal of the American Veterinary Medical Association*, *261*(12), 1838–1846. DOI: 10.2460/javma.23.06.0326 PMID: 37607680

Köhn, D., Lessmann, S., & Schaal, M. (2020). Predicting online shopping behaviour from clickstream data using deep learning. *Expert Systems with Applications*, *150*, 113342. DOI: 10.1016/j.eswa.2020.113342

Kong, H., Yin, Z., Baruch, Y., & Yuan, Y. (2023). The impact of trust in AI on career sustainability: The role of employee–AI collaboration and protean career orientation. *Journal of Vocational Behavior, 146*, 103928. DOI: 10.1016/j.jvb.2023.103928

Koohang, A., Nord, J. H., Ooi, K.-B., Tan, G. W.-H., Al-Emran, M., Aw, E. C.-X., Baabdullah, A. M., Buhalis, D., Cham, T.-H., Dennis, C., Dutot, V., Dwivedi, Y. K., Hughes, L., Mogaji, E., Pandey, N., Phau, I., Raman, R., Sharma, A., Sigala, M., & Wong, L.-W. (2023). Shaping the Metaverse into Reality: A Holistic Multi-disciplinary Understanding of Opportunities, Challenges, and Avenues for Future Investigation. *Journal of Computer Information Systems, 63*(3), 735–765. DOI: 10.1080/08874417.2023.2165197

Lalicic, L., & Weismayer, C. (2021). Consumers' reasons and perceived value co-creation of using artificial intelligence-enabled travel service agents. *Journal of Business Research, 129*, 891–901. DOI: 10.1016/j.jbusres.2020.11.005

Laranjo, L., Tudor Car, L., Payne, R. E., Neves, A. L., Kidd, M., & Miranda, J. J. (2025). Artificial intelligence in primary care: Innovation at a crossroads. *The Lancet Primary Care, 100078*. Advance online publication. DOI: 10.1016/j.lanprc.2025.100078 PMID: 41969643

Laria, G., & Pantano, E. (2011). Immersive environments for an advanced technology-based store. In *The 7th International Conference on Networked Computing and Advanced Information Management* (pp. 218-221). IEEE.

Lawrence, C., Cui, I., & Ho, D. (2023). The bureaucratic challenge to AI governance: An empirical assessment of implementation at US federal agencies. In *Proceedings of the 2023 AAAI/ACM Conference on AI, Ethics, and Society* (pp. 606-652). DOI: 10.1145/3600211.3604701

Ledro, C., Nosella, A., & Vinelli, A. (2022). Artificial intelligence in customer relationship management: Literature review and future research directions. *Journal of Business and Industrial Marketing, 37*(13), 48–63. DOI: 10.1108/JBIM-07-2021-0332

Lee, H. (2021). Changes in workplace practices during the COVID-19 pandemic: The roles of emotion, psychological safety and organisation support. *Journal of Organizational Effectiveness: People and Performance, 8*(1), 97–128. DOI: 10.1108/JOEPP-06-2020-0104

Lee, J. D., & See, K. A. (2004). Trust in automation: Designing for appropriate reliance. *Human Factors, 46*(1), 50–80. DOI: 10.1518/hfes.46.1.50.30392 PMID: 15151155

Lemon, K. N., & Verhoef, P. C. (2016). Understanding customer experience throughout the customer journey. *Journal of Marketing*, *80*(6), 69–96. DOI: 10.1509/jm.15.0420

Lepak, D. P., & Snell, S. A. (1999). The human resource architecture: Toward a theory of human capital allocation and development. *Academy of Management Review*, *24*(1), 31–48. DOI: 10.2307/259035

Lessmann, S., Haupt, J., Coussement, K., & De Bock, K. W. (2021). Targeting customers for profit: An ensemble learning framework to support marketing decision-making. *Information Sciences*, *557*, 286–301. DOI: 10.1016/j.ins.2019.05.027

Lharti, R. (2026). The Role of AI in Facilitating Value Co-Creation in Service Industries. In *Transforming Humanities and Social Sciences Through AI* (pp. 435–464). IGI Global Scientific Publishing.

Li, M., & Bitterly, T. B. (2024). How perceived lack of benevolence harms trust of artificial intelligence management. *The Journal of Applied Psychology*, *109*(11), 1794–1816. DOI: 10.1037/apl0001200 PMID: 38815093

Lind, E. A., & Tyler, T. R. (1988). *The social psychology of procedural justice*. Plenum Press. DOI: 10.1007/978-1-4899-2115-4

Li, Y. (2012). Theories in online information privacy research: A critical review and an integrated framework. *Decision Support Systems*, *54*(1), 471–481. DOI: 10.1016/j.dss.2012.06.010

Mabrouk, A. (2024). Human resouce management in the age of Artificial Intelligence: Concepts tools and steps. *Solo International Collaboration and Publication of Social Sciences and Humanities*, *3*(01), 1–12. DOI: 10.61455/sicopus.v3i01.216

Madanchian, M., & Taherdoost, H. (2025). Ethical theories, governance models, and strategic frameworks for responsible AI adoption and organizational success. *Frontiers in Artificial Intelligence*, *8*, 1619029. DOI: 10.3389/frai.2025.1619029 PMID: 40741285

Maindola, S., Bangwal, D., Singh Oberoi, S. S., & Kumar, R. (2026). Transforming hospitality 5.0: A systematic review of AI's impact on employee experience and well-being. *International Journal of Quality and Service Sciences*, *18*(2), 1–26. DOI: 10.1108/IJQSS-09-2025-0245

Ma, J., Guo, X., & Zhao, X. (2022). Identifying purchase intention through deep learning. *Annals of Operations Research*, *314*, 1–20.

Makker, R., & Kapoor, A. (2026). Decoding Greenwashing: Consumer Skepticism and Trust in Decathlon's Sustainability Claims. In *Futureproofed Sustainability Amidst Climate Change Polycrisis: Advancing SDGs and ESG for the Cities of Tomorrow* (pp. 73-96). IGI Global Scientific Publishing.

Makridakis, S. (2017). The forthcoming artificial intelligence (AI) revolution: Its impact on society and firms. *Futures*, *90*, 46–60. DOI: 10.1016/j.futures.2017.03.006

Maleki, A. (2026). Rethinking ethical academic integrity ecosystems in higher education in the age of artificial intelligence. *Discover Artificial Intelligence*, *6*(1), 145. DOI: 10.1007/s44163-026-00887-z

Malik, A., Budhwar, P., & Kazmi, B. A. (2023). Artificial intelligence (AI)-assisted HRM: Towards an extended strategic framework. *Human Resource Management Review*, *33*(1), 100940. Advance online publication. DOI: 10.1016/j.hrmr.2022.100940

Malik, N., Tripathi, S. N., Kar, A. K., & Gupta, S. (2022). Impact of artificial intelligence on employees working in industry 4.0 led organizations. *International Journal of Manpower*, *43*(2), 334–354. DOI: 10.1108/IJM-03-2021-0173

Manser Payne, E. H., Dahl, A. J., & Peltier, J. (2021). Digital servitization value co-creation framework for AI services: A research agenda for digital transformation in financial service ecosystems. *Journal of Research in Interactive Marketing*, *15*(2), 200–222. DOI: 10.1108/JRIM-12-2020-0252

Marinova, D., de Ruyter, K., Huang, M. H., Meuter, M. L., & Challagalla, G. (2017). Getting smart: Learning from technology-empowered frontline interactions. *Journal of Service Research*, *20*(1), 29–42. DOI: 10.1177/1094670516679273

Marr, B. (2023). *Future skill: The 20 skills and competencies everyone needs to succeed in a digital world*. Wiley.

Marsh, E., Vallejos, E. P., & Spence, A. (2022). The digital workplace and its dark side: An integrative review. *Computers in Human Behavior*, *128*, 107118. DOI: 10.1016/j.chb.2021.107118

Ma, Y., Li, X., Hu, S., Liu, S., & Cheong, K. H. (2025). Trustworthy AI in education: Framework, cases, and governance strategies. *Innovation and Emerging Technologies*, *12*(2550026), 2550026. Advance online publication. DOI: 10.1142/S2737599425500264

McCradden, M. D., Joshi, S., Anderson, J. A., & London, A. J. (2023). A normative framework for artificial intelligence as a sociotechnical system in healthcare. *Patterns (New York, N.Y.)*, *4*(11), 100864. Advance online publication. DOI: 10.1016/j.patter.2023.100864 PMID: 38035190

McKinsey & Company. (2023). What is personalization? https://www.mckinsey.com/featured-insights/mckinsey-explainers/what-is-personalization

Mehmetoglu, M., & Engen, M. (2011). Pine and Gilmore's Concept of Experience Economy and Its Dimensions: An Empirical Examination in Tourism. *Journal of Quality Assurance in Hospitality & Tourism*, *12*(4), 237–255. DOI: 10.1080/1528008X.2011.541847

Mehrabi, N., Morstatter, F., Saxena, N., Lerman, K., & Galstyan, A. (2022). A Survey on Bias and Fairness in Machine Learning. In *ACM Computing Surveys* (Vol. 54, Number 6). Association for Computing Machinery. DOI: 10.1145/3457607

Mehter, A. K., Kumar, V. R., & Mehta, M. (2025, October). A hybrid intelligence approach for customer-centric product development and marketing. In *2025 2nd International Conference on Artificial Intelligence and Knowledge Discovery in Concurrent Engineering (ICECONF)* (pp. 1–8). IEEE. DOI: 10.1109/ICECONF65644.2025.11379515

Mesinovic, M., Watkinson, P., & Zhu, T. (2025). Explainability in the age of large language models for healthcare. *Communications Engineering*, *4*(1), 128. Advance online publication. DOI: 10.1038/s44172-025-00453-y PMID: 40676176

Meyer, J. W., & Rowan, B. (1977). Institutionalized organizations: Formal structure as myth and ceremony. *American Journal of Sociology*, *83*(2), 340–363. DOI: 10.1086/226550

Mikalef, P. C., & Gupta, M. (2021). Artificial intelligence capability: Conceptualization, measurement calibration, and link to competitive advantage. *MIS uarterly*, *45*(1), 335–359.

Milgram, P. (1994). A taxonomy of mixed reality visual displays. In *IEICE Transactions on Information Systems* (Number 12). http://vered.rose.utoronto.ca/people/paul_dir/IEICE94/ieice.html

Mishra, R., & Jadeja, D. (2025). A literature review on the impact of AI-enhanced HRIS on employee retention and engagement. In *Intersecting Natural Language Processing and FinTech Innovations in Service Marketing* (pp. 11–20). IGI Global Scientific Publishing., DOI: 10.4018/979-8-3693-9944-6.ch002

Misra, S., Barik, K., & Kvalvik, P. (2025). A Comprehensive Review of Human-Centric AI, Regulatory Frameworks, and Their Role in Shaping Industry 5.0. *Procedia Computer Science*, *259*, 1672–1681. DOI: 10.1016/j.procs.2025.04.122

Mitchell, R. K., Agle, B. R., & Wood, D. J. (1997). Toward a theory of stakeholder identification and salience: Defining the principle of who and what really counts. *Academy of Management Review*, *22*(4), 853–886. DOI: 10.2307/259247

Mohsen, S. E., Hamdan, A., & Shoaib, H. M. (2025). Digital transformation and integration of artificial intelligence in financial institutions. *Journal of Financial Reporting and Accounting*, *23*(2), 680–699. DOI: 10.1108/JFRA-09-2023-0544

Mökander, J., & Floridi, L. (2023). Operationalising AI governance through ethics-based auditing: An industry case study. *AI and Ethics*, *3*(2), 451–468. DOI: 10.1007/s43681-022-00171-7 PMID: 35669570

Mökander, J., Sheth, M., Gersbro-Sundler, M., Blomgren, P., & Floridi, L. (2022). Challenges and best practices in corporate AI governance: Lessons from the biopharmaceutical industry. *Frontiers of Computer Science*, *4*, 1068361. Advance online publication. DOI: 10.3389/fcomp.2022.1068361

Moore, P. V. (2019). OSH and the future of work: Benefits and risks of artificial intelligence tools in workplaces. *Policy and Practice in Health and Safety*, *17*(2), 1–15. DOI: 10.1080/14773996.2019.1657171

Morley, J., Floridi, L., Kinsey, L., & Elhalal, A. (2020). From what to how: An initial review of publicly available AI ethics tools, methods and research to translate principles into practices. *Science and Engineering Ethics*, *26*(4), 2141–2168. DOI: 10.1007/s11948-019-00165-5 PMID: 31828533

Mortati, M., & Viana Mundstock Freitas, G. (2026). AI in service design: A new framework for hybrid human–AI service encounters. *Journal of Service Research*, *29*(1), 81–96. Advance online publication. DOI: 10.1177/10946705251344387

Mosaku, I., Ajewole, O., Adegoke, S., & Hosseinian-Far, A. (2025). Data-driven future: A review of technologies and applications in the era of industry 5.0. In *Symbiotic intelligence: Advancing forecasting through human-AI collaboration*. CRC Press., DOI: 10.1201/9781003540373-8

Mourtzis, D., Panopoulos, N., Angelopoulos, J., Wang, B., & Wang, L. (2022). Human centric platforms for personalized value creation in metaverse. *Journal of Manufacturing Systems*, *65*, 653–659. DOI: 10.1016/j.jmsy.2022.11.004

Muridzi, G., & Dhliwayo, S. (2026, February). Satisfaction: Systematic literature review. In *Embracing technological agility in accounting and business (*Vol. 2*): Proceedings of the 6th International Conference of Accounting and Business iCAB, Cape Town 2025* (p. 249). Springer Nature.

Mustak, M., et al. (2021). Deep learning in marketing: A review and research agenda.

Nakavachara, V. (2025). AI and worker well-being: Differential impacts across generational cohorts and genders [Preprint]. arXiv.

Neal, S. V., Rudmann, D. G., & Corps, K. N. (2025). Artificial intelligence in veterinary clinical pathology – An introduction and review. *Veterinary Clinical Pathology*, *54*(S2), S13–S29. DOI: 10.1111/vcp.70012 PMID: 40462415

OECD. (2023). *OECD employment outlook 2023: Artificial intelligence and the labour market*. OECD Publishing.

Olawade, D. B., Weerasinghe, K., Teke, J., Msiska, M., Boussios, S., & Hatzidimitriadou, E. (2025). Evaluating AI adoption in healthcare: Insights from information governance professionals in the United Kingdom. *International Journal of Medical Informatics*, *194*, 105909. Advance online publication. DOI: 10.1016/j.ijmedinf.2025.105909 PMID: 40198930

Osnat, B. (2025). Patient perspectives on artificial intelligence in healthcare: A global scoping review of benefits, ethical concerns, and implementation strategies. *International Journal of Medical Informatics*, *196*, 106007. Advance online publication. DOI: 10.1016/j.ijmedinf.2025.106007 PMID: 40494217

Owoyemi, A., Osuchukwu, J., Salwei, M. E., & Boyd, A. (2025). Checklist approach to developing and implementing AI in clinical settings: Instrument development study. *JMIRx Med*, *6*, e65565. Advance online publication. DOI: 10.2196/65565 PMID: 39977249

Oyeyemi, B. B., John, A. O., & Awodola, M. (2025). Infrastructure and regulatory barriers to AI supply chain systems in Nigeria vs. the US. *Engineering Science and Technology*, *6*(4), 155–172. DOI: 10.51594/estj.v6i4.1912

Pacholec, C., Flatland, B., Xie, H., & Zimmerman, K. (2025a). Harnessing artificial intelligence for enhanced veterinary diagnostics: A look to quality assurance, Part I – Model development. *Veterinary Clinical Pathology*, *54*(S2), S30. DOI: 10.1111/vcp.13401 PMID: 39638756

Pacholec, C., Flatland, B., Xie, H., & Zimmerman, K. (2025b). Harnessing artificial intelligence for enhanced veterinary diagnostics: A look to quality assurance, Part II – External validation. *Veterinary Clinical Pathology*, *54*(S2), S43. DOI: 10.1111/vcp.13407 PMID: 39843399

Pal, D., Arpnikanondt, C., & Razzaque, M. A. (2020). Personal information disclosure via voice assistants: The personalization–privacy paradox. *SN Computer Science*, *1*(5), 280. DOI: 10.1007/s42979-020-00287-9

Pandey, J., Kumar, M., & Singh, S. (2024). Organizational ethical climate: Influence on employee meaning and well-being. *Management Decision*, *62*(10), 3235–3260. DOI: 10.1108/MD-10-2023-1823

Pantano, E., Pizzi, G., Scarpi, D., & Dennis, C. (2020). Competing during a pandemic? Retailers' ups and downs during the COVID-19 outbreak. *Journal of Business Research*, *116*, 209–213. DOI: 10.1016/j.jbusres.2020.05.036 PMID: 32501307

Papadopoulou, I., & Kotsi, M. (2025). Customer experience in the era of AI: Harnessing AI and technology for a human future that works. *Journal of Airport Management*, *20*(1), 6–26. DOI: 10.69554/GPJS4492

Papagiannidis, E., Mikalef, P., & Conboy, K. (2025). Responsible artificial intelligence governance: A review and research framework. *The Journal of Strategic Information Systems*, *34*(2), 101885. DOI: 10.1016/j.jsis.2024.101885

Papanikolaou, N., Boufounou, P., & Eriotis, N. (2025). Determinants of Fintech Adoption: A Systematic Review Integrating Trust, Security, and User Perceptions within Technology Acceptance Frameworks.

Para, R., Bhatia, R., & Sandiri, S. (2025). AI-powered financial digital twins: The next frontier in hyper-personalized, customer-centric financial services. *Journal of Next-Generation Research 5.0.*

Parker, S. K., & Grote, G. (2022). Automation, algorithms, and beyond: Why work design matters more than ever in a digital world. *Applied Psychology*, *71*(4), 1171–1204. DOI: 10.1111/apps.12241

Parker, S. K., & Knight, C. (2024). The SMART model of work design: A higher order structure to help see the wood from the trees. *Human Resource Management*, *63*(2), 265–291. DOI: 10.1002/hrm.22200

Pasmore, W., Winby, S., Mohrman, S. A., & Vanasse, R. (2019). Reflections: Sociotechnical systems design and organization change. *Journal of Change Management*, *19*(2), 67–85. DOI: 10.1080/14697017.2018.1553761

Passalacqua, M., Pellerin, R., Magnani, F., Doyon-Poulin, P., Del-Aguila, L., Boasen, J., & Léger, P. M. (2025). Human-centred AI in Industry 5.0: A systematic review. *International Journal of Production Research*, *63*(7), 2638–2669. DOI: 10.1080/00207543.2024.2406021

Pepple, D., & Muthuthantrige, N. (2026). Artificial intelligence, innovation and the new architecture of exploitation: Towards reconfiguring humanness in the age of algorithmic labour. *Journal of Innovation & Knowledge*, *11*, 100878. DOI: 10.1016/j.jik.2025.100878

Petronio, S. (2002). *Boundaries of privacy: Dialectics of disclosure*. State University of New York Press. DOI: 10.1353/book4588

Plaskoff, J. (2017). Employee experience: The new human resource management approach. *Strategic HR Review*, *16*(3), 136–141. DOI: 10.1108/SHR-12-2016-0108

Polisetty, A., Chakraborty, D. G. S., Kar, A. K., & Pahari, S. (2024). What determines AI adoption in companies? Mixed-method evidence. *Journal of Computer Information Systems*, *64*(3), 370–387. DOI: 10.1080/08874417.2023.2219668

Porlezza, C., & Schapals, A. K. (2024). AI ethics in journalism (studies): An evolving field between research and practice. *Emerging Media*, *2*(3), 356–370. DOI: 10.1177/27523543241288818

Prabagar, S., Mothkur, R., Swetha, C. B., Kurian, A., Pavithra, K., & Aarthi, S. (2025). Generative AI for inclusive special education. In *Advances in Computational Intelligence and Robotics* (pp. 205–236). IGI Global Scientific Publishing. DOI: 10.4018/979-8-3373-3745-6.ch008

Prahalad, C. K., & Ramaswamy, V. (2004). Co-creation experiences: The next practice in value creation. *Journal of Interactive Marketing*, *18*(3), 5–14. DOI: 10.1002/dir.20015

Presbitero, A., & Teng-Calleja, M. (2023). Job attitudes and career behaviors relating to employees' perceived incorporation of artificial intelligence in the workplace: A career self-management perspective. *Personnel Review*, *52*(4), 1169–1187. DOI: 10.1108/PR-02-2021-0103

Puffer, S. M., McCarthy, D. J., & Jaeger, A. M. (2016). Institution building and institutional voids: Can Poland's experience inform Russia and Brazil? *International Journal of Emerging Markets*, *11*(1), 18–41. DOI: 10.1108/IJoEM-02-2015-0027

Putri, K. M. H., & Werdini, Y. E. (2025). Artificial intelligence adoption, job insecurity, and psychological resilience: Challenges for employee adaptation in future work environments. *International Journal of Issue Science*, *1*(5).

Raghavan, M., Barocas, S., Kleinberg, J., & Levy, K. (2020). Mitigating bias in algorithmic hiring: Evaluating claims and practices. *Proceedings of the 2020 Conference on Fairness, Accountability, and Transparency*, 469–481. DOI: 10.1145/3351095.3372828

Rai, A. (2020). Explainable AI: from black box to glass box. In *Journal of the Academy of Marketing Science* (Vol. 48, Number 1, pp. 137–141). Springer. DOI: 10.1007/s11747-019-00710-5

Raisch, S., & Krakowski, S. (2021). Artificial intelligence and management: The automation–augmentation paradox. *Academy of Management Review*, *46*(1), 192–210. DOI: 10.5465/amr.2018.0072

Ramadugu, R., & Doddipatla, L. (2022). Emerging trends in fintech: How technology is reshaping the global financial landscape. *Journal of Computational Innovation*, *2*(1), 573–380. DOI: 10.53555/8fp9w410

Ramkissoon, T., Jairam, A., & Hosein, P. (2025, October). AI-driven personalization as a disruptive strategy for the creation of new business models. In *2025 IEEE International Conference on Technology Management, Operations and Decisions (ICTMOD)* (pp. 1–6). IEEE. DOI: 10.1109/ICTMOD66732.2025.11371941

Ranjan, B., Sivanesan, I., & Bernie, S. B. (2026). Artificial intelligence and anxiety: The human price of adapting to a smarter workplace. *Inspire Intelligence Journal (ISSN: 3110-942X), 1*(1), 52-67.

Rathinavel, P., Ravikumar, R. N., Aarthi, S., Habib, M., Salaeva, N., & Pardaev, J. (2025). Augmenting human capabilities. In *Advances in Computational Intelligence and Robotics* (pp. 1–30). IGI Global Scientific Publishing. DOI: 10.4018/979-8-3373-2372-5.ch001

Ravikumar, R. N., & Aarthi, S. (2025a). AI-driven governance. In *Advances in Computational Intelligence and Robotics* (pp. 343–372). IGI Global Scientific Publishing. DOI: 10.4018/979-8-3373-3760-9.ch012

Ravikumar, R. N., & Aarthi, S. (2025c). Mind meets machine. In *Advances in Computational Intelligence and Robotics* (pp. 143–172). IGI Global Scientific Publishing. DOI: 10.4018/979-8-3373-5747-8.ch006

Ravikumar, R. N., & Aarthi, S. (2025d). The role of educational developers in AI integration at scale. In *Advances in Computational Intelligence and Robotics* (pp. 289–322). IGI Global Scientific Publishing. DOI: 10.4018/979-8-3373-4129-3.ch011

Ravikumar, R. N., & Aarthi, S. (2025b). Integrating machine learning with human decision making in HR. In *Empowering Human Resources Through Human-Computer Interaction* (pp. 115–146). IGI Global Scientific Publishing., DOI: 10.4018/979-8-3373-1676-5.ch005

Reddy, S. M., & Kumar, B. R. (2025). Artificial intelligence and the human experience: Impacts on social behavior and mental processes. *Chinese Medicine*, *25*(1), 89–111. PMID: 40524220

Regona, M., Yigitcanlar, T., Hon, C., & Teo, M. (2026). Building Trust in Artificial Intelligence: A Systematic Review through the Lens of Trust Theory. *ACM Computing Surveys*, *58*(9), 1–39. DOI: 10.1145/3789256

Reinhardt, K. (2023). Trust and trustworthiness in AI ethics. *AI and Ethics*, *3*(3), 735–744. DOI: 10.1007/s43681-022-00200-5

Riandhi, A. N., Arviansyah, M. R., & Sondari, M. C. (2025). AI and consumer behavior: Trends, technologies, and future directions from a scopus-based systematic review. *Cogent Business & Management*, *12*(1), 2544984. DOI: 10.1080/23311975.2025.2544984

Ricci, F., Rokach, L., & Shapira, B. (Eds.). (2015). *Recommender systems handbook* (2nd ed.). Springer. DOI: 10.1007/978-1-4899-7637-6

Richardson, J. P., Smith, C., Curtis, S., Watson, S., Zhu, X., Barry, B., & Sharp, R. R. (2021). Patient apprehensions about the use of artificial intelligence in healthcare. *NPJ Digital Medicine*, *4*(1), 140. DOI: 10.1038/s41746-021-00509-1 PMID: 34548621

Riedl, M. O. (2019). Human-centered artificial intelligence and machine learning. *Human Behavior and Emerging Technologies*, *1*(1), 33–36. DOI: 10.1002/hbe2.117

Rosso, B. D., Dekas, K. H., & Wrzesniewski, A. (2010). On the meaning of meaningful work: A theoretical integration and review. *Research in Organizational Behavior*, *30*, 91–127. DOI: 10.1016/j.riob.2010.09.001

Rostamzadeh, R., Alizadeh, F. K., Keivani, S., & Isavi, H. (2025). The role of artificial intelligence in improving organizational behavior: A systematic study. *Human Behavior and Emerging Technologies*, *2025*(1). DOI: 10.1155/hbe2/8094428

Russell, S., & Norvig, P. (2021). *Artificial intelligence: A modern approach* (4th ed.). Pearson.

Ryan, M., Christodoulou, E., Antoniou, J., & Iordanou, K. (2022). An AI ethics 'David and Goliath': Value conflicts between large tech companies and their employees. *AI & Society*. Advance online publication. DOI: 10.1007/s00146-022-01430-1

Sadeghi, S. (2024). Employee well-being in the age of AI: Perceptions, concerns, behaviors, and outcomes [Preprint]. arXiv.

Sadeghi, S. (2024). Employee well-being in the age of AI: Perceptions, concerns, behaviors, and outcomes. *arXiv preprint arXiv:2412.04796*.

Saini, M., Singh, D., Kataria, A., & Singh, R. (2025). Digital transformation and environmental sustainability: Reviewing the role of human capital. *Journal of Organizational Change Management*, •••, 1–24. DOI: 10.1108/JOCM-03-2025-0289

Saiyed, A. (2025). AI-Driven Innovations in Fintech: Applications, challenges, and future trends. *International Journal of Electrical and Computer Engineering Research*, *5*(1), 8–15. DOI: 10.53375/ijecer.2025.437

Saldaña, J. (2021). *The coding manual for qualitative researchers*. SAGE Publications.

Sartori, L., & Theodorou, A. (2022). A sociotechnical perspective for the future of AI: Narratives, inequalities, and human control. *Ethics and Information Technology*, *24*(1), 4. Advance online publication. DOI: 10.1007/s10676-022-09624-3

Schmager, S., Pappas, I. O., & Vassilakopoulou, P. (2025). Understanding human-centred AI: A review of its defining elements and a research agenda. *Behaviour & Information Technology*, *44*(15), 3771–3810. DOI: 10.1080/0144929X.2024.2448719

Schneider, B., White, S. S., & Paul, M. C. (1998). Linking service climate and customer perceptions of service quality: Test of a causal model. *The Journal of Applied Psychology*, *83*(2), 150–163. DOI: 10.1037/0021-9010.83.2.150 PMID: 9577232

Shaikh, M., Joseph, A., Zhao, H., Al Assadi, A., Bluemel, J. H., Diaz, D., & Zaki, M. (2026). AI agents in service experience: Towards autonomous and conscious agency. *Journal of Service Management*, *37*(3), 1–24. DOI: 10.1108/JOSM-04-2025-0187

Sharipudin, M. N. S., Rejab, M. M., Tugiman, N., Indiyati, D., C Andriani, A. D. (2024). The influence of digital communication technology on university branding: An understanding of open and distance learning (ODL) from students' perspectives. Jurnal Komunikasi: Malaysian Journal of Communication.

Sharma, R., & Kapoor, A. (2026). From Automation to Innovation: The Transformative Impact of AI on Business Functions in India. *Management Dynamics*, *26*(1), 4. DOI: 10.57198/2583-4932.1366

Sharma, R., Srivastva, S., & Fatima, S. (2023). E-commerce and digital transformation: Trends, challenges, and implications. *International Journal of Multidisciplinary Research*, *5*(5).

Shehu, H., Ogunleye, E., Atilola, M. O., Eromosele, E. I., Lawal, A. B., & Chukwuma, T. T. (2025). Ethical and responsible AI in engineering and construction projects: Governance, trust, and human-centered design. *Scientific. Journal of Engineering Technology*, *2*(2), 53–62. DOI: 10.69739/sjet.v2i2.833

Shen, S. Y., & Hong, Y. (2025). Bridging the Trust Gap: Exploring the Role of Trust in AI Integration Within the Workplace. In *Academy of Management Proceedings* (Vol. 2025, No. 1, p. 18789). Academy of Management.

Shneiderman, B. (2020). Human-centered artificial intelligence: Reliable, safe and trustworthy. *International Journal of Human-Computer Interaction*, *36*(6), 495–504. DOI: 10.1080/10447318.2020.1741118

Shneiderman, B. (2020). Human-centered artificial intelligence: Three fresh ideas. *AIS Transactions on Human-Computer Interaction*, •••, 109–124. DOI: 10.17705/1thci.00131

Shopify. (2022, Apr. 29). *The ROI on AR: How augmented reality is boosting ecommerce sales*. https://www.shopify.com/blog/ar-shopping

Siamagka, N. T., Christodoulides, G., Michaelidou, N., & Valvi, A. (2015). Determinants of social media adoption by B2B organizations. *Industrial Marketing Management*, *51*, 89–99. DOI: 10.1016/j.indmarman.2015.05.005

Sigfrids, A., Leikas, J., Salo-Pöntinen, H., & Koskimies, E. (2023). Human-centricity in AI governance: A systemic approach. *Frontiers in Artificial Intelligence*, *6*, 976887. DOI: 10.3389/frai.2023.976887 PMID: 36872934

Sigfrids, A., Nieminen, M., Leikas, J., & Pikkuaho, P. (2022). How should public administrations foster the ethical development and use of artificial intelligence? A review of proposals for developing governance of AI. *Frontiers in Human Dynamics*, *4*, 858108. Advance online publication. DOI: 10.3389/fhumd.2022.858108

Siu, E. (2026, Feb. 23). AR experiences that boosted conversion rates by 189%. *Single Grain*. https://www.singlegrain.com/digital-marketing/ar-experiences-that-boosted-conversion-rates-by-189/

Sobkowich, K. E. (2025). Demystifying artificial intelligence for veterinary professionals: Practical applications and future potential. *American Journal of Veterinary Research*, *86*(S1), S6–S15. DOI: 10.2460/ajvr.24.09.0275 PMID: 39842402

Solberg, E., Kaarstad, M., Eitrheim, M. H. R., Bisio, R., Reegård, K., & Bloch, M. (2022). A conceptual model of trust, perceived risk, and reliance on AI decision aids. *Group & Organization Management*, *47*(2), 187–222. DOI: 10.1177/10596011221081238

Solnet, D., Subramony, M., Ford, R. C., Golubovskaya, M., Kang, H. J., & Hancer, M. (2019). Leveraging human touch in service interactions: Lessons from hospitality. *Journal of Service Management*, *30*(3), 392–409. DOI: 10.1108/JOSM-12-2018-0380

Soulami, M., Benchekroun, S., & Galiulina, A. (2024). Exploring how AI adoption in the workplace affects employees: A bibliometric and systematic review. *Frontiers in Artificial Intelligence*, *7*, 1473872. DOI: 10.3389/frai.2024.1473872 PMID: 39610851

Sreejesh, S., Ghosh, T., & Dwivedi, Y. K. (2021). Moving beyond the content: The role of contextual cues in the effectiveness of gamification of advertising. *Journal of Business Research*, *132*, 88–101. DOI: 10.1016/j.jbusres.2021.04.007

Stahl, B. C., Timmermans, J., & Mittelstadt, B. D. (2016). The ethics of computing: A survey of the computing-oriented literature. *ACM Computing Surveys*, *48*(4), 55. Advance online publication. DOI: 10.1145/2871196

Staley, I., & Amankwa, E. (2025). Bridging blockchain and digital asset gaps: A comparative policy analysis of regulatory practices in emerging markets. *The Institution of Engineering and Technology (IET). IET Blockchain*, *5*(1), e70019. DOI: 10.1049/blc2.70019

Statista. (2024). *Statistics & facts on augmented reality (AR)*. https://www.statista.com/topics/3286/augmented-reality-ar

Supriyadi, T., Sulistiasih, S., Rahmi, K. H., Pramono, B., & Fahrudin, A. (2025). The impact of digital fatigue on employee productivity and well-being: A scoping literature review. *Environment and Social Psychology*, *10*(2), 1–13. DOI: 10.59429/esp.v10i2.3420

Susser, D., Roessler, B., & Nissenbaum, H. (2019). Technology, autonomy, and manipulation. *Internet Policy Review*, *8*(2). Advance online publication. DOI: 10.14763/2019.2.1410

Szenftner, A., Stumpp, S., & Knopf, T. (2024). Exploring the potential of AI to increase productivity in small marketing teams. In *European Conference on Innovation and Entrepreneurship* (Vol. 19, No. 1, pp. 970–977). Academic Conferences International Limited. DOI: 10.34190/ecie.19.1.2468

Szostak, M. (2025). Aesthetic insight into humanistic management and AI: Research perspectives. In *AI and humanistic management* (pp. 13–58).

Tabata, M., Wildermuth, C., Bottomley, K., & Jenkins, D. (2025). Generative AI integration in leadership practice: Foundations, challenges, and opportunities. *Journal of Leadership Studies*, *18*(4), 41–54. DOI: 10.1002/jls.70005

Tarafdar, M., Cooper, C. L., & Stich, J. F. (2019). The technostress trifecta—Techno eustress, techno distress and design: Theoretical directions and an agenda for research. *Information Systems Journal*, *29*(1), 6–42. DOI: 10.1111/isj.12169

Tariq, M. U. (2025). Harnessing Technology to Combat Bias: Innovative Tools and Techniques in HR. In Kanwal, S. (Ed.), *Navigating Bias in Human Resource Management* (pp. 155–184). IGI Global Scientific Publishing., DOI: 10.4018/979-8-3693-7132-9.ch006

Tariq, M. U. (2026). Bridging the Digital and Human Divide: Fostering Inclusion and Well-Being in Tech-Driven Workplaces. In Achour, Z. (Ed.), *Leading Inclusive Workplaces Through Digital Transformation and Organizational Change* (pp. 139–168). IGI Global Scientific Publishing., DOI: 10.4018/979-8-3373-5127-8.ch005

Tasleem, N., & Gangadharan, S. (2022). Navigating stakeholder dynamics in large-scale transformations. *Journal of Advance Multidisciplinary Research*, *1*(2), 48–56. DOI: 10.54660/.JAMR.2022.1.2.48-56

Teece, D. J., Pisano, G., & Shuen, A. (1997). Dynamic capabilities and strategic management. *Strategic Management Journal*, *18*(7), 509–533. DOI: 10.1002/(SICI)1097-0266(199708)18:7<509::AID-SMJ882>3.0.CO;2-Z

The Hindu Business Line. (2023). *Kerala's domestic tourist arrivals at record 21.87 crore in 2023: Minister Riyas*. https://www.thehindubusinessline.com/news/keralas-domestic-tourist-arrivals-at-record-218-crore-in-2023-minister-riyas/article67912764.ece

Tokic, V., & Csivre, A. (2026). Shaping tomorrow's digital banking: From technology to human-centric transformation. *Journal of Digital Banking*, *10*(3), 202–213. DOI: 10.69554/IBDY8945

Torraco, R. J. (2005). Writing integrative literature reviews: Guidelines and examples. *Human Resource Development Review*, *4*(3), 356–367. DOI: 10.1177/1534484305278283

Trist, E. L., & Bamforth, K. W. (1951). Some social and psychological consequences of the Longwall method of coal-getting. *Human Relations*, *4*(1), 3–38. DOI: 10.1177/001872675100400101

Trunk, A., Birkel, H., & Hartmann, E. (2020). On the current state of combining human and artificial intelligence for strategic organizational decision making. *Business Research*, *13*(3), 875–919. DOI: 10.1007/s40685-020-00133-x

Tursunbayeva, A., Di Lauro, S., & Pagliari, C. (2022). People analytics—A scoping review of conceptual boundaries and value propositions. *International Journal of Human Resource Management*, *33*(2), 357–388. DOI: 10.1080/09585192.2019.1659492

Uddin, A. S. M. A. (2023). The era of AI: Upholding ethical leadership. *Open Journal of Leadership*, *12*(04), 400–417. DOI: 10.4236/ojl.2023.124019

Usmani, A., Happonen, A., & Watada, J. (2023). Human-centered artificial intelligence: Designing for user empowerment and ethical considerations. In *2023 5th International Congress on Human-Computer Interaction, Optimization and Robotic Applications (HORA)* (pp. 1–7). IEEE. DOI: 10.1109/HORA58378.2023.10156761

Uzoamaka, N.-O. P., Amujiogu, A. A., & Blessing, E. O. (2025). Governance and ethical oversight of agentic artificial intelligence in business process management: Balancing human-autonomy, organizational accountability and algorithmic transparency. *Journal of Basic and Applied Research International*, *31*(6), 121–133. DOI: 10.56557/jobari/2025/v31i610028

Valtonen, A., Kimpimäki, J. P., & Savela, N. (2026). Employee wellbeing: A computational review on the consequences of workplace automation. *Technovation*, *152*, 103424. DOI: 10.1016/j.technovation.2025.103424

Valtonen, A., Saunila, M., Ukko, J., Treves, L., & Ritala, P. (2025). AI and employee wellbeing in the workplace: An empirical study. *Journal of Business Research*, *199*, 115584. DOI: 10.1016/j.jbusres.2025.115584

van Kessel, R., Wong, B. L. H., Rubinić, I., O'Nuallain, E., & Czabanowska, K. (2022). Is Europe prepared to go digital? Making the case for developing digital capacity: An exploratory analysis of Eurostat survey data. *PLOS Digital Health*, *1*(2), e0000013. DOI: 10.1371/journal.pdig.0000013 PMID: 36812527

Vanu, N., Farouk, M. O., Samiun, M., Sharmin, S., Billah, M., & Hossain, S. (2024). The Innovations and Trends of Information Technology with AI: Weapons to Reassemble the Future World. *Journal of Computer and Communications*, *12*(12), 34–54. DOI: 10.4236/jcc.2024.1212003

Vargo, S. L. C., & Lusch, R. F. (2020). Service-dominant logic 2025. *International Journal of Research in Marketing*, *37*(1), 1–10.

Vargo, S. L., & Lusch, R. F. (2008). Service-dominant logic: Continuing the evolution. *Journal of the Academy of Marketing Science*, *36*(1), 1–10. DOI: 10.1007/s11747-007-0069-6

Vashishth, T. K., Sharma, V., Sharma, K. K., Kumar, B., Kumar, A., & Panwar, R. (2024). Artificial intelligence (AI)–powered chatbots: Providing instant support and personalized recommendations to guests 24/7. In *Technology and luxury hospitality* (pp. 211–236). Routledge. DOI: 10.4324/9781003488248-15

Vaska, S.. (2021). Digital transformation: Lessons from organizations that have successfully balanced exploration and exploitation. *Frontiers in Psychology*, *12*, 629864.

Venigandla, K., Vemuri, N., & Vemuri, N. (2024). Hybrid intelligence systems combining human expertise and AI/RPA for complex problem solving. [IJISRT]. *International Journal of Innovative Science and Research Technology*, *9*(3), 2066–2075. DOI: 10.38124/ijisrt/IJISRT24MAR2039

Verhoef, P. C., Broekhuizen, T., Bart, Y., Bhattacharya, A., Dong, J. ., Fabian, N., & Haenlein, C. (2021). Digital transformation: A multidisciplinary reflection and research agenda. *Journal of Business Research*, *122*, 889–901. DOI: 10.1016/j.jbusres.2019.09.022

Vial, G. (2019). Understanding digital transformation: A review and a research agenda. *The Journal of Strategic Information Systems*, *28*(2), 118–144. DOI: 10.1016/j.jsis.2019.01.003

Viljakainen, A., Silmukari, J., Roto, V., Čaić, M., & Aromaa, S. (2025). AI and the future of industrial work: A framework for enhancing employee experience from satisfaction to flourishing. *Behaviour & Information Technology*, •••, 1–13. DOI: 10.1080/0144929X.2025.2596889

Vrontis, D., Christofi, M., Pereira, V., Tarba, S., Makrides, A., & Trichina, E. (2022). Artificial intelligence, robotics, advanced technologies and human resource management: A systematic review. *International Journal of Human Resource Management*, *33*(6), 1237–1266. DOI: 10.1080/09585192.2020.1871398

Walter, Y. (2024). Managing the race to the moon: Global policy and governance in Artificial Intelligence regulation: A contemporary overview and an analysis of socioeconomic consequences. *Discover Artificial Intelligence*, *4*(1), 14. DOI: 10.1007/s44163-024-00109-4

Wang, Q., Qi, Y., & Li, R. (2026). Artificial intelligence and corporate sustainability: Shaping the future of ESG in the age of industry 5.0. *Sustainable Development (Bradford)*, *34*(1), 1–26. DOI: 10.1002/sd.70200

Wang, Y., Zhong, M., Sharma, P., & Niu, D. F. (2026). The impact of human-centred artificial intelligence on firms' workforce demand in Industry 5.0 transition. *Enterprise Information Systems*, *20*(2), 2595706. DOI: 10.1080/17517575.2025.2595706

Warner, K. S. C., & Wäger, M. (2020). Building dynamic capabilities for digital transformation: An ongoing process of strategic renewal. *Long Range Planning*, *53*(3), 101910.

Wedel, M., Bigné, E., & Zhang, J. (2020). Virtual and augmented reality: Advancing research in consumer marketing. *International Journal of Research in Marketing*, *37*(3), 443–465. DOI: 10.1016/j.ijresmar.2020.04.004

Wells, B. J., Saef, J., & Green-Saxena, A.. (2025). A practical framework for appropriate implementation and review of artificial intelligence (FAIR-AI) in healthcare. npj. *Digital Medicine*, *8*(1), 514. Advance online publication. DOI: 10.1038/s41746-025-01900-y PMID: 40790350

Westover, J. H. (2025). How to become an effective AI-augmented leader. *Human Capital Leadership Review*, *20*(4), 2–10. DOI: 10.70175/hclreview.2020.20.4.2

Wilson, H. J., Daugherty, P. R., & Morini-Bianzino, N. (2017). The jobs that artificial intelligence will create. *MIT Sloan Management Review*, *58*(4), 14–16. https://sloanreview.mit.edu/article/will-ai-create-as-many-jobs-as-it-eliminates/

World Economic Forum. (2023). The future of jobs report 2023. World Economic Forum.

World Economic Forum. (2024). The future of jobs report 2024. Geneva: WEF.

Xavier, D. F., Korunka, C., & Reiter-Palmon, R. (2025). AI integration and workforce development: Exploring job autonomy and creative self-efficacy in a global context. *PLoS One*, *20*(6), e0319556. DOI: 10.1371/journal.pone.0319556 PMID: 40465594

Xu, W. (2026). Human-centered artificial intelligence (HCAI): Foundations and approaches. *arXiv preprint arXiv:2601.01247.*

Yadav, A., & Sondhi, H. (2023). Systematic Literature Review on Sustainable Marketing and Artificial Intelligence. *Proceedings of the 17th INDIACom; 2023 10th International Conference on Computing for Sustainable Global Development, INDIACom 2023*, 583–588.

Yaşar, T. (2024). Artificial intelligence in business operations: Exploring how AI technologies are reshaping processes, enhancing decision-making, and driving efficiency across various industries. *Human-Computer Interaction*.

Yin, R. K. (2018). *Case study research and applications* (vol. 6). Sage.

Ying, T., Tang, J., Ye, S., Tan, X., & Wei, W. (2022). Virtual Reality in Destination Marketing: Telepresence, Social Presence, and Tourists' Visit Intentions. *Journal of Travel Research*, *61*(8), 1738–1756. DOI: 10.1177/00472875211047273

Yin, R. K. (2018). *Case study research and applications: Design and methods* (6th ed.). Sage., https://uk.sagepub.com/en-gb/eur/case-study-research-and-applications/book250150

Zarifis, A., & Cheng, X. (2023). The five emerging business models of Fintech for AI adoption, growth and building trust. In *Business digital transformation: selected cases from industry leaders* (pp. 73–97). Springer International Publishing.

Zhang, C., Chen, S., Zhang, D., & Zhang, Q. (2026). The Impact of Artificial Intelligence Usage on Affective Work Well-Being: A Self-Determination Theory Perspective. *Behavioral Sciences (Basel, Switzerland)*, *16*(5), 670. DOI: 10.3390/bs16050670 PMID: 42193549

Zhang, S., Yao, L., Sun, A., & Tay, Y. (2019). Deep learning based recommender system: A survey and new perspectives. *ACM Computing Surveys*, *52*(1), 1–38. DOI: 10.1145/3158369

Zhao, H. (2025). Artificial intelligence in social governance: Global insights from theoretical frameworks to practical applications using CiteSpace. *Global Review of Humanities, Arts, and Society*, *1*(4), 26–37. DOI: 10.63802/grhas.v1.i4.74

Zhao, Y., Chen, Y., Sun, Y., & Shen, X. L. (2024). Understanding users' voice assistant exploration intention: Unraveling the differential mechanisms of the multiple dimensions of perceived intelligence. *Internet Research*, *34*(6), 2096–2122. DOI: 10.1108/INTR-10-2022-0807

Zirar, A., Ali, S. I., & Islam, N. (2023). Worker and workplace Artificial Intelligence (AI) coexistence: Emerging themes and research agenda. *Technovation*, *124*, 102747. Advance online publication. DOI: 10.1016/j.technovation.2023.102747

About the Contributors

Nasser Al Harrasi is a senior academic and researcher in Human Resource Management, currently leading the HRM Program at the University of Technology and Applied Sciences in Oman. He holds a PhD in Management from Binary University and is a Fellow of the UK Higher Education Academy. With over 10 years of experience in higher education and industry, Dr. Al Harrasi has published extensively on HRM, university–industry collaboration, and the integration of AI in education. He has led national research projects funded by Oman's Ministry of Higher Education and contributed to several academic books and conferences, including at Cambridge and Edinburgh. In addition to his academic leadership, he serves as a Research Associate at Oxford Business College (UK) and is a board member at the Global College of Engineering and Technology. He is also a recipient of national awards recognizing his contributions to research and education in Oman.

Zahra Alhabsi is a Senior Lecturer at the University of Technology and Applied Sciences (UTAS), Oman, with extensive experience in marketing, branding, and stakeholder communication. She holds a PhD from Brunel University London, where her research examined value co-creation and employer branding in the context of corporate social responsibility. Her academic work focuses on branding strategies, CSR, innovation in higher education, and the emerging role of generative AI in organisations and learning environments. She has led national-level initiatives related to graduate employability, institutional branding, and digital transformation, and has contributed to international publications and conferences, including work on ethical AI and AI-driven brand equity.

***

Mona Abdulla is a Maths Tutor in the School of Professional Development at Bahrain Polytechnic. A founding member of the institution since 2008, she previously served as Maths Programme Manager in the Faculty of Foundation for over six years and brings extensive experience in developing Mathematics and Engineering Physics courses. She has taught a wide range of Maths courses across foundation and degree levels, including Data Analysis, Engineering Mathematics, Mathematics for Business and ICT, and Technical Mathematics. She also served for seven years as a Maths and Science Senior Tutor at Bahrain Training Institute. Her professional interests include integrating Problem-Based Learning into Maths curricula. She has strong leadership and management experience and has actively contributed to several Quality Department projects.

Ranya Alesh is a Senior English Lecturer at Bahrain Polytechnic. She has been teaching English as a Second Language, developing curricula, and ensuring that quality standards and policies are implemented in alignment with Quality Matters standards. Her research interests include Quality Education Best Practices and Success Stories, Effectiveness of Asynchronous Activities in English Learning and Teaching, Comparative Literature, and Change Management Techniques.

Astri Andriani is an Associate Professor in Communication Studies and currently serves as the Rector of Putra Indonesia University, Indonesia. Dr. Andriani has authored 15 copyrighted books and published more than 120 scholarly articles in national and international journals, including Scopus-indexed publications. Her research contributions have received over 1,800 citations, with an H-index of 16 and an iH-index of 21. In recognition of her academic impact, she was awarded a Bronze Medal at the International Research Invention Innovation Exhibition (IRIEX). Beyond academia, she serves as an editor at Communicatus, acts as a master trainer for the Ministry of Communication and Digital Affairs of the Republic of Indonesia, and leads community-based digital literacy initiatives such as Digimom Indonesia and Next Generation Indonesia. Her leadership and advocacy for gender equality have earned her multiple regional awards, including recognition as one of the top 10 influential women in the field of education.

Arun Arora is a transformative and visionary Operations and Supply Chain Management Leader with decades of distinguished industry experience driving manufacturing business excellence through Lean Management, Total Productive Maintenance (TPM), Business Process Reengineering and Total Quality Management (TQM). Proven track record of delivering measurable business outcomes ranging from significant Cost reduction and Productivity enhancement to Revenue growth and Operational turnaround across high-impact roles in leading organizations including International Tractors Ltd., Mahindra & Mahindra Ltd and Escorts Limited. Currently, Dr. Arora is working as PROFESSOR (Operations and Supply Chain Management) & Dean-Students Welfare with Lloyd Business School, Greater Noida (India). Recognized for strategic leadership in Global Manufacturing Operations, including heading the Export Tractor Assembly business at International Tractors, where he led large-scale transformations by optimizing processes, enhancing quality systems, and integrating digitization for performance gains. Adept at aligning operational goals with broader business objectives, while fostering a Culture of Continuous Improvement, Innovation, and Capability building. Holds a Ph.D. in Operations under Mechanical Engineering, MTech. in Manufacturing Management from BITS PILANI, and PGDBA with Specialization in Operations Management and Human Resource Management from Symbiosis, Pune, complemented by a strong academic presence as Guest Faculty at BITS Pilani. A published researcher and patent holder, Dr. Arora brings deep technical acumen and thought leadership to complex operational challenges. Skilled in stakeholder engagement, cross-functional leadership, and global collaboration, he is driven by a commitment to Operational Excellence, Sustainable Growth, and Innovation. He has contributed in 10 Indian design patents and author of 3 books. He has published 9 research papers in SCOPUS indexed SCI journal. He has also contributed 2 book chapters published in LNME, Springer, which is Scopus indexed. He is active reviewer and reviewed 182 manuscripts so far, which has testimonial in Web of Science. Key competencies include: Strategic Planning, Lean Transformation, TPM, Cost Optimization, Digitization in processes, Quality Systems, Employee Development, and Safety & Compliance (OHSAS 18001). With a proven ability to lead high-performing teams and large-scale operations, Dr. Arora stands out as a trusted advisor and catalyst for enterprise wide value creation and a researcher.

Khalil Ebrahim is an English Language Lecturer and Course Coordinator specializing in academic literacy, digital pedagogy, and AI-enhanced assessment. He holds an MA in Linguistics from the UK and is known for designing innovative, student-centered learning experiences and integrating intelligent feedback tools into higher education. His research focuses on improving writing assessment accuracy and feedback effectiveness through human–AI collaboration, positioning him as an emerging voice in the intersection of linguistics, learning design, and educational technology.

Manika Garg is a visionary Research Analyst, Author, Career Coach, and Mentor with a proven track record of publishing numerous research papers in reputable international journals including Springer, ABDC and Scopus. With expertise in multidisciplinary research, academic writing, and career development, Dr. Manika has made significant contributions to various fields, including Financial Engineering, Banking Digitalisation, Artificial Intelligence in Banking Sector,

Financial Inclusion, Financial Modelling and FinTech. As an author, Dr. Manika has written and published several books and book chapters on topics related to Working Capital Management, Portfolio Management and Financial Engineering etc, showcasing their ability to communicate complex ideas to diverse audiences. As a career coach and mentor, She has provided guidance and support to students and professionals, helping them navigate their academic and professional pursuits. With a strong background in research design, data analysis, and interpretation, She is well-equipped to conduct high-quality research and provide expert mentorship. Through their work, she aims to inspire and empower individuals to achieve their full potential and make a positive impact in their respective fields. She has touched the lives of countless individuals, empowering them to achieve remarkable success and make a lasting impact in their respective fields. What sets Dr. Manika apart is their unique ability to transcend geographical boundaries, providing research coaching to working professionals across the world. From corporate executives to industry leaders, She has worked with diverse professionals, helping them to develop research skills, craft compelling narratives, and drive innovation in their organizations. Their expertise in bridging the gap between academia and industry has made them a sought-after expert in the global research community. Her exceptional expertise, coupled with their passion for knowledge sharing and mentorship, has earned them numerous prestigious awards and recognition from esteemed institutions. As a true trailblazer, Dr. Manika continues to push the frontiers of knowledge, inspiring others to join them on this extraordinary journey of discovery and growth. With a legacy that spans continents and industries, She remains committed to empowering individuals to achieve excellence and make a meaningful difference in the world.

Khidirov Nodir Giyosalievich is a Professor in the Department of Finance and Financial Technologies at Tashkent State University of Economics, Uzbekistan. He has extensive academic and research experience in finance, with expertise in financial management, banking systems, and modern financial technologies. His research interests include digital finance, financial markets, investment strategies, and the application of advanced analytical tools in financial decision-making. He is actively involved in teaching, research supervision, and curriculum development, contributing to the academic and professional growth of students. Professor Khidirov has published scholarly works and participated in national and international conferences, promoting innovation in financial education and research. His work emphasizes the integration of theoretical knowledge with practical financial applications, contributing to the advancement of financial systems and economic development.

Mansi Kapoor is an Assistant Professor in the area of Marketing with University of Delhi and holds a PhD in Management from the prestigious Indian Institute of Foreign Trade, New Delhi. Her research interests include customer engagement, digital marketing, social media marketing, trade shows and advertising. She has published in ABDC list journals and peer-reviewed journals. She is actively involved in teaching, research, and academic mentoring.

Shikha Khullar is an academician and researcher specializing in Artificial Intelligence, Computational Intelligence, and Intelligent Systems. Her research focuses on AI-powered fraud detection, IoT-enabled smart systems, cybersecurity, and sustainable agriculture technologies. She has contributed to edited books and research publications with international publishers such as IGI Global, Wiley–Scrivener, and CRC Press. Dr. Khullar's work emphasizes integrating machine learning and swarm intelligence to solve real-world challenges across finance, healthcare, and smart infrastructure. She is actively involved in academic research, reviewing, and mentoring in advanced computing and emerging AI technologies.

Andrii Klietsov is a Doctor of Veterinary Medicine and the owner of the "VetDopomoga" chain of veterinary clinics in Sumy, Ukraine. He serves as Head of the NGO "Society of Veterinary Business Owners," which brings together practitioners and licensed business owners across Ukraine. Over more than 20 years of practice, Dr Klietsov has combined small-animal clinical work with managing veterinary teams, developing service standards and building resilient business models. His professional interests include One Health, staff wellbeing and burnout prevention in veterinary medicine, the practical use of digital tools and AI to improve diagnostics, client communication and decision-making. He has been invited as a keynote speaker at the World Veterinary Association Congresses in Taipei (2023) and Cape Town (2024), as well as events in Bacolod (2024), Washington, DC (2025), and Tokyo (2026).

Nataliia Klietsova is a Senior Lecturer in Human Resource Management at the University of Hertfordshire Business School (UK) and the Associate Professor in the Department of Private Law and Social Welfare at Sumy National Agrarian University (Ukraine). A chartered HR specialist, international employment relations lawyer and certified auditor, she has over 17 years' experience in lecturing, research and consulting, particularly in the fields of international HRM, labour relations and organisational resilience. Her research focuses on economic, social and legal approaches to HRM in veterinary medicine and allied sectors, including under conditions of digitalisation, and turbulent environment, within a broader sustainability and One Health perspective. Dr Klietsova has consulted for private veterinary practices, and has authored more than 100 scientific publications. She actively collaborates on interdisciplinary projects that link HRM, wellbeing and sustainability, and contributes to international academic and professional networks in Ukraine and the UK. She has also been invited as a keynote speaker at the World Veterinary Association Congresses in Taipei (2023) and Cape Town (2024), as well as events in Bacolod (2024), Washington, DC (2025), and Tokyo (2026).

Sakshi Mann is an Assistant Professor of Human Resource Management at School of Business, Indira University, Pune. With a Ph.D. in HR and over 11 years of combined industry and academic experience, she brings a practical edge to her teaching. Her expertise spans Organizational Behavior, Recruitment & Selection, Employee Engagement, and Leadership. Having managed HR operations across various organizations, she seamlessly integrates real-world insights into academia. Passionate about research, she explores contemporary HR challenges to contribute valuable insights to the field. Committed to bridging academia and industry, Dr. Mann fosters critical thinking and practical application, equipping students for the evolving HR landscape.

Shikha Mann is an award-winning academician, certified leadership coach, and organizational consultant currently serving as Controller of Examinations at Indira University (IU), Pune. Previously, she held the role of Deputy Director and HOD–HR at Indira School of Business Studies PGDM, where she led academic, administrative, and accreditation initiatives. A recipient of Business World's 40under40 Leaders in Education award, Dr. Mann brings a decade-plus of experience at the intersection of education, leadership development, and institutional strategy. She holds a Ph.D. in Organizational Behavior from Symbiosis International University and is an ICF-certified PCC coach, with additional accreditations in MBTI, FIRO-B, TIFF, TA 101, Enneagram, and psychometric assessments. Dr. Mann has conducted high-impact MDPs and consulting interventions for reputed organizations like Tata Motors, RBI, Jabil, Thermax, Lupin, and the Maharashtra Police. She has played a pivotal role in leading NBA and AIU accreditation processes and in designing outcome-based curricula, assessment centers, and CXO-level talent strategy blueprints.

Bobur Mirzayev is the Head of the Department of Finance at Alfraganus University, Tashkent, Uzbekistan. He has significant academic and administrative experience in finance, with expertise in financial management, investment analysis, and economic policy. His research interests include capital markets, corporate finance, and the application of modern financial technologies in decision-making processes. As a departmental head, he plays a key role in academic leadership, curriculum development, and fostering a research-oriented environment. He is actively involved in teaching and mentoring students, supporting their academic and professional growth in finance-related disciplines. Mirzayev has contributed to scholarly research through publications and participation in academic conferences. His work emphasizes bridging theoretical knowledge with practical financial applications, contributing to the advancement of financial education and institutional development.

Reza Naji is a Senior Lecturer at the University of Hertfordshire Business School. His work focuses on strategic management, human resource management, and the role of technology in sustainability. He teaches undergraduate and postgraduate students, including MBA programmes, and is actively engaged in research on digital transformation and student engagement in higher education.

Dusmuxammedova Nozima is a faculty member in the Department of Accounting and Statistics at Termez University of Economics and Service, Uzbekistan. She is actively engaged in teaching and research in the fields of accounting, financial reporting, and statistical analysis. Her academic interests include financial accounting, auditing, data analytics, and the application of statistical methods in economic decision-making. She contributes to curriculum development and student mentoring, supporting the development of analytical and practical skills among learners. Dusmuxammedova participates in academic research, publications, and collaborative initiatives that promote innovation and knowledge dissemination in accounting and statistics. Her work emphasizes the integration of theoretical concepts with real-world applications, contributing to the advancement of accounting education and data-driven economic analysis.

Sumayia Pouransari is a Senior Lecturer in Human Resource Management at the University of Hertfordshire Business School, where she leads and delivers postgraduate modules in HRM, Information Systems, and research methods. Her recent work focuses on HRIS, student engagement and sustainability in online learning, and energy-efficient management. She has contributed to different research projects and collaborates on variety of studies in HRM. Dr Pouransari is an active member of research groups dedicated to sustainability, technology, and inclusive learning.

Ravikumar R N is currently a Postdoctoral researcher at Universiti Malaysia Perlis, Malaysia. Also, working as an Assistant Professor (Sr. Grade) in the Department of Computer Science and Engineering at Jain (Deemed-to-be University), Bangalore, Karnataka. He has 13+ years of national and international teaching experience. He completed his PhD at Amity University, Rajasthan, M.E at VMRF Deemed University, B.E at Anna University, Chennai. He also holds a

MiniMBA certificate from Swiss eLearning Institute, Switzerland. He has published numerous research articles in Scopus, SCI journals, Book chapters, and Conference papers. Also, he hold several patents and authored books. His specialization is ML, DL, Federated Learning, Recommendation Systems, and Optimization Techniques.

Sini Rahuman is an Assistant Professor of Mathematics at Bahrain Polytechnic, where she teaches a range of mathematics courses, including Mathematics for Computing, Technical Mathematics, Business Mathematics and Foundation Mathematics. She is also actively involved in course development and material preparation. Her research interests include Computational Fluid Dynamics (CFD), Applied Mathematics, Artificial Intelligence, Machine Learning, Deep Learning, and Reinforcement Learning.

Daniel Rufai is a research assistant working with the main author. He holds an MSc in Industrial Relations and Human Resource Management and is aspiring to pursue PhD opportunities in Organisational Behaviour, Human Resource Management, and Strategic Management. His research interests include Workplace Technology, Organisational Behaviour, Human Resource Management, Leadership, Organisational Change, Quality of Work Life, and Work Culture.

Aarthi S is a dedicated Assistant Professor in Computer Science with over six years of teaching experience. She is currently pursuing her Ph.D. at Marwadi University, Gujarat, and holds an M.Phil. and MCA from Bharathiar University, Tamil Nadu. Throughout her academic career, Aarthi has specialized in programming languages such as C++, Java, and C, and contributed to research in recommender systems and AI-related data privacy. She has published journal articles, contributed to book chapters, and actively participated in technical workshops. Known for her student mentorship and engagement in academic events, Aarthi remains committed to fostering innovation and excellence in computer science education.

Sai Simhadri is an accomplished Data and AI Leader with 18+ years of experience architecting and executing enterprise-wide data solutions that drive business transformation. Proven track record in leading cross-functional teams and delivering complex, multi-million-dollar data initiatives across global organizations. Strategic expertise spans Data Architecture, Data Governance, AI/ML integration, and Business Intelligence. Adept at designing modern data platforms—including Data Lakes, Data Warehouses, and Customer Data Hubs—across both cloud and on-premise environments. Hands-on leadership in implementing scalable ETL/ELT frameworks using tools like Informatica, Talend, SSIS, AWS DMS, and GoldenGate. Deep technical proficiency with Redshift, Oracle, SQL Server, and MongoDB, combined with advanced SQL and PL/SQL expertise. Visionary in establishing enterprise-wide Data Quality frameworks, MDM solutions, and integrating systems like Salesforce and Oracle ERP. Experience managing CI/CD pipelines, Agile delivery, and version control across diverse data environments. Recognized for strategic thinking, stakeholder engagement, and aligning data initiatives with core business objectives. Successfully reduced data pipeline complexity, enhanced data accessibility, and enabled actionable insights through platforms such as Tableau, OBIEE, MicroStrategy, and SAP BO.

Muhammad Usman Tariq is a strategic higher education leader and scholar with more than 18 years of international experience across academia, research, and industry. He holds dual doctorates, a PhD in Artificial Intelligence and a Doctorate in Business Administration and has published extensively as the author of research articles, case studies, book chapters, and academic texts. His contributions also include several patents, reflecting his applied research in technology, business, and education. He is the Founder and CEO of TheCaseHQ.com, a global hub for professional certification programmes, narrative and video case studies, and digital learning innovation. In addition, he serves as President of the Gulf Higher Education Network (Gulf HE), an initiative dedicated to advancing academic practice, faculty development, and institutional collaboration across the region. He is a Principal Fellow of Advance HE (UK), Chartered Fellow of the CIPD (UK), Senior Fellow of SEDA (UK), and a Senior Member of IEEE, reflecting his standing as both an academic innovator and a global professional leader.

Fatema Wali is an Associate Professor of English at Bahrain Polytechnic, and she has been teaching English as a Second Language, developing curricula, designing e-learning courses, and managing teams. Her research interests include On-line language learning, English as a Second Language, Computer Assisted Language Learning, Interdisciplinary Education, Entrepreneurship Education and Problem Based Learning.

Shodiyeva Yulduz is a faculty member in the Department of Biomedical Engineering, Biophysics, and Informatics at Bukhara State Medical Institute, Uzbekistan. She has a multidisciplinary academic background that integrates biomedical engineering with biophysical sciences and medical informatics. Her research interests include biomedical signal processing, health data analytics, computational modeling, and the application of intelligent systems in healthcare. She is actively engaged in teaching and curriculum development, contributing to the education of students in emerging areas such as digital health, biomedical technologies, and data-driven healthcare solutions. Shodiyeva participates in academic research, publications, and collaborative initiatives that promote innovation in healthcare engineering. Her work aims to enhance diagnostic accuracy, improve patient care, and support the integration of advanced technological solutions in modern healthcare systems.

Index

P

R

S

T

U

V

www.ingramcontent.com/pod-product-compliance
Lightning Source LLC
LaVergne TN
LVHW081536300926
849161LV00006B/1451